The Original
WOLFHOUND

Guide to EveningClasses

2003/2004

in Dublin City & County

WOLFHOUND PRESS

ACKNOWLEDGMENTS

Our thanks to all who have assisted and facilitated our research on this year's edition, including school authorities and organisers of adult education courses at the various centres.

Details are correct at time of going to press. While every effort has been made to ensure accuracy and comprehensive listings, the editor and publisher accept no responsibility for any inaccuracies that may appear herein or any changes in prices, days, times, or venues or other changes to the courses we have listed.

Design and Layout © 2003Merlin Publishing

Published by
Wolfhound Press
An imprint of Merlin Publishing
16 Upper Pembroke Street, Dublin 2
Tel: (01) 676 4373
Fax: (01) 676 4568
e-mail: publishing@merlin.ie
www.merlin-publishing.com

Cover Design by M & J Graphics
Printed and bound by Nørhaven Paperback A/S

Westmoreland College
for Management and Business

11 Westmoreland Street, Dublin 2.
Tel: 6795324/6797266 Fax: 6791953
Email: admissions@westmorelandcollege.ie

Marketing & International Studies
• Dip. & Adv. Dip. in Marketing, Advertising & PR (ICM)
• Dip. in Journalism & Media Studies (ICM)
• Cert. In Travel & Tourism (ICM)

Business & Management Programmes
• Dip. HR Mgt. (ICM) • Dip. Corporate Mgt. (ICM)
• Cert. in Safety & Health Practice at Work (ICM)
• Cert. & Dip. in Business Studies (ICM)
• Dip. Health Services Mgt. (ICM)

Financial & Postgraduate Programmes
• Accounting Technicians (IATI)
• Dip. in Financial Mgt. (ACCA)
• Grad. Dip. Mgt. (ICM)
• Adv. Dip. in Project Mgt. (ICM)

Legal Studies Programmes
• Dip. Legal Studies (ICM)

Westmoreland College for Management and Business

Readers & booklovers, young and old
visit & browse
a wonderworld of books at

www.merlin-publishing.com

including

Biography, Fiction, True Crime, History, Politics,
Humour, Children's Books

INTRODUCTION

Welcome to the twenty-ninth edition of the original & bestselling *Wolfhound Guide to Evening Classes & Leisure Activities*. This edition contains more options and information than ever before to help locate the most suitable evening classes for you. The *Wolfhound Guide* continues to be the market leader and has by far the most comprehensive coverage of evening classes - plus many part-time day courses - and leisure activities throughout Dublin and surrounding areas. Choose now from over 4,600 courses, workshops - classroom or home study based - and rejoin the knowledge age - there is a course here for you, from computers & keep-fit to art, philosophy and history, from the traditional to the myriad of new alternatives. All are here in an easy to use subject sequence - A to Z.

We include prices where possible, but be forewarned that not all centres had finalised prices, or in some cases times of courses & activities, when we went to press. However, days, times and prices will be available the relevant centre by early September or before. Most evening courses begin at 7pm or 7.30 (and are of from 1-2 hours duration). But again, 6.30pm is not an infrequent start time. Early registration is always advisable as places are often limited. For the more expensive courses, it is vital to make a definite decision before paying in full as fees are usually non-refundable. Bear in mind also that in spite of some significant euro-uping price increases this year, most courses remain extraordinarily inexpensive and good value.

The *Wolfhound Guide* also includes a directory of e-mail and web addresses, but the telephone remains the most effective means of contact next to calling in to enroll. Enrolment days/ evenings generally take place from the second week of September, and most courses begin from mid- to late September.

Most of the classes in this guide are held in the evening. Some are also available during the day and others can be taken by correspondence, online or e-mail. Some courses continue or restart again in January, so be sure to keep the *Wolfhound Guide* close at hand throughout the year.

We hope that you enjoy your course.

ACCORDION see also Music

Comhaltas Ceoltoiri Eireann 32 Belgrave Sq Monkstown (2800295) - button

Dun Laoghaire Music Centre 130A Lr George's St Dun Laoghaire (2844178)

Nolan School of Music 3 Dean St 8 (4933730) - also day

Walton's New School of Music 69 Sth Gt George's St 2 (4781884) - button & piano, also day, see ad page 173.

ACCOUNTANCY / ACCOUNTS see also Book-keeping / Business / Computerised Accounts / Management / PAYROLL / PAYE

ACCA (Assoc of Chartered Certified Accountants) 9 Leeson Pk 6 (4988900) - chartered certified accountancy; also day / dip in financial management - nationwide

DIT Faculty: Business Aungier St 2 (4023040/3445) - ACCA exam, €700 per stage/ CIMA exam, 1&2 €700 per stage

Dorset College 64a Lr Dorset St/ 8 Belvedere Pl 1 (8309677) - accounting & finance cert/dip - ICM, Mon-Fri, 9.30-1.30, 30 wks; Mon & Wed, 6.30-9.30, 1-2 yrs

Dublin Business School 13/14 Aungier St 2 (4177500) - ACCA, Mon to Fri, 6pm-10pm, 3-4 years, also revision/ BA (hons) Acc & Finance, 3-4 yrs/ CIMA, 3-4 yrs, certified dip in financial management, ACCA, 1 eve per wk, 1 yr/ revision w/end/ all 6.15-9.30pm/ DBS dip accounting & finance, 1 yr

Dublin City University Registry office Glasnevin 9 (7005338)

Eden Computer Training Rathfarnham 16, or MACRO Centre, 1 Green St 7 (4953155) - Tasbooks/ Sage/ Take 5

FAS Training Centre Loughlinstown (2043600) - manual & computerised

FAS Training Centre Tallaght 24 (4045284) - manual, C&G, 10wk

Greendale Community School Kilbarrack 5 (8322735/6) - wages, PAYE, PRSI, VAT, P&L, Tbal etc, Tues, 7.30-9.30pm, 10wks, €55

Griffith College Dublin Sth Circular Rd 8 (4150400) - ACCA & CPA, p/t revision, both 3 stages over 3 yrs, 2 eves per wk/ also available w/ends/ IATI & ACA revision, both 2 stages over 2 yrs, 2 eves per wk/ BA in accounting & finance, 3yrs HETAC p/time

Hartstown Community School Clonsilla 15 (8209863) - & accounts beginners/intermediate 10wks, €60 each

Inst of Certified Public Accountants in Ireland 9 Ely Pl 2 (6767353) - CPA centres of ed at Griffith College & Plunket College, w/end & eve courses, Sept - April

Institute of Technology Tallaght 24 (4042000) - BBS/ nat dip/ nat cert

Irish Payroll Association (IPASS) Clifton House Lower Fitzwilliam St 2 (6617200) - certified payroll technician, 1 eve x 10 wks, stage 1 & 2/ dip in payroll management, 4 modules, 2 day each: various venues: city centre, Griffith Ave, Blanchardstown, Tallaght, Dun Laoire

Kilroy's College 25 Kingram Place 2 (1850 700700) - tutor supported home study: book-keeping & accounts, self-employed accounts, farm acounts, dip course

Kylemore College Kylemore Rd 10 (6265901) - basic manual & computerised accounts, Wed 2-4pm 10 wks

Plunket College Swords Rd, Whitehall 9 (8371689) - IATI cert, accounting/taxation - €113.50 each/ Certified Public Accountant, economics & business environment/ legal framework/ accounting framework/ taxation/ IT/ management accounting - €166 per subject, 25 wks/ also leaving cert(H,O), Tues, 27 wks, €143

Dorset College

66 (Head Office) Lower Dorset Street, Dublin 1

Tel: (01) 8309677   E-Mail: info@dorset-college.ie   www.dorset-college.ie

EXCELLENCE THROUGH LIFE-LONG LEARNING

Full-Time Courses
- Office Technology / Back To Work Course
- Business Administration - IT and Communications
- Business Administration, Diploma in Computers & Communications
- Diploma in Accounting & Finance
- Computer Systems Professional – A+, Network+, MCP

Part-Time Computer Courses
- Using The Internet Certificate - e-Quals City & Guilds
- Computer Applications Certificate – e-Quals City & Guilds Level 1
- ECDL - European Computer Driving Licence (also Full-Time)
- Diploma Computer Applications – e-Quals C&G & Microsoft Office Specialist
- Advanced Diploma Computer Applications - e-Quals City & Guilds Level 3
- Computerised Accounts Certificate - e-Quals City & Guilds
- Microsoft Office Specialist (MOS) Core Level / (MOS) Expert Level
- Desk Top Publishing Certificate - e-Quals City & Guilds (Level 1-3)

• Computer Aided Design – Beginner & Intermediate

• Teachers' Diploma Information Communication Technology – Skills (JEB)

• Web Page Design – Master Designer
CompTIA I-Net   * CIW Site Designer   * CIW E-Commerce Designer

• I.T. Professional
- CompTIA A+ / Network+ Diploma for IT Practitioners (System Support) e-Quals City & Guilds Level 2 • CompTIA - Security+ / Server+ / Linux+ / Project+
- MCSA - Microsoft Certified System Administrator • MCSE - Microsoft Certified System Engineer • MCDBA – Microsoft Certified Database Administrator

Programming – Software Development
- Certificate / Diploma Computer Programming - e-Quals City & Guilds
- Advanced Certs/ Diploma Computer Programming - e-Quals City & Guilds/Sun
- CIW JAVA Programming • CIW Web Languages – JavaScript / Perl

• Keyboarding

Business Courses (P/T)
- Business Studies Certificate & Diploma • Diploma Human Resource Development
- Diploma Marketing, Advertising and PR • Psychology Certificate & Diploma
- Accounting & Finance Certificate & Diploma • Legal Studies Certificate & Diploma

Tel: (01) 8309677   E-Mail: info@dorset-college.ie   www.dorset-college.ie

Portobello School Rere 40 Lr Dominick St 1 (8721277) - p/time eve

Senior College Dun Laoghaire CFE Eblana Ave Dun Laoghaire (2800385) - professional accounting formation 2 CPA, 25 wks €200

Westmoreland College for Management Studies 11 Westmoreland St 2 (6795324/7266) - ACCA dip in Financial Management

ACCOUNTING TECHNICIAN see also PAYROLL

ACCA 9 Leeson Pk 6 (4988900) - certified - nationwide, also day

Ashfield College Main St Templeogue 6W (4900866) - certified, 2 yr p/time, from Sept

Ballsbridge College of Business Studies Shelbourne Rd 4 (6684806) - IATI course, Mon, 6pm €420

Ballyfermot College of Further Education Ballyfermot Rd 10 (6269421) - IATI cert foundation yr 1, 20 wks, Mon & Wed, 7-10pm, €405/ admission yr 2, 20 wks, Mon, Wed, 7-10pm, €480

Colaiste Ide Cardiffsbridge Rd Finglas West 11 (8342333) - admission/foundation, Tues & Thurs, 7-9pm, each 25 wks, €450, IATI

Crumlin College of Further Education Crumlin Rd 12 (4540662) - IATI - 2 yr course: Yr 1: business management & IT, accounting, level 1, business law, taxation, level 1/ yr 2: IT in business, computerised accounts (TAS books), company law, accounting level 2, taxation, level 2 - 2 eves per week

DIT Faculty: Business Aungier St 2 (4023040/3445) - IATI exams, 2 yrs, €700 per stage

Dublin Business School 13/14 Aungier St 2 (4177500) - IATI, 2 eves per wk, 6.15-9.30pm, 2yrs

Inchicore College of Further Education Emmet Rd 8 (4535358) - day

Institute of Accounting Technicians in Ireland 87/89 Pembroke Rd 4 (6377363) - information on accredited courses

Institute of Technology Tallaght 24 (4042000) - yrs 1 & 2

Institute of Technology, Blanchardstown Blanchardstown Road North 15 (8851100) - IATI cert, 8 hrs wkly, 2 yr €735 pa

McKeon Murray Business Training Services Elm House Leopardstown Office Pk 18 (2959089) - correspondence, Inst of Acc Tech Foundation,& Admission exams, €450

Plunket College Swords Rd, Whitehall 9 (8371689) - IATI, Accounting/ Taxation/ Business Management & Law/IT/ Company Law/ Computerised Accounts/ Costing & Budgeting - 27 wks €113.50 each

Senior College Dun Laoghaire CFE Eblana Ave Dun Laoghaire (2800385) - IATI foundation/admission, 1yr/25 wks, €400 each/various, €120 f/time & p/time

St Thomas Community College Novara Ave Bray (2866111) - IATI cert, yr 2, €400 pa

Stillorgan College of Further Education Old Road Stillorgan (2880704) - 2 eve a wk, 20 wks IATI

Westmoreland College for Management Studies 11 Westmoreland St 2 (6795324/7266) - IATI/foundation & admission

ACRYLIC PAINTING

Brian Byrnes Art Studio 3 Upr Baggot St 4 (6671520 / 6711599) - 8wk, €130, also day

Cabinteely Community School Johnstown Rd 18 (2857455) - improvers, 10wk, €75

Colaiste Eanna Kilkieran Rd Cabra 7 (8389577) - 10wk, Tues, 7-9pm

Jean Strong (2892323) - ongoing, beginners-improvers, 10wks, €140/also day - Blackrock

Meridian Art Group c/o St Paul's College Raheny 5 (8310688)

ACTING Drama / Speech & Drama / Theatre

Betty Ann Norton Theatre School 11 Harcourt St 2 (4751913) - performance / acting dip / adult foundation course

Colaiste Dhulaigh Barryscourt Rd Coolock 17 (8481337) - 'act now!' personal development, Tues, 8 wks, 7.15-9.15 / Auditions! Auditions, Tue 10 wks

Connolly House Nth Strand (by 5 Lamps) 1 (8557116) - comedy & improvisation, 10 wks Wed, 7pm €66

Corporate Club 24 Elmcastle Green Kilnamanagh 24 (4610935)

Donahies Community School Streamville Rd 13 (8482217) - informal for beginners, Tue, 10 wks, €55

Drama League of Ireland Carmichael House Nth Brunswick St 7 (8749084) - take to the stage, Autumn & Spring modules, drama classes for all - 10 wk module focussing on acting styles, improv nights, voice work, movement & creating characters, Tues or Thurs 7.30-9.30pm €90

Gaiety School of Acting Sycamore St Meeting House Sq Temple Bar 2 (6799277) - Performance course/ Foundation course: each 1 yr €1750, / intro to drama / acting for camera/ advanced acting for camera/ page to stage/ advanced page to stage: each €290/ wkend workshops, Voice, €135/ making a short 'short', €310/ easter courses, acting for camera, €290/ adult improvisation, €310

Leinster School of Music & Drama Griffith College Campus South Circular Rd 8 (4150467)

Malahide Community School Malahide (8460949)

Network Sports & Social Club 24 Elmcastle Green Kilnamanagh 24 (4524415)

Plunket College Swords Rd, Whitehall 9 (8371689) - explore through performance Wed, 10 wks 7.30 €66

Pobalscoil Rosmini Adult Ed Grace Pk Rd 9 (8371015) - comedy workshop, 8.30, Wed €80

UCD Adult Education Office (7061695) - dramatic communication, 10 wks

ACUPUNCTURE see also Medicine

Acupuncture Foundation Training School Milltown Pk College (1850 577405) - traditional Chinese acupuncture licentiate 3yr p/time, €3533 pa

Irish College of Traditional Chinese Medicine Dublin (01-4967830) - licentiate in traditional Chinese medicine, 3 yrs, p/time course

ADDICTION STUDIES see also Drugs & Alcohol Abuse

Addiction Training Institute Neptune House Strand Road Bray, Co. Wicklow (2964218/ 2828537) - 2 wk part-time dip / home study, 6 mth cert: addiction studies/ counselling, psychotherapy & psychoanalysis/ eating disorders/ parent-child psychology

Department of Adult & Community Education NUI Maynooth (7084500) - NUI cert; also at Arklow (2803335); Bray, St Killian's (2864646); Drogheda (9836084); Dublin, Clonliffe (8360911); Stillorgan (2803335)

Institute of Technology Tallaght 24 (4042000) - community addiction studies, 1 yr

ADMINISTRATION see also Hospital & Health Services / Leisure / Teachers

Kilroy's College 25 Kingram Place 2 (1850 700700) - tutor supported home-study dip courses

Westmoreland College for Management Studies 11 Westmoreland St 2 (6795324/7266) - ICM dip in business studies/ ICM dip corporate management/ ICM dip health services management

ADULT EDUCATION see also Teachers

Further Education & Training Awards Council (FETAC East Point Plaza East Point Business Park 3 (8659500) - national certification body

Holistic Healing Centre 38 Dame St 2 (6710813)

Kilroy's College 25 Kingram Place 2 (1850 700700) - tutor supported home study: personal development, careers, computer skills, leaving cert, dip courses

UCD Adult Education Office (7061695) - adults & learning/ contemporary issues in ad ed/ course delivery/ designing the learning experience/ philosophy of ad ed/ planning skills/ supporting the adut learner/ facilitation skills & group learning/ new ideas in ad ed: all 12 wks

ADULT EDUCATOR'S TRAINING COURSE see also Teachers

Ballymun Comprehensive School Adult Ed Centre Ballymun Rd 9 (8420654/ 8425828 night) - literacy tutor training course (8622402)

Ballymun Comprehensive Schools Adult Ed Centre Ballymun Rd 9 (8420654/ 8425828 night) - literacy tutor training, €free

Colaiste Eoin Cappagh Rd 11 (8340893) - literacy tutor training

Crumlin College of Further Education Crumlin Rd 12 (4540662) - for adult literacy tutors, Mon (4547054)

ADULT LITERACY see also English Literacy / Basic Education

Ballymun Comprehensive School Adult Ed Centre Ballymun Rd 9 (8420654/ 8425828 night) - tutor training course, €free, spell well - improve your spelling skills, 10 wks free/ reading & writing group, free classes tel 8622402

Colaiste Eanna College of Business & Technical Stu Kilkieran Rd Cabra 7 (8389577) - literacy, numeracy, computers - day (tel 8688342/8389577/ FETAC English spelling, maths, etc

Crumlin College of Further Education Crumlin Rd 12 (4540662) - various adult reading & writing courses: one-to-one, spelling groups, numeracy, FETAC foundation in communications, spelling through computers; junior cert English; Tues & Thurs 7.45-9.45/ guidance service 4540662 ext119

Dublin Adult Learning Centre 3 Mountjoy Sq 1 (8787266) - Read, Write, Spell - various courses; also tutor training

Irish Deaf Society 30 Blessington St 7 (8828001/Minicom: 8828002) - literacy classes for Deaf adults, €free

Kilroy's College 25 Kingram Place 2 (1850 700700) - tutor supported home study: English, words study, spelling & arithmetic, general education, dip courses

KLEAR Grange Park View Kilbarrack 5 (8671845) - self-esteem/ computer literacy/ parent to parent/ spelling group/ basic maths/ sums/ learn through cookery/ reading & writing/ reading with children: day courses

Rathmines Snr College Town Hall 6 (4975334) - literacy service Tue eves

Ringsend Technical Institute Cambridge Rd 4 (6684498) - numeracy, various times, ongoing, free

St Mark's Community School Cookstown Road Tallaght 24 (4519399)

ADVENTURE SKILLS

Clondalkin Sports & Leisure Centre Nangor Rd Clondalkin 22 (4574858) - day

St Kevins College Clogher Rd Crumlin 12 (4536397) - ISA, ICU, NCVA, 1yr, day

ADVENTURE SPORTS & HOLIDAYS

An Oige 61 Mountjoy Street 7 (8304555) - walking, hiking, photography, cycling, hostelling, voluntary work, conservation

Corporate Club 24 Elmcastle Green Kilnamanagh 24 (4610935) - snow skiing abroad

Kylemore College Kylemore Rd 10 (6265901) - rock climbing beginners, Mon & Tue 8 wks

Network Sports & Social Club 24 Elmcastle Green Kilnamanagh 24 (4524415) - hillwalking, walking, sailing, windsurfing, canoeing, orienteering, snow skiing (abroad)

Portmarnock Sub-Aqua Club John Kirwan Diving Instructor (2987932-pm) - scuba diving

ADVERTISING see also Graphics / Marketing

DIT Faculty: Business Aungier St 2 (4023040/3445) - professional dip: executive/ creative, 1 yr €700 each

Dublin Business School 13/14 Aungier St 2 (4177500) - dip in marketing, advertising & PR, 2 eves wkly1 yr/14wks/ also advanced dip, 2 eves wkly, 1 yr 6.30-9.30

Fitzwilliam Institute Ltd Temple Court Temple Rd Blackrock (2834579) - dip in advertising, 1 yr, €1,520 + 130 PRII, exam fees, Mon & Wed, 6.30-9.15/ also postgrad dip in advertising, day, €3606+ €190 exam fees, AAI accred

Westmoreland College for Management & Business 11 Westmoreland St 2 (6795324/7266) - ICM dip, marketing, advertising & PR

AEROBICS see also Keep Fit / Exercise

Bodyline Studio Rere Brady's Terenure Pl 6W (4902038) - & gym, 6 days, membership from €199

Cabinteely Community School Johnstown Rd 18 (2857455) - intermediate, €40 step, €40 10wk each

Clondalkin Sports & Leisure Centre Nangor Rd Clondalkin 22 (4574858) - & step aerobics, also day

Coolmine Community School Clonsilla 15 (8214583) - Wed, 7-8pm, 8.10-9.10pm, €40

Corporate Club 24 Elmcastle Green Kilnamanagh 24 (4610935) - aqua

Greendale Community School Kilbarrack 5 (8322735/6) - Tues, 7-8pm, 10wks, €35

Hartstown Community School Clonsilla 15 (8209863) - 10wk, €40

Holy Family Community School Rathcoole (4580766)

Jackie Skelly's Fitness 42 Clarendon St, 2; Park West Bus Pk, Nangor Rd, 12 & Applewood Village, Swords (6770040 / 6301456 / 8075620) - step, pump, spin, toning, taebo, pilates, body sculpt - membership includes classes, €47-59 per mth

Marino College 14-20 Marino Mart 3 (8332100) - Tues, 6.15pm 10wks, €33

Motions Health & Fitness Training City West Leisure Centre (4588179/ 087 2808866)

National College of Exercise & Health Studies 16a St Joseph's Parade Dorset St 7 (8827777) - Nat Qual in exercise to Music, 18 wks €1640, also day / step aerobics, spincycle, 1 day - Nat Qual

Network Sports & Social Club 24 Elmcastle Green Kilnamanagh 24 (4524415) - aqua

Palmerstown Community School 20 (6260116) - Mon, 10 wks, 8-9pm €55

Phibsboro Gym 1st floor, Phibsboro SC 7 (8301849) - step/boxercise

Portmarnock Community School Carrickhill Rd (8038056) - & body conditioning, 8wk, €30

Portmarnock Sports & Leisure Club Blackwood Lane Carrickhill Portmarnock (8462122) - also aqua fit

Saint Paul's Swimming Pool Sybil Hill Raheny 5 (8316283) - aqua

Salsa Dublin East Hill Newtownmountkennedy Co Wicklow (087 9172939) - cardiosalsa, beginners/ intermediate. €8 per class various Dublin venues

St MacDara's Community College Wellington Lane Templeogue 6W (4566216) - Mon beginners/ Wed, 7.30& 8.15 10 wks, €46

St Thomas Community College Novara Ave Bray (2866111) - 8wks, €40

St Tiernan's Community School Parkvale Balally 16 (2953224) - Mon/ Wed, 7.30-9.30pm, 10 wks, €40

AEROMODELLING
Malahide Community School Malahide (8460949) - build your plane from scratch, 10 wks, no fee

AERONAUTICAL ENGINEERING and related courses See also Aviation
DIT Faculty: Engineering Bolton St 1 (4023649/3445) - aeronautical maintenance engineers' type courses, 1 yr €700/ jet engine overhaul, 1 yr €500/ basic aeronautical knowledge; also catagory A: €500, 1 eve wk modules; €700 2 eve wk modules/ fundamentals of avionics, 10 wks €500

Kilroy's College 25 Kingram Place 2 (1850 700700) - tutor supported home study: avionics - basic aircraft electronics, dip course

AESTHETICIAN see Beauty Therapy

AFRIKAANS
Dublin Public Libraries Admin Hq, 138-144 Pearse St 2 (6644800) - central library Ilac Centre, D1, (8734333) or Library HQ for details (6744800)- self-learning €free Sth Dublin Co Libraries Languages & Computers: Ballyroan/Clondalkin/ Castletymon, Lucan & Co Library (4597834-admin only) - self learning

AIKIDO see also Karate / Martial Arts
Irish Aikido Federation 1 Parklane E Pearse St 2 (6718454) - 10wk, €100/ 3 months, €150

Natural Health Training Centre 1 Park Lane E Pearse St 2 (6718454) - intro, 10wks, €100/ 3 mths, €170/ 6mths €300

Phibsboro Gym 1st floor, Phibsboro SC 7 (8301849)

Public Service Aikido Club St Andrew's Resource Cntr Pearse St 2 (4947787 Paul/Joan) - all yr except bank hols, Mon & Thurs, 8 classes, €30 / unwaged €20

Whitefriar Aikido Dojo Whitefriar Community Centre Aungier St 2 (4535509) - basic, 20wks, €50/intermediate, 40wks, €100/advanced €3 per class/mixed, €3 per class

AIRLINE STUDIES see AVIATION
Portobello School Rere 40 Lr Dominick St 1 (8721277) - airline studies, p/time eve; also f/time

ALARM INSTALLATIONS
FAS Training Centre Finglas Jamestown Rd 11 (8140243)

Hi-Tech Training 4 Nth Gt George's St 1 (1850-759759) - 50% practical, hands-on, 7-10pm, 15 wks, cert

ALCOHOL ABUSE see Drugs
St Anthony's House St Lawrence Rd Clontarf 3 (8335300) - AA, also Sat

ALEXANDER TECHNIQUE
Alexander Technique Postural Re-education Frank Kennedy 35 Callary Rd Mt Merrion (2882446) - also day/ stress management

ALTERNATIVE & COMPLEMENTARY THERAPIESsee also Holististic/ Homoeopathy/Healing/Kineasology/Meditation/Reiki, etc.
BASE Ballyboden Adult Social Education Whitechurch Library Taylor's Lane 16 (4935953) - release energy through colour movement, paint

Cabinteely Community School Johnstown Rd 18 (2857455) - medicine, 10wk, €75

Cocoon Reiki Centre Howth (8321255; 086 2312684) - reiki & seichim, levels 1 &

2 mastership, Reiki: 12 wks, Seichem: 2 wks, cert

Coolmine Community School Clonsilla 15 (8214583) - 7.30-9.30, 9 wks €60

Greenhills College Limekiln Ave Walkinstown 12 (4507779/4507138) - angel therapy, Mon, 8wks, €73

Hartstown Community School Clonsilla 15 (8209863) - holistic life skills/just for me - 10wks, €60 each

Healing House 24 O'Connell Ave Berkeley Rd 7 (8306413) - wide range of courses & therapies

Holistic Sourcing Centre 67 Lr Camden St 2 (4785022) - meridian energy psychotherapy (Ir Ass of Adv Meridian Techniques) 086 8168834

Institute of Celtic, Shamanic Development Sacred Hoop Lodge 64 Sth William Street 2 (4577839)

KAIROS Therapy Training Ellen Smith (6286466) Kairos emotioinal release therapy

Killester College of Further Education Collins Ave 5 (8337686) - Tues 7.30 10 wks €60; Fri morn 10-12, 10 wks €75

Margaret Macken Stephen's Gr/Adelaide Rd/Clontarf (8332954) - Iyengar Yoga, 6 wk course; also relaxation, stress management and meditation

Motions Health & Fitness Training City West Leisure Centre (4588179/ 087 2808866)

Newpark Adult & Continuing Ed. Centre Newtownpark Ave Blackrock (2884376)

OBUS Healing Centre 53 Beech Grove Lucan (6282121) - accupressure 8 day course, day / chakra, 1 day €150

Portobello School Rere 40 Lr Dominick St 1 (8721277) - complementary therapies dip, p/time eve, 1 day release; also full time

Rathmines Snr College Town Hall 6 (4975334) - holistic lifestyle - yoga, massage, indian head massage, stress management, shiatsu, armoatherapy, reflexology: 10 wks, Wed, €65/ health & alternative nutrition, Tue 10 wks €65

Shiatsu Ireland classes Ranelagh & Leixlip/ individ treatments (6109110) - shiatsu & massage, - beginners & advanced

Walmer College & Holistic Centre First Floor, Raheny SC Howth Rd 5 (8475410/338) - auragraphics, wkend workshops/ body spirit/ various massage courses/ relaxation - meditation, etc

AMHARIC (language of Ethiopia)

Dublin Public Libraries Admin Hq, 138-144 Pearse St 2 (6644800) - central library Ilac Centre (8734333) or Library HQ for details (6744800), self-learning €free

ANATOMY

Bronwyn Conroy Beauty School 10 The Crescent Monkstown (2804020) - anatomy, physiology & massage

Complementary Healing Therapies 136 New Cabra Rd 7 (8681110) - & physiology, ITEC dip, w/ends, 7 months

Crumlin College of Further Education Crumlin Rd 12 (4540662) - ITEC dip in anatomy & physiology & body massage, for registered nurse

Healing House 24 O'Connell Ave Berkeley Rd 7 (8306413) - anatomy & physiology diploma course, ITEC, Tues, Thurs or w/end, €700

Irish Academy of Massage & Complementary Therapies 33 Monkstown Lawns, Clondalkin,22 Walkinstown/ Celbridge centres (4640126 /086 8494660) - anatomy and physiology, 60hrs; also wkends; €600, ITEC dip; venues - Walkinstown, Celbridge, Dundrum, Swords, Tullamore

Motions Health & Fitness Training City West Leisure Centre (4588179/ 087 2808866)

Senior College Dun Laoghaire CFE Eblana Ave Dun Laoghaire (2800385) - dip in anatomy, physiology and body massage, CIBTAC, 25 wks, €475

Walmer College & Holistic Centre First Floor, Raheny SC Howth Rd 5 (8475410/338) - & physiology, ITEC dip

ANGELS see Meditation, Personal Development

ANGLING

Irish Federation of Sea Anglers c/o H O'Rourke 67 Windsor Drive Monkstown (2806873)

ANIMALS / ANIMAL CARE

Brian Byrnes Art Studio 3 Upr Baggot St 4 (6671520 / 6711599) - painting/drawing, 8wk, €130, also day

Colaiste Dhulaigh & College of Further Education Barryscourt Rd Coolock 17 (8481337) - animal welfare program, Mon 7-9.30, 10 wks

Killester College of Further Education Collins Ave 5 (8337686) - per care & animal grooming, 10 wks, Mon, Tue 7.30-9.30 €110

Plunket College Swords Rd, Whitehall 9 (8371689) - animal welfare theory & practice, Wed 7.30 10wks €66

St Thomas Community College Novara Ave Bray (2866111) - wildlife conservatin, 30 wks €200

ANIMATION see also Computer Aided Graphics/ Graphic

Ballyfermot College of Further Education Ballyfermot Rd 10 (6269421) - computeranimation, 3D Max, 10 wks, Mon & Weds, 7-10pm, €60

New Media Technology Training 13 Harcourt St 2 (4780905) - macromedia flash

ANTHROPOLOGY

AAA Counselling Dr MJ Brennan PhD c/o 48 Connaught St Phibsboro 7 (8380014) - Time Research and Cosmology

UCD Adult Education Office (7061695) - family, gender, sexuality in Euro history, 10 wks/

ANTIQUES see also Furniture Restoration

Irish Auctioneers & Valuers Institute 38 Merrion Sq E 2 (6611794) - fine art appreciation, 6wks, €200/advanced course, 9wks, €220

Newpark Adult Education Centre Newtownpark Ave Blackrock (2884376) - restoration & repair, 10wks, €102, Mon, tur, Thurs

UCD Adult Education Office (7061695) - 8 wks

APIARY see Bee-Keeping
APPLIQUE see Patchwork
APTITUDE TESTS
AAA Counselling Dr MJ Brennan PhD c/o 48 Connaught St Phibsboro 7 (8380014) - aptitude determinations, also day
Kilroy's College 25 Kingram Place 2 (1850 700700) - general aptitude and intelligence tests
ARABIC Languages
Dublin Public Libraries Admin Hq, 138-144 Pearse St 2 (6644800) - central library
Ilac Centre, D1. (8734333) or Library HQ for details (6744800) self-learning €free
Maynooth College Language Centre NUI Maynooth Co Kildare (7083737) - beginners, 9wk, €110
Sandford Language Institute Milltown Pk Sandford Rd 6 (2601296) - language and culture, all levels, 14 wks, €250 each
Sth Dublin Co Libraries Languages & Computers: Ballyroan/Clondalkin/Castletymon, Lucan & Co Library (4597834-admin only) - self learning
UCD Adult Education Office (7061695) - intro to modern Arabic literature & culture, 10 wks
ARCHAEOLOGY
Old Bawn Community School Tallaght 24 (4526137) - appreciating Ireland, past & present, with 2 field trips, Tues, 7.30-9.30pm, 10 wks
People's College 32 Parnell Sq 1 (8735879) - €40
Royal Soc of Antiquaries of Ireland 63 Merrion Sq 2 (6761749) - individual lectures, outings, talks
UCD Adult Education Office (7061695) - arch of medieval & post-medieval Ireland/curent themes & approaches in arch/ 9 wks ea/ death & our ancestors, 10 wks
ARCHERY
Clondalkin Sports & Leisure Centre Nangor Rd Clondalkin 22 (4574858)
Greendale Community School Kilbarrack 5 (8322735/6) - Tue, 6-8pm, 10wks, €55
Inchicore College of Further Education Emmet Rd 8 (4535358) - Tues, 10wks
Kylemore College Kylemore Rd 10 (6265901) - beginners, Thurs, 7wks
ARCHITECTURE see also Art History / Draughtsmanship
Irish Georgian Society 74 Merrion Sq 2 (6767053) - lectures, tours, visits to historic houses etc, for members
Pearse College Clogher Rd 12 (4536661/4541544) - draughting, day
Trinity College 2 (6772941) - (6083061), extra mural, intro to European, €205, 22 wks
UCD Adult Education Office (7061695) - understanding, 10 wks
AROMATHERAPY
Ann Prendergast Rosebud Salon Rathgar Ave 6 (4920856) - intro, 8wk, €127, Sun morning, Rathgar/Rthfarnham
Ashfield College Main St Templeogue 6W (4900866) - 7.30-9.30, 8 wks
Aspen's Beauty Clinic & College 83 Lr Camden St 2 (4751079/ 4751940) - wkend, Sun 11-4pm, 16 wks €1795
Berni Grainger 21 Grangemore Ave 13 (8472943) - massage & use of oils, intro, w/end, €140

Colaiste Dhulaigh Barryscourt Rd Coolock 17 (8481337) - & body massage for women, Mon, 10 wks, 7.45-9.30

Coolmine Community School Clonsilla 15 (8214583) - 7.30-9.30, 9 wks €60

Crumlin College of Further Education Crumlin Rd 12 (4540662) ITEC dip, 25 wks

Dun Laoghaire College of Further Education 17 Cumberland St Dun Laoghaire (2809676) - Wed, 10 wks, 7.30-9.30pm, €100

Galligan College of Beauty 109 Grafton St 2 (6703933) - ITEC & CIBTAC, c.30wks

Greenhills College Limekiln Ave Walkinstown 12 (4507779/4507138) - 8wks, €87

Hartstown Community School Clonsilla 15 (8209863) - 10wks, €60

Healing House 24 O'Connell Ave Berkeley Rd 7 (8306413) - international dip - Sept to June, Tues 8-10pm €1325; also wkend / essential oils 1 & 2 day workshops €75/ €125

Holistic Healing Centre 38 Dame St 2 (6710813) - dip

Irish College of Complementary Medicine 6 Main St Donnybrook 4 (2696588/086-2500617) - ITEC, dip

KLEAR Grange Park View Kilbarrack 5 (8671845) - Mon, 9.30am

Lucan Community College Esker Drive (6282077) - 6wk, €53

Marie Oxx Pearse College, Clogher Rd 12 (4536661) - ITEC dip, day

Newpark Adult Education Centre Newtownpark Ave Blackrock (2884376) - 10wks, €99 Tue

OBUS Aromatherapy Training 53 Beech Grove Lucan (6282121) - professional, 1yr, dip, also day @ Lucan & Leixlip/ home use, 6wks, cert, also day, various centres

Old Bawn Community School Tallaght 24 (4526137) - beginners, Thurs, 7.30-9.30pm, 10 wks

Palmerstown Community School 20 (6260116) - for home use: level 1, €60/level 2, €65

People's College for Continuing Education & Traini 32 Parnell Sq 1 (8735879) - & Indian head massage, €60

Pobalscoil Rosmini Adult Ed Grace Pk Rd 9 (8371015) - beginners, 1&2, Wed, 7pm, 10 wks, €85

Portobello School Rere 40 Lr Dominick St 1 (8721277) - ITEC dip, part-time eve

Senior College Dun Laoghaire CFE Eblana Ave Dun Laoghaire (2800385) - CIB-TAC dip,1 yr, 25 wks, €475/ intro to aromatherapy & massage, 10 wks, €100

St Thomas Community College Novara Ave Bray (2866111) - 10wks, €70/ 30 wks, €130, day

Tallaght Community School Balrothery 24 (4515566) - intro to massage & aromatherapy, 7.30 8 wks €45

Walmer College & Holistic Centre First Floor, Raheny SC Howth Rd 5 (8475410/338) - aromatherapy ITEC dip

ART see also Acrylics / Animation / Architecture / Design / Drawing / Graphics / Oil Painting / Painting / Picture Framing / Portrait / Sketching / Watercolours

Balbriggan Community College Pine Ridge Chapel St (8412388/9) - watercolours, 8 wks, Wed 7.30-9.30, €73

Ballsbridge College of Business Studies Shelbourne Rd 4 (6684806) - mixed media, Thurs 7.45, 10 wks, €60

Ballyfermot College of Further Education Ballyfermot Rd 10 (6269421) -drawing & painting, 10 wks, Mon, 7-9.30pm, €80; portfolio preparation 15 wks, Mon&Wed, 7-9.30pm, €240

Ballymun Comprehensive Schools Adult Ed Centre Ballymun Rd 9 (8420654/ 8425828 night) - oils, watercolours, painting, beginners/improvers, Mon Tue 10wk, €75, €80 / mosaics & stained glass, beginners, Tue 10 wk, €85

Ballymun Mens Centre LS4 Shangan Rd Ballymun 9 (8623117/8623409) - day

BASE Ballyboden Adult Social Education Whitechurch Library Taylor's Lane 16 (4935953) - beginners / improvers

Botanic Art School 28a Prospect Avenue Glasnevin 9 (8304720) - all media, for adults & children, also day, figure & portrait, drawing & watercolours

Brenda Bigger Killiney (2849675) - hand-painted porcelain, 5wk, 2.5 hours per class, €85, materials extra, day

Brian Byrnes Art Studio 3 Upr Baggot St 4 (6671520 / 6711599) - 8wk, €130, also day, landscapes, animals, portraits, flowers & gardens

Colaiste Eanna Kilkieran Rd Cabra 7 (8389577) - sketching/painting, 10wk, Tues, 7-9pm / also day (Finbars Court) 10-12

Colaiste Eoin Cappagh Rd 11 (8340893) - 10wk

College of Further Education Main St Dundrum 14 (2951376) - drawing, sketching, watercolours, 8 wks Tue

Coolmine Community School Clonsilla 15 (8214583) - paint & draw, Mon, Tue, Wed, 9wks, €60 each

DATE College of Further Education Dundrum 14 (2964322) - beginners/ flower painting: each 10 wks, €66, day

DIT Faculty: Applied Arts Aungier St 2 (4023465/3445) - finding your own direction, 5 wks

Dublin School of Art 18 Butterfield Ave Rathfarnham 14 (4943303) - art studies dip, open learning, 10-12 mths €850 / master class portfolio, eve, 8wks €180 / art holiday in France, 1 wk €360 / tuition class, one to one, day, 2.5hr €45 / art therapy, day, 2.15 hrs €30

Dunboyne Village Co Meath (8222929) - drawing & painting (watercolours &

acrylics) Thurs, 8 wks all yr; also courses for children

FAS Training Centre Cabra Bannow Rd 7 (8821400) - art & mural painting, day

Finglas Adult Reading & Writing Scheme Colaiste Eoin Finglas 11 (8340893) - for leaving cert, day, 30wks, free

Grange Community College Grange Abbey Rd Donaghmede 13 (8471422) - water colours, 8wks, €73

Greenhills College Limekiln Ave Walkinstown 12 (4507779/4507138) - 10 wks, €79

Hartstown Community School Clonsilla 15 (8209863) - 10wks/watercolour 10wks €60

Holy Family Community School Rathcoole (4580766)

Inchicore College of Further Education Emmet Rd 8 (4535358) - & design, day/ drawing & painting, Tues 10 wks

Jean Strong (2892323) - ongoing, beginners-improvers, 10wks, €140/also day - Blackrock

Kilternan Adult Ed. Group Ballybetagh Rd 18 (2952050) - all mediums Thurs. 10 wks £72.

Knocklyon Youth & Community Centre, 16 (4943991)

Kylemore College Kylemore Rd 10 (6265901) - can't paint, can't draw, Tue / various creative art techniques, Wed / clay modelling Thurs/ print techniques Mon/ water colours Wed: all 7-9pm 10 wks/ art & design, FETAC cert, 12 wks Mon 7-9pm

Melt, Temple Bar Natural Healing Centre 2 Temple Ln 2 (6798786) - art experience, day wkend, €100

Meridian Art Group c/o St Paul's College Raheny 5 (8310688)

Newpark Adult & Continuing Education Centre Newtownpark Ave Blackrock (2884376) - painting/drawing/watercolours, sketching pen & ink

Old Bawn Community School Tallaght 24 (4526137) - intro to drawing, design, watercolours & oils, materials not incl., Tues, 7.30-9.30, 10wks

Plunket College Swords Rd, Whitehall 9 (8371689) - beginners, Tues 7.30, €66/ painting/sketching for active retired, day only

Pobalscoil Rosmini Adult Ed Grace Pk Rd 9 (8371015) - beginners, Mon&Tue €85/ continuation/ landscape/ painting for pleasure,Wed, day €85/ watercolour & oils €90; portfolio preparation: €83, 10 wks each

Portmarnock Community School Carrickhill Rd (8038056) - & painting 8 wks €50

RAVE Good Shepherd School Churchtown 14 (2981052) - painting with Hazel / painting & drawing, each 10 wks Mon 7.30, €79

St Mac Dara's Community College Wellington Lane Templeogue 6W (4566216) - Mon beginners/ art club, Tue: 7.30-9.30pm, 10 wks, €79

St Tiernan's Community School Parkvale Balally 16 (2953224) - watercolours/ acrylic, 10 wks, €70

Stillorgan Senior College Old Road Stillorgan (2880704) - mixed ability, mixed experience, Mon/ sketching & painting, beginners/improvers, Thurs - 8 wks, €70 each

TACT St Dominic's School St Dominic's Rd Tallaght 24 (4596757) - beginners/advanced, 10wks, €55 day

Taney Parish Centre Taney Rd Dundrum 14 (2985491) - Mon 2981853/ art zone childrens, Thurs

Trinity College 2 (6772941) - (6081116) - extra mural, contemporary art, 8wks, free lunchtime lectures

UCD Adult Education Office (7061695) - for beginners 1 & 2 10 wks

ART APPRECIATION see also Art History

Institute of Professional Auctioneers & Valuers 129 Lr Baggot St 2 (6785685) - fine & decorative arts, cert, 15 wks €750

Irish Auctioneers & Valuers Institute 38 Merrion Sq E 2 (6611794) - fine art appreciation, 6wks, €200/advanced course, 9wks, €220

National Gallery of Ireland Merrion Sq W 2 (6615133) - lectures over 2 terms, 22 wks, Season Ticket €140; €7 per talk

People's College 32 Parnell Sq 1 (8735879) - exploring modern Irish art, €50

TACT St Dominic's School St Dominic's Rd Tallaght 24 (4596757) - the artist's way, 13 wks, €78/ leaving cert art 30 wks free

Trinity College 2 (6772941) - (6083061) - extra mural, intro to Euro painting, €205 / the Arts of Japan, 22 wks, €105

UCD Adult Education Office (7061695) - an introduction to, 10 wks, day/ 'The Arts' - a guide, 10 wks

ART HISTORY see also Art Appreciation

Ballyfermot College of Further Education Ballyfermot Rd 10 (6269421) - Weds, 7-9, 10 wks €65

Connolly House Nth Strand (by 5 Lamps) 1 (8557116) - history & appreciation of art, 10 wks Wed, 8pm €50

DATE College of Further Education Dundrum 14 (2964322) - history & appreciation, 10 wks, €79, day

DIT Faculty: Applied Arts Aungier St 2 (4023465/3445) - critical theory: construction of the Irish Landscape 1850-2000 (4024138)

National Gallery of Ireland Merrion Sq W 2 (6615133) - lectures over 2 terms, 22 wks, Season Ticket €140; €7 per talk

Old Bawn Community School Tallaght 24 (4526137) - past & present, Thurs, 10 wks

Trinity College 2 (6772941) - (6081039/1072) - Euro painting, dip, 22wks

Trinity College 2 (6772941) - (6083061) - modernism & post-modernism, day, 22 wks, €105 / the Italian renaissance, day 22 wks €105 / (6082480) Irish art & its contexts, eve 18 wks, €90

UCD Adult Education Office (7061695) - history of European painting, ye 2 dip

ART METAL WORK see also Jewellery

DIT Faculty: Engineering Bolton St 1 (4023649/3445) - art metal casting, 8 wks eve

Gemcraft Design Studio 5 Herbert St 2 (2883796) - & jewellery making, 2 eve per wk, 7-9.30, 10 wks

National College of Art & Design in Art & Design 100 Thomas Street 8 (6364214) - & jewellery, all levels, c.22wk

The Centre for Continuing Education in Art and Design
NCAD, 100 Thomas Street, Dublin 8

The Centre for Continuing Education in Art and Design, NCAD, promotes a broad selection of art, craft and design classes for people who wish to explore their creative potential, learn new skills, and deepen their understanding of visual art processes. People interested in developing an art practice are encouraged to progress from Introductory to Intermediate classes, on a year to year basis.

This Autumn, CEAD are offering a wide range of classes, including:

- **Drawing/Painting from Life**
- **Bronze Casting**
- **Stained Glass**
- **Etching and Dry Point Technique**
- **Sculpture**
- **Photography**
- **Jewellery and Metalwork**
- **Ceramics**
- **Fashion Design**
- **Pottery**
- **Textiles**
- **Portfolio Prep.**
- **History of Art and Cultural Studies**

Courses are 21/22 weeks long. Students attend one evening a week from 6.45pm to 9.15pm. CEAD courses cater for a range of interests, level of skill and ability. Closing date for application is 5th September 2003.

For further information please contact CEAD at: 01-6364214 or E-mail: cead@ncad.ie

Ringsend Technical Institute Cambridge Rd 4 (6684498) - 10 wks €65
ARTS/CRAFTS see also Crafts; Jewellery
Ballymun Mens Centre LS4 Shangan Rd Ballymun 9 (8623117/8623409) -day
Colaiste Eanna College of Business & Technical Stu Kilkieran Rd Cabra 7 (8389577) - day (tel 8688342/8389577)
Connolly House Nth Strand (by 5 Lamps) 1 (8557116) - Wed, 7pm €66
Coolmine Community School Clonsilla 15 (8214583) - mosaic magic, 7.30-9.30, 9 wks €60
Dunboyne Village Co Meath (8222929) - art with crafts for children
Kilroy's College 25 Kingram Place 2 (1850 700700) - tutor supported home study, dressmaking
KLEAR Grange Park View Kilbarrack 5 (8671845) - creative arts, day
Kylemore College Kylemore Rd 10 (6265901) - papier mache/ paper sculpture/ paper craft, Thurs/ mocaics: 10 wk each

Newpark Adult Education Centre Newtownpark Ave Blackrock (2884376) - intro to mosaics, 10wks, €99

School of Practical Child Care Blackrock Campus Carysfort Ave Blackrock (2886994) - for children, city centre, 3 day, SPCC cert

St Thomas Community College Novara Ave Bray (2866111) - for people needing care, 30 wks, €200 FETAC cert

Tracy Miley 13b Dodder View Cottages Ballsbridge 4 (086 8485394) - mosaic, 7-9pm, 8 wks/ hand built ceramics: 8 wks €120 ea materials supplied

UCD Adult Education Office (7061695) - papercrafting, 10 wks, Sats

ASSERTIVENESS see also Enneagram / Personal Development

Ballsbridge College of Business Studies Shelbourne Rd 4 (6684806) - Thurs, 6.30 10 wks, €65

Cabinteely Community School Johnstown Rd 18 (2857455) - 10wk, €75

Centre for Professional & Personal Development Coach Centre 44 Westland Row 2 (6612291) - women's wealth within, wkend, €500

Colaiste Eanna Kilkieran Rd Cabra 7 (8389577) - confidence building 10 wks, Tue.

Communication & Personal Development 30/31 Wicklow St 2 (6713636/6613225)

Donahies Community School Streamville Rd 13 (8482217) - for men & women, Wed, 10 wks, €55

Eden Computer Training Rathfarnham 16, or MACRO Centre, 1 Green St 7 (4953155) - communications, motivation, decision making: customised

Froebel College of Education Sion Hill, Blackrock & Nurture Inst 140 Meadowgrove Dundrum (2963795) - for parents, Tues, 7 wks, €80

Keytrainer Ireland 33/34 Dame St 2 (6714000) - tailored courses

Killester College of Further Education Collins Ave 5 (8337686) - intro to, Mon, Tue, 7.30, 10 wks €60

Marino College 14-20 Marino Mart 3 (8332100) - level 1&2, Tue & Thurs, 10wks, €26

MD Communications 38 Spireview Lane off Rathgar Rd 6 (4975866)

Newpark Adult Education Centre Newtownpark Ave Blackrock (2884376) - stress management, life skills, €95

Old Bawn Community School Tallaght 24 (4526137) - self discovery, Tue, 7.30-9.30, 10wks

Quantum Communications Ken McCready 39 Emerald Sq, Dolphin's Barn 8 (086 1502604) - courses in city centre, 6 wk

St Thomas Community College Novara Ave Bray (2866111) - 10 wks, €70

Star Consulting PO Box 8796 2 (086 6061639) - 2 day €350

Yvonne Stewart Park House Library Road Dun Laoire (2802150) - for women, 8wks, €70, day

ASTROLOGY

Astrological Assoc of Ireland Astral House Lr Rathmines 6 (4969440) - planets & signs, Mon / rules in interpretation, Tues / forecasting & future trends: each 10 wks €150 / also held at Old Bawn Com School & Ballymun comprehensive

Ballymun Comprehensive School Adult Ed Centre Ballymun Rd 9 (8420654/ 8425828 night) - Wed, 7.30 10 wks €80

House of Astrology 9 Parliament St 2 (8641697) - astroleg, beginners / intermediate

Old Bawn Community School Tallaght 24 (4526137) - as a tool for self awareness, Tue, 10 wks

Star Consulting PO Box 8796 2 (086 6061639) - beginners/ advanced, 8 wks €250 ea

ASTRONOMY

Astronomy Ireland PO Box 2888 5 (8470777) - introduction to 10wks, members €75, non-m €105 - venue Old Bawn CS

Dunsink Observatory Dunsink Lane Castleknock 15 (838 7911/7959) - Public open nights 1st/3rd Wed of each month, Oct-Mar, 8pm. Must send SAE for free tickets

ATHLETICS

Athletics Association of Ireland 11 Prospect Rd Glasnevin 9 (8308925) - the national body, 320 clubs

AUCTIONEERING

Institute of Professional Auctioneers & Valuers 129 Lr Baggot St 2 (6785685) - estate agent practical, cert

AUTOGENIC TRAINING

IICH Education 118 Stillorgan Road 4 (2600118) - 3-day foundation skills course, €245. Thought Field Therapy (Algorithms Levels I &II), Applied Behavioural Medicine/ Health Crisis Counselling. Classes at Milltown Pk, 6 and other south-city locations

Institute of Autogenic Training 118 Stillorgan Rd 4 (2600118) - 3-day, weekend courses with Manfred Hillmann

AUTOMOBILE ENGINEERING see Engineering

AVIATION

DIT Faculty: Engineering Bolton St 1 (4023649/3445) - flight ops officer dispatcher, 2yr €975/ fundamentals of avionics, 10 wks €397/ private aircraft pilot licence theory, 1 yr €750

Eircopter Helicopters Weston Aerodrome Celbridge (6280088) - helicopter private pilot licence, ground school, 7.30-10pm, 16 wks €550/ also, introductory flying lessons, 30 min €185, 60min €363

Kilroy's College 25 Kingram Place 2 (1850 700700) - tutor supported home study: avionics - basic aircraft electronics, dip course

Old Bawn Community School Tallaght 24 (4526137) - private pilot's licence, foundatin course, 10 wks

AYURVEDA

Coolmine Community School Clonsilla 15 (8214583) - 9 wks, Wed 7.30-9.30 €60

BABYSITTING see TRANSITION YEAR

BADMINTON

Badminton Union of Ireland, Leinster Branch Terenure Centre Whitehall Rd 6

(4508101/ Baldoyle Centre (8393355) - beginners, 10 wks, €65/ also improvers, 10wks, €65

Colaiste Dhulaigh & College of Further Education Barryscourt Rd Coolock 17 (8481337) - for beginners, Mon 6.30

Corporate Club 24 Elmcastle Green Kilnamanagh 24 (4610935)

Network Sports & Social Club 24 Elmcastle Green Kilnamanagh 24 (4524415)

Pobalscoil Rosmini Adult Ed Grace Pk Rd 9 (8371015) - beginners/ improvers, Tue/ players;continuation, Thurs: 10 wks, €80 each

Portmarnock Sports & Leisure Club Blackwood Lane Carrickhill Portmarnock (8462122)

Ringsend Technical Institute Cambridge Rd 4 (6684498) - begineers, 10wks, €65

Taney Parish Centre Taney Rd Dundrum 14 (2985491) - Tues, Thurs (2981583)

BAKERY STUDIES

DIT Faculty: Tourism & Food Cathal Brugha St 1 (4024349/3445) - School of Bakery: German masterclass in professional bread baking, for graduates, based in Weinheim, with simultaneous English trans (4024566)

BALLET Classical & Jazz : see also Dance

Dublin School of Dance 13 Stamer St Portobello 8 (4755451) - ballet, for adults, 40 wks, €7 per class

Inchicore College of Further Education Emmet Rd 8 (4535358) - Tue, 10 wks, 6-7.30

Ingrid Nachstern (2600663) - classical, beginners, 10 wk, Tues, Sandymount, €65 per term

BALLROOM DANCING see also Dancing / Old Time

Beginners Dance Centre 54 Parnell Sq W 1 (8304647) - waltz, €7 per class

Cabinteely Community School Johnstown Rd 18 (2857455) - quickstep, foxtrot, waltz, tango 10wk, €45

Dance Club Rathmines & Rathgar (2893797) - beginners

Hartstown Community School Clonsilla 15 (8209863) - beginners/intermediate, 10wks, €55

Just Dance Owen Cosgrave (4628857 087 8473518) - Whitefriar St community centre, Aungier St

Morosini-Whelan School of Dancing 46 Parnell Sq W 1 (8303613) - incl waltz, rock- 'n'roll, quickstep, swing, Mon & Wed 8-9pm €8

Palmerstown Community School 20 (6260116) `- Tue 10 wks €60

Pobalscoil Rosmini Adult Ed Grace Pk Rd 9 (8371015) - oldtime: beginners, 10 wks, €80

Portmarnock Community School Carrickhill Rd (8038056) - & Latin American & Salsa, 8wks, €45 each

Prodancer Presentation Primary School Terenure 6 (6211514/ 087 2484890) - waltz, quickstep, tango & slow foxtrot - all levels & teacher training, Fri, €7 per class

St Thomas Community College Novara Ave Bray (2866111) - 10 wks €60

BANJO

Comhaltas Ceoltoiri Eireann 32 Belgrave Sq Monkstown (2800295)

Walton's New School of Music 69 Sth Gt George's St 2 (4781884) - also day, see ad page 173.

BANKING AND FINANCE see also Financial Services / Money Management
Dublin Business School 13/14 Aungier St 2 (4177500) - Institute of Bankers dip, Mon to Fri, 2 yrs/ cert in Mutual Funds, 1 eve per wk - both 6.15-9.30pm / stock-market trading, DBS p/time 14 wks dip

Dun Laoghaire College of Further Education 17 Cumberland St Dun Laoghaire (2809676) - banking operations, IBI cert, 7-10pm, Mon 13wks €350

electronic Business School of Ireland (094-81444) - elearning course

Westmoreland College for Management Studies 11 Westmoreland St 2 (6795324/7266) - ACCA Dip in financial management

BASIC EDUCATION may include English / Irish / Maths / Writing see also Adult Literacy
Adult Education Centre Adult Ed Centre Ballymun Rd 9 (8420654/ 8425828 night) - spell well/basic numeracy - 10wk, €free

Colaiste Dhulaigh Barryscourt Rd Coolock 17 (8481337) - basic English, Mon, 10 wks

Colaiste Eanna College of Business & Technical Stu Kilkieran Rd Cabra 7 (8389577) - wide range of courses, day & eve

Colaiste Eoin Cappagh Rd 11 (8340893) - adult reading & writing / tutor training courses

Crumlin College of Further Education Crumlin Rd 12 (4540662) - adult reading & writing courses, one-to-one, spelling groups, numeracy, also day

Dublin Adult Learning Centre 3 Mountjoy Sq 1 (8787266) - basic English/ jnr cert English/ leaving cert English

Finglas Adult Reading & Writing Scheme Colaiste Eoin Finglas 11 (8340893) - one-to-one, day, eve, 30 wks, free: reading & writing / basic english group

Kilroy's College 25 Kingram Place 2 (1850 700700) - tutor supported home study: English, word study, spelling & arithmethic, general adult education, dip

KLEAR Grange Park View Kilbarrack 5 (8671845) - general knowledge,/ basic English/Maths group/ spelling - phonics & pronounciation; day only

Kylemore College Kylemore Rd 10 (6265901)

Palmerstown Community School 20 (6260116) - reading & writing, Tues 7-8, €50

Pearse College Clogher Rd 12 (4536661/4541544) - English & maths, day

People's College for Continuing Education & Traini 32 Parnell Sq 1 (8735879) - €15

Plunket College Swords Rd, Whitehall 9 (8371689) - basic reading & writing, 25 wks, day

Ringsend Technical Institute Cambridge Rd 4 (6684498) - spellwell & numeracy, various times,ongoing, free

Southside Adult Literacy Scheme 3 Ashgrove Tce Dundrum 14 (2964321) - range of basic one-to-one up to leaving cert courses incl. English, maths, geography, history: FETAC cert foundation & level 1

St Mark's Community School Cookstown Road Tallaght 24 (4519399)

BASKET-MAKING see Crafts
BASKETBALL
Irish Basketball Assoc National Basketball Arena Tallaght 24 (4590211)
Network Sports & Social Club 24 Elmcastle Green Kilnamanagh 24 (4524415)

Portmarnock Sports & Leisure Club Blackwood Lane Carrickhill Portmarnock (8462122)

BEAUTICIAN see also Beauty Therapy

Aspen's Beauty Clinic & College of Beauty Therapy 83 Lr Camden St 2 (4751079/ 4751940) - beautician course, Mon, Wed, Thurs, Fri, 9.30-3.30, 9mths €2,195; also Sat 9.30-3.30pm

Bronwyn Conroy Beauty School 10 The Crescent Monkstown (2804020) - beautician / also f/time CIDESCO/ CIBTAC / p/time CIBTAC

Coogan-Bergin Clinic & College of Beauty Therapy Glendenning Hse 6-8 Wicklow St 2 (6794387) - CIBTAC Mon & Wed 6.30-9.30, €1778/also 1 day weekly/ beautical body &electrolysis CIBTAC Tue, day €4127/ day Tue-Fri, €4888/ 1-day weekly €1778

Galligan College of Beauty 109 Grafton St 2 (6703933) - ITEC & CIBTAC, c.30wks

Portobello School Rere 40 Lr Dominick St 1 (8721277) - image consultancy, p/time morn or eve

BEAUTY CARE (GROOMING, MAKE-UP, etc.) Grooming / Manicure & Pedicure / Skin Care

Ann Prendergast Rosebud Salon Rathgar Ave 6 (4920856) - aroma & beauty intro course, w/end, one-day workshop, €65, small classes

Ashfield College Main St Templeogue 6W (4900866) - colour, image & style, 7.30-9.30, 8 wks

Ballymun Comprehensive School Adult Ed Centre Ballymun Rd 9 (8420654/ 8425828 night) - Mon 6 wks, €60/ nails & make-up Wed, 10 wks €60 / beauty secrets, Tue €60

Cabinteely Community School Johnstown Rd 18 (2857455) - simply beautiful course, 8wk, €65

Colaiste Dhulaigh Barryscourt Rd Coolock 17 (8481337) - skin care & make-up, Tues, 10 wks, 7.15-9.15

Colour & Image Professionals 2 Terenure Rd Nth 6W (4905751) - personal colour analysis, style & make-up, 5 wks x 1 night / also intensive consultant training in colour analysis, style analysis & make-up appli

Coolmine Community School Clonsilla 15 (8214583) - image makeover, Wed 7.30-9.30 €60

Crumlin College of Further Education Crumlin Rd 12 (4540662) - CIBTAC course, skin treatments dip 20 wk, Mon & Wed 6.45; nail treatments dip 13 wks, / waxing dip 13 wks, Tues & Thurs 6.45 each; stress management dip 13 wks Mon & Wed, 6.45

Donahies Community School Streamville Rd 13 (8482217) - colour & style, Mon 7.30 5wks €35

Geraldine Brand Style Image Consultant City Centre (8327332) - courses or individual consultation for men, women & teenagers

Greenhills College Limekiln Ave Walkinstown 12 (4507779/4507138) - colour me beautiful, Tue, 8wks, €79 / make up, skin care, 8wks Mon, €73

Hartstown Community School Clonsilla 15 (8209863) - 5wks, €40

Killester College of Further Education Collins Ave 5 (8337686) - Tue 7.30-9, 10 wks €60

KLEAR Grange Park View Kilbarrack 5 (8671845) - make up - make-over, day

Marino College 14-20 Marino Mart 3 (8332100) - personal grooming, 10wk, €50/ colour & image counselling, Thurs €50

Old Bawn Community School Tallaght 24 (4526137) - colour me beautiful, Tues, 7.30-9.30pm, 10 wks

Palmerstown Community School 20 (6260116) - colour me beautiful, 7wks €89

Plunket College Swords Rd, Whitehall 9 (8371689) - make-over coursel, 4wks Mon 7pm €26

Pobalscoil Rosmini Adult Ed Grace Pk Rd 9 (8371015) - make-over, Thurs 7.30 10 wks €95

Portmarnock Community School Carrickhill Rd (8038056) - colour me beautiful, 2wk, Tue 7-9.20, €55

Portobello School Rere 40 Lr Dominick St 1 (8721277) - make-up artistry, f/time; also 1 day release/ facial make-up, p/time eve, morn/ spa & body treatments, 1 day release

RAVE Good Shepherd School Churchtown 14 (2981052) - colour image & style, 10 wks 7.30 €73

Senior College Dun Laoghaire CFE Eblana Ave Dun Laoghaire (2800385) - make-up, products, skin care 10 wks €100

BEAUTY THERAPY & THERAPIST

Aspen's Beauty Clinic & College of Beauty Therapy 83 Lr Camden St 2 (4751079/ 4751940) - full beauty therapy course (beautician, body massage, electrolysis, nail course), day, Mon-Fri, 9.30-3.30, 9mths €4995

Bronwyn Conroy Beauty School 10 The Crescent Monkstown (2804020) - beautician/ also f/time CIDESCO / CIBTAC / p/time CIBTAC

Coogan-Bergin Clinic & College of Beauty Therapy Glendenning Hse 6-8 Wicklow St 2 (6794387) - CIBTAC courses; also day, wkend, dip

Galligan College of Beauty 109 Grafton St 2 (6703933) - CIDESCO 38wks, day

National Training Centre 16a St Joseph's Parade Off Dorset Street 7 (8827777) - myofascial therapy, soft tissue dysfunction, one w/end per month, 15 mths, €3268, national qualification

Portobello School Rere 40 Lr Dominick St 1 (8721277) - beauty specialist, ITEC cert, full time, part-time day or eve, also wkend / waxing, part-time wkend; manicure/pedicure, nail technology, each part-time eve, day wkend, ITEC certs

BEE-KEEPING

Fingal-Nth Dublin Beekeepers Assoc Sec. John McMullan 34 Ard Na Mara Cr Malahide (8450193) - beginners bee-keeping course, February/March 2004, 5wk, 2hrs pw + outdoor demonstration

Portmarnock Community School Carrickhill Rd (8038056) - eve, 7.30-9.20, 5wks, €31, in spring only

BELLY DANCING

BASE Ballyboden Adult Social Education Whitechurch Library Taylor's Lane 16 (4935953)

Dance Theatre of Ireland Bloomfields Centre, Lr George St Dun Laoghaire (2803455) - Tue 10-11.30am / Body Weather, Thurs 10-11.30

Hartstown Community School Clonsilla 15 (8209863) - 10wks, €45

Malahide Community School Malahide (8460949) - for beginners, 10 wks €65

Marino College 14-20 Marino Mart 3 (8332100) - Thurs 6.30 10 wks €50

Old Bawn Community School Tallaght 24 (4526137) - for women of all ages & sizes (bring hip scarves), Tues, 7.30-9.30pm, 10 wks

Rakassah School for Egyptian Belly Dance 2 (087 6841492) - beginners to advanced levels; also workshops, phone Valerie for syllabus

St Thomas Community College Novara Ave Bray (2866111) - 8 wks €50

Valarie Larkin, Bellydance Ireland Tymon Bawn Community Centre Tallaght 24 (2963856) - ongoing, 8pm, 10 wks/ also Old Bawn Tue 7.30

Veronica Coughlan (087 7785127) - various venues

BEREAVEMENT (Aspects of dealing with loss)

Donahies Community School Streamville Rd 13 (8482217) - life after loss, healing and moving forward, Wed 9.30-11.30, 10 wks €55

St Thomas Community College Novara Ave Bray (2866111) - bereavement counselling / pet bereavement: each 10 wks €70

BIBLE STUDIES see also Scripture / Theology / Religion

Chris Harkins (045 866710) - bible studies, by e-mail only

Institute for Feminism & Religion www.instituteforfeminismandreligion.org 6w (4624504)

UCD Adult Education Office (7061695) - old testament studies, 10 wks

Watchtower Bible & Tract Society Watchtower Hse Newcastle, Greystones Co Wicklow (2810692) - knowledge for life, 6mth, €free, also day

BIOLOGY

Kilroy's College 25 Kingram Place 2 (1850 700700) - tutor supported home study: leaving cert course

Plunket College Swords Rd, Whitehall 9 (8371689) - leaving cert(h,o), 27 wks, €215

BIRDS & BIRDWATCHING

Birdwatch Ireland (2804322)

BODHRAN

Comhaltas Ceoltoiri Eireann 32 Belgrave Sq Monkstown (2800295)

Old Bawn Community School Tallaght 24 (4526137) - beginners, Tues, 10 wks, 7.15 or 8.30

Walton's New School of Music 69 Sth Gt George's St 2 (4781884) - also day, see ad page 173

BODY BUILDING see also Keep Fit, PE etc.

Tony Quinn Centre 66/67 Eccles St 7 (8304211) - annual membership

BODY CONDITIONING see also Exercise / Keep Fit, etc

Dun Laoghaire College of Further Education 17 Cumberland St Dun Laoghaire (2809676) - toning, Wed, 10 wks, 7-8pm, €70

Greendale Community School Kilbarrack 5 (8322735/6) - Thurs, 7-8pm, 10wks, €35

Hegarty Fitness Centre 53 Middle Abbey St 1 (8723080) - cellulite removal/slimming/figure therapy, 10-15 wks, from €120 ea, also day

Kilroy's College 25 Kingram Place 2 (1850 700700) - tutor supported home study: diet, fitness & health, dip course

BODY THERAPY

NTC 16a St Joseph's Parade 7 (8827777) - advanced dip, body work & movement therapy, w/ends, 2 yrs, nat qual

BODY WEATHER see BELLY DANCING

BOOK CLUB/ READING GROUPS see also Literature, Libraries, etc

TACT St Dominic's School, Tallaght 24 (4596757) - book club, 10 wks, €50 day

Kilternan Adult Ed. Ballybetagh Rd 18 (2952050) – Monthly 2nd Fri.

BOOK-KEEPING see also Accounts / Computerised Accounts / Farm Accounts / PAYE/ Payroll

Ballsbridge College of Business Studies Shelbourne Rd 4 (6684806) - practical, Tues 7.30, 10 wks, €75

Ballyfermot College of Further Education Ballyfermot Rd 10 (6269421) - 10 wks, Mon, 7-10.30pm, €80

Cabinteely Community School Johnstown Rd 18 (2857455) - European Institute of Technology, calculator required, 10wks, €90

Colaiste Dhulaigh Barryscourt Rd Coolock 17 (8481337) - small business accounts, manual, Mon 7.30, 10 wks

Dorset College 64a Lr Dorset St/ 8 Belvedere Pl 1 (8309677) - computerised - Sage/ Tas, Mon & Wed, 6.30-9pm, 12 wks

FAS Training Centre 10 (6055900/ 5933) - manual; Baldoyle 13 (8167460) - manual basic; Tallaght 24 (4045284) - manual, C&G, 10wk; Loughlinstown, Wyatville Rd (2043600)

Greenhills College Limekiln Ave Walkinstown 12 (4507779/4507138) - VAT, PAYE, purchases, sales, etc made easy, 8 wks, €73

Hartstown Community School Clonsilla 15 (8209863) - & accounts, beginners/

intermediate 10wks, €60 each

Irish Payroll Association (IPASS) Clifton House Lower Fitzwilliam St 2 (6617200) - certified payroll technician, 1 eve x 10 wks, stage 1 & 2/ dip in payroll management, 4 modules, 2 day each: various venues: city centre, Griffith Ave, Blanchardstown, Tallaght, Dun Laoire

Kilroy's College 25 Kingram Place 2 (1850 700700) - tutor supported home-study, & accounts, dip

Lucan Community College Esker Drive (6282077) - & accounts, 10wk, €79

Marino College 14-20 Marino Mart 3 (8332100) - wages, PAYE, VAT, personal tax, 10wks, €50

Old Bawn Community School Tallaght 24 (4526137) - PAYE, PRSI & VAT, 10 wks, Tues of Thurs, 7.15

Pitman Training Centre 6-8 Wicklow St 2 (6768008) - basic skills, cert, 10 hrs, €210, also day

St Mark's Community School Cookstown Road Tallaght 24 (4519399)

St Thomas Community College Novara Ave Bray (2866111) - 10wks, €70

BOOK-PRODUCTION see Desktop Publishing

BOUZOUKI

Waltons New School of Music 69 Sth Gt George's St 2 (4781884) - also day, see ad page 173

BOWLING (LAWN)

Saint Anthony's House St Lawrence Rd Clontarf 3 (8335300) - indoor, annual membership, also day

BOWLING (TEN-PIN)

Leisureplex Malahide Rd, Coolock (8485722); Leisureplex Stillorgan (2881656); Leisureplex, Blanchardstown (8223030); Leisureplex, Tallaght (4599411)

Network Sports & Social Club 24 Elmcastle Green Kilnamanagh 24 (4524415)

BRAILLE

Pobalscoil Rosmini Adult Ed Grace Pk Rd 9 (8371015) - beginners, Wed 7pm, 10 wks €80

BREATHING EXERCISES

Holistic Healing Centre 38 Dame St 2 (6710813)

BRIDGE (BASIC - ADVANCED)

Ballymun Comprehensive Schools Adult Ed Centre Ballymun Rd 9 (8420654/ 8425828 night) - beginners / continuation, 10wk, €75

Brian's Bridge School Brian or Elizabeth at (4501541) - home tuition & absolute beginners a speciality, expert tutor (25+yrs exp), also day, wkend, 6wks

Cabinteely Community School Johnstown Rd 18 (2857455) - 10wk, €75

Civil Service Bridge Club 72 Heytesbury St 8 (4750083 eve; 6282729 day) - beginners 10wk, €75

Colaiste Eanna College of Business & Technical Stu Kilkieran Rd Cabra 7 (8389577) - 10wks, Tue 7-9pm

Coolmine Community School Clonsilla 15 (8214583) - beginners, Mon, Tue/ improvers Wed: 9wk, €60

DATE College of Further Education Dundrum 14 (2964322) - improvers 10 wks €70/ bridge club €3 per session

Donahies Community School Streamville Rd 13 (8482217) - beginners, Wed, 10am €70 / improvers day Wed

Dun Laoghaire College of Further Education 17 Cumberland St Dun Laoghaire (2809676) - beginners, Mon, 10 wks, 7.30-9.30pm, €100

Foxrock Institute Kill O' the Grange School Kill Lane Blackrock (4939506/4939629) - 8 wks, €85

Greendale Community School Kilbarrack 5 (8322735/6) - beginners Tue 7.30 €55/ also Mon morn 10.30 10 wks €55

KAIES-Knocklyon Community Centre, 16 (4943991)

KLEAR Grange Park View Kilbarrack 5 (8671845) - for beginners, day / club 10 wks supervised play, day

Lucan Community College Esker Drive (6282077) - beginners, 10wk, €79/ improvers, advanced, 10 wks €66

Malahide Community School Malahide (8460949) - for novice/ improvers, 10 wks €75

Marino College 14-20 Marino Mart 3 (8332100) - beginners, €66/ improvers, €50, Tues, 10 wks each

Newpark Adult Education Centre Newtownpark Ave Blackrock (2884376) - basic/improved, 10wks, €99, Mon, Tue

Palmerstown Community School 20 (6260116) - level 1&2, 10 wks, €60 each

Plunket College Swords Rd, Whitehall 9 (8371689) - for active retired, day only

Pobalscoil Neasain Baldoyle 13 (8063092) - Wed 2-4pm, 10 wks €75

Pobalscoil Rosmini Adult Ed Grace Pk Rd 9 (8371015) - intro, Tue, 10 wks, €100

Saint Tiernan's Community School Parkvale Balally 16 (2953224) - beginners Mon 7.30-9.30pm, 10 wks, €70

St Anthony's House St Lawrence Rd Clontarf 3 (8335300) - club, 7-11pm

St Thomas Community College Novara Ave Bray (2866111) - beginners/improvers, 10wks, €70

Taney Centre Taney Rd Dundrum 14 (2985491) - Mon, Wed & Fri (2788340) day/ capricorn Wed 2884020

Templeogue Castle Community Bridge Club Templeogue House 6W (4943255 / 4902908) -beginners classes commence Sept in Templeogue Bridge Centre

BROADCASTING see also Communications / Media / Writing

Dublin Media Centre 2nd floor, 31 Ranelagh 6 (4970900) - foundation skills, 5 wks, Tue / Wed 7.30

Hartstown Community School Clonsilla 15 (8209863) - radio broadcasting, 10 wks €60

BRONZE CASTING

National College of Art & Design in Art & Design 100 Thomas Street 8 (6364214) - intro & advanced mouldmaking & waxwork, 21-22wk

BUDDHISM

Dublin Meditation Centre 42 Lr leeson St (Basement) 2 (6615934)

Shambhala Meditation Group Upstairs at The Davis Gallery 11 Capel St 1 (8533782) - Meditation & Shambhala teachings, Wed, 8pm, €free

Tara Buddhist Centre 32 Whitebarn Rd Churchtown 14 (2983314) - €8 per class: at 67 Lr Camden St 2, Tue, 7.30 / Chinese Med Centre, Clarinda Pk W, Dun Laoghaire, Thurs, 7.30 / Northside - phone for details

BUDGETING see Money Management

BUILDING CONSTRUCTION Construction / House Maintenance / Surveying

DIT Faculty: Built Environment Bolton St 1 (4023711/3445) - construction technology cert, 3yr p/time, 1 day+ 2eve weekly, 800pa/ building maintenance management, 5 modules/ building technology, 2yr, €700, cert/ site management cert, 3 yr, 1 day & eve wkly, €800 pa/ safety management, 5 wks

BUILDING TRADES see also Construction/ House Maintenance/ Surveying/ Building Construction

FAS Training Centre Tallaght 24 (4045284) - building maintenance, 10wk

St Kevins College Clogher Rd Crumlin 12 (4536397) - pre-apprenticeship, 1yr, day

BULGARIAN

Dublin Public Libraries Admin Hq, 138-144 Pearse St 2 (6644800) - central library Ilac Centre (8734333) or Library HQ for details (6744800), self-learning €free

BULLYING

Campaign Against Bullying 72 Lakelands Ave Stillorgan (2887976) - anti-bullying courses in workplace/school

BUSINESS ADMINISTRATION / STUDIES see also Banking / Computer/ Ebusiness / Finance / Management / Office Procedure / Secretarial

Cabinteely Community School Johnstown Rd 18 (2857455) - future studies (computer, office, busniess skills) NCVA cert, 9.15-12.30, Sept-May, €100

Colaiste Dhulaigh Barryscourt Rd Coolock 17 (8481337) - small business accounts/ manual, 20wks, Wed 11.00-1.00

DIT Faculty: Business Aungier St 2 (4023040/3445) - MBA - core: edonomics, business law, entrepreneurial, project; plus international, entrepreneurship or facilitiles management; plus group project, 2yr p/time, 4 semesters €7500 pa

Dorset College 64a Lr Dorset St/ 8 Belvedere Pl 1 (8309677) - business studies cert & dip ICM, Tue & Thurs 6.30-9.30 1-2 yrs/ bus admin information technology & communications, Mon-Fri, day 30 wks/ business excutive programme, Mon-Fri 9.30-2.30 30 wks/ dip in computers & communications, 9.30-2.30, 30 wks

Dublin Business School 13/14 Aungier St 2 (4177500) - BA(hons), 3-4years, fax: 4177543/ dip in business studies, 2 eves per wk, 1 yr/14 wks/ graduate dip in business studies/ bs &IT/ bs & HR management/ bs & e-business, 2 eves plus some Sats, 16 mt hs each/ MBS, 2 eves and some Weds, 18 mths; all 6.30 -8pm

Dublin City University Registry office Glasnevin 9 (7005338)

Eden Computer Training Rathfarnham 16, or MACRO Centre, 1 Green St 7 (4953155) - ecommerce/ ebusiness, project management, start your own business training

FAS Net College www.fas-netcollege.com (info@fas-netcollege.com/ 2043600) - elearning: e-Commerce, intro €120/ project management, €80/ business plan guidelines, €40/ finance for the non-financial, €100; online tutor option €80

Fitzwilliam Institute Ltd Temple Court Temple Rd Blackrock (2834579) - post-grad dip in communications & media skills, 17 wks+ 8wks arranged work experience, f/time day €3990+€190 fees

Griffith College Dublin Sth Circular Rd 8 (4150400) - national cert, 2 yrs, HETAC, f/t, Mon to Fri/ BA in Business Studies, 3 yrs, HETAC, p/t, 3 eves per wk, also available f/t, Mon to Fri/ Dip in Business Admin 18 mths APE f/time/ ABE cert f/time 15 wks

Inchicore College of Further Education Emmet Rd 8 (4535358) - business admin with legal studies, day

Institute of Public Administration 57-61 Lansdowne Rd 4 (6686233)

Institute of Technology Tallaght 24 (4042000) - Management/ Accounting/ Marketing - BBS/nat dip/ nat cert in Business Studies (administration)/ nat dip in Business Studies (community enterprise & development)

Institute of Technology, Blanchardstown Blanchardstown Road North 15 (8851100) - IT & business interdisciplinary studies HETAC cert: modules - business management; human resource management; psychology; operating systems; softward development; networking & maths - from 240 to 485 per module/ also HETAC project management 6-10; from 350 per module

Irish Management Institute Sandyford Rd 16 (2078400) - Henley Masters in Busines Admin, 3 yr prog, €19995

Kilroy's College 25 Kingram Place 2 (1850 700700) - tutor supported home study: leaving cert, also business admin, dip

National College of Ireland Mayor St IFSC 1 (4060500/ 1850 221721) - Grad Dip Business Studies/Grad Dip Human Resource Management; each 1 yr p/time day

Pearse College Clogher Rd 12 (4536661/4541544) - & international trade/& retail management, day

Pitman Training Centre 6-8 Wicklow St 2 (6768008) - business skills, 10 hrs €210, cert/ effective business communication, 18 hrs €280, cert/ business skills dip, 5 wks €996: day eve Sats

Plunket College Swords Rd, Whitehall 9 (8371689) - BBS, IPA degree: yr 1, Mon & Wed/ also p/time day IATI cert, accounts / taxation/ business management, IT/ €113.50 per subject/ LC bus org, Tue 7-9pm

Senior College Dun Laoghaire CFE Eblana Ave Dun Laoghaire (2800385) - ICM cert, €400/dip, €200 - 25 wks each/ single subject €120

Star Consulting PO Box 8796 2 (086 6061639) - networking skills, 1 day €200/ empowerment for women, 2 day €350/ business essentials, 1 wk, cert Corporate Coach USA

The Open University Enquiry & Advice Centre Holbrook House, Holles St 2 (6785399)

Transactional Analysis in Ireland (4511125) - in everyday situations, mthly workshop, donation

Trinity College 2 (6772941) - (6081532) - & IT, BSc hons, 4yr, 24wks per yr

UCD Adult Education Office (7061695) - business & finance courses, 12 wks each/ intro to stock market, 10 wks

Westmoreland College for Management Studies 11 Westmoreland St 2 (6795324/7266) - ICM cert, dip, business studies/ ICM dip corporate management/ICM dip, health services management/ ICM grad dip management

Whitehall College of Further Education Swords Rd 9 (8376011) - financial services foundation; business & finance; fund management; insurance & banking - day

Whitehall College of Further Education Swords Rd 9 (8376011) - for adults

BUSINESS, SMALL see also Book-keeping / Coaching

Kilroy's College 25 Kingram Place 2 (1850 700700) - tutor supported home study: book-keeping & accounts, self-employed accounts & tax, business admin, dip

Pobalscoil Rosmini Adult Ed Grace Pk Rd 9 (8371015) - finance & accounts for

small business, 7.30 €80

St Tiernan's Community School Parkvale Balally 16 (2953224) - small business tax & accounts, Mon, 7.30-9.30pm, 10 wks, €70

BUSINESS, START YOUR OWN

Ashfield College Main St Templeogue 6W (4900866) - 7.30-9.30, 8 wks

College of Further Education Main St Dundrum 14 (2951376) - Tue 8 wks

Donahies Community School Streamville Rd 13 (8482217) - comprehensive course, 7-10 Wed, 10 wks €150

Dun Laoghaire College of Further Education 17 Cumberland St Dun Laoghaire (2809676) - running your own business, 20 wks, 7.30-9.30pm, €170

Eden Computer Training Rathfarnham 16, or MACRO Centre, 1 Green St 7 (4953155) - management, start your own, payroll

FAS Training Centre Baldoyle 13 (8167460); Baldoyle 13 (8167460); Ballyfermot 10 (6055900/ 5933); Finglas 11 (8140243); Jervis St 1 (8044600); Tallaght 24

(4045284) - 10wk; Wyatville Rd (2043600)

Greenhills College Limekiln Ave Walkinstown 12 (4507779/4507138) - 10 wks, €79

Hartstown Community School Clonsilla 15 (8209863) - 10wks, €60

Holy Family Community School Rathcoole (4580766)

Killester College of Further Education Collins Ave 5 (8337686) - picture framing, 2 days weekly CDVEC cert €300

Kilroy's College 25 Kingram Place 2 (1850 700700) - tutor supported home study: book-keeping & accounts, self-employed accounts & tax, business admin, dip

Lucan Community College Esker Drive (6282077) - Mon, 10 wks €79

Marino College 14-20 Marino Mart 3 (8332100) - Thurs, 6.30 10 wks €50

Newpark Adult Education Centre Newtownpark Ave Blackrock (2884376) - 10wks, €99. Mon 7.30

Old Bawn Community School Tallaght 24 (4526137) - developing the idea, Tues, 10 wks

Pitman Training Centre 6-8 Wicklow St 2 (6768008) - business start up dip, 5 wks €996, cert; day eve Sats

Pobalscoil Rosmini Adult Ed Grace Pk Rd 9 (8371015) - practical, business plan, etc, Mon, 7.30 €80

Positive Success Group Mary O'Driscoll NPL (087 7640385) - business & life coaching, dip course (incl foundation, start your own business, branding & marketing, getting clients, NPL core skills)

St Thomas Community College Novara Ave Bray (2866111) - 10wks, €70

UCD Adult Education Office (7061695) - entrepreneurship & management theory, 12 wks

Campanology

Theory, Practice, History of Bell-ringing in Christ Church Cathedral. Phone 6778099

CALLANETICS
Taney Centre Taney Rd Dundrum 14 (2985491) - Wed (087 2445425)

CALLIGRAPHY
Ballymun Comprehensive School Adult Ed Centre Ballymun Rd 9 (8420654/ 8425828 night) - Wed, 7.30, €80

Colaiste Eanna College of Business & Technical Stu Kilkieran Rd Cabra 7 (8389577) - 8wks, Tue 7-9pm

Coolmine Community School Clonsilla 15 (8214583) - beginners/ improvers Mon, 9wk, €60

DATE College of Further Education Dundrum 14 (2964322) - beginners/ advanced: each 10 wks, €79, day

Dun Laoghaire College of Further Education 17 Cumberland St Dun Laoghaire (2809676) - & poster design, Tues, 10 wks, 7.30-9.30pm, €100

Foxrock Institute Kill O' the Grange School Kill Lane Blackrock (4939506/4939629) - 8wks, €85

Holy Family Community School Rathcoole (4580766)

Marino College 14-20 Marino Mart 3 (8332100) - Thurs, 10wks €50

Old Bawn Community School Tallaght 24 (4526137) - italic handwriting, scroll making, ribbons & seasonal cards, 10 wks

Peannairi, Irish Scribes St Mary's Haddington Rd 4 (8337621/ 2897541) - beginners cert, €58/ intermediate dip, Weds, €80/ advanced dip, €120/ all 7.30-9.30pm, 10wks, autumn & spring

Pobailscoil Iosolde 20 (6260116) - Thurs, 7.30 10 wks €60

Pobalscoil Rosmini Adult Ed Grace Pk Rd 9 (8371015) - beginners, Tues, 10 wks, €90

Saint Tiernan's Community School Parkvale Balally 16 (2953224) - traditional & modern, Tues, 7.30-9.30pm, 10 wks, €70

St Thomas Community College Novara Ave Bray (2866111) - 10 wks €70

CAMBODIAN
Dublin Public Libraries Admin Hq, 138-144 Pearse St 2 (6644800) - central library Ilac Centre (8734333) or Library HQ for details (6744800), self-learning €free

CAMOGIE
Cumann Camogaiochta na nGael Pairc an Chrocaigh St Joseph's Ave 3 (8364619)

CAMPANOLOGY(Art & Science of Bell/Change-Ringing)
Society of Change Ringers Christchurch Cathedral 8 (6778099) - lectures, demos & participation, 12wk, also day

CANOEING see also Adventure Sports
Clondalkin Sports & Leisure Centre Nangor Rd Clondalkin 22 (4574858) - also day

Go further with a *FETAC* award

As the national awarding body for further education and training in Ireland, FETAC gives people the opportunity to gain recognition for learning in education or training centres, in the work place and in the community.

For employers, FETAC guarantees quality assured recognisable qualifications.

We make awards previously certified by BIM, CERT/NTCB, FÁS, NCVA and Teagasc.

To find out more visit our website at **www.fetac.ie**.

FETAC
Further Education and Training Awards Council
Comhairle na nDámhachtaini
Breisoideachais agus Oiliúna

Funded by the Irish Government under the National Development Plan 2000 to 2006.

Colaiste Dhulaigh & College of Further Education Barryscourt Rd Coolock 17 (8481337) - Wed 9.30-5pm,

Corporate Club 24 Elmcastle Green Kilnamanagh 24 (4610935)

Irish Canoe Union House of Sport Long Mile Rd 12 (4509838) - introductory courses summer and spring, 7-9.30pm, 6 wks; assessment for Kayak proficiency cert can be arranged at end of each course, €150, all technical equipment supplied, at Strawberry Beds, Chapelizod

Network Sports & Social Club 24 Elmcastle Green Kilnamanagh 24 (4524415)

CANTONESE

Sandford Language Institute Milltown Pk Sandford Rd 6 (2601296) - all levels, 14 wks, €250

CAR ALARM INSTALLATION

Hi-Tech Training 4 Nth Gt George's St 1 (1850-759759) - practically based, Sat, 10am-5pm, 1 day, cert

CARD PLAYING see also Bridge

Network Sports & Social Club 24 Elmcastle Green Kilnamanagh 24 (4524415)

Saint Anthony's House St Lawrence Rd Clontarf 3 (8335300) - Tues

CAREERS/CAREER GUIDANCE see also Job / Coaching / Parents Courses

AAA Counselling Dr MJ Brennan PhD c/o 48 Connaught St Phibsboro 7 (8380014) - career difficulties, life coaching, mentoring, also day

ABM Business Training 54 North St, Swords (8902348) - and interview prep; all yr, also day, Sat

Bi-Aura Foundation De Light House Corlurgan Bailieboro, Co Cavan (087-2317984) - complementary career, bi-aura therapy dip, w/ends 9mths, €3500

Centre for Professional & Personal Development Coach Centre 44 Westland Row 2 (6612291) - find the career you love, eve/ w/end, €400, cert

ETC Consult 17 Leeson Pk 6 (4972067) - comprehensive career guidance report & discussion

Irish Payroll Association (IPASS) Clifton House Lower Fitzwilliam St 2 (6617200) - certified payroll technician, 1 eve x 10 wks, stage 1 & 2/ dip in payroll management, 4 modules, 2 day each: various venues: city centre, Griffith Ave, Blanchardstown, Tallaght, Dun Laoire

Keytrainer Ireland 33/34 Dame St 2 (6714000) - CV & job prep skills

Kilroy's College 25 Kingram Place 2 (1850 700700) - home study

Milltown Institute of Theology & Philosophy Milltown Pk 6 (2698388) personal opportunity to explore alternative leadership styles, 6 wks, Wed, €530, cert

Pearse College Clogher Rd 12 (4536661/4541544) -soccer coaching, day, 1 yr FETAC/FAI cert

UCD Adult Education Office (7061695) - career planning & personal development, day

CARERS, COURSES FOR - incl Caring for the Elderly

Inchicore College of Further Education Emmet Rd 8 (4535358) - caring services (social care); cert in social studies; caring for people with disabilities

School of Practical Child Care Blackrock Campus Carysfort Ave Blackrock (2886994) - community & residential care, UCD SPCC cert; 30 wks+3 Sats/ caring skills NCFE & SPCC home study, internet course

CARING FOR THE ELDERLY

School of Practical Child Care Blackrock Campus Carysfort Ave Blackrock (2886994) - community & residential care, UCD SPCC cert; 30 wks+3 Sats/ caring skills NCFE & SPCC home study, internet course

CARPENTRY see also Furniture / Woodwork

DIT Faculty: Built Environment Bolton St 1 (4023711/3445) - CNC machining, 10 wks €230/ advanced carpentry, joinery, 1 yr €700/ woodcutting machinery, 1 yr €700 / updating for Phase 4, 6 syllabi carpentery joinery, 10 wks €230

CARTOONING see Animation/ Graphics

CATECHETICS see Religion

CATERING see also Cookery / Management / Hospitality

DIT Faculty: Tourism & Food Cathal Brugha St 1 (4024349/3445) - professional restaurant service 1 & 2, cert, 16 wks €265 each/ cert in: advanced kitchen, 16 wks €590 per module: cold; pastry; internatinal cuisine 1&2; ethnic; kitchen management/ culinary arts, 3 yrs €700 pa/ bar management 2yrs €500 pa/ meat a pprentice, 3yrs dip/ bar tending supervision, 1 yr dip

Institute of Technology Tallaght 24 (4042000) - nat cert in supervisory development, 28 wks/ adv nat cert in advanced kitchen & garden, 18 wks

CCTV INSTALLATION

Hi-Tech Training 4 Nth Gt George's St 1 (1850-759759) - 2-day practical course, cert

CEARD-TEASTAS GAEILGE see Teaching

CEILI DANCING see also Dancing / Irish Dancing

Pobalscoil Iosolde 20 (6260116) - Mon 8.20 10 wks €60

CELLO

Bray Music Centre Florence Rd Bray (2866768)

Dun Laoghaire Music Centre 130A Lr George's St Dun Laoghaire (2844178)

Leinster School of Music & Drama Griffith College Campus South Circular Rd 8 (4150467)

Newpark Music Centre Newtownpark Ave Blackrock (2883740) - also day

Walton's New School of Music 69 Sth Gt George's St 2 (4781884) - also day, see ad page 173

CELTIC STUDIES

Saor-Ollscoil na hEireann 55 Prussia St 7 (8683368) - BA, early Irish History

CERAMICS Pottery

National College of Art & Design in Art & Design 100 Thomas Street 8 (6364214) - advanced, c.22wk

Tracy Miley 13b Dodder View Cottages Ballsbridge 4 (086 8485394) - hand built, beginners, 7-9pm 8 wks, €120, materials supplied

CERTIFICATION

FETAC – Further Education & Training Awards East Point Plaza East Point Business Park 3 (8659500) - national certification body

CHEMISTRY

DIT Faculty: Engineering Bolton St 1 (4023649/3445) - introduction to chemical engineering, 5 day (4024777)

DIT Faculty: Science Kevin St 8 (4024585/3445) - dip, 2 yr €835pa/ BSc chemical sciences, 2 yr €835pa

Dublin City University Registry office Glasnevin 9 (7005338) - chemical & pharmaceutical sciences/ Chemistry & German/French

Institute of Technology Tallaght 24 (4042000) - BSc in Applied Chemistry

Kilroy's College 25 Kingram Place 2 (1850 700700) - tutor supported home study: leaving cert, dip course

Plunket College Swords Rd, Whitehall 9 (8371689) - leaving cert, 27 wks, €215

CHESS

Corporate Club 24 Elmcastle Green Kilnamanagh 24 (4610935)

Network Club, The 24 Elmcastle Green Kilnamanagh 24 (4524415)

CHILD CARE AND DEVELOPMENT see also Montessori / Parents / Pre-School / Teachers

Adult Education Centre Adult Ed Centre Ballymun Rd 9 (8420654/ 8425828 night) - childcare, cert 20 wks/classroom assistant training, 12 wks, Arts & crafts for children, 6 wks/ understanding & managing difficult behaviour, (Ph: 2886999)

Campaign Against Bullying 72 Lakelands Ave Stillorgan (2887976) - anti-bullying policies

College of Further Education Main St Dundrum 14 (2951376) - caring for children / working in childcare / care of the special child / each FETAC, eve, 20 wks €199

Coolmine Community School Clonsilla 15 (8214583) - FETAC cert in childcare

Dun Laoghaire College of Further Education 17 Cumberland St Dun Laoghaire (2809676) - play & the developing child, IPPA cert, Wed, 10 wks 7-9, €110

FAS Training Centre Finglas Jamestown Rd 11 (8140243)

Greenhills College Limekiln Ave Walkinstown 12 (4507779/4507138) - play & developing child, Tue, 10wks €79

Inchicore College of Further Education Emmet Rd 8 (4535358) - child-care, pre-nursing/ nursery studies: day

IPPA - the Early Childhood Organisation Unit 4 Broomhill Business Complex Broomhill Rd 24 (4630010) - play & the developing child, raising awareness, practical ways to support children's play - attendance cert

Kilroy's College 25 Kingram Place 2 (1850 700700) - tutor supported home study: child care, child psychology, dip courses

KLEAR Grange Park View Kilbarrack 5 (8671845) - child development

Kylemore College Kylemore Rd 10 (6265901) - art & craft for child care, 15 wk Mon 7-9pm/ caring for children, 20 wk Tue/ child development, 20 wk Thurs: all 7-9pm FETAC cert

Liberties Vocational School Bull Alley St 8 (4540044) - FETAC level 2, Mon & Wed, 7-9pm, each module €115

Malahide Community School Malahide (8460949) - play & the developing child, Tues, 10 wks €70 - IPPA course

Marino College 14-20 Marino Mart 3 (8332100) - childcare management, 2 yr Tue 6.30, €198/ FETAC cert 2, Tues 7.30 €198/ play & the developing child, Thurs €66

Montessori Education Centre 41-43 Nth Gt George's St 1 (8780071) - Montessori teacher training dip: course (1) 0-6 yrs, (2) 6-9 yrs, (3) 9-12 yrs: 29 wks, €1800 each/ also by distance learning, 36 wks, €1250

Old Bawn Community School Tallaght 24 (4526137) - SPCC courses: childcare practice, 20 wks / child psychology 15 wks + 3 Sats/ understanding & managing behavious/ classroom assistants, 12 wks/ special needs dip/ working with special needs child in creche or playgroup: apply direct to 2886994

Portobello School Rere 40 Lr Dominick St 1 (8721277) - childcare studies c&g/ managing a childcare facility/ special needs cert: all part-time day and or eve

School of Practical Child Care 27-29 Carysfort Ave Blackrock (2886994) - childcare & education, cert 30 wks/ after school care cert 10 wks/ childminding in the home: all NCFE & SPCC cert/ also home study & internet courses - - Classroom Assistant, advanced studies in, nursery managing, montessori foundation/ undestanding

School of Practical Child Care

LEADERS IN CARE TRAINING SINCE 1986

We have a variety of training courses available to introduce you to, or to further develop your CAREER IN CHILDCARE.

Full Time Course: Childcare & Early Education Course for Childcare Workers & Carers of Children with Special Needs. (Including a free accommodation scheme)

Full-time day, evening, morning, weekend, correspondence and on-line courses available.

Certificate in Business Skills for the Crèche/Playgroup *NEW*	Montessori Method of Education
Crèche Management	First Aid for Children and Infants
Special Needs Assistant Certificate and Diploma	Certificate in Child Psychology. *NEW*
Certificate in After School Care	Creative Activities and Arts and Crafts for Children
Child minding in the Home	The Professional Nanny Training Course *NEW*
Child Protection	Childcare and English Language Training for the Au-pair. *NEW*
Certificate in Caring for the Child with Special Needs in the Crèche/Playgroup. *NEW*	Certificate in Play Therapy *NEW*
Teaching English as a Second Language to the Child in the Crèche / Playgroup *NEW*	Training Course for Adults to Teach Adults.*NEW*
Certificate in Team Leadership in Crèche/Pre-School *NEW*	Certificate in First-Line Management in Early Years Settings *NEW*

Dublin Venues: Ballymun; Bray; Blackrock; Baldoyle; Tallaght; Lucan, Palmerstown; Dundrum; Dublin City,

ON-SITE GROUP TRAINING AVAILABLE BY ARRANGEMENT

For details on our complete course list contact:

The School of Practical Child Care
27-29 Carysfort Ave
Blackrock, Co. Dublin

E-mail: info@practicalchildcare.com
WEB: www.practicalchildcare.com
Phone: +353 1 2886994
Fax : +353 1 2886995

difficult behaviour, 6 wks SPCC cert/ professional nanny cert/ play therapy cert/ also day. Cert in: Out Of School Care/ in Caring for the Child with Special Needs in the Crèche / Playgroup / Training for Adults to Teach Adults.

St Peter's College Collins Ave 5 (8337686) - FETAC level 3, Mon & Tue 7-10 Sept-May, €480

St Tiernan's Community School Parkvale Balally 16 (2953224) - cert in childcare for classroom assistants & special education, Wed, 7.30-9.30 €750/ also cert, 20 wks, €750/ introductory course, Tues 12 wks €150

Transactional Analysis in Ireland (4511125) - in everyday situations, mthly workshop, donation

UCD Adult Education Office (7061695) - SPCC - afterschool care; creche management/ nursery management NCNA dip

CHILD CARE LANGUAGE COURSES

School of Practical Child Care 27-29 Carysfort Ave Blackrock (2886994) - Teaching English as a Second Language to the Child in the Crèche / Playgroup Childcare and English Language Training for the Au-pair.

CHILD CARE MANAGEMENT

School of Practical Child Care 27-29 Carysfort Ave Blackrock (2886994) Cert in Business Skills for the Crèche/Playgroup / Crèche Management / Cert in Team Leadership in Crèche/Pre-School / Cert in First-Line Management in Early Years Settings/ Outreach courses available

CHILD PROTECTION STUDIES

School of Practical Child Care 27-29 Carysfort Ave Blackrock (2886994) – Child protection in the Early Years, 1 day SPCC cert City Centre

CHINESE CULTURE/LANGUAGE

Aisling Language Services Languages for Business & Pleasure 137 Lr Rathmines Rd 6 (4971902) - beginners, 10 wks €185

Dublin Public Libraries Admin Hq, 138-144 Pearse St 2 (6644800) - Mandarin / Cantonese, central library Ilac Centre, D1. (8734333) or Library HQ for details (6744800) - self-learning €free

Irish Chinese Cultural Society 3 Pacelli Ave Sutton 13 (8394194) - monthly meetings on Chinese culture, Wed, September to May at The Institute of Engineers, 22 Clyde Road, Ballsbridge, D. 4

Newpark Adult & Continuing Education Centre Newtownpark Ave Blackrock (2884376) - 10 WKS €99

Sandford Language Institute Milltown Pk Sandford Rd 6 (2601296) - Mandarin language and culture, all levels, 14 wks, €250

Trinity College 2 (6772941) - (6081560) - extra mural, intro to language & culture, 24wk, €320/ post-beginners/language, 24wks, €320

CHOIR/CHORAL SINGING see also Music

Cor Duibhlinne Foras Na Gaeilge 7 Merrion Sq 2 (8371605) - women's, as Gaeilge, rehersals Mon eves

Dun Laoghaire Music Centre 130A Lr George's St Dun Laoghaire (2844178)

Goethe Institut 62 Fitzwilliam Sq 2 (6801110) - Goethe Institute Choir

Walton's New School of Music 69 Sth Gt George's St 2 (4781884) - see ad page 173

CHRISTIANITY see also Bible / Meditation / Religion
Chris Harkins (045 866710) - bible studies, by e-mail only
CINEMA see also Film Appreciation / Media / Video / Writing, Creative
Corporate Club 24 Elmcastle Green Kilnamanagh 24 (4610935)
Film Institute of Ireland Irish Film Centre 6 Eustace St Temple Bar 2 (6795744)
CIVIL DEFENCE see First Aid/ Rescue
CIVIL SERVICE (confined and open)
Kilroy's College 25 Kingram Place 2 (1850 700700) - course
CLARINET see also Music
Abbey School of Music 9b Lr Abbey St 1 (8747908) - Peter Ogram
Bray Music Centre Florence Rd Bray (2866768)
Dun Laoghaire Music Centre 130A Lr George's St Dun Laoghaire (2844178)
Leinster School of Music Griffith College Campus South Circular Rd 8 (4150467)
Newpark Music Centre Newtownpark Ave Blackrock (2883740) - also day
Nolan School of Music 3 Dean St 8 (4933730) - also day
Walton's New School of Music 69 Sth Gt George's St 2 (4781884) - also day, see ad page 173
CLASSICAL STUDIES
Colaiste Eanna College of Business & Technical Stu Kilkieran Rd Cabra 7 (8389577) - day (tel 8688342/8389577
College of Further Education Main St Dundrum 14 (2951376) - introduction to, Thurs
DATE College of Further Education Dundrum 14 (2964322) - intro, 10 wks, €66, day
Saor-Ollscoil na hEireann 55 Prussia St 7 (8683368) - BA, Tues
UCD Adult Education Office (7061695) - history of gardenst/ Roman Empire - the daily life; also, wining & dining in/ old testament studies: each 10 wks
CLASSROOM ASSISTANT see also Teachers Courses
Old Bawn Community School Tallaght 24 (4526137) - SPCC courses - classroom assistant cert/ Special Needs cert & dip: apply 2886994
School of Practical Child Care 27-29 Carysfort Ave Blackrock (2886994) Cert - classroom assistant, 12 wks/ Cert & dip in special needs assistant, 30 wks + 5, City Centre & Countrywide SPCC & NCFE/ cert in developing skills for crèche/playgroup workers 20 wks + 3 Sats; City Centre & Countrywide
CLAY MODELLING see also Arts/Crafts
Connolly House Nth Strand (by 5 Lamps) 1 (8557116) - 10 wks Wed, 7pm €80
Kylemore College Kylemore Rd 10 (6265901) - Thurs 7-9pm 10 wks
CLAY PIGEON SHOOTING
Fassaroe Sporting Club (087 2243829)
CLIMBING see Adventure Sports
COACHING see also Life Skills, Personal Development
ABM Business Training 54 North St, Swords (8902348) - coaching & mentoring skills, also day, Sat
Athletics Association of Ireland 11 Prospect Rd Glasnevin 9 (8308925) - courses in coaching, introductory & levels 1-3, NCTC
Centre for Professional & Personal Development Coach Centre 44 Westland Row 2

(6612291) - accredited dip in life & business coaching, 6 mths €2035

Dun Laoghaire College of Further Education 17 Cumberland St Dun Laoghaire (2809676) - intro to life coaching, 7-9.30, 10 wks €115

FAS Training Centre Ballyfermot 10 (6055900/ 5933) - sports coaching & fitness leaders, day

FAS Training Centre Cabra Bannow Rd 7 (8821400) - tennis coach, day

Football Assoc of Ireland 80 Merrion Sq Sth 2 (6766864) - FAI tech dept AUL Complex, Clonshaugh, D17 (8900700)

Irish Basketball Assoc National Basketball Arena Tallaght 24 (4590211)

Positive Success Group Mary O'Driscoll NPL (087 7640385) - business & life coaching, dip course (incl foundation, start your own business, branding & marketing, getting clients, NPL core skills)

Star Consulting PO Box 8796 2 (086 6061639) - life coaching, 2 days €350/ corporate coaching day, 3 wks, Corp. Coach USA cert

The Professional Training and Coaching Consultancy (087 6379765/ 045 865783) - fulfil your goals & ambitions, be successful: Grainne Carrickford-Kingston, Accredited Life Coach

COLOUR THERAPY

Colour & Image Professionals 2 Terenure Rd Nth 6W (4905751) - colour analysis, personal style & make-up / consultant training in colour, style & make-up

Newpark Adult Education Centre Newtownpark Ave Blackrock (2884376) - ladies colour analysis, Tue 5wks, €90/ reveal your colour, Auro-Soma, Thurs, €99

Old Bawn Community School Tallaght 24 (4526137) - colour healing - aurosoma, Thurs, 10 wks

School of Reiki Ivy House Sth Main St Naas (045 8982343 086 3084657) introductory

COMEDY see Acting

COMMERCIAL STUDIES see also Business / Book-keeping

Kilroy's College 25 Kingram Place 2 (1850 700700) - tutor supported home study

COMMUNICATION SKILLS see also Drama / Media / Personal Development / Public Speaking / Facilitation

Ballymun Men's Centre LS4 Shangan Rd Ballymun 9 (8623117/8623409) - BTEI course in communications, social studies & computer, Mon, Wed, Thurs mornings

Centre for Professional and Personal Development Coach Centre 44 Westland Row 2 (6612291) - personal effectiveness & communication skills, 6 wks, €380, cert

Corporate Club 24 Elmcastle Green Kilnamanagh 24 (4610935)

Eden Computer Training Rathfarnham 16, or MACRO Centre, 1 Green St 7 (4953155) - communicatin & personal development

Finglas Adult Reading & Writing Scheme Colaiste Eoin Finglas 11 (8340893) - FETAC course, 30 wks, free

Kilroy's College 25 Kingram Place 2 (1850 700700) - tutor supported home study: writing, communication skills, dip course

Leinster School of Music Griffith College Campus South Circular Rd 8 (4150467)

MD Communications 38 Spireview Lane off Rathgar Rd 6 (4975866)

Network Sports & Social Club 24 Elmcastle Green Kilnamanagh 24 (4524415)

Newpark Adult Education Centre Newtownpark Ave Blackrock (2884376) - public speaking, 10wks, €95

Ringsend Technical Institute Cambridge Rd 4 (6684498) - FETAC cert courses at various times,ongoing, free

Star Consulting PO Box 8796 2 (086 6061639) - 2 day €350

UCD Adult Education Office (7061695) - comm skills across the life span/ dramatic comm/ IT & PR comm/ intercultural comm/ mass comm/ public comm/ psychology of comm: each c 12 wks/ effective interpersonal skills, 8 wks/ reading skills/ speak with confidence, also workshop/ writing skills 12 wks

COMMUNICATION SKILLS IN BUSINESS

Communication & Personal Development 30/31 Wicklow St 2 (6713636/6613225)

FAS Training Centre Ballyfermot 10 (6055900/ 5933)

FAS Training Centre Jervis St 1 (8044600)

Fitzwilliam Institute Ltd Temple Court Temple Rd Blackrock (2834579) - post-grad dip in communications & media skills, 17 wks+ 8wks arranged work experience, f/time day €3990+€190 fees

Keytrainer Ireland 33/34 Dame St 2 (6714000) - tailored courses in customer care, assertiveness, report writing & many more

Kilroy's College 25 Kingram Place 2 (1850 700700) - tutor supported home-study dip course

COMMUNICATION STUDIES

Communication & Personal Development 30/31 Wicklow St 2 (6713636/6613225)

Dublin City University Registry office Glasnevin 9 (7005338)

Kilroy's College 25 Kingram Place 2 (1850 700700) - tutor supported home study: freelance journalism, communication skills, dip course

KLEAR Grange Park View Kilbarrack 5 (8671845) - Thurs eve; also day

COMMUNITY CARE

Dun Laoghaire College of Further Education 17 Cumberland St Dun Laoghaire (2809676) - FETAC cert, Mon & Wed, 20 wks, 7-9.30pm, €360

FAS Training Centre Finglas Jamestown Rd 11 (8140243)

COMMUNITY DEVELOPMENT

Department of Adult & Community Education NUI Maynooth (7084500) - & Leadership, Ballymun Axix Arts Centre (8832134) day; Leixlip, Colaiste Ciaran (6247624)

FAS Training Centre Finglas 11 (8140243), Jervis St 1 (8044600) - community training workshop, community service: day

UCD Adult Education Office (7061695) - drugs & drug counselling skills, 10 wks / crime & criminality 1 & 2, 12 wks/ project & community development, 20 wks various locations

COMMUNITY GAMES

National Community Games Tower 2 Fumbally Court 8 (4544424) - info

COMMUNITY INFORMATION CENTRES

Community & Youth Info Centres: - Ashbourne 8351806/ Balbriggan 8414600/ Ballyfermot 6264313/Ballymun 8421890/Blanchardstown 8220449/ Bray 2869590/ Clondalkin 4579045/ Crumlin 4546070/ Dun Laoghaire 2844544/ Dundrum 2960713/ Finglas 8641970/Killester 8511438/Lucan 6241975/ Malahide 8450627/ Palmerstown 6263050/ Rialto 4539965/ St Vincents 8305744/ Liberties 4536098/ Skerries 8494443/ Stillorgan 2885629/ Swords 8406877/ Tallaght 4515911/ Nat Assn for Deaf People 8723800

COMMUNITY WORK, Voluntary see Voluntary Work

COMPETITION WINNING

Old Bawn Community School Tallaght 24 (4526137) - hints & tips, Tues, 7.30-9.30pm, 10 wks, - incl crosswords, quizzes etc

COMPUTER (INTRODUCTION TO THE) see also Computer Training / ECDL / Keyboard / Word Processing

ABM Computer Training 54 North St, Swords (8902348) - all yr, also day & Sat

Balbriggan Community College Pine Ridge Chapel St (8412388/9) - computer literacy & pc skills/ wp basic skills - 8 wks, Mon & Wed 7.30-9.30 / also Stage 2, Tues: €99 each

Ballinteer Community School Ballinteer 16 (2988195) - basic, 10 wks €100, Wed 6.45/ intermediate, €165

Ballsbridge College of Business Studies Shelbourne Rd 4 (6684806) - computers for beginners, Mon 7.45, 10wks €80/ exce for beginners, Mon 6pm €80/ powerpoint for beginners, Tue 10 wks €80/ for older adults, Thurs 6 & 7.45 10 wks €80

Ballyfermot College of Further Education Ballyfermot Rd 10 (6269421) - everything you want to know about set up assembly, installatioin, beginners & advanced, Mon 7pm & 8.30, each 10 wks, €50

Ballymun Comprehensive Schools Adult Ed Centre Ballymun Rd 9 (8420654/8425288 night) - beginners, 10wk, €90

Blackrock College (2888681) - beginners, Tue 7.30-9, 6 wks €65

Cabinteely Community School Johnstown Rd 18 (2857455) - intro to ms office 97, windows, 10wk, €95

CITAS Computer & I.T. Training 54 Middle Abbey St 1 (8782212) - computer skills - word, keyboard, windows, internet, Tue morn, 10-12 €320/ windows, 1 day €170/ word, excel, access, powerpoint - each 1 day, €199

Colaiste Dhulaigh Barryscourt Rd Coolock 17 (8481337) - intro for retired people, Feb 2004, Tues, 6.30 / day courses: & the internet, 10wks/ pre-ECDL, 10 wks

Colaiste Eanna Kilkieran Rd Cabra 7 (8389577) - explore windows, 10 wks, Tues, 7-9pm / also day courses for beginners

Colaiste Eoin Cappagh Rd 11 (8340893) - basic, 10wk

Colaiste Ide Cardiffsbridge Rd Finglas West 11 (8342333) - beginners, pitman cert, pre-ECDL, Thurs, 7pm, 15 wks, €150

College of Further Education Main St Dundrum 14 (2951376) - for absolute beginners, Tue & Thurs

Computeach AXIS, Main St Ballymun 9 (8832167)

Coolmine Community School Clonsilla 15 (8214583) - beginners word processing 9wks €90

Crumlin College of Further Education Crumlin Rd 12 (4540662) - beginners, general introduction, 10 wks / pocket PCs for business people, Tue 5 wks 8.15

Donahies Community School Streamville Rd 13 (8482217) - intro,Mon, 7 wks / for the older adult, day only, levels 1, 2 & 3, 10wks / for home use, Wed 10 wks / improve your skills 1o wks / for the modern office Wed 10 wks each €100

Dun Laoghaire College of Further Education 17 Cumberland St Dun Laoghaire (2809676) - beginners/ improvers: incl word & email, Mon 5 & 6.45; Tue & Wed, 6.45 & 8.45, €100 ea

Eden Computer Training Rathfarnham 16, or MACRO Centre, 1 Green St 7 (4953155) - intro; beginners: word, internet, email/ ECDL

FAS Training Centre Baldoyle 13 (8167460); Ballyfermot 10 (6055090/ 5933); Cabra Bannow Rd 7 (8821400); Finglas Jamestown Rd 11 (8140243); Tallaght 24 (4045284) - C&G cert, 10wk; Wyatville Rd (2043600)

Greendale Community School Kilbarrack 5 (8322735/6) - for absolute beginners, Tue 10 wks 7pm €100

Greenhills College Limekiln Ave Walkinstown 12 (4507779/4507138) - 10 wks, €106

Greenhills College Limekiln Ave Walkinstown 12 (4507779/4507138) - European cert in E-literacy, Tue, 20wks, €330

Griffith College Dublin Sth Circular Rd 8 (4150400) - understanding computers, ITEB cert, p/t, end user, 1 eve per wk

Hartstown Community School Clonsilla 15 (8209863) - beginners/intermediate, 10wks, €80 each

Holy Family Community School Rathcoole (4580766)

Inchicore College of Further Education Emmet Rd 8 (4535358) - intro, Mon, 10 wks

Irish Academy of Computer Training 98 St Stephen's Grn 2 (4347600) - IACT webmaster dip, 12 wks €1998/ intro to programming; C; visual basic: ea 8 wks €795 cert/ access 8 wks €645 cert/ word; excel; powerpoint: ea 4 wks €275 cert/ C++, 10 wks; VC++; java 12 wks: ea €1295 cert / ECDL bootcamp, 10 wks €395

Keytrainer Ireland 33/34 Dame St 2 (6714000) - foundation course incl windows/ filemanagement/ computer appreciation, word & email, day & p/time

Killester College of Further Education Collins Ave 5 (8337686) - intro to & improvers: each 10 wk Mon 7.30-9.30 €110

Kilroy's College 25 Kingram Place 2 (1850 700700) - tutor supported home study: basics, ECDL, data processing

Kilternan Adult Ed Centre Ballybetagh Rd Kilternan 18 (2952050) – for fun / improvers

KLEAR Grange Park View Kilbarrack 5 (8671845) - computer literacy, eve/ also day

Knocklyon Youth & Community Centre, 16 (4943991)

Kylemore College Kylemore Rd 10 (6265901) - FETAC computer applications, 15 wk / for beginners, for older adults, for the terrified, further skills, each 10 wks

Lucan Community College Esker Drive (6282077) - 8wk, €99

Malahide Community School Malahide (8460949) - Wed, day, 10 wks €100; Tues, 10 wks €120

Malahide Community School Malahide (8460949) - for those with some knowledge, incl internet, email, 10 wks €140

Marino College 14-20 Marino Mart 3 (8332100) - beginners/improvers

Newpark Adult Education Centre Newtownpark Ave Blackrock (2884376) - 10wks, €130/ ECDL, 20wks, €520/ ms office beginners, 5.10pm Tue €130

Old Bawn Community School Tallaght 24 (4526137) - basic introductory & intermediate courses - word, excel, internet: 10 wks each/ also, introduction for over 50s, Wed 10 wks

Open Learning Centre at Crumlin College FE 12 (4531202) - self-learn with software self-tuition, day & eve

Pearse College Clogher Rd 12 (4536661/4541544) - work skills, day/ also advanced skills, day, Sept-May €14 or VTOS, FETAC cert

People's College 32 Parnell Sq 1 (8735879) - €55

Pitman Training Centre 6-8 Wicklow St 2 (6768008) - intro to, day, eve Sats, 45 hrs €468, cert

Plunket College Swords Rd, Whitehall 9 (8371689) - beginners, Tues, €108/ intermediate, Wed, €108 - 10 wks, each

Pobalscoil Iosolde 20 (6260116) - for absolute beginners/ also level 2: each 10 wks €55

Pobalscoil Neasain Baldoyle 13 (8063092) - beginners, mon 7.30 10 wks €120/

everyday use of, 8pm 10 wks €120

Pobalscoil Rosmini Adult Ed Grace Pk Rd 9 (8371015) - beginners 1 & 2, Mon-Wed / for mature learners, Wed 10 wks / MOUS core/ expert. Mon: all €130

Portmarnock Community School Carrickhill Rd (8038056) - introduction to, €80

Rathmines Snr College Town Hall 6 (4975334) - applications for beginners & improvers, 10 wks, €80/ 20 wks, €160

RAVE Good Shepherd School Churchtown 14 (2981052) - 10 wks 7.30, €99

Saint Finian's Community College Swords (8402623) - 10wk, €106

School of Computer Technology 21 Rosmeen Gdns Dun Laoghaire (2844045) - intro to - unix; linux; java; C++; SQL; perl; PHP; visual basic; website design: each €35 per hr, C&G

Senior College Dun Laoghaire CFE Eblana Ave Dun Laoghaire (2800385) - computer applications (beginners)using ms office, FETAC 25 wks, €250

St Kevin's College Clogher Rd Crumlin 12 (4536397) - 10wks

St MacDara's Community College Wellington Lane Templeogue 6W (4566216) - beginners Mon, Tue, 10 wks, €106 each

St Mark's Community School Cookstown Road Tallaght 24 (4519399)

St Thomas Community College Novara Ave Bray (2866111) - beginners / stage 2/ 10 eks €70 each/ beginners 20 wks C&G cert €250

St Tiernan's Community School Parkvale Balally 16 (2953224) - level 1 how to use, Mon €100/ level 2 Thurs, €100/ level 3 €120, Wed: all 7.30, 10 wks / computers & the internet & web pages, Mon 7.30 10 wks €120

Sth Dublin Co Libraries Languages & Computers: Ballyroan/Clondalkin/ Castletymon, Lucan & Co Library (4597834-admin only) - self learning

Stillorgan Senior College Old Road Stillorgan (2880704) - beginners, internet & email, Mon, 7.30pm, 6wk, €75/ pre-ECDL Thurs 8wks €95

TACT St Dominic's School St Dominic's Rd Tallaght 24 (4596757) - beginners/intermediate, 8wks, €85 day

Tallaght Community School Balrothery 24 (4515566) - intro to office 97, 10wk, €110

COMPUTER AIDED DESIGN see also Design, Graphic

Ashfield Computer Training Main St Templeogue 6W (4926708) - AutoCAD 2000

Colaiste Dhulaigh Barryscourt Rd Coolock 17 (8481337) - CAD, C&G cert, Mon/Tues, wks. 7 - 9.30

Colaiste Ide Cardiffsbridge Rd Finglas West 11 (8342333) - C&G computer aided draughting & design, 2D, Tues, 7-10pm, 25 wks, €300

DIT Faculty: Engineering Bolton St 1 (4023649/3445) - intro to com aid draughting, 10 wks €320

Dorset College 64a Lr Dorset St/ 8 Belvedere Pl 1 (8309677) - autoCAD - beginners & intermediate

Dublin Institute of Design 25 Sufflok St 2 (6790286) - AutoCad 2D, c&g cert, 12 wks, €550

Dun Laoghaire College of Further Education 17 Cumberland St Dun Laoghaire (2809676) - basic & advanced, AutoCAD 2000 2D, 20wks 7-10pm, €400

Eden Computer Training Rathfarnham 16, or MACRO Centre, 1 Green St 7 (4953155) - autocad 2000/ autocad lite, p/time

FAS Training Centre Baldoyle 13 (8167460); Ballyfermot 10 (6055900/ 5933); Cabra Bannow Rd 7 (8821400); Finglas 11 (8140243)

FAS Training Centre Tallaght 24 (4045284) - AutoCAD, 10wk / 2D draughting & design, 30 wks

Greendale Community School Kilbarrack 5 (8322735/6) - autocad intro, 2d draughting, 3d modelling, Tue 7.30 10 wks €100

Griffith College Dublin Sth Circular Rd 8 (4150400) - AutoCAD - 2D C&G/ AutoCAD - 3D, C&G, both p/t, end user, 1 eve per wk

Irish Academy of Computer Training 98 St Stephen's Grn 2 (4347600) - quarkxpress, corel draw, ms publisher, adobe photoshop, framemaker, intro to CAD design for engineers: all 8 wks €695, cert/ powerpoint, 4 wks €295, cert/ desktop publishing master course 12 wks, dip, €1995; also day

New Media Technology Training 13 Harcourt St 2 (4780905) - 3D studio Max/ 2 dreamweaver; 3 java, CGI scripts, style sheets/ digital imaging, adobe photoshop/ animation - flash, director / also p/time day

Newpark Adult & Continuing Education Centre Newtownpark Ave Blackrock (2884376) - autocad beginners/ photoshop beginners: each 10 wks€140

Portobello School Rere 40 Lr Dominick St 1 (8721277) - autocad, eve

Ringsend Technical Institute Cambridge Rd 4 (6684498) - autoCAD, 10wks, €95

St Kevin's College Clogher Rd Crumlin 12 (4536397) - autoCAD, 20wks

St Thomas Community College Novara Ave Bray (2866111) - Autocad, C&G cert,

25wks, €350, also day/ photoshop 10 wks €150

COMPUTER APPRECIATION

Ballyfermot College of Further Education Ballyfermot Rd 10 (6269421) - for absolute beginners, Mon 7-8.30pm & 8.30-10pm, 10 wks ea, €75/ for improvers 1&2, Wed 7-830pm & 8.30-10pm, 10 wks ea, €75

Business Computer Training Institute Central Dublin (6616838 LoCall 1890 564039) - introductory computers & computing

Irish Academy of Computer Training 98 St Stephen's Grn 2 (4347600) - PC survival, 2 wks €195 cert/ internet & email, 3 wks, €195 cert/ becoming computer literate/powerpoint: 4 wks €295 cert each/ word, excel: 4 wks €275 cert/ office smart suite, 4-8 wks €795 cert/ dtp 6 wks €495 cert/ ms frontpage, access: 8 wks €645

Kilroy's College 25 Kingram Place 2 (1850 700700) - tutor supported home study: ECDL, MOUS, PC repair, A+, networking, visual basic 6.0, i.Net+

COMPUTER MAINTENANCE / Technical Support

Ashfield Computer Training Main St Templeogue 6W (4926708) - PC maintenance, CompTia's A+ computer technician

Ballsbridge College of Business Studies Shelbourne Rd 4 (6684806) - the computer hospital, Mon 6pm 10 wks €108

Business Computer Training Central Dublin (6616838 LoCall 1890 564039) - pc installaton & mainteance, 10 wks €445 cert; A+ hardward pc technician, 10 wks, €475; A+ software technician, 12 wks €570

Colaiste Dhulaigh Barryscourt Rd Coolock 17 (8481337) - A+ & A Net cert, maint technician course, Mon, 20wks 7-9.30; also day

Colaiste Ide Cardiffsbridge Rd Finglas West 11 (8342333) - Sat, 10-1pm, 10 wks, €250/ A+ CompTia cert technician core module, 7-10, 25 wks €800

Dorset College 64a Lr Dorset St/ 8 Belvedere Pl 1 (8309677) - cert computer professioinal: CompTIA A+, network+, mcp70-210, Mon-Fri 9.30-1.30, 35 wks/ compTIA A+ dip for information technology practitioners c&g e-Quals, Mon-Fri 6.30-9pm 20 wks/ compTIA qualifications: A+ computer technician leading cert, Mon & Wed; network+ Tue & Thurs; security+ Mon; linux+ Wed; server+, Tue; project+ Thurs; I-net: each 6.30-9, 15 wks

Eden Computer Training Rathfarnham 16, or MACRO Centre, 1 Green St 7 (4953155) - network+, A+, NT4, windows 2000, cisco networking

FAS Net College www.fas-netcollege.com (info@fas-netcollege.com/ 2043600) - elearning: technical support certs: A+ service technician; iNet+; internetworking professional; network+; server admin; security professional; SQL 7.0 system admin; windows 2000 instal, configure, admin - all €120 excl exam fees. Online tutor support option €80

FAS Training Centre Ballyfermot 10 (6055900/ 5933); Finglas 11 (8140243); Loughlinstown (2043600)

Hi-Tech Training 4 Nth Gt George's St 1 (1850-759759) - levels 1, 2, 50% practical hands-on, 7-10pm, 15wks each; cert

Institute of Technology Tallaght 24 (4042000) - national cert in maintenance technology - modular basis

Irish Academy of Computer Training 98 St Stephen's Grn 2 (4347600) - pc troubleshooting & repair, 8 wks €755 cert/ A+ , network+ : certs 20 wks €1995 each/ windows NT server, 12 wks €1495 MCSA cert/ Linux+ admin / also day

Kilroy's College 25 Kingram Place 2 (1850 700700) - pc assembly & A+

Pitman Training Centre 6-8 Wicklow St 2 (6768008) - A+ computer technician, cert, 120hrs, €1,491, day, eve, Sats

Plunket College Swords Rd, Whitehall 9 (8371689) - intro, Thurs, 10 wks, €66

COMPUTER NETWORKS see also Computer Training, IT etc

Business Computer Training Institute Central Dublin (6616838 LoCall 1890 564039) - networking, 12 wks €570 cert/ dip, 32 wks €1460; cisco associate, ccna cert, 14 wks €760/ cisco professional - ccna routing cert & ccna switching cert / ccnp routing cert: - 10wks, €1050 each/ ms windows 2000 - professional mcp70-210, 10 wks €475; ms managing windows 2000, network mcp70-218, 11 wks, €660/ ms admin exchange 200 server mcp70-224, 10 wks €570/ ms certified systems admin, 43 wks €2365, mcsa cert mcp70-216 admin ms win2000 network infrastructure; mcp70-217 admin ms win2000 directory services infrastructure: each 12 wks €660, cert / mcp70-270 ms winXP Pro, 10 wks €475/ security+ & network engineer; server+ network engineer: each 12 wks €825

Colaiste Dhulaigh Barryscourt Rd Coolock 17 (8481337) - A+ & A Net cert, maint & net technician course, Mon, 20wks 4-6.00; 7-9.30; also day

Colaiste Ide Cardiffsbridge Rd Finglas West 11 (8342333) - introduction to, Thurs 7-10pm, 10 wks €90

DIT Faculty: Engineering Bolton St 1 (4023649/3445) - network cabling course, 10 wks €360

Eden Computer Training Rathfarnham 16, or MACRO Centre, 1 Green St 7 (4953155) - mcsa, mcse, ccna

FAS Training Centre Ballyfermot 10 (6055900/ 5933)

I.T. Blanchardstown Blanchardstown Road North 15 (8851100) - cisco certified network academy prog CCNA, 10 mths €3700 CCNP prog 4 13 wk modules €1900 each

Kilroy's College 25 Kingram Place 2 (1850 700700) - tutor supported home study, network+

Moresoft Computers Ltd 44 Lr Lesson St 2 (6621711) - PC Networking, ICM cert, 12 wks €952

School of Computer Technology 21 Rosmeen Gdns Dun Laoghaire (2844045) - C&G dip in networking, 4 wks €1600, day

COMPUTER PROGRAMMING see also Systems Analysis

Ashfield Computer Training Main St Templeogue 6W (4926708) - VB, C++, C, SQL

Business Computer Training Central Dublin (6616838 LoCall 1890 564039) - eve or home study courses C+G cert: program design techniques & data processing, 12 wks €445/ systems analysis, 14 wks €635/ programming in C++, 10 wks €445/ prog in java, 12 wks €505/ visual basic prog, stage 1, 10 wks €445; stage 2 12 wks €505; s

CITAS Computer & IT Training 54 Middle Abbey St 1 (8782212) - Oracle SQL, PL/SQL 7 wks x 2 days, 6.30-9.30, €2000/ oracle forms & reports, 7 wks x 2days 6.30-8.30/ C++ programming, 7 wks Tue & Thurs eve, €1200/ oracle DBA, €4000/ dip in IT, €2500, 1 yr f/time

Colaiste Dhulaigh Barryscourt Rd Coolock 17 (8481337) - Visual Basic, part 1, Mon 6.30-8.30, 10 wks/ HTML & java script pt 1 basics, 8 wks Tues 6.45-8.45; continuation Spring 2004

Crumlin College of Further Education Crumlin Rd 12 (4540662) - dip in prog level 2 C&G(7261) - visual basic, java, Tue & Wed 6.45; also level 2 in jan 2004: 10 wks each

DIT Faculty: Engineering Bolton St 1 (4023649/3445) - programming, cert, 3yr p/time €800/ programmable logic controllers, 10wks €320 per stage; also 1 yr course

Dorset College 64a Lr Dorset St/ 8 Belvedere Pl 1 (8309677) - prog cert & prog dip: C++, visual basic, java/ also CIW adv dip level 3: design & analysis, C++, VB, java, SQL

Dun Laoghaire College of Further Education 17 Cumberland St Dun Laoghaire (2809676) - using visual basic, 20 wks 7-10pm €400

Eden Computer Training Rathfarnham 16, or MACRO Centre, 1 Green St 7 (4953155) - visual basic, C++, java, Ms SQL server

FAS Net College www.fas-netcollege.com (info@fas-netcollege.com/ 2043600) - various - see under Web Design/ visual basic 6 - desktop applications; online tutor option €80

FAS Training Centre Baldoyle 13 (8167460); Ballyfermot 10 (6055900/ 5933); Finglas Jamestown Rd 11 (8140243)

Fitzwilliam Institute Ltd Temple Court Temple Rd Blackrock (2834579) - dip in java programming/ dip in oracle database programming: each course hands-on, 2 eve wkly,10 wks, 6.30-9.30pm, €1263, Ely Place 2 / postgrad dip in software development, networking & website development, ICM,f/time day, €3810/ 4540 Eu non-resident/ 5835 non EU nationals, all + €190 exam fees

Griffith College Dublin Sth Circular Rd 8 (4150400) - Visual Basic, ITEB cert/ business systems devel, ITEB cert/ programming intro/advanced/ C prog intro & advanced/ C++, intro/advanced, C&G, all p/t, end user, 1 eve per wk

Irish Academy of Computer Training 98 St Stephen's Grn 2 (4347600) - intro to programming; C; visual basic primer: each 8 wks €795, cert/ visual basic for programmers; advanced visual basic; visual basic MCP prep; VB.net prog: each 8 wks €1195 cert/ ms access 8 wks €645 cert/; C++; visual C++;java; VB script & ASP prog: 10 wks €1295 cert / IACT webmaster course in web design, 12 wks €1995, dip

Kilroy's College 25 Kingram Place 2 (1850 700700) - home study visual basic 6.0

Moresoft Computers Ltd 44 Lr Lesson St 2 (6621711) - Java & advanced Java, ICM cert 12 wks €950 each

New Media Technology Training 13 Harcourt St 2 (4780905) - web programming, active server pages

Ringsend Technical Institute Cambridge Rd 4 (6684498) - visual basic, 10 wks €95

School of Computer Technology 21 Rosmeen Gdns Dun Laoghaire (2844045) - unix/linux LPI cert, €825/ java; C++; visual basic: C&G certs/ SQL; perl; PHP: all 36 hrs, €750 ea/ also day

COMPUTER SCIENCE / ELECTRONICS see also Digital / Information Technology

Cabinteely Community School Johnstown Rd 18 (2857455) - ECDL, 20 wks, €450

DIT Faculty: Engineering Bolton St 1 (4023649/3445) - MSc applied computing for technologists; MSc engineering computation: each 2yr p/t 6 modules, €1373pa/ electronic & copmputer systems, dip 2yr €700/ cert 3yr €800pa

Griffith College Dublin Sth Circular Rd 8 (4150400) - BSC in computing science, 4 yr, HETAC, p/t, 3 eves per wk/ also f/t/ MSc, 18 mths, p/t, 3 eves per wk/ MSc 1 yr f/time / graduate dip, 18 mths, p/t, 3 eve wkly, also 1 yr f/time/ cert in computing, 2 yrs, HETAC, Mon to Fri, also 3 eve per wk

Irish Academy of Computer Training 98 St Stephen's Grn 2 (4347600) - IATC webmaster, 12 wks €1995 dip/ programming; PB troubleshooting & repair: each 8 wks €795, cert/ A+; network+: 20 wks €1995, cert each

Kilroy's College 25 Kingram Place 2 (1850 700700) - tutor supported home study

National College of Ireland Mayor St IFSC 1 (4060500/ 1850 221721) - BSc in Software Systems, HETAC, 4 yrs eve & Sats

The Open University Enquiry & Advice Centre Holbrook House, Holles St 2 (6785399)

Trinity College 2 (6772941) - (6081039/3644) - BSc hons, 4yr, 24wks per yr

COMPUTER TRAINING

ABM Computer Training 54 North St, Swords (8902348) - intro to computers, word processing, spreadsheets, database, internet, powerpoint, ECDL and advanced ECDL, web design, internet marketing, accounts, ms office specialist, access JEB, outlook

Adelaide Computers 14 Pembroke Lane Ballsbridge 4 (2696213) - Windows Applications, Dreamweaver, HTML, FrontPage, Networks, etc; one-to-one training at your office/home or our offices, small groups, beginners to advanced / full training programmes also

Ashfield Computer Training Main St Templeogue 6W (4926708) - Ms Office applications all levels & versions/ ECDL/ MOS all morns, eves, acelerated/ MS MCP,

MCSA, MSCE / CompTIA - A+, Network+, Security+, Linux+,Server+/ Cisco , CCNA, CCNP, Citrix - CCA/ CIW - webmaster Track/ Oracle - OCP

Ballinteer Community School Ballinteer 16 (2988195) - ECDL advanced, Mon 20 hrs, €240

Ballymun Comprehensive School Adult Ed Centre Ballymun Rd 9 (8420654/ 8425828 night) - ECDL complete course Sat 10-3.30pm, 10 wks €460

Bray Business College Florence Rd Bray (2829936) - Ms Word, Excel, Access, 2 wks, €250/ Sage accounts, 2 wks, €250

Business Computer Training Central Dublin (6616838 LoCall 1890 564039) - ECDL 12wks €475; ECDL word processing advanced 10wk €445, cert/ ECDL spreadsheets advanced, 10 wks €4445/ computing basics, 10 wks €445 cert/ dip in computer applications, 34 wks €1585

CITAS Computer & I.T. Training 54 Middle Abbey St 1 (8782212) - courses in: windows €170/ word processing; excel; access; powerpoint, outlook, €199 each; ms office user - MOUS, 6 wks €210 per module 1 day 03 3 eve/ dip in software applications, 2 yr, €2500pa

Colaiste Dhulaigh Barryscourt Rd Coolock 17 (8481337) - ECDL, 22 wks; also 10 & 15 wks/ computers & computing, C&G cert, Tues, 20 wks/ MCAS - cert systems administrator, Mon 6.30, 25 wks

Colaiste Ide Cardiffsbridge Rd Finglas West 11 (8342333) - ECDL, Thurs, 7pm, cert/ advanced (excel) Thurs/ advanced (word); 20 wks €400 each

College of Further Education Main St Dundrum 14 (2951376) - intro to excel, Tue, Thurs, 8 wks

Computeach AXIS, Main St Ballymun 9 (8832167)

Crumlin College of Further Education Crumlin Rd 12 (4540662) - Mon & Thurs, MS office MOS/ word, powerpoint, excel - spreadsheets/ access - database/ ECDL Tues & Wed, 6.45-9.45, 20 wks

DIT Faculty: Engineering Bolton St 1 (4023649/3445) - computer applications, 3 yr cert, €800/ BTech computing, 6 modules 2y €1500pa

DIT Faculty: Science Kevin St 8 (4024585/3445) - British Computer Soc exams, 4 yrs, cert & dip €870, prof grad dip €915

Donahies Community School Streamville Rd 13 (8482217) MOS office / word, cert €100

Dorset College 64a Lr Dorset St/ 8 Belvedere Pl 1 (8309677) - ECDL, all 7 modules, day, eve Sats/ office technology 10 wks/ computer applications beginners, C&G e-Quals cert, Tue & Thurs, 15 wks/ MOS & e-Quals core level & expert level adv dip/

Dublin Business School 13/14 Aungier St 2 (4177500) - dip in IT, 1 eve per wk, 1 yr,14 wks/ JEB teachers dip in IT, 2 eves, 10 wks; both 6.30-9.30pm/ grad dip in business studies/ IT, 2 eves per wk plus some Sats, 6.15-9.30pm, 16 mths/ grad dip in business studies/ e-Business, 2 eves per wk plus some Sats, 6.15-9.30/ dip in web design 1 eve wkly 6.30-9.30, 10 wks/ advanced pc applications ICM dip, intensive p/time

Dublin City University Registry office Glasnevin 9 (7005338) - applications-day/computer-aided mechanical & manufacturing engineering

Dun Laoghaire College of Further Education 17 Cumberland St Dun Laoghaire

(2809676) - ECDL, 22 wks, Mon & Wed, 7.30 €320 ea/ advanced ECDL 22 wks, Wed 7.30, €135 ea

Eden Computer Training Rathfarnham 16, or MACRO Centre, 1 Green St 7 (4953155) - word, excel, access, powerpoint, ECDL, MOS, JEB teacher's dip, web design, MCP, A+, Network+, MCSE, MCSA, server+ / ebusiness, also day

Educational Multimedia Corporation The Digital Hub 157 Thomas St Blackrock 8 (4806400) - providers of ECDL & Microsoft approved training courseware

FAS Net College www.fas-netcollege.com (info@fas-netcollege.com/ 2043600) - MOUS cert courses - €120 each: access 2000 core; ECDL; excel 2000 core/ expert; project 2000 core; word 2000 core/expert; outlook 2000 core; also computer fundamentals - €free/ tutor support €80 extra

FAS Training Centre Baldoyle 13 (8167460); Ballyfermot 10 (6055900/ 5933); Cabra Bannow Rd 7 (8821400); Finglas Jamestown Rd 11 (8140243); Jervis St 1 (8044600); Tallaght 24 (4045284) - MOS 10 wks; Wyatville Rd (2043600)

Fingal Co Libraries County Hall Main St Swords (8905520) - self-learning computer courses: Balbriggan: 8411128; Blanchardstown: 8905563; Howth: 8322130; Malahide: 8452026; Rathbeale: 8404179; Mobile Library HQ: 8221564; Schools Library:8225056; Housebound Service: 8604290

Fitzwilliam Institute Ltd Temple Court Temple Rd Blackrock (2834579) - website development/ computer programming/ databases

Foxrock Institute Kill O' the Grange School Kill Lane Blackrock (4939506/4939629) - beginners/intermediate/advanced certs 6-8wks, from €127 - also Sat

Grange Community College Grange Abbey Rd Donaghmede 13 (8471422) - ms word/ ms access/ms excel, 10wks, €93 each

Greendale Community School Kilbarrack 5 (8322735/6) - applications - excel, access, powerpoint, 10 wks, Thurs €100 / ECDL, mod 5 &7, 12 wks €140

Greenhills College Limekiln Ave Walkinstown 12 (4507779/4507138) - ECDL, 20wks, €330

Griffith College Dublin Sth Circular Rd 8 (4150400) - xcel/ powerpoint, all ITEB cert, p/t end user, 1 eve per wk

Holy Family Community School Rathcoole (4580766)

Inchicore College of Further Education Emmet Rd 8 (4535358) - computer studies/applications, day/ ECDL, Tue, 20 wks 7-9pm

Institute of Technology Tallaght 24 (4042000) - ECDL, 20 wks

Institute of Technology, Blanchardstown Blanchardstown Road North 15 (8851100) - ECDL, 7 modules, cert, 15 wks €510

Irish Academy of Computer Training 98 St Stephen's Grn 2 (4347600) - IACT webmaster, 12 wks €1995, dip/ word processing; spreadsheets: 4 wks €275 cert, ea/ graphics, freelance, powerpoint; presentation tools: ea €295, cert/ programming €1195, cert/ operating systems; networking: ea €1495, cert/ dtp 24 wks €1995, cert; also quark, corel, ms pub, photoshop, illustrator framemaker 8 wks €695/ new technologies €1995, cert/ ms, lotus, ibm, corel, sun, €395 ea wind 2000, xp, linux €1495 cert: all also day

Keytrainer Ireland 33/34 Dame St 2 (6714000) - applications training: Word, Excel,

Powerpoint, Access - all levels/ ECDL, JEB, MOUS/ Web Design/ Keyboard skills

Kilroy's College 25 Kingram Place 2 (1850 700700) - tutor supported home study: beginners, ECDL, MOUS, PC repair/assembly, networking, data processing, visual basic 6.0, A+, i.Net+

Malahide Community School Malahide (8460949) - ECDL qualification, 3 modules 10 wks Thurs €200

Marino College 14-20 Marino Mart 3 (8332100) - intro to access/ excel spreadsheets, 10wk, €81

Milltown Institute Milltown Pk 6 (2698388) - ECDL, word, excel, internet, email, IT concepts & access powerpoint & file mngt, 26 wks, 6.30-9pm, €500

Moresoft Computers Ltd 44 Lr Lesson St 2 (6621711) - ECDL, 16 wks cert €750/ Unix fundamentals & Unix administration, ICM cert 12 wks, €952 each/ Cisco professional ICM cert, 12 wks €1009/ MOUS master, ICM cert, 16 wks €1000

Old Bawn Community School Tallaght 24 (4526137) - ECDL, all 7 modules, Tues & Thurs, 14 wks, 5-7.10, or Tues or Thurs, 28 wks, 7.30-9.40

Palmerstown Community School 20 (6260116) - ECDL, 7 modules 10 wks €65 each/ computer architecture systems, FETAC cert Mon 7pm €140

Pearse College Clogher Rd 12 (4536661/4541544) - ECDL, 10wk, day/fast track into technology (FIT), 30wk, VTOS

Pitman Training Centre 6-8 Wicklow St 2 (6768008) - Windows, 12 hrs, €240/ Ms Office specialist dip, 6 wks /ECDL, various courses, €752/ MS Skills dip, 4 wks €780/ Ms office applications, 16-20 hrs €300, cert/ day, eve, Sats

Plunket College Swords Rd, Whitehall 9 (8371689) - ECDL, all 7 IT modules, Mon & Wed, 24 wks, €420

Pobalscoil Neasain Baldoyle 13 (8063092) - ECDL Mon 8pm 10 wks €385

Pobalscoil Rosmini Adult Ed Grace Pk Rd 9 (8371015) - ECDL, modules 1-7, Wed, Thurs, 5 wks, €165 each/ special classes, Wed, 1.30&3pm, 10 wks, €130/ MOUS Mon 7pm €135

Portobello School Rere 40 Lr Dominick St 1 (8721277) - Galileo computer system/ Sabre, part time eve

Prism Computer Taining 3 George's Ave Blackrock (2781270) - EDCL, 13 wks, one-to-one, €500, cert; also day

Rathmines Snr College Town Hall 6 (4975334) - applications, intermediate, 10 wks, €80 Tue, Wed/ for foreign students, Wed 10 wks €80

Ringsend Technical Institute Cambridge Rd 4 (6684498) - ECDL, 25wks, €420/ word processing; excel spreadsheets 7-9pm MOUS core cert €185 each

School of Computer Technology 21 Rosmeen Gdns Dun Laoghaire (2844045) - unix/linux LPI cert, €825/ java; C++; visual basic: C&G certs/ SQL; perl; PHP; website design: all 36 hrs, €750 ea/ also day/ dip in networking C&G cert 4 wks €1600 day

Senior College Dun Laoghaire CFE Eblana Ave Dun Laoghaire (2800385) - computer applications beginners, FETAC cert, €250/intermediate (access & excel) cert, €260, 25 wks each

St Mark's Community School Cookstown Road Tallaght 24 (4519399)

St Peter's College Collins Ave 5 (8337686) - ECDL/ ECDL improvers: each 20 wks €365

St Thomas Community College Novara Ave Bray (2866111) - ECDL cert, 20wks, €400/C&G cert, 20wks, €250/ MOS office, 20 wks €400

Sth Dublin Co Libraries Languages & Computers: Ballyroan/Clondalkin/ Castletymon, Lucan & Co Library (4597834-admin only) - a wide range of self-learning packages available

Stillorgan College of Further Education Old Road Stillorgan (2880704) - intro, Mon/ internet & email, 6 wks €75/ WP 8 wks €95/ECDL 10 wks €95/pre-ECDL 8 wks/ MOS Tue 20 wks

Tallaght Community School Balrothery 24 (4515566) - ECDL, 25wk, €370, 3 terms (payable €155, €155, €80)

TARGET St Kevin's School Newbrook Rd, Donaghmede 13 (8671967) - day only, intro to; Pre-ECDL / ECDL

Whitehall College of Further Education Swords Rd 9 (8376011) - MS certified professional MCPwin2000/ spreadsheets/ Excel (MOS)

COMPUTERISED ACCOUNTS

ABM Computer Training 54 North St, Swords (8902348) - TAS, Quickbooks, Sage: all yr, also day

Adelaide Computers 14 Pembroke Lane Ballsbridge 4 (2696213) - one-to-one training at your office/home or our offices, small groups, beginners to advanced, full training programmes also

Ashfield Computer Training Main St Templeogue 6W (4926708) - Tas Books / Sage, Quickpay

CITAS Computer & I.T. Training 54 Middle Abbey St 1 (8782212) - Sage & Tas Books, Tas Payroll, €199 per module, Weds / Oracle Financials €4000 f/time

Crumlin College of Further Education Crumlin Rd 12 (4540662) - TAS books for windows, Tues, 10 wks, 8.15-9.45

Dorset College 64a Lr Dorset St/ 8 Belvedere Pl 1 (8309677) - computerised - Sage/ Tas, Mon & Wed, 6.30-9pm, 12 wks

Eden Computer Training Rathfarnham 16, or MACRO Centre, 1 Green St 7 (4953155) - Tasbooks/ Sage. Take 5; all payroll packages

FAS Training Centre Baldoyle 13 (8167460) - plus Payroll; Ballyfermot 10 (6055900/ 5933); Finglas Jamestown Rd 11 (8140243); Jervis St 1 (8044600); Tallaght Cookstown Indl Est 24 (4045284) - 10 wks

FAS Training Services Wyatville Rd (2043600)

Greendale Community School Kilbarrack 5 (8322735/6) - Tas books, Tue 10 wks €100

Irish Academy of Computer Training 98 St Stephen's Grn 2 (4347600) - excel; lotus 1-2-3; ea 4 wks €275 cert; also day

Plunket College Swords Rd, Whitehall 9 (8371689) - IATI course, Wed, 8.30-10

Plunket College Swords Rd, Whitehall 9 (8371689) - IATI cert, Fri 11am €113.50

Senior College Dun Laoghaire CFE Eblana Ave Dun Laoghaire (2800385) - Tas Books, IATI, 12 wks, €150

St Thomas Community College Novara Ave Bray (2866111) - Tas, 30 wks, €200, FETAC, day / Take 5, 20 wks, €400 FETAC

COMPUTERS, FOR ELECTRICIANS, ENGINEERS see also Computer Maintenance

Business Computer Training Central Dublin (6616838 LoCall 1890 564039) - network+ engineer foundation: 12 wks €660 cert; Linux+, 12 wks €825, cert/ mcse cert systems engineer, 79 wks €4.345, cert

Crumlin College of Further Education Crumlin Rd 12 (4540662) - ICM cert in operating systems, ms & linus, Mon 6.45 20 wks/ c&g dipl in electronic & computing sys 1 (hardware), Wed 6.45 20 wks

Dorset College 64a Lr Dorset St/ 8 Belvedere Pl 1 (8309677) - MS certified professional - MCP; systems administrator; systems engineer - mcse; database admin - mcdba

Eden Computer Training Rathfarnham 16, or MACRO Centre, 1 Green St 7 (4953155) - windows 2000 admin, NT server

Kilroy's College 25 Kingram Place 2 (1850 700700) - home study PC repair & upgrading, Assembly & A+

CONCERTINA see also Music

Comhaltas Ceoltoiri Eireann 32 Belgrave Sq Monkstown (2800295)

Na Piobairi Uileann 15 Henrietta St 1 (8730093) - Weds

CONFECTIONERY / CAKE MAKING / DECORATION

DIT Faculty: Tourism & Food Cathal Brugha St 1 (4024349/3445) - cake design & decor: royal icing/ sugar paste/ sugar flowers, each, 2 yr cert €500pa/ professional baking, cake 1 yr €250 per module

Hartstown Community School Clonsilla 15 (8209863) - sugar craft & cake decoration, 10wk, €60

Newpark Adult Education Centre Newtownpark Ave Blackrock (2884376) - cake icing, beginners, Mon 7.30 10wks, €99

Old Bawn Community School Tallaght 24 (4526137) - cake icing/ sugar art, beginners/advanced/ 10 wks, Tues/Thurs, 7.30

St Finian's Community College Swords (8402623) - sugar craft, Mon, 10 wks €79

St MacDara's Community College Wellington Lane Templeogue 6W (4566216) - sugar craft, cake decoration, Mon, 7.30-9.30pm, 10 wks, €79

CONFLICT RESOLUTION see also Social / Personnel

Colaiste Dhulaigh & College of Further Education Barryscourt Rd Coolock 17 (8481337) - dealing with conflict creatively, Mon 7-9pm, 10 wks

Trinity College 2 (6772941) - conflict & dispute resolution studies, 1yr, postgrad dip, 24 wks (2601144)

CONSERVATION see also Environment

An Taisce- The National Trust for Ireland The Tailors Hall Back Lane 8 (4541786) - info, lectures, seminars, exhibitions

Birdwatch Ireland (2804322)

Irish Peatland Conservation Council 119 Capel St 1 (8722397) - wet, wild & wonderful bogs & fens, 6 wks, Spring 2004, €150;lectures, workshops & full day field trips

CONSTRUCTION see also Building

DIT Faculty: Built Environment Bolton St 1 (4023711/3445) - construction economics & management (BSc Surveying), 6 yrs p/time, €1350 pa

Trinity College 2 (6772941) - (6081007) - construction law & contract admin, 1yr postgrad dip, 24wks, also Sat

CONSTRUCTION TECHNICIANS see Surveying

CONSUMER EDUCATION see also Law / Know Your Rights

AAA Counselling Dr MJ Brennan PhD c/o 48 Connaught St Phibsboro 7 (8380014) - conducting research, also day

Consumer's Assoc of Ireland 45 Upr Mount St 2 (6612466) - independent non-profitmaking org working for the Irish consumer, publish Consumer Choice monthly

KLEAR Grange Park View Kilbarrack 5 (8671845) - consumer awareness, day

Ringsend Technical Institute Cambridge Rd 4 (6684498) - FETAC cert courses at various times,ongoing, free

CONTEMPORARY DANCE Dance / Modern Dance

Dance Theatre of Ireland Bloomfields Centre, Lr George St Dun Laoghaire (2803455) - beginnersThurs 6.54-8pm/ intermediate Tue, Wed 6.45-8pm; Sats 10-11.15am

COOKERY / FAMILY COOKING see also Catering / Confectionery / Health Food / Hostess / Hotel / Vegetarian

Alix Gardner Catering 71 Waterloo Road 4 (6681553) - intermediate 1 around the world cuisine / 10wks, 6.30-9pm, €525 ea, cert

Ashfield College Main St Templeogue 6W (4900866) - gourmet cookery & wine selection / entertaining at home, new recipes / 7.30-9.30, 8 wks each

Ballymun Comprehensive Schools Adult Ed Centre Ballymun Rd 9 (8420654/ 8425828 night) - for all, Tues 8wk, €80/ oriental, Mon 10 wks €90

Blackrock College (2888681) - Thurs, 7.30-9, 6 wks, €65

Cabinteely Community School Johnstown Rd 18 (2857455) - for special occasions, 8wk, €90 /oriental, 8wk, €90

Cafe Fresh Mary Farrell Powerscourt Townhouse Centre 2 (6719669/ 086 8115519) - vegetarian, 6 wks

Colaiste Dhulaigh Barryscourt Rd Coolock 17 (8481337) - Chinese, Tues, 10 wks, 7.30-9.00

Colaiste Eanna College of Business & Technical Stu Kilkieran Rd Cabra 7 (8389577) -introduction to catering, 10wks Tues 7-9pm

Coolmine Community School Clonsilla 15 (8214583) - healthy home fare, €75 9wk 7.30-9.30/ Indian, Wed 9 wks €75

Crumlin College of Further Education Crumlin Rd 12 (4540662) - beginners/ healthy eating/ international/ vegetarian:all 10 wks/meals in minutes/ christmas cookery, 5 wks each

DIT Faculty: Tourism & Food Cathal Brugha St 1 (4024349/3445) - professional baking: bread 2 yr/ cake 1 yr, €250 per module/ sweetbreads; pastries & snacks, each 2 modules €250 ea

Donahies Community School Streamville Rd 13 (8482217) mediterranean, Mon, 5 wks €90

Greendale Community School Kilbarrack 5 (8322735/6) - cuisine international, 10 wks mornings, €65/ can cook, will cook 10 wks €65

Hartstown Community School Clonsilla 15 (8209863) - joy of cooking/ holistic

Coolmine Community School
Clonsilla, Dublin 15
General evening courses for leisure/social activities
Extra Mural Certificates and Diploma Courses (NUI, IMI, NCI).
Tel/Fax: 8214583 (during September)
EMail: adulted@coolminecs.ie

nutrition/ thai: each 10wks, €60/ Indian eve 5wks €45 / Thai, eve 10 wks €60

Institute of Technology Tallaght 24 (4042000) - national cert in professional cookery/ nat dip in culinary arts

Kylemore College Kylemore Rd 10 (6265901) - latin & South American, Tue 7-9pm 7 wks/ FETAC food cookery nutrition, cert, 12 wks Wed, 1.30-4pm

Lucan Community College Esker Drive (6282077) - kick start to cooring, Mon/ the gourmet club, Tue: each s €79

Marino College 14-20 Marino Mart 3 (8332100) - for all, Tues/ vegetarian/ Chinese/ Indian, Thurs: 10wks, €70-85 range

Newpark Adult Education Centre Newtownpark Ave Blackrock (2884376) - basic, for all/ Chinese/ Indian Vegetarian: €102 each, 10wks/ gourmet eve at home €125/ Italian, €110

Palmerstown Community School 20 (6260116) - beginners/ healthy options: each Thurs 7-9pm 10 wks €76

Pobalscoil Neasain Baldoyle 13 (8063092) - chinese, Mon 7.30 10 wks €110

Ringsend Technical Institute Cambridge Rd 4 (6684498) - dinner party ideas 10 wks €85

Saint Finian's Community College Swords (8402623) - demo, Tue, 10wk, €93

St Kevins College Clogher Rd Crumlin 12 (4536397) - 10wks

St Thomas Community College Novara Ave Bray (2866111) - for the family/ East Asian cookery; 10 wks, €80/ basic everyday; imaginative everyday: 10 wks €90 each

St Tiernan's Community School Parkvale Balally 16 (2953224) - hands-on, vegetarian, fish cuisine, pastry, Tues, 7.30-9.30pm, 10 wks €120

Tallaght Community School Balrothery 24 (4515566) - 10wk, €80

TARGET St Kevin's School Newbrook Rd, Donaghmede 13 (8671967) - colourful creative cooking, 10 wks, day only

CORRESPONDENCE SCHOOLS & HOME STUDY see also Distance Learning

ACCEPT Counselling Assoc of Ireland PO BOX 6989 Newpark Adult Education Centre Blackrock - 1 yr cert in counselling, psychology & therapy, send large SAE for details

Esperanto Assoc of Ireland 9 Templeogue Wood 6W (4945020) - Esperanto, €free

International Foundation of Adult Education PO Box 93 Eglinton St Cork (022-29358/ 0818 365305) - social studies/ psychology/ anthropology/ sociology: IFAE-Netherlands

Irish Academy of Public Relations (2780802) - intro to PR, cert/practical journalism, cert, 8wks, €355 each - both by correspondence or e-mail

Irish Payroll Association (IPASS) Clifton House Lower Fitzwilliam St 2 (6617200) - certified payroll technician, , stage 1 & 2/ dip in payroll management, 4 modules: also at various venues, city centre, Griffith Ave, Blanchardstown, Tallaght, Dun Laoire

Kilroy's College 25 Kingram Place 2 (1850 700700) - adult education dip courses, personal devel., hobbies, careers, computer skills, leaving cert, PC repair & upgrading, languages, tutor support

McKeon Murray Business Training Services Elm House Leopardstown Office Pk 18 (2959089) - Inst of Accounting Tech Foundation & Admission exams, €450

National College of Communications Park Hse Cabinteely Vlg 18 (2352657) - home study: alternative therapies, beauty therapy, counselling, general, management, publishing, sports & fitness, stress, writing, yoga

National Training Authority Park House, Cabinteeley 18 (2350451) - various courses

Portobello School Rere 40 Lr Dominick St 1 (8721277) - montessori teaching cert, dip & higher dip/ classroom assistant dip/ playgroup leader cert/ creche management dip/ childcare cert, dip/ special needs cert & dip

School of Practical Child Care Blackrock Campus Carysfort Ave Blackrock (2886994) - home study for child care related courses

The Open University Enquiry & Advice Centre Holbrook House, Holles St 2 (6785399) - BA/BSc degrees/ dips/ postgrad degrees/ professional training progs in management, education, health & social welfare

COUNSELLING SKILLS see also Bereavement, Psychology, etc

AAA Counselling Dr MJ Brennan PhD c/o 48 Connaught St Phibsboro 7 (8380014) - self-esteem life skills, also day

Ballsbridge College of Business Studies Shelbourne Rd 4 (6684806) - NUI Maynooth course, Tue 7.30 pm €1155/ intro to, Tue 6p, 10 wks €75

Ballyfermot College of Further Education Ballyfermot Rd 10 (6269421) - NUI Maynooth cert, 20 wks, Mon, Wed, 7.30-10pm, €1,175

Ballymun Comprehensive School Adult Ed Centre Ballymun Rd 9 (8420654/ 8425828 night) - NUI cert, Wed 7-10pm, 25 wks €1300

Business Coach Ireland 28 Grange Pk Walk Raheny 5 (8478391) - dip business & executive coaching, 1 yr eves, €2500

Clanwilliam Institute 18 Clanwilliam Tce 2 (6761363) - marital & family therapy: foundation, 1yr/ professional, 3yrs; mediation training, 1yr

Colaiste Dhulaigh Barryscourt Rd Coolock 17 (8481337) - intro NCS cert, Thurs 10-12.30, 20 wks/ what's it all about? Mon 7.30-9.30, 20 wks

Colaiste Eanna College of Business & Technical Stu Kilkieran Rd Cabra 7 (8389577) - intro to theory, styles, practices, 10 wks Tues

Coolmine Community School Clonsilla 15 (8214583) - NUI Maynooth cert - foundation in counselling, 1 yr Mon 7-10, €1160

Department of Adult & Community Education NUI Maynooth (7084500) - NUI cert: also at Ballsbridge (6684806); Ballyfermot (6269421); Ballymun (8420654); Bray (2866111); Coolmine (8473522); Dunlaoghaire (2809676); Drogheda (9836084); Knocklyon (4943991); Naas (045 897885); Old Bawn (4526137) €1155 to €1312

Donahies Community School Streamville Rd 13 (8482217) - NUI Maynooth course, Tues+4Sats, 100 hrs tuition, €1155

Dublin Business School 13/14 Aungier St 2 (4177500) - BA in counselling & psychotherapy, 4 yrs/ national cert in Applied Social Studies/ Counselling, 2 yrs, both 6.30-9.30pm / dip in counselling skills for early childhood/adolescent care, 10 wks

Dun Laoghaire College of Further Education 17 Cumberland St Dun Laoghaire (2809676) - NUI Maynooth cert, foundation in counselling skills, 1 year, Mon 7.30-10pm also 4 Sats, €1190

Hanly Centre Eblana Ave Dun Laoghaire (2807269) - pre-intervention counselling/ one-to-one

IICH Education 118 Stillorgan Road 4 (2600118) - 3-day foundation skills course, €245. Thought Field Therapy (Algorithms Levels I &II), Applied Behavioural Medicine/ Health Crisis Counselling. Classes at Milltown Pk, 6 and other south-city locations

Institute of Creative Counselling & Psychotherapy 82 Upr George's St Dun Laoghaire (2802523) - intro course, October, 10 wks €260/ also day courses

Irish Association of Holistic Medicine 66 Eccles St 7 (8500493) - & psychotherapy wkend foundation course, €250/ 2 yr dip, 11 wkends per year, €2000pa

Knocklyon Youth & Community Centre, 16 (4943991)

Kylemore College Kylemore Rd 10 (6265901) - intro to, 7 wks, ties 7-9pm

Marino College 14-20 Marino Mart 3 (8332100) - skills, €66 10wks

Old Bawn Community School Tallaght 24 (4526137) - foundation, NUI Maynooth cert, 1yr, 26 wks

People's College 32 Parnell Sq 1 (8735879) - €60

Roebuck Counselling Centre 59 Rathgar Rd 6 (4971929) - counselling skills & group dynamics, cert, Wed & Thurs 6-9pm, 20 wks; also day/ dip in counselling & psychotherapy, 3 yrs, Fri 4-10pm; Sat 8am-2pm

St Thomas Community College Novara Ave Bray (2866111) - NUI cert, 1yr €1050/ intro to counselling process & skills, 30 wks, €200, day

CRAFTS GENERAL see also Arts & Crafts / Crochet / Jewellery/ Lace / Patchwork / Quilting / Tapestry, etc

Ballymun Mens Centre LS4 Shangan Rd Ballymun 9 (8623117/8623409) - wirecraft, day

Balymun Comprehensive School Adult Ed Centre Ballymun Rd 9 (8420654/ 8425828 night) - mosaic & stained glass, beginners, Tues 10 wks €95

BASE Ballyboden Adult Social Education Whitechurch Library Taylor's Lane 16 (4935953) - decorating tile mosaics/ hand made cards/ handbag making

Botanic Art School 28a Prospect Avenue Glasnevin 9 (8304720)

Colaiste Dhulaigh Barryscourt Rd Coolock 17 (8481337) - for christmas, Thurs, day / icing christmas cakes 10-12.00

Colaiste Ide Cardiffsbridge Rd Finglas West 11 (8342333) - decoupage, 7.30 Thurs 10wks €90 cdvec cert/ also leisure course, €65

DATE College of Further Education Dundrum 14 (2964322) - pressed flowers; making cards, etc 10 wks € 66 day

Donahies Community School Streamville Rd 13 (8482217) - cross stitch & design, Mon 7.30 10 wks €55

Hartstown Community School Clonsilla 15 (8209863) - sewing & craftwork/decoupage -10wks, €60 each/ stained glass skills, 10 wks, €80

Holy Family Community School Rathcoole (4580766)

Kilroy's College 25 Kingram Place 2 (1850 700700) - tutor supported home study: dressmaking

KLEAR Grange Park View Kilbarrack 5 (8671845) - creative crafts, day

Old Bawn Community School Tallaght 24 (4526137) - beginners, original handbag making, handmade cards, etc, Tues, 7.30-9.30, 10wks/ decorative tile mosaics, practical, Tues, 7.30-9.30, 10wks

Palmerstown Community School 20 (6260116) - mosaic, Tues 7.30, 10 wks €65

St Thomas Community College Novara Ave Bray (2866111) mosaic art/ jewellery, 10 wks €70ea

St Tiernan's Community School Parkvale Balally 16 (2953224) - mosaics to decorate home, garden, Wed, 7.30-9.30pm, 10 wks, €80/ leather carving crafts, Thurs 7.30 10 wks €120

Yellow Brick Road 8 Bachelors Wlk 1 (8730177) - heirloom beadwork, wkend workshops €150/ jewellery making all levels, €250 incl materials, 8 wks Wed 7.30-9.30; multimedia necklace / netting & chips, Wed €25 not incl mats / also in Spring 2004

CREATIVE TEXTILES

Quilt Art Workshops 4 Mill Wood Naas (045-876121) - classes & workshops, SAE for info

CREATIVE THINKING – The Artist's Way
Catriona Mitchell 8 Longwood Ave 8 (087-2367084) - The Artist's Way, 12 wks, €175, also day
Old Bawn Community School Tallaght 24 (4526137) - the artist's way, Thurs, 10 wks
Sam Young, Howth area (8322803) - 'The Artist's Way' based courses on being creative
TACT St Dominic's School St Dominic's Rd Tallaght 24 (4596757) - the artist's way, 13 wks €78

CREATIVE WRITING see also Writing / Creative Thinking
Ballsbridge College of Business Studies Shelbourne Rd 4 (6684806) - beginner, Tues, 7.45pm €50
Colaiste Dhulaigh Barryscourt Rd Coolock 17 (8481337) - Mon, 9 wks, 7.15-9.15
Colaiste Eanna College of Business & Technical Stu Kilkieran Rd Cabra 7 (8389577) - day (tel 8688342/8389577)/ also creative writing for men
DATE College of Further Education Dundrum 14 (2964322) - writers group/ beginners & improvers: each 10 wks €79 day
Donahies Community School Streamville Rd 13 (8482217) - introductory, Wed, 10 wks, €55
Greendale Community School Kilbarrack 5 (8322735/6) - Tue, 7.30 10 wks €55
Hartstown Community School Clonsilla 15 (8209863) - 10 wks, €60
Irish Writers' Centre 19 Parnell Sq 1 (8721302)
Kilroy's College 25 Kingram Place 2 (1850 700700) - tutor supported home study
KLEAR Grange Park View Kilbarrack 5 (8671845) day only

Old Bawn Community School Tallaght 24 (4526137) - informal, Tues, 7.30-9.30pm, 10 wks

Plunket College Swords Rd, Whitehall 9 (8371689) - Tues, 10 wks, €66

Pobalscoil Rosmini Adult Ed Grace Pk Rd 9 (8371015) - beginners & continuation, short story, Wed 10 wks, €95 each

Rathmines Snr College Town Hall 6 (4975334) - with a view to getting published, Wed 10 wks, €65

St Thomas Community College Novara Ave Bray (2866111) - beginners & intermediate, 10 wks, €70 each

CREDIT CONTROL see Accountancy, etc

CRICKET

Leinster Cricket Union Hon Sec: Mary Sharpe 20 Dornden Park Booterstown (2698953) - list of clubs available

CRIME / CRIMINOLOGY

Colaiste Dhulaigh Barryscourt Rd Coolock 17 (8481337) - Mon, 10 wks, 7.15-9.15

Pobalscoil Rosmini Adult Ed Grace Pk Rd 9 (8371015) - & the law, Thurs 10 wks, €80

UCD Adult Education Office (7061695) - crime & criminality 1 & 2, 12 wks, cert

CROATIAN see also Serbo-Croatian

Marino College 14-20 Marino Mart 3 (8332100) - Tuesday, 6-7.30, €50

CROCHET see also Crafts

Ballymun Comprehensive Schools Adult Ed Centre Ballymun Rd 9 (8420654/ 8425828 night) - & hand knitting, embroidery - candlewick, cross stitch, Mountmellick, tapestry, all levels, Mon 10wk, €70

Donahies Community School Streamville Rd 13 (8482217) - crochet and knitting, Wed 7.30 10 wks €55

Marino College 14-20 Marino Mart 3 (8332100) - Thurs, 10wks €50

CULTURAL STUDIES

Development Studies Centre Holy Ghost College Whitehall Rd 12 (4064386/4064380) - Understanding Cultures & Cultural Differences, eve, 10wk, €90, cert

Greendale Community School Kilbarrack 5 (8322735/6) - intro to languages & culture, Germanic languages, 8.30 Thurs €50

National College of Ireland Mayor St IFSC 1 (4060500/ 1850 221721) - FETAC Foundation Cert, 1 yr p/time day

UCD Adult Education Office (7061695) - world of Islam, 8 wks/ wisdom of the east/rediscovering the bible/ the clash of civilizations/ hist of Arab-Israeli conflict: each 10 wks

CURRENT AFFAIRS see also Political Studies

DATE College of Further Education Dundrum 14 (2964322) - 8 wks, €53 day

KLEAR Grange Park View Kilbarrack 5 (8671845) - day

People's College 32 Parnell Sq 1 (8735879) - €40

CURTAIN MAKING see also Sewing / Soft Furnishing

Tallaght Community School Balrothery 24 (4515566) - 10wk, €55

CUSTOMER CARE

ABM Business Training 54 North St, Swords (8902348) - improving services; also day, Sat

DIT admissions office Dublin (4023445) - Nat Institute for transport & Logistics courses (4023115): management course:understancing cust service, 20hrs

DIT Faculty: Tourism & Food Cathal Brugha St 1 (4024349/3445) - communications and customer excellence, 12 wks, €265

FAS Training Centre Tallaght 24 (4045284) - sales rep / customer care

Keytrainer Ireland 33/34 Dame St 2 (6714000) - tailored courses

St Thomas Community College Novara Ave Bray (2866111) - 12 wks cert, €130

UCD Adult Education Office (7061695) - - cont. professional development course, Bord Gais

CYCLING see also Adventure Sports

Colaiste Eanna Kilkieran Rd Cabra 7 (8389577) - racing & leisure, theory based, diet training progs, 10 wks Thurs 7-9pm

Corporate Club 24 Elmcastle Green Kilnamanagh 24 (4610935)

Network Sports & Social Club 24 Elmcastle Green Kilnamanagh 24 (4524415)

CZECH

Dublin Public Libraries Admin Hq, 138-144 Pearse St 2 (6644800) - central library Ilac Centre (8734333) or Library HQ for details (6744800), self-learning €free

Sandford Language Institute Milltown Pk Sandford Rd 6 (2601296) - all levels, 14 wks, €250

DANCE see also Aerobics / Ballet / Ballroom / Belly / Contemporary / Disco / Folk / Irish / Jive / Latin American / Line / Modern / Old Time / Tap / Waltz / Set

Beginners Dance Centre 54 Parnell Sq W 1 (8304647) - beginners/ improvers, €6/€7 per class, ballroom, latin american, salsa, cha-cha, etc

Brooks Academy 15 Henrietta St 1 (8730093) - set dancing

Dance Club Rathmines & Rathgar (2893797)

Dance Theatre of Ireland Bloomfields Centre, Lr George St Dun Laoghaire (2803455) - modern/ hip-hop, contemporary, salsa, cardio salsa, yoga, jazz belly dance, body weather: all ages, eves, w'ends, also 'dance all day' summer course intensive; also youth dance company based at centre

Donahies Community School Streamville Rd 13 (8482217) - for fun, to all music, Tue 7.30, 10 wks €55

Dublin Folk Dance Group 48 Ludford Drive Ballinteer 16 (2987929) - sets/figure/solo (step)/ step for beginners/international dances

Dublin School of Dance 13 Stamer St Portobello 8 (4755451) - adult beginners / improvers, ballet & jazz, 40 wks €7 per class

Hartstown Community School Clonsilla 15 (8209863) - latino & salsa, 10 wks €60

Ingrid Nachstern (2600663) - ballet, beginners, 10wk, Tues, Sandymount

Just Dance Owen Cosgrave (4628857 087 8473518) - salsa, latino, ballroom, hip-hop, street: venues Dublinwide

Killester College of Further Education Collins Ave 5 (8337686) - salsa & cha cha, 10 wks Mon 7 & 8.30 €50

Knocklyon Youth & Community Centre, 16 (4943991)

Lakelands Folk Dance Club 72 Lakelands Ave Stillorgan (2887976) - folkdance, beginners, 5wks/ advanced Greek dancing

Marino College 14-20 Marino Mart 3 (8332100) - hip-hop, Tue 5pm 10 wks €33

Morosini-Whelan School of Dancing 46 Parnell Sq W 1 (8303613) - ballroom/ waltz/ rock 'n roll/ quickstep/ swing/ salsa/ Argentinian/Tango - also private lessons by appointment

Pobalscoil Rosmini Adult Ed Grace Pk Rd 9 (8371015) - salsa, ballroom, set - 10 wks, €80 each

Ringsend Technical Institute Cambridge Rd 4 (6684498) - hip hop; jazz dance: each 10 wks €50

Salsa Dublin East Hill Newtownmountkennedy Co Wicklow (087 9172939) - salsa, various Dublin venues, €8 per class

St Mark's Community School Cookstown Road Tallaght 24 (4519399)

St Thomas Community College Novara Ave Bray (2866111) - ballroom, bellydance; tap: 8wks each

Taney Parish Centre Dundrum 14 (2985491) - hip hop, Fri (2986309)/ ballroom, Wed (2882455/087 2205022), day only/ ballet, Sat (8385264)/ Irish, Thurs 086 8170292

The Sanctuary Stanhope Street 7 (6705419) - & meditation

DANISH

Dublin Public Libraries Admin Hq, 138-144 Pearse St 2 (6644800) - central library

Ilac Centre, D1. (8734333) or Library HQ for details (6744800) self-learning €free

Sandford Language Institute Milltown Pk Sandford Rd 6 (2601296) - all levels, 14 wks, €250

Sth Dublin Co Libraries Languages & Computers: Ballyroan/Clondalkin/ Castletymon, Lucan & Co Library (4597834-admin only) - self learning

DATA INPUT COURSES see also Keyboarding

Kilroy's College 25 Kingram Place 2 (1850 700700) - tutor supported home study: data processing, keyboard + typing skills

DATABASES see also Computer Training / Computer Programming, etc

ABM Computer Training 54 North St, Swords (8902348) - intro, also day & Sat / ms access, cert

Business Computer Training Institute Central Dublin (6616838 LoCall 1890 564039) - database methods, 10 wks €445, cert

CITAS Computer & I.T. Training 54 Middle Abbey St 1 (8782212) - Access, 1 day; €199/ Oracle DBA, €1900, 1 yr full time

Colaiste Eanna College of Business & Technical Stu Kilkieran Rd Cabra 7 (8389577) - intro to access dbase & excel spreadsheet, Thurs 7-9

Eden Computer Training Rathfarnham 16, or MACRO Centre, 1 Green St 7 (4953155) - beginners to advanced - relational databases

Fitzwilliam Institute Ltd Temple Court Temple Rd Blackrock (2834579) - dip in oracle database programming, ICM, 20 evesover 10 wks, 6.30-9.30pm, Ely Place 2

Grange Community College Grange Abbey Rd Donaghmede 13 (8471422) - ms access, 10wks, €93

Griffith College Dublin Sth Circular Rd 8 (4150400) - Access, ITEB cert, p/t end user, 1 eve per wk

Kilroy's College 25 Kingram Place 2 (1850 700700) - tutor supported home study: ECDL, access, visual basic 6

Moresoft Computers Ltd 44 Lr Lesson St 2 (6621711) - Oracle DBA ICM cert, 12 wks €1100

DEAFNESS see Sign Language

Henry Pollard email: wendyland@eircom.net (Fax: 2853126) - for sign language private tuition, deaf awareness training

UCD Adult Education Office (7061695) - dip in aural rehabilitation, dip/ hearing aid audiology, dip, 30 wks

DEBATING see Public Speaking

DEGREE & POST-GRADUATE COURSES

Dublin Business School 13/14 Aungier St 2 (4177500) - BA(hons) 3-4yrs each: Accounting & Finance / Financial Services/ Marketing/ Management & Information systems/ BA specialisms: Anthroplogy, Literature & Drama, Philosophy, Psychoanalysis, 3-4yrs/ grad dip in business studies, 2eve +some Sats,16 mths MBS (Masters of Business Studies) 2 eves, some Weds, 2yrs; all 6.15-9.30pm/ Grad dip specialism in IT/ HRM/ eBusiness, 2eve, 16mths/ Grad dip in Psychoanalytic Studies, 1yr p/time

National College of Ireland Mayor St IFSC 1 (4060500/ 1850 221721) - Grad, Postgrad, Degree, Diploma, and Cert courses in: Human Resource Management; Personnel Practice; Industrial Relations & Personnel Management; eCommerce; Management & Employee Relations; Software Systems; eLearning/MA or PHd by Research

Oscail - National Distance Education Centre DCU 9 (7005481) - BSc IT, via distance learning, 4-6 years, BSc awarded by DCU/ graduate dip/MSc management and applications of IT in Accounts, 2-3 yrs, awarded by DCU/ BA in Humanities, 3-6 yrs, awarded by one of 6 participating Irish Universities, distance learning

The Open University Enquiry & Advice Centre Holbrook House, Holles St 2 (6785399) - BA/BSc degrees/ dips/ postgrad degrees/ professional training progs in management, education, health & social welfare

Saor-Ollscoil na hÉireann, 55 Prussia St 7 (8683368) – BA in the Liberal Arts

DESIGN Computer Aided Design / Dress / Engineering / Graphic / Interior / Printing / Web

DIT Faculty: Applied Arts Aungier St 2 (4023465/3445) - display design, 10 wks, (4024138) / MA in design in digital media, 2yr p/time, €1800 pa

DIT Faculty: Built Environment Bolton St 1 (4023711/3445) - p/time design studies cert, 2 yr 2 eve weekly, €800 pa/ visual design in building work, 2 eve weekly 30 wks, €700, cert/ signwork, advanced, 1 & 2, 30 wks each pt, €700

Irish Academy of Computer Training 98 St Stephen's Grn 2 (4347600) - IACT webmaster 12 wks dip, €1995/ desktop pub 20 wks, €1995 cert; also day/ quarkxpress; corel draw; ms pub; adobe photoshop & illustrator; framemaker: ea 8 wks €695 cert/

powerpoint; freelance graphics: 4 wks €295 each cert/ also day
St Kevins College Clogher Rd Crumlin 12 (4536397) - & art, 1yr, day

DESK-TOP PUBLISHING

ABM Computer Training 54 North St, Swords (8902348) - all yr, also day, Sat

Adelaide Computers 14 Pembroke Lane Ballsbridge 4 (2696213) - one-to-one training at your office/home or our offices, small groups, beginners to advanced, full training programmes also / Dreamweaver, HTML, FrontPage, Networks, etc

Ballyfermot College of Further Education Ballyfermot Rd 10 (6269421) - & photoshop, 10 wks, Mon, 7-9pm, €155

Business Computer Training Central Dublin (6616838 LoCall 1890 564039) - dtp methods, 12 wks, €570 cert

CITAS Computer & I.T. Training 54 Middle Abbey St 1 (8782212) - QuarkXpress, photoshop, illustrator, Thurs 6-9pm €600

Colaiste Dhulaigh Barryscourt Rd Coolock 17 (8481337) - pt 1, Mon 7-9.30, 10 wks

Colaiste Ide Cardiffsbridge Rd Finglas West 11 (8342333) - Tue 7-10pm, 20 wks, €300 c&g cert

Crumlin College of Further Education Crumlin Rd 12 (4540662) - Quarkxpress, Thurs, 10 wks/ ICM cert in DTP Thurs, 20 wks

Dorset College 64a Lr Dorset St/ 8 Belvedere Pl 1 (8309677) - incl photoshop, illustrator, Mon & Wed 12 wks

Eden Computer Training Rathfarnham 16, or MACRO Centre, 1 Green St 7 (4953155) - ms publisher, corel draw, quarkexpress

FAS Training Centre Ballyfermot 10 (6055900/ 5933); Cabra Bannow Rd 7 (8821400); Tallaght 24 (4045284) - 10wk, introd & level 2; Wyatville Rd (2043600)

Irish Academy of Computer Training 98 St Stephen's Grn 2 (4347600) - dtp course 24 wks €1995, cert/ quarkxpress; corel draw; ms pub; adobe photoshop & illustrator; framemaker: ea 8 wks €695, cert/ IACT webmaster 12 wks €1995 dip/ also day

Keytrainer Ireland 33/34 Dame St 2 (6714000) - tailored & scheduled

Moresoft Computers Ltd 44 Lr Lesson St 2 (6621711) - DTP master, 10 wks ICM cert €571

Newpark Adult & Continuing Education Centre Newtownpark Ave Blackrock (2884376) - 10 wks €140

Plunket College Swords Rd, Whitehall 9 (8371689) - DTP, NCVA level 2, Tues 25 wks, €166

Ringsend Technical Institute Cambridge Rd 4 (6684498) - intro to, 10wks, €95

St Thomas Community College Novara Ave Bray (2866111) - 30 wks, €200, cert, FETAC

DEVELOPMENT STUDIES Third World Studies

Comhlamh 10 Upr Camden St 2 (4783490) - options and issues for those with at home or overseas evelopment interest

Development Studies Centre Holy Ghost College Whitehall Rd 12 (4064386/4064380) - MA / Grad Dip & National Dip, 9-12 months, day / Understanding Development, eve, 20wk, €180, cert / Understanding Cultures & Cultural Differences, eve, 10wk, €90, cert / Community Capacity Building, eve, 10 wk €90, cert

DIET see also Nutrition / Food / Health
AAA Counselling Dr MJ Brennan PhD c/o 48 Connaught St Phibsboro 7 (8380014) - obesity control
Bodyline Studio Rere Brady's Terenure Pl 6W (4902038) - clinic, 4wk plan, €80
Holistic Healing Centre 38 Dame St 2 (6710813)
Irish College of Complementary Medicine 6 Main St Donnybrook 4 (2696588/086-2500617) - ITEC diet & nutrition, dip
Kilroy's College 25 Kingram Place 2 (1850 700700) - tutor supported home study: & health & fitness, dip
Taney Parish Centre Taney Rd Dundrum 14 (2985491) - weightwatchers, Mon/Thurs (2989844)
Tony Quinn Centre 66/67 Eccles St 7 (8304211)
DIGITAL ELECTRONICS & MICRO PROCESSORS see also Computer Maintenance
Dublin City University Registry office Glasnevin 9 (7005338) - digital media engineering
Hi-Tech Training 4 Nth Gt George's St 1 (1850-759759) - levels 1-3, 50% practical hands-on, 7-10pm, 15 wks each/ digital communicators, 50% practical hands-on, Sat, 1 day, 10am-5pm: C&G cert
Kilroy's College 25 Kingram Place 2 (1850 700700) - home study: PC Assembly & A+

DISABILITIES, PEOPLE WITH, Courses for – see also Learning
FAS Training Centre Ballyfermot 10 (6055900/ 5933) - vocational skills; access to IT
FAS Training Centre Jervis St 1 (8044600) - wide range of day courses: skills training; woodwork; amenity horticulture; teleservices; computer programming & applications; hotel & tourism; printing; desktop publishing; business admin; graphic design; electronic assembly; pottery; welding; coo kery; retail sales; etc
FAS Training Centre Loughlinstown Wyatville Rd (2043600) - various incl busines studies; computers; programming; professional cookery
DISCO-DANCING see Dance / Keep-Fit
DISTANCE LEARNING see also Teachers/ Corresponcence
Bluefeather School of Languages 35 Montpelier Parade Monkstown (2806288) - preliminary TEFL
DIT admissions ofice Dublin (4023445) - various education & training modules
DIT Faculty: Applied Arts Aungier St 2 (4023465/3445) - online, theory & practice, French, German, Spanish, 1 yr €950, Kevin St 8 (4024673 / 4024944)
DIT Faculty: Engineering Bolton St 1 (4023649/3445) - online: vehical parts personnel, C&G cert, €500
Dublin City University Registry office Glasnevin 9 (7005338)
Dublin School of Art 18 Butterfield Ave Rathfarnham 14 (4943303) - dip in art studies, open learning, 10-12 mths €850
electronic Business School of Ireland (094-81444) - elearning course, online support
FAS Net College www.fas-netcollege.com (info@fas-netcollege.com/ 2043600) - variety of courses online with optional tutor support
Institute of International Trade of Ireland 28 Merrion Square 2 (6612182) - dangerous goods safety advisor / air cargo security
Institute of Public Administration 57-61 Lansdowne Rd 4 (6686233)
Institute of Technology Tallaght 24 (4042000) - dip/degree in IT/ dip/degree in Arts - Humanities/IT (distance learning DCU)
International Foundation of Adult Education PO Box 93 Eglinton St Cork (022-

29358/ 0818 365305) - social studies/ psychology/ anthropology/ sociology: IFAE-Netherlands

Irish Academy of Public Relations (2780802) - intro to PR, cert/practical journalism cert, €355 each - both correspondence or e-mail

Irish Payroll Association (IPASS) Clifton House Lower Fitzwilliam St 2 (6617200) - certified payroll technician, , stage 1 & 2/ dip in payroll management, 4 modules/ also at various venues: city centre, Griffith Ave, Blanchardstown, Tallaght, Dun Laoire

Kilroy's College 25 Kingram Place 2 (1850 700700) - tutor supported adult ed dip courses, personal devel., hobbies, careers, computer skills, leaving cert

Marketing Institute Sth Co Business Pk, Leopardstown 18 (2952355) - marketing, cert 2 yrs, dip 3 yrs, graduate 4 yrs, by attending college or by distance learning

Milltown Institute Milltown Pk 6 (2698388) - online theology courses, credits, 13 wk, €520 each

Montessori Education Centre 41-43 Nth Gt George's St 1 (8780071) - distance learning Montessori teacher training, 36 wks €1,250; also 2 yr option, dip

National College of Communications Park Hse Cabinteely 18 (2352657) - home study: alternative health, beauty therapy, counselling, general, management, publishing, sports & fitness, stress, writing, yoga

National College of Ireland Mayor St IFSC 1 (4060500/ 1850 221721) - National Dip in Personnel Management, home study with workshops

National Training Authority Park House, Cabinteeley 18 (2350451) - various courses

New Media Technology Training 13 Harcourt St 2 (4780905) - interactive media production, e-learning course, 1 yr in assoc with Eur Broadcasting Union

Oscail - National Distance Education Centre DCU 9 (7005481) - dip in IT, 2-3 yrs/BSc in IT, 4-6 yrs/ Bachelor of Nursing studies, 2-3 yrs/ grad dip/ MSc management & applications of IT in Accounting, 2-3 yrs/grad dip MSc Management of Operations, 3-4 yrs - all awarded by DCU/dip in Arts, 2-3 yrs/ BA Humanities, 3-6 yrs - both awarded by one of 6 participating Irish Universities

Saor-Ollscoil na hEireann 55 Prussia St 7 (8683368) - BA, environmental studies/ peace & conflict studies

School of Practical Child Care Blackrock Campus Carysfort Ave Blackrock (2886994) - various child care related courses

St Thomas Community College Novara Ave Bray (2866111) - Open Uni courses BA, BSc in psychology/social science, heath &social care

TEFL Training Institute of Ireland 38 Harrington St 8 (4784035) - TEFL: preliminary ATTcert, €350/ advanced ATTcert, €750

The Open University Enquiry & Advice Centre Holbrook House, Holles St 2 (6785399) - BA/BSc degrees/ dips/ postgrad degrees/ prof training progs in management, education, health & social welfare

Whitehall College of Further Education Swords Rd 9 (8376011) - online MOS / and advanced MOS master

DIVING see Adventure Sports / Scuba Diving

DIY COURSES

Ballsbridge College of Business Studies Shelbourne Rd 4 (6684806) - home maintenance, Mon 6.30, 8 wks, €55

Cabinteely Community School Johnstown Rd 18 (2857455) - beginners, 8wk, €65

Colaiste Dhulaigh Barryscourt Rd Coolock 17 (8481337) - various, Tues, 7.30-9.30

Hartstown Community School Clonsilla 15 (8209863) - home maintenance, 10wks, €60

Kylemore College Kylemore Rd 10 (6265901) - caretakers maintenance skills, Wed; DIY home decorating, improving, Thurs: 12 wks day

Newpark Adult Education Centre Newtownpark Ave Blackrock (2884376) - 10wks, €99, home maintenance

Pobalscoil Iosolde 20 (6260116) - introduction Tue 7.30, 10 wks €70

Pobalscoil Rosmini Adult Ed Grace Pk Rd 9 (8371015) - beginners, Mon, 7-8.30pm, 10 wks, €80

Ringsend Technical Institute Cambridge Rd 4 (6684498) - home maintenance, €65

St Thomas Community College Novara Ave Bray (2866111) - home maintenance, 10wks, €70

DOG TRAINING

Tagnrye Dog Services 20 church Grove Aylesbury 24 (4513324) - any breed, age, problem - learn in your own home

DOMESTIC HEATING ENGINEERING

DIT Faculty: Built Environment Bolton St 1 (4023711/3445) - oil fired, 10 wks €230 / gas installation & safety, 1 yr

DRAMA see also Acting / Literature / Personal Development / Speech and Drama / Theatre / Voice

1000 FACES: International School of Stage, TV & Film (8368201/ 087 2261479) - make-up for stage, tv, film - fashion, special effects, costume, etc, diploma course

Abbey School of Music 9b Lr Abbey St 1 (8747908) - Kathleen Yeates

Ballymun Mens Centre LS4 Shangan Rd Ballymun 9 (8623117/8623409) - day

Betty Ann Norton Theatre School 11 Harcourt St 2 (4751913) - performance / acting dip / adult foundation course

Colaiste Dhulaigh Barryscourt Rd Coolock 17 (8481337) - NCVA foundation cert, Mon, 7.15-9.30, 20 wks

Connolly House Nth Strand (by 5 Lamps) 1 (8557116) - 10 wks Wed, 6.30pm €50

DIT Faculty: Applied Arts Aungier St 2 (4023465/3445) - drama in education (for social/community workers), 1 yr €500, Rathmines, cert; also level 2

DIT Faculty: Applied Arts Aungier St 2 (4023465/3445) - creative drama, level 1 & 2 (4023464)

Gaiety School of Acting Sycamore St Meeting House Sq Temple Bar 2 (6799277) - intro to drama / acting for camera/ advanced acting for camera/ page to stage/ advanced page to stage: each €290/ wkend workshops

Hartstown Community School Clonsilla 15 (8209863) - acting, 10 wks, €60

Network Sports & Social Club 24 Elmcastle Green Kilnamanagh 24 (4524415)

New Directions 16 Carmichael Cntr Nth Brunswick St 7 (8723181) - creative drama, 6wk

Newpark Adult Education Centre Newtownpark Ave Blackrock (2884376) - beginners, workshop, 10wks, €99

Pobalscoil Rosmini Adult Ed Grace Pk Rd 9 (8371015) - part 1, 10 wks €90/ play production €60

Ringsend Technical Institute Cambridge Rd 4 (6684498) - theatre studies, 10 wks €65

Tallaght Community School Balrothery 24 (4515566) - 10wk, €45

Taney Centre Taney Rd Dundrum 14 (2985491) - Encore, Mon 087 9085913; Tues 2951709; Thurs 2987641/ speech & drama, Thurs 4069758, day only

Trinity College 2 (6772941) - (6082885) - The Abbey Theatre, 1904-2004, 9 wks, €40

UCD Adult Education Office (7061695) - contemporary Theatre, 10 wks/ intro do modern drama, 12 wks

DRAUGHTSMANSHIP see also Computer Aided Design/ Graphics

FAS Training Centre Finglas Jamestown Rd 11 (8140243)

Pearse College Clogher Rd 12 (4536661/4541544) - architectural, day

DRAWING / FROM LIFE / STILL LIFE see also Art

Brian Byrnes Art Studio 3 Upr Baggot St 4 (6671520 / 6711599) - 8wk, €130, also day

Cabinteely Community School Johnstown Rd 18 (2857455) - beginners/improvers, 10wk, €75

DIT Faculty: Applied Arts Aungier St 2 (4023465/3445) - drawing as information gathering, 6 wks (4024138)

Hartstown Community School Clonsilla 15 (8209863) - 10wks, €60

Kilternan Adult Education Centre Glencullen Rd Kilternan 18 (2952050)

National College of Art & Design in Art & Design 100 Thomas Street 8 (6364214) - drawing & painting from life, intro & advanced/ drawing with pastels/ 2D work studio, intro & advanced/ 'seeing is believing'/ drawing advanced/ the human figure, intro, advance: each c 22 wks

National Gallery of Ireland Merrion Sq W 2 (6615133) - practical in 3 parts, autumn, autumn & spring, 10 wks, €150 each part, summer €75; - day

Rathmines Snr College Town Hall 6 (4975334) - beginners, continuation, improvers: 7pm, Mon, Tue & Wed, 20 wks €130/ life drawing(h) leaving cert, Tues 10 wks €40/ life 6pm 10 wks €40

St Thomas Community College Novara Ave Bray (2866111) - - 10 wks €70

UCD Adult Education Office (7061695) - art of drawing, 12 wks / drawing & painting workshop 10 wks

DRAWING AND PAINTING see also Art / Oil Painting / Portrait / Sketching / Water Colours

Ballymun Comprehensive School Adult Ed Centre Ballymun Rd 9 (8420654/ 8425828 night) - Wed, day 2-4pm 10 wks €75

Botanic Art School 28a Prospect Avenue Glasnevin 9 (8304720) - Tues/Thurs, 6.30-9pm, also day

Brian Byrnes Art Studio 3 Upr Baggot St 4 (6671520 / 6711599) - 8wk, €130, also day

Colaiste Dhulaigh Barryscourt Rd Coolock 17 (8481337) - FETAC cert Wed 10-12, 10 wks/ beginners, Mon 9 wks/ visual skills foundation, Mon 9 wks/ also day levels 1-3, Mon & Wed, 11am 10 wks, Mon 7-9.30

Dublin School of Art 18 Butterfield Ave Rathfarnham 14 (4943303) - master class portfolio, eve, 8wks €180 / art holiday in France, 1 wk €360 / tuition class, one to one, day, 2.5hr €45 / art therapy, day, 2.15 hrs €30

Dunboyne Village Co Meath (8222929) - Thurs, 8 wks, all yr

Inchicore College of Further Education Emmet Rd 8 (4535358) Tue, 7.30 10 wks

Meridian Art Group c/o St Paul's College Raheny 5 (8310688)

National College of Art & Design in Art & Design 100 Thomas Street 8 (6364214) - from life/ 2D work studio intro/ advanced drawing, c.22wk each

Plunket College Swords Rd, Whitehall 9 (8371689) - & sketching, beginners, 10wks, €66

Rathmines Snr College Town Hall 6 (4975334) - beginners/ continuation/ improvers, 20 wks, €130

Ringsend Technical Institute Cambridge Rd 4 (6684498) - aide to portfolio prep, 10 wks €75

St Kevins College Clogher Rd Crumlin 12 (4536397) - NCVA, 20wks

DREAM INTERPRETATION

Complementary Healing Cntr 91 Terenure Rd N 6W (4929077) - dream analysis, 6 wks €150/ also wkend workshop

Harvest Moon Centre 24 Lr Baggot St 2 (6627556)

Institute of Celtic, Shamanic Development Sacred Hoop Lodge 64 Sth William Street 2 (4577839)

DRESSMAKING see also Patternmaking / Sewing

Ballsbridge College of Business Studies Shelbourne Rd 4 (6684806) - Fri, 2.30pm day only, 10 wks €65

Crumlin College of Further Education Crumlin Rd 12 (4540662) - beginners, Mon, 10 wks 7.30-9.30

Grafton Academy of Dress Designing 6 Herbert Place 2 (6763653) - from commercial patterns, 10 classes €205/ summer courses 1 wk €225, 2 wk €395/ felt workshop, 2 day €225

Kilroy's College 25 Kingram Place 2 (1850 700700) - tutor supported home-study dip courses

Marino College 14-20 Marino Mart 3 (8332100) - Tues, 10wks, €66

Ringsend Technical Institute Cambridge Rd 4 (6684498) - & designing, 10wks, €65
St Mac Dara's Community College Wellington Lane Templeogue 6W (4566216) - Mon, Tue, 7.30-9.30pm, 10 wks, €79
St Tiernan's Community School Parkvale Balally 16 (2953224) - introd to textiles, dyeing, batik etc, Tues 10 wks €80

DRIVING

Colaiste Dhulaigh Barryscourt Rd Coolock 17 (8481337) - new driving theory test, Tue 6pm; also pt 1 & 2, Wed, day; HAZCHEM pt 1 Tue 7-9.15: 10 wks each/ advanced driving, Tue 7.15-8.45, also Sat/Sun, 3 wks

Colaiste Eanna College of Business & Technical Stu Kilkieran Rd Cabra 7 (8389577) - driving test theory support, Wed, 2-4pm

FAS Training Centre Ballyfermot 10 (6055900/ 5933) - rigid truck / articulated truck/ minibus; Cabra Bannow Rd 7 (8821400) - heavy goods vehicles; Tallaght 24 (4045284) - advanced defensive, 10 wks/ heavy goods, day

Greenhills College Limekiln Ave Walkinstown 12 (4507779/4507138) - education, 6wks, €51

KLEAR Grange Park View Kilbarrack 5 (8671845) - rules of the road, day

DRIVING INSTRUCTOR TRAINING

Colliers Driving Instructor College 116 Ballygall Rd W Finglas E 11 (8340329)

National Register of Driving Instructors Road Safety House 39/41 Glasnevin Hill 9 (8570377) - info centre only

DRUGS & ALCOHOL ABUSE

Coolmine Community School Clonsilla 15 (8214583) - drug awareness, 7.30-9.30, 9 wks €50

Hanly Centre Eblana Ave Dun Laoghaire (2807269) - counselling for alcoholics & other addicts, or family/adult children of, level 1, 10wk, €190

Hartstown Community School Clonsilla 15 (8209863) - drug questions - local answers, 10 wks €20

UCD Adult Education Office (7061695) - community drugs work/ drugs, counselling & intervention skills/

DRUMS see also Music / Percussion

Melody School of Music 178E Whitehall Rd W Perrystown 12 (4650150) - also day; also w/ends Sat-Sun, 12 wks

Walton's New School of Music 69 Sth Gt George's St 2 (4781884) - also day, see ad page

DUBLIN see History / Archaeology

DUTCH, Elementary & Intermediate

Dublin Public Libraries Admin Hq, 138-144 Pearse St 2 (6644800) - central library Ilac Centre (8734333) or Library HQ for details (6744800), self-learning €free

Language Centre NUI Maynooth Co Kildare (7083737) - for beginners, 9 wks, €110

Marino College 14-20 Marino Mart 3 (8332100) - Tues 6.30 10 wks €50

Newpark Adult & Continuing Education Centre Newtownpark Ave Blackrock (2884376) - conversation, 10 wks €90

Sandford Language Institute Milltown Pk Sandford Rd 6 (2601296) - all levels, 14 wks, €250

WORDS Language Services 44 Northumberland Rd 4 (6610240) - beginners, advanced & commercial, cert, individual tuition only

DYSLEXIA

Dyslexia Association of Ireland 1 Suffolk St 2 (6790276) - individual remedial tuition for adults/ group or individual tuition for children

E-BUSINESS see also Distance Learning, Business, etc

Dublin Business School 13/14 Aungier St 2 (4177500) - graduate dip in Business Studies/ E-Business, 2 eves per wk plus some Sats, 6.15-9.30pm, 16 months / dip in e-business, 1 eve a wk 6.30-9.30 1 yr

Dun Laoghaire College of Further Education 17 Cumberland St Dun Laoghaire (2809676) - doing busines on the web, Wed 7-9.30 10 wks €135

Eden Computer Training Rathfarnham 16, or MACRO Centre, 1 Green St 7 (4953155) - & web marketing, ICM accred / also day

FAS Net College www.fas-netcollege.com (info@fas-netcollege.com/ 2043600) - elearning: e-business, €120; online tutor option €80

Institute of International Trade of Ireland 28 Merrion Square 2 (6612182) - prof. dip in global trade & e-Business/

National College of Ireland Mayor St IFSC 1 (4060500/ 1850 221721) - Grad Dip in Business Studies, HETAC 1 yr, p/time day/Grad Dip in eLearning, HETAC 1 yr, p/time day

Pearse College Clogher Rd 12 (4536661/4541544) - dip

E-LEARNING see also Distance Learning / Online / Correspondence

Kilroy's College 25 Kingram Place 2 (1850 700700) - tutor supported home study

New Media Technology Training 13 Harcourt St 2 (4780905)

ECDL (European Computer Driving Licence) see also Computer Training etc

ABM Computer Training 54 North St, Swords (8902348) - basic ECDL; advanced word & spreadsheets/ also day

ABM Computer Training 54 North St, Swords (8902348) - ECDL and advanced; all yr, also day, Sat

Ballsbridge College of Business Studies Shelbourne Rd 4 (6684806) - foundation, Mon, Tue, 6pm 10 wks €160/ ECDL Mon 20 wks/ Tue & Thurs 10 wks: 6pm €420

Balymun Comprehensive School Adult Ed Centre Ballymun Rd 9 (8420654/ 8425828 night) - EDCL 10 wks each: Mon: basic concepts, €50; file management ; word processing ; & Tues; €100 each: database, powerpoint; Wed, spreadsheets, internet €100 ea/ Wed, advanced wp, 20 wks €210 each

Blackrock College (2888681) - ecdl 1 & 2, 6.30-9, 10 wks

Business Computer Training Institute Central Dublin (6616838 LoCall 1890 564039) - 12 wks, €475 cert

CITAS Computer & IT Training 54 Middle Abbey St 1 (8782212) - 8 wk, morn 10-12.30; eve 6-8pm, €468 + tests & card €182/ ECDL full time 10am, 6 mths/ tests, ongoing daily

Colaiste Dhulaigh Barryscourt Rd Coolock 17 (8481337) - ECDL 7 modules, Tue 6.15 22 wks; 4 modules, 10 wks; pre-ECDL foundation, 10 wks / also day, Wed & Thurs

Colaiste Eanna College of Business & Technical Stu Kilkieran Rd Cabra 7 (8389577) - day (tel 8688342/8389577)

Computeach Computer Centre AXIS, Main St Ballymun 9 (8832167)

Connolly House Nth Strand (by 5 Lamps) 1 (8557116) - 10 wks Wed, 6.30-9.30, €360

Donahies Community School Streamville Rd 13 (8482217) - 7 modules, Mon & Tue; also Fri, day: 17 wks €400

Dorset College 64a Lr Dorset St/ 8 Belvedere Pl 1 (8309677) - all 7 modules, day, eve, Sats

Dun Laoghaire College of Further Education 17 Cumberland St Dun Laoghaire (2809676) - ECDL, 22 wks, Mon & Wed, 7.30 €320 ea/ advanced ECDL 22 wks, Wed 7.30, €135 ea

FAS Training Centre Baldoyle 13 (8167460); Ballyfermot 10 (6055900/ 5933); Cabra Bannow Rd 7 (8821400); Finglas Jamestown Rd 11 (8140243); Jervis St 1 (8044600)

FAS Training Centre Tallaght 24 (4045284) - ECDL all 7 modules; also ECDL advanced website technology/ 10 wks each

FAS Training Services Loughlinstown Wyatville Rd (2043600)

Irish Academy of Computer Training 98 St Stephen's Grn 2 (4347600) - basic concepts of IT; using computer, managing files; wp; spreadsheets; databases; presentations & drawing; info network services: each €95, cert/ ECDL bootcamp 10 wks €395/ ECDL multimedia guide 10 wks €195

Keytrainer Ireland 33/34 Dame St 2 (6714000) - day, eve, summer specials

Killester College of Further Education Collins Ave 5 (8337686) - ECDL/ ECDL improvers: each 20 wks €365

Kilroy's College 25 Kingram Place 2 (1850 700700) - tutor supported home study

Milltown Institute Milltown Pk 6 (2698388) - 7 modules, 26 wks, 6.30-9pm, €500

Moresoft Computers Ltd 44 Lr Lesson St 2 (6621711) - cert, 16 wks €750

Newpark Adult Education Centre Newtownpark Ave Blackrock (2884376) - ECDL, 20wks, €520

Palmerstown Community School 20 (6260116) - ECDL modules: €65 each, all 10 wks

Pitman Training Centre 6-8 Wicklow St 2 (6768008) - ECDL - various courses €752 / ECDL & MOUS exams, day & eve

Pitman Training Centre 6-8 Wicklow St 2 (6768008) - various courses, cert; €752; day, eve, Sats

Plunket College Swords Rd, Whitehall 9 (8371689) - Mon, Wed, 24 wks 7-10pm, €420 each

Pobalscoil Neasain Baldoyle 13 (8063092) - Mon 8=9.30 10 wks €385

Rathmines Snr College Town Hall 6 (4975334) - all 7 modules, Mon/ Tue/ Wed: 25 wks €370

Ringsend Technical Institute Cambridge Rd 4 (6684498) - ECDL 25 wks Wed 7-10, €420

St Finian's Community College Swords (8402623) - ECDL database & internet modules, Mon, 10 wks €160 each

St Tiernan's Community School Parkvale Balally 16 (2953224) - 7 modules, 20 wks, the €380

Stillorgan College of Further Education Old Road Stillorgan (2880704) - pre-ECDL Thurs 8 wks €95/ ECDL Thurs 10 wks 2 terms

Whitehall College of Further Education Swords Rd 9 (8376011) - ECDL/ also advanced: Tue & Thurs, 6.30-9.30 each

ECOLOGY see also Environment

St Tiernan's Community School Parkvale Balally 16 (2953224) - basics of, Mon 7.30 10 wks €70

ECONOMICS see also History / Leaving Cert / Social Studies

Kilroy's College 25 Kingram Place 2 (1850 700700) - home study: & economic history, leaving cert

Plunket College Swords Rd, Whitehall 9 (8371689) - leaving cert, 27 wks, €143

ECUMENICS see also Religion

Irish School of Ecumenics Bea House Milltown Pk 6 (2601144) - ecumenical studies: variousvenues in city incl Cabinteely & Drundrum; 8wks eve €40

EDUCATION & TRAINING see also Return to Learning

College of Further Education Main St Dundrum 14 (2951376) - early childhood education, Tues 20 wks

Department of Adult & Community Education NUI Maynooth (7084500) - NUI cert in Continuing Education, contact (8210016)

DIT admissions ofice Dublin (4023445) - industry services in, various courses

Further Education & Training Awards Council (FETAC East Point Plaza East Point Business Park 3 (8659500) - national certification body

Kilroy's College 25 Kingram Place 2 (1850 700700) - tutor supported home study: personal development, careers, computer skills, leaving cert, adult education, dip courses

UCD Adult Education Office (7061695) - adults teaching adults learning, 10 wks / CRC course - assistive computer applications

ELECTRICAL ENGINEERING

DIT Faculty: Engineering Bolton St 1 (4023649/3445) - electrical systems, 1 yr €700/ & electronic technicians, 3 yr, dip, €700/ BE electrical engineering Pt 1, 4 yr €800; Pt 2, 4 yr, 6 courses €320 each/ updating electrical installation technology: intermediate, advanced, network cabling €360 each 10 wks/ updating p[hase 4 electrical science/ craft practice, 10 wks €265 per module; phase 6 10 wks €265 per mod/ services technician, 3yr €800pa, cert

ELECTRICAL INSTALLATION

FAS Training Centre Baldoyle 13 (8167460)

FAS Training Centre Tallaght 24 (4045284) - basic & advanced, 10 wks each

ELECTRICITY

Blackrock College (2888681) - diy course, 6 wks, 7.30-9, €65

ELECTROLYSIS see also Beauty Therapy

Aspen's Beauty Clinic & College of Beauty Therapy 83 Lr Camden St 2 (4751079/ 4751940) - electrolysis, Thurs 9.30-12/ also Sat 3.30-5.30: each 9 mths, €1,695/

Coogan-Bergin Clinic & College of Beauty Therapy Glendenning Hse 6-8 Wicklow St 2 (6794387) - CIBTAC Tue 6.30-9.30 €1397

Galligan College of Beauty 109 Grafton St 2 (6703933) - ITEC & CIBTAC, 30wks

ELECTRONIC ENGINEERING

Dublin City University Registry office Glasnevin 9 (7005338) - also electronic systems

Institute of Technology Tallaght 24 (4042000) - BEng/ nat dip, also cert, yrs 1 & 2

ELECTRONICS see also Digital / Computer Maintenance etc

Colaiste Dhulaigh Barryscourt Rd Coolock 17 (8481337) - C&G certs: electronic servicing, Mon, 20 wks/ computing systems, Mon & Tues, 20 wks

DIT Faculty: Engineering Bolton St 1 (4023649/3445) - electrical & electronic technicians, 3 yr €700/ programmable logic controllers, 10 wks €320 per stage/ electronic & computer systems, dip, 2yrs €700; also cert 3yrs €800pa

FAS Training Centre Baldoyle 13 (8167460); Ballyfermot 10 (6055900/ 5933); Cabra Bannow Rd 7 (8821400); Finglas 11 (8140243)

Griffith College Dublin Sth Circular Rd 8 (4150400) - dip, C&G, p/t, end user, 2 eves per wk/ software engineering, GCD, p/t, 1 yr, 3 eves per wk

Hi-Tech Training 4 Nth Gt George's St 1 (1850-759759) - levels 1,2,3, 50% practical hands-on, 7-10pm, 15wks each: C&G cert

Kilroy's College 25 Kingram Place 2 (1850 700700) - tutor supported home study: basic aircraft electronics, avionics, dip/ PC Assembly & A+

Kylemore College Kylemore Rd 10 (6265901) - FETAC 1 cert, 12 wks Mon 7-9pm

Plunket College Swords Rd, Whitehall 9 (8371689) - basic, Tues, €66/ assembly, Tues, 25 wks

ELOCUTION see Public Speaking / Speech and Drama

EMAIL see INTERNET & EMAIL

EMBROIDERY / CREATIVE see also Crafts

Colaiste Dhulaigh Barryscourt Rd Coolock 17 (8481337) - & textile art, Tue 7.15, 8 wks

Grafton Academy of Dress Designing 6 Herbert Place 2 (6763653) - Mon, 6wk day €150/ beading workshop, 2 day 225

Marino College 14-20 Marino Mart 3 (8332100) - Tue 6-8pm, €66

National College of Art & Design in Art & Design 100 Thomas Street 8 (6364214) - exploring, intro & intermediate, c. 22wk

Quilt Art Workshops 4 Mill Wood Naas (045-876121) - classes & workshops, SAE for info

EMPLOYMENT-SEEKING / APPLICATION see Careers

ENGINEERING see also Computers / Electronic Engineering / Industrial / Management / Mathematics / Telecommunications

DIT admissions office Dublin (4023445) - fibre optic technology/ advanced optictal network design

DIT Faculty: Engineering Bolton St 1 (4023649/3445) - foundation, 1yr €800; BE degree, 3 yr p/time €1350; civil engineering technician, cert & dip, 3 yr/5 yr, €800pa; building services technician, cert & dip, €800

Dublin City University Registry office Glasnevin 9 (7005338) - digital media engineering/ computer-aided mechanical & manufacturing engineering/ manufacturing engineering with business/ mechatronic engineering/ electronic engineering/ medical mechanical engineering/ mechanical engineering common entry/ medical engineering common entry

Graduate School of Engineering Studies O'Reilly Institute TCD 2 (6081007) - post-

grad dips in: physical planning/computers for engineers/construction law & contract admin/highway & geotech engineering/project management/fire safety practice (buildings & other structures) / environmental engineering/ BSc Hons in business & Institute of Technology Tallaght 24 (4042000) - BEng/ nat dip in manufacturing engineering, also cert yrs 1 & 2 / computer engineering, cisco, 1 yr

Institution of Fire Engineers 77 Ballyroan Road 16 (4943669) - fire safety/engineering

St Kevin's College Clogher Rd Crumlin 12 (4536397) - mechanical, all day/electronic, FETAC, 1yr, day

Trinity College 2 (6772941) - (6081007) - computers for engineers, 1yr postgrad dip, 22wks/environmental, 1yr postgrad dip, 24wks/highway & geotechnical, 1yr, postgrad dip, 24wks /physical planning, 1yr, postgrad dip, 24wks, also Sat

UCD Adult Education Office (7061695) - engineering access course, 20 wks

ENGLISH (EFL-English as a Foreign Language) see also English TEFL

Aisling Ireland Languages for Business & Pleasure 137 Lr Rathmines Rd 6 (4971902) - intermediate to advanced, 20 wks

Alpha College of English city centre venue (8747024) - Tue & Thurs, 7-9pm, 10 wks/ afternoons 1.30-5.30 20hrs, from €130 per wk/ exam prep, IELTS, TOEFL, TOEIC, Cambridge/ also morn & wkend

Ashfield College Main St Templeogue 6W (4900866) - 7-8.30pm, 10 wks

Balbriggan Community College Pine Ridge Chapel St (8412388/9) - 8 wks, Wed, 7.30-9.30, €73

Ballsbridge College of Business Studies Shelbourne Rd 4 (6684806) - intermediate & advvanced, Mon, Tues, Thurs, 6-9pm 10 wks, €100

Balymun Comprehensive School Adult Ed Centre Ballymun Rd 9 (8420654/ 8425828 night) - Wed, 10 wks free for refugees, assylum seekers, migrant workers

Bluefeather School of Languages 35 Montpelier Parade Monkstown (2806288) - EFL general & specialist, also day

Colaiste Dhulaigh Barryscourt Rd Coolock 17 (8481337) - for the business environment, Mon 6.45, 15 wks

Colaiste Eanna College of Business & Technical Stu Kilkieran Rd Cabra 7 (8389577) - for non-nationals, Wed, 2-4pm

College of Further Education Main St Dundrum 14 (2951376) - spoken, for foreign students, Thurs, beginners/ improvers

Connolly House Nth Strand (by 5 Lamps) 1 (8557116) - business English (BCE), Wed 10 wks €99/ also advanced Cambridge and cambridge proficiency certs, €99 each

Coolmine Community School Clonsilla 15 (8214583) - 7.30, 9 wks €40

DATE College of Further Education Dundrum 14 (2964322) - beginners/ improvers 10 wks €33, day

Dublin Public Libraries Admin Hq, 138-144 Pearse St 2 (6644800) - central library Ilac Centre (8734333) or Library HQ for details (6744800), self-learning €free

Dublin School of English 10-12 Westmoreland St 2 (6773322) - various courses, day, pm, eve; Cambridge, IELTS certs; 24 lessons 1 wk €245 morn; eve, 4 wks, 6 lesson wkly € 180/ 12 lesson €360 - also p/time day

Dun Laoghaire College of Further Education 17 Cumberland St Dun Laoghaire (2809676) - for foreign students, Mon, 20 wks, 7-9pm, €210

English Language Institute 99 St Stephen's Green 2 (4752965)

Finglas Adult Reading & Writing Scheme Colaiste Eoin Finglas 11 (8340893) - day, eve, 30 wks, free

Fitzwilliam Institute Ltd Temple Court Temple Rd Blackrock (2834579) - dip in English language & computer skills for overseas students, 40 wks + 4wks work experience arranged, p/time day, 9am-1pm or 1.30-5.30, €4000

Hartstown Community School Clonsilla 15 (8209863) - 10wks, €60

Institute of Technology Tallaght 24 (4042000) - 1 yr HETAC cert

International Study Centre 67 Harcourt St 2 (478 2766/2845) - day

Irish College of English 6 Church Rd Malahide (8453744) - 2 per wk ongoing, €125 per mth; also full time day

Killester College of Further Education Collins Ave 5 (8337686) - Level 2, for foreign students, Mon 7-9, 10 wks €70

Kylemore College Kylemore Rd 10 (6265901)

Language learning International 1 Clarinda Pk Nth Dun Laoghaire (2801729) - standard & intensive, general English classes/EFL exams/1st cert/Cambridge advanced proficiency/TOEFL/TOEIC/IELTS, also day

Marino College 14-20 Marino Mart 3 (8332100) - levels 1,2,3 & Cambridge cert, 10-20 wks, €99 each

COURSES IN TEFL

(Teaching English as a Foreign Language)
are held full time (Day) and part time (Evenings)
throughout the year at

DUBLIN SCHOOL OF ENGLISH

The school was founded in 1968 and recognised
by the Department of Education in the same year
We know how to teach English to foreigners –
Let us show you how to do it also

**Starting dates for courses in 2003/2004
available on request**

ALL COURSES 100 HOURS
With observation and practice teaching

All successful candidates are awarded the RELSA Cert. in TEFL.

RELSA – Recognised English Language Schools Association – is the
representative body of TEFL in Ireland. More than 90% of people coming
to Ireland on English Language courses study at RELSA member schools.

**DUBLIN SCHOOL OF ENGLISH
10/11/12, Westmoreland Street
Temple Bar, Dublin 2
Telephone: 6773322.   Fax: 6795454
E-Mail: Admin@dse.ie   Web: www.dse.ie**

**CLASSES IN ENGLISH FOR FOREIGNERS? OF COURSE!
MORNING, AFTERNOON AND EVENING COURSES
FULL DETAILS OF CLASS TIMES AVAILABLE ON REQUEST**

Maynooth College Language Centre NUI Maynooth Co Kildare (7083737) - intermediate/advanced, 9wk, €110

Plunket College Swords Rd, Whitehall 9 (8371689) - English for non-nationals, Tues, 10 wks, €66/English for refugees, Wed 9.30-1130 am

Pobalscoil Neasain Baldoyle 13 (8063092) - Mon 7.30 1o wks €50

Pobalscoil Rosmini Adult Ed Grace Pk Rd 9 (8371015) - introductory, Wed, 7.30 €80

Rathmines Snr College Town Hall 6 (4975334) - advanced/prep for Cambridge cert/ general/ elementary/ inter/advanced: each 10 wks, €70, Mon, Tue, Wed 7pm

Ringsend Technical Institute Cambridge Rd 4 (6684498) - introductory, 10 wks free

Sandford Language Institute Milltown Pk Sandford Rd 6 (2601296) - English for foreigners, all levels, 14 wks, €336/ English for the workplace, 14 wks, €336

St Thomas Community College Novara Ave Bray (2866111) - learn to speak English, 10 wks €70

St Tiernan's Community School Parkvale Balally 16 (2953224) - beginners, Wed 7.30 10 wks €70

U-Learn 205 New St Mall Malahide (8451619) - cert, €175 per week

Whitehall College of Further Education Swords Rd 9 (8376011) - for overseas students

WORDS Language Services 44 Northumberland Rd 4 (6610240) - individual tuition

ENGLISH - teaching as a foreign language TEFL

Alpha College of English city centre venue (8747024) - Tue & Thurs, 7-9pm, 10 wks/ afternoons 1.30-5.30 20hrs, from €130 per wk/ exam prep, IELTS, TOEFL, TOEIC, Cambridge/ also morn & wkend

Bluefeather School of Languages 35 Montpelier Parade Monkstown (2806288) - all ATT TEFL, also day - prelim 40hr, 1 wk, cert, €300 / foundation, 70hr, 2wks, €490 / advanced, ACELS Cert 115hr, 3.5wks, €780

Cabinteely Community School Johnstown Rd 18 (2857455) - 10 wks, €75

Colaiste Dhulaigh Barryscourt Rd Coolock 17 (8481337) - improve oral & written skills, also exam prep

CITAS Computer and IT Training, 54 Middle Abbey St 1 (8782212) – C&G ESOL f/time

Dublin Business School 13/14 Aungier St 2 (4177500) - English communications for business, DBS dip, p/time, 12 wks

Dublin School of English 10-12 Westmoreland St 2 (6773322) - TEFL various courses; 4 wks, 6 lesson wkly € 180/ 12 lesson €360 - also p/time day

English Language Institute 99 St Stephen's Green 2 (4752965)

Hibernian School of English 69 Emmet Road 8 (086 3789688) - all courses & levels, exam prep, one-to-one tuition

Language Learning International 1 Clarinda Pk Nth Dun Laoghaire (2801729) - cert, €680 / also day /RELSA prep cert, day 3wk, f/time/ eve, 12wk, p/time

Marino College 14-20 Marino Mart 3 (8332100) - 20wks, €231

Phoenix A.B.C. TEFL (8208462) - cert, 2.5 days, €180,classes in 36 Parnell Sq

St Thomas Community College Novara Ave Bray (2866111) - TEFL, 10 wks, €70, cert

TEFL Training Institute of Ireland 38 Harrington St 8 (4784035) - foundation, 2/5 wks, €550 ATT cert/ advanced Dept Ed cert 3/5 wks, €699/ distance courses: preliminary ATTcert, €350/ advanced ATTcert, €750

U-Learn 205 New St Mall Malahide (8451619) - international cert, 100 hrs, 2wk, €550

WORDS Language Services 44 Northumberland Rd 4 (6610240) - by correspondence & e-mail

ENGLISH incl English as a Second / Foreign language EFL see also Basic Education / Junior Cert / Languages / Leaving Cert / Literature / Writing, Creative

Alpha College of English city centre venue (8747024) - Tue & Thurs, 7-9pm, 10 wks/ afternoons 1.30-5.30 20hrs, from €130 per wk/ exam prep, IELTS, TOEFL, TOEIC, Cambridge/ also morn & wkend

Ballymun Comprehensive Schools Adult Ed Centre Ballymun Rd 9 (8420654/ 8425828 night) - jnr cert 30wk, €free/ leaving cert, 25wk, €150

Colaiste Dhulaigh Barryscourt Rd Coolock 17 (8481337) - basic, 12 classes 10-12.00, 8 wks/ leaving cert (O), Tue, 22 wks/ brush up English, 25 wks, Tue day

Colaiste Eanna College of Business & Technical Stu Kilkieran Rd Cabra 7 (8389577) - day basic English / one-to-one English (tel 8688342/ 8389577)

Crumlin College of Further Education Crumlin Rd 12 (4540662) - junior cert, also day/leaving cert (O), Mon & Thurs

DATE College of Further Education Dundrum 14 (2964322) - basic English, 10 wks free, day

DIT Faculty: Applied Arts Aungier St 2 (4023465/3445) - english for oral communication, 2 semesters (4024712)/ for academic purposes (4024673)

Dublin Public Libraries Admin Hq, 138-144 Pearse St 2 (6644800) - central library Ilac Centre D.1 (8734333) or Library HQ for details (6744800), self-learning €free

English Language Institute 99 St Stephen's Green 2 (4752965) - for business purposes: engineering, legal, secretarial, banking, marketing, medical, telecommunications/ basic, for work/ for academic purposes

FAS Training Centre Baldoyle 13 (8167460) - specialised with IT, day

FAS Training Centre Jervis St 1 (8044600) - specialised with IT, day/ vocational English for work

FAS Training Centre Tallaght 24 (4045284) - specialised with IT, day

Greenhills College Limekiln Ave Walkinstown 12 (4507779/4507138) - leaving cert(O), 20 wks, €79

Kilroy's College 25 Kingram Place 2 (1850 700700) - tutor supported home study: basic English, also literature, leaving cert & junior cert

Kilternan Adult Education Centre Glencullen Rd Kilternan 18 (2952050)

KLEAR Grange Park View Kilbarrack 5 (8671845) - junior cert/ leaving cert/ exploring English/ ESOL; day

People's College 32 Parnell Sq 1 (8735879) - basic, €15 / as a foreign language, €45

Plunket College Swords Rd, Whitehall 9 (8371689) - junior cert, 25 wks, also day/ leaving cert, 27 wks, €215

Ringsend Technical Institute Cambridge Rd 4 (6684498) - leaving cert (O), 25wks, €132

TACT St Dominic's School St Dominic's Rd Tallaght 24 (4596757) - language classes 10 wks €30

TARGET St Kevin's School Newbrook Rd, Donaghmede 13 (8671967) - basic, 10wk, day only, CDVEC/junior cert, 10 wks, CDVEC

ENGLISH LITERACY SCHEME see also Adult

Colaiste Eoin Cappagh Rd 11 (8340893) - adult reading & writing, 1-to-1/ tutor training courses

Dublin Adult Learning Centre 3 Mountjoy Sq 1 (8787266) - basic English/jnr cert English/leaving cert English

Pearse College Clogher Rd 12 (4536661/4541544) - day drop-in centre

Southside Adult Literacy Scheme 3 Ashgrove Tce Dundrum 14 (2964321) - range of basic one-to-one up to leaving cert courses: FETAC cert foundation & level 1

ENNEAGRAM see also Assertiveness / Personal Development

Adult Education Centre Adult Ed Centre Ballymun Rd 9 (8420654/ 8425828 night) - personality types, Mon 10wk, €65

Cabinteely Community School Johnstown Rd 18 (2857455) - Tues, 10 wks, €75

Killester College of Further Education Collins Ave 5 (8337686) - intro to, Tues 7.30, 10 wks €65

Newpark Adult & Continuing Education Centre Newtownpark Ave Blackrock (2884376) - intro to personality types, 10 wks, €99

Old Bawn Community School Tallaght 24 (4526137) - why do I always do that? Thurs, 7.30-9.30, 8 wks

Pobalscoil Rosmini Adult Ed Grace Pk Rd 9 (8371015) - Thurs, 7pm 10 wks €80

Rathmines Snr College Town Hall 6 (4975334) - understanding personality types, Wed 10 wks €65

Ringsend Technical Institute Cambridge Rd 4 (6684498) - 10 wks €65

TACT St Dominic's School St Dominic's Rd Tallaght 24 (4596757) - personal discovery, 4 wks €25

ENTREPRENEURIAL SKILLS see also Business, start your own

UCD Adult Education Office (7061695) - & management theory, 12 wks

ENVIRONMENT

An Oige 61 Mountjoy Street 7 (8304555) - environmental group

An Taisce- The National Trust for Ireland The Tailors Hall Back Lane 8 (4541786) - info, lectures, seminars, exhibitions

ENFO - Information on the Environment 17 St Andrew St 2 (1890 200191) - dept of the environment & local government - free public info service on environmental matters

European Movement 32 Nassau St 2 (6714300) - European training course - EU environmental policy

Greendale Community School Kilbarrack 5 (8322735/6) - awareness, 7.30, Thurs 10 wks €55

People's College 32 Parnell Sq 1 (8735879)

Saor-Ollscoil na hEireann 55 Prussia St 7 (8683368) - environmental studies, BA, Mon

St Thomas Community College Novara Ave Bray (2866111) - discover co Wicklow - 10 wks €70

The Open University Enquiry & Advice Centre Holbrook House, Holles St 2 (6785399)

UCD Adult Education Office (7061695) - Irish birds/ orchid cultivation/ the shaping of Dublin/ wet wild & wonderful: bogs & fens - 10 wks each

ESPERANTO

Esperanto Assoc of Ireland 9 Templeogue Wood 6W (4945020) - correspondence/monthly meetings, €free

ETCHING and Related Techniques

National College of Art & Design in Art & Design 100 Thomas Street 8 (6364214) - & dry point techniques, c. 22wk

ETHICS see also ECUMENICS

Colaiste Dhulaigh Barryscourt Rd Coolock 17 (8481337) - an insight, Tue 7pm, 8wks

UCD Adult Education Office (7061695) - the eternal questions of ethics, 10 Wed

EUROPEAN STUDIES/ AFFAIRS

DIT Faculty: Applied Arts Aungier St 2 (4023465/3445) - European perspectives, 1 yr modular (4024673)

Dublin City University Registry office Glasnevin 9 (7005338) - business - French/German/Spanish/transatlantic studies / economics, politics & law/ international relations

European Movement 32 Nassau St 2 (6714300) - European training courses: EU environmental policy/ EU employment & social policy/ access to EU funding/ Europe explained, an easy guide to the EU

People's College 32 Parnell Sq 1 (8735879)

EXERCISE see also Keep Fit, etc

Cabinteely Community School Johnstown Rd 18 (2857455) - pilates, Tues, 10 wks, €40

Colaiste Dhulaigh Barryscourt Rd Coolock 17 (8481337) - Taebo & toning, 8wks Tues 7.15-9.15

Killester College of Further Education Collins Ave 5 (8337686) - Fri morn, 10-20, 10 wks €60, movement for well being

Kilroy's College 25 Kingram Place 2 (1850 700700) - tutor supported home study: diet, fitness & health, dip courses

Kilroy's College 25 Kingram Place 2 (1850 700700) - tutor supported home study

Newpark Adult & Continuing Education Centre Newtownpark Ave Blackrock (2884376) - chi kung - gentle exercise, 10 wks €80

EXPORT see International Trade

FACILITATION SKILLS see also Teamwork

Comhlamh 10 Upr Camden St 2 (4783490) - on development issues

Old Bawn Community School Tallaght 24 (4526137) - NUI maynooth cert, group work theory & practice, Thurs + some Sats, 100hrs

FAMILY LAW see Law

FAMILY RELATIONSHIPS

Froebel College of Education Sion Hill, Blackrock & Nurture Inst 140 Meadowgrove Dundrum (2963795) - parenting: family management Tue, 30 wks cert/ dip, €290/ what a parent can do/ Teen parenting/ from pram to primary/ assertiveness for parents: Tues, 7 wks, €80 each

Hanly Centre Eblana Ave Dun Laoghaire (2807269) - adult children of dysfunctional families, modules 1 & 2; 12 steps study series, moldule 3; group therapy, module 4

FAMILY TREE see Genealogy

FARM ACCOUNTS

Kilroy's College 25 Kingram Place 2 (1850 700700) - tutor supported home study: & tax, dip course

FASHION

Crumlin College of Further Education Crumlin Rd 12 (4540662) - portfolio prep for work or college, Mon 6.45-9.45, 10 wks

Grafton Academy of Dress Design 6 Herbert Place 2 (6763653) - design, pattern making, assembly, p/time day 4 yr dip €3485/ to make own clothes, 18 wks €370/ summer fashion design, day €450; fashion drawing, 18 wks 7-9, €370

Marino College 14-20 Marino Mart 3 (8332100) - & dressmaking, Tue 5.30m 10 wks €66

National College of Art & Design in Art & Design 100 Thomas Street 8 (6364214) - design & pattern construction, c. 22wk

Portobello School Rere 40 Lr Dominick St 1 (8721277) - fashion merchandising & retail styling, part-time eve

Ringsend Technical Institute Cambridge Rd 4 (6684498) - fashion design, 10 wks €65

FELDENKRAIS

Newpark Adult & Continuing Education Centre Newtownpark Ave Blackrock (2884376) - feldenkrais body awareness for all ages, Thurs 10 wks €99

FEMINISM

www.instituteforfeminismandreligion.org / (4624504)

FENCING

Hartstown Community School Clonsilla 15 (8209863) - 10wks beginners/ improvers, €50 each

Salle d'Armes Duffy Salle d'Armes St John's Rd Sandymount 4 (2693720) - beginners & experienced, children & adults

FENG SHUI see also Chinese Culture / Interior Design

Ashfield College Main St Templeogue 6W (4900866) - 7.30-9.30 8 wks

Greendale Community School Kilbarrack 5 (8322735/6) - inrto, Wed morn 10.30, 10 wks €60

Hartstown Community School Clonsilla 15 (8209863) - 10wks, €60

Harvest Moon Centre 24 Lr Baggot St 2 (6627556)

Phil McNally Portmarnock (8462259)

Ringsend Technical Institute Cambridge Rd 4 (6684498) - 10 wks €65

St Finian's Community College Swords (8402623) - home & gardens Mon €79
The Irish School of Feng Shui Milltown Pk 6 (4921534) - p/t courses, consultations & workshops
FICTION see CREATIVE THINKING/ CREATIVE WRITING / WRITING
Dun Laoghaire-Rathdown Co Council Public Library Service () - free monthly book clubs; novels discussed, informal, new members welcome: the library at: Cabinteely (2855363), Dalkey (2855277), Dun Laoghaire (2801147), Dundrum (2985000), Shankill (2823081), Stillorgan (2889655)
FIDDLE see also Music
Clontarf School of Music 6 Marino Mart 3 (8330936) - Irish, 12wk - also day
Comhaltas Ceoltoiri Eireann 32 Belgrave Sq Monkstown (2800295)
Melody School of Music 178E Whitehall Rd W Perrystown 12 (4650150) - all day W/S & Sat; w/ends, Sat-Sun, 12 wks
Na Piobairi Uileann 15 Henrietta St 1 (8730093) - Mon
Walton's New School of Music 69 Sth Gt George's St 2 (4781884) - also day, see ad page 173
FILM APPRECIATION see also Cinema / Writing, Creative
DIT admissions ofice Dublin (4023445) - MA in film & TV/ professional level courses for audio visual personnel
Film Institute of Ireland Irish Film Centre 6 Eustace St Temple Bar 2 (6795744)
Marino College 14-20 Marino Mart 3 (8332100) - Tue 7.30m 10 wks €66
New Media Technology Training 13 Harcourt St 2 (4780905) - digital film production

Newpark Adult & Continuing Education Centre Newtownpark Ave Blackrock (2884376) - intro to film history, 10 wks €99

Saor-Ollscoil na hEireann 55 Prussia St 7 (8683368) - BA, film & theatre studies

St Kevins College Clogher Rd Crumlin 12 (4536397) - 10wks

St Thomas Community College Novara Ave Bray (2866111) - world cinema (Jan 04) - 10 wks €70

FINANCIAL SERVICES / FINANCE

Dublin Business School 13/14 Aungier St 2 (4177500) - stockbroker trading, ICM dip, p/time, 1yr

Institute of Public Administration 57-61 Lansdowne Rd 4 (6686233)

Institute of Technology Tallaght 24 (4042000) - postgrad dip in financial management (ACCA), 1 yr

Newpark Adult Education Centre Newtownpark Ave Blackrock (2884376) - successful investment, 10wks, €101

UCD Adult Education Office (7061695) - finance for the non-financial manager, 12 wks/ stock market: an introduction, 10 wks

Westmoreland College for Management Studies 11 Westmoreland St 2 (6795324/7266) - ACCA dip in financial management

FINE ARTS see also Art Appreciation

Institute of Professional Auctioneers & Valuers 129 Lr Baggot St 2 (6785685) - fine & decorative arts, cert, 15 wks €750

Irish Auctioneers & Valuers Institute 38 Merrion Sq E 2 (6611794) - fine art appreciation, 6wks, €200/advanced course, 9wks, €220

FINNISH

Dublin Public Libraries Admin Hq, 138-144 Pearse St 2 (6644800) - central library Ilac Centre, D1. (8734333) or Library HQ for details (6744800), self-learning €free

Sandford Language Institute Milltown Pk Sandford Rd 6 (2601296) - all levels, 14 wks, €250

FIRE FIGHTING

Civil Defence Esplanade Wolftone Qy 7 (6772699) - various centres

FIRE PREVENTION

Institution of Fire Engineers 77 Ballyroan Road 16 (4943669) - fire safety/engineering

Trinity College 2 (6772941) - (6081007) - fire safety practice (buildings & other structures), 1yr postgrad dip, 24wks, also Sat

FIRST AID

Adult Education Centre Adult Ed Centre Ballymun Rd 9 (8420654/ 8425828 night) - Wed 10wk, cert, €65, Order of Malta

Ballyfermot College of Further Education Ballyfermot Rd 10 (6269421) - 8 wks, Wed, 8-10pm, €55

Civil Defence Esplanade Wolftone Qy 7 (6772699) - various centres

Colaiste Dhulaigh Barryscourt Rd Coolock 17 (8481337) - Mon, 8 wks, cert

Colaiste Eanna Kilkieran Rd Cabra 7 (8389577) - dealing with emergencies, ABC cert, 10 wks, Thurs, 7-9pm

Connolly House Nth Strand (by 5 Lamps) 1 (8557116) - refresher course, 5 wks Wed, 7pm €45

Coolmine Community School Clonsilla 15 (8214583) - basic, 9wk, €60

Dun Laoghaire College of Further Education 17 Cumberland St Dun Laoghaire (2809676) - Tues, 10 wks, 7.30-9.30pm, €100

FAS Training Centre Ballyfermot 10 (6055900/ 5933) - & manual handling

Greendale Community School Kilbarrack 5 (8322735/6) - Tues, 7-9pm, 7wks, €70

Hartstown Community School Clonsilla 15 (8209863) - cert, 9wks, €60

Holy Family Community School Rathcoole (4580766)

Irish Red Cross Society 16 Merrion Sq 2 (6765135/6/7) - basic, cert, 10wk, €70/ also, IRC Dublin Borough course at 47 Mountjoy Sq 1, 8603819 / ircs@ireland.com in Occupational First Aid, cert, day, 3.5 days, €250

Marino College 14-20 Marino Mart 3 (8332100) - red cross, Tues, 10 wks, €90

Newpark Adult Education Centre Newtownpark Ave Blackrock (2884376) - Irish Red Cross, 9wks, €90

Old Bawn Community School Tallaght 24 (4526137) - Irish Red Cross, basic cert, Tues, 10wks, 7.30-9.30/ caring for the sick, cert 12wks, Thurs, 7.30-9.30

Order of Malta Ambulance Corps St John's House 32 Clyde Rd 4 (6684891) - up to 10 wks, cert

Palmerstown Community School 20 (6260116) - Order of Malta, cert, 10 wks €65

Plunket College Swords Rd, Whitehall 9 (8371689) - Tues, 12 wks, €79

Pobalscoil Rosmini Adult Ed Grace Pk Rd 9 (8371015) - Irish Red Cross tutor, beginners, Wed, 10 wks, €95, cert

Portmarnock Community School Carrickhill Rd (8038056) - civil defence, 8wks

Ringsend Technical Institute Cambridge Rd 4 (6684498) - 10wks, €65

Saint Finian's Community College Swords (8402623) - Tue, Irish Red Cross, 10wk, €79

Saint John's Ambulance Brigade 29 Upr Leeson St 4 (6688077) - 8 wks, cert, various venues

School of Practical Child Care Blackrock Campus Carysfort Ave Blackrock (2886994) - for children & infants, 2 days, SPCC cert

Sea & Shore Safety Services Ltd Happy Valley Glenamuck Rd 18 (2955991) - elementary first aid, 1 day €75/ medical, 3 day €145

Sea-Craft 3 Newcourt Ave Bray (2863362) - ISA/HSA cert, first aid at sea, 2 days, €140

St Kevin's College Clogher Rd Crumlin 12 (4536397) - REC rescue & emergency care (Ireland), cert

St MacDara's Community College Wellington Lane Templeogue 6W (4566216) - Mon, 7.30-9.30pm, 10 wks, €79, cert

St Thomas Community College Novara Ave Bray (2866111) - beginners Order of Malta, 10 wks, €70, cert/ for the childcare worker/ for the community worker, 30 wks, €130 each, cert

St Tiernan's Community School Parkvale Balally 16 (2953224) - for the home, Wed 10 wks €70

Tallaght Community School Balrothery 24 (4515566) - community CPR, 2wk, €10

Taney Parish Centre Taney Rd Dundrum 14 (2985491) - Red Cross, Tues (2981117) day

FISHING see also Angling

Network Sports & Social Club 24 Elmcastle Green Kilnamanagh 24 (4524415)

FITNESS - HEALTH/LEISURE see Health / Keep-Fit / Exercise

Hegarty Fitness Centre 53 Middle Abbey St 1 (8723080) - dynamic health, from €120,home/office/city centre, also day

Holistic Sourcing Centre 67 Lr Camden St 2 (4785022) - pilates (086 3416995)

Jackie Skelly's Fitness 42 Clarendon St, 2; Park West Bus Pk, Nangor Rd, 12 & Applewood Village, Swords (6770040 / 6301456 / 8075620) - gym membership, €47-59 per mth - aerobics, spin, toning, taebo, pilates, yoga

Kilroy's College 25 Kingram Place 2 (1850 700700) - tutor supported home study: diet, fitness & health, dip courses

Motions Health & Fitness Training City West Leisure Centre (4588179/ 087 2808866)

National College of Exercise & Health Studies 16a St Joseph's Parade Dorset St 7 (8827777) - exercise & health studies, nat. qual, 18wks, €1640, also day/ nat qual in Personal Training, 18wks € 1640

NTC 16a St Joseph's Parade 7 (8827777) - Pilates teacher training. p/time, Nat Qual

Phibsboro Gym 1st floor, Phibsboro SC 7 (8301849) - body sculpting / pilates, Sats 10-11am, 6 wks, beginners

Pobalscoil Rosmini Adult Ed Grace Pk Rd 9 (8371015) - incl circuit training for men & women, Mon, 8.30pm, 10 wks, €80

Susan Church (087 6210402) - pilates: Phibsboro, Church St, Baggot St, Sandymount

Taney Parish Centre Taney Rd Dundrum 14 (2985491) - gentle exercise, League of Health: Mon, Wed, Fri, day only, 0404 66423

FLAMENCO see also dance

Ballymun Comprehensive School Adult Ed Centre Ballymun Rd 9 (8420654/ 8425828 night) - Wed, 8-9pm, 10 wks €55

Marino College 14-20 Marino Mart 3 (8332100) - Thurs, 10wks €50

FLORISTRY COURSE

Crescent Flower Studios 15 Ballyroan Cres 16 (4947507) - start your own business, floristry course & intensive day workshops

Crumlin College of Further Education Crumlin Rd 12 (4540662) - FETAC course practical class - intro, funeral, occasion, Wedding flowers: p/time day

Dublin School of Floristry 4 (6681887) - commercial - also day

FLOWER ARRANGING

Ashfield College Main St Templeogue 6W (4900866) - fresh, 7.30-9.30, 8 wks

Ballinteer Community School Ballinteer 16 (2988195) - Wed 8pm, 15 hrs€100

BASE Ballyboden Adult Social Education Whitechurch Library Taylor's Lane 16 (4935953)

Cabinteely Community School Johnstown Rd 18 (2857455) - 10wk, €75

Colaiste Dhulaigh Barryscourt Rd Coolock 17 (8481337) - dried & fresh flowers, Mon, 8 wks 7.30-9.30

Colaiste Eanna College of Business & Technical Stu Kilkieran Rd Cabra 7 (8389577) - 10wks, Tue 7-9pm

Coolmine Community School Clonsilla 15 (8214583) - Mon, 7.30-9.30 €60

Crumlin College of Further Education Crumlin Rd 12 (4540662) - for seasonal & special occasions, Tues, 10 wks 7.30-9.30

Donahies Community School Streamville Rd 13 (8482217) - beginners/improvers, Tues, 10 wks, €55

Grange Community College Grange Abbey Rd Donaghmede 13 (8471422) - floral design, Wed, 10 wks €93

Greendale Community School Kilbarrack 5 (8322735/6) - basic floral design, Tue 7.30 / Mon morn 10.30: each 10 wks €55

Greenhills College Limekiln Ave Walkinstown 12 (4507779/4507138) - beginners/intermediate 8wks, €87

Killester College of Further Education Collins Ave 5 (8337686) - beginners, Tue 7.30-9, 10 wks 60

KLEAR Grange Park View Kilbarrack 5 (8671845) - day

Knocklyon Youth & Community Centre, 16 (4943991)

Lucan Community College Esker Drive (6282077) - beginners/ improvers, 10wk, €79 each

Malahide Community School Malahide (8460949) - floral art, 10 wks €70

Marino College 14-20 Marino Mart 3 (8332100) - Thurs, 10wks, €66

Newpark Adult Education Centre Newtownpark Ave Blackrock (2884376) - beginners/ improvers, 10 wks, €99 each

Old Bawn Community School Tallaght 24 (4526137) - designing with flowers, Thurs, 7.30-9.30pm, 10 wks

Pobalscoil Iosolde 20 (6260116) - 8 wks Thurs 7.30 €60

Portmarnock Community School Carrickhill Rd (8038056) - 8wk

St Kevins College Clogher Rd Crumlin 12 (4536397) - 10wks

St Mac Dara's Community College Wellington Lane Templeogue 6W (4566216) - Mon, Tue, 7.30-9.30pm, 8 wks, €73

St Thomas Community College Novara Ave Bray (2866111) - 10 wks, €70

St Tiernan's Community School Parkvale Balally 16 (2953224) - Wed 10 wks €80

Stillorgan College of Further Education Old Road Stillorgan (2880704) - Thurs, 7.30-9.30pm, 8 wks, €83

TACT St Dominic's School St Dominic's Rd Tallaght 24 (4596757) - beginners/intermediate, 10wks, €55 day

FLUTE see also Music

Abbey School of Music 9b Lr Abbey St 1 (8747908) - Michael McGrath

Bray Music Centre Florence Rd Bray (2866768)

Clontarf School of Music 6 Marino Mart 3 (8330936) - & tin whistle, Irish, 12wk - also day

Comhaltas Ceoltoiri Eireann 32 Belgrave Sq Monkstown (2800295)

Dun Laoghaire Music Centre 130A Lr George's St Dun Laoghaire (2844178)

Leinster School of Music Griffith College Campus South Circular Rd 8 (4150467)

Na Piobairi Uileann 15 Henrietta St 1 (8730093)

Newpark Music Centre Newtownpark Ave Blackrock (2883740) - also day

Pobalscoil Rosmini Adult Ed Grace Pk Rd 9 (8371015) - tin whistle & flute, Thurs 7.30 €80

Walton's New School of Music 69 Sth Gt George's St 2 (4781884) - classical & trad, also day, see ad page 173

FLYING see Aviation

FOCUSING SKILLS

Pobalscoil Neasain Baldoyle 13 (8063092) - mon 7.30, 10 wks, €70

FOLK ACTIVITIES/ MUSIC see also Singing / Traditional

Dublin Folk Dance Group 48 Ludford Drive Ballinteer 16 (2987929) - international dance, ongoing

Walton's New School of Music 69 Sth Gt George's St 2 (4781884) - also day, see ad page

FOOD SCIENCE Nutrition

DIT admissions ofice Dublin (4023445) - new product development

DIT Faculty: Science Kevin St 8 (4024585/3445) - BSc in food science, 3 yr p/time €1350

DIT Faculty: Tourism & Food Cathal Brugha St 1 (4024349/3445) - MSc food safety management, 2yrs €2900pa/ food product development courses, 1/2 days each / gastronomy, jan-june (4024344)

Hartstown Community School Clonsilla 15 (8209863) - food hygiene & safety: 10 wks €60; 10 wks €120; 20 wks €200; cert (RIPH) foundation, intermediate, advanced

Institute of Technology Tallaght 24 (4042000) - management of food hygiene in the hospitality industry, 9 wks

Ringsend Technical Institute Cambridge Rd 4 (6684498) - food & nutrition, FETAC cert courses at various times,ongoing, free

FOOTBALL see Gaelic / Rugby / Soccer

Football Assoc of Ireland 80 Merrion Sq Sth 2 (6766864) - soccer

FOREIGN TRADE see International Trade

FORK LIFT TRUCK TRAINING

FACTS Training 49 Cherry Orchard Ind. Est 10 (6260388) - forklift driving safety, 8 eve cert €710; 4 eve cert, €395 /day 5 days cert, €710; 2 day cert €395

FAS Training Centre Baldoyle 13 (8167460); Ballyfermot 10 (6055900/ 5933); Tallaght 24 (4045284) - in-company only

FRENCH (BEGINNERS to ADVANCED)

Aisling Language Services Languages for Business & Pleasure 137 Lr Rathmines Rd 6 (4971902) - intermediate, 10 wks €145

Alliance Francaise 1 Kildare St 2 (6761632); Alliance-Sud Foxrock Ave 18 (2898760) - groups and one-to-one 32 hrs €285/ conversation classes / dip, cert / workshops

Ashfield College Main St Templeogue 6W (4900866) - beginners / improvers 8wks each 7.30-9.30pm

Balbriggan Community College Pine Ridge Chapel St (8412388/9) - beginners, 10wks, Mon 7.30-9pm, €66

Ballymun Comprehensive Schools Adult Ed Centre Ballymun Rd 9 (8420654/ 8425828 night) - beginners/improvers, Tue 10wk, €75 each

Blackrock College (2888681) - Wed, beginners 7pm/ advanced 8.30, 6 wks €65 each

Cabinteely Community School Johnstown Rd 18 (2857455) - beginners/improvers, 10wk, €75 each

Colaiste Dhulaigh Barryscourt Rd Coolock 17 (8481337) - for beginners, Mon, 10 wks

Colaiste Eanna College of Business & Technical Stu Kilkieran Rd Cabra 7 (8389577) - beginners conversation, 10 wks Tues

College of Further Education Main St Dundrum 14 (2951376) - beginners, Tues, Thurs, 8 wks

Coolmine Community School Clonsilla 15 (8214583) - beginners Mon/improvers Tue, 2 terms, 18wk, €120 each

Crumlin College of Further Education Crumlin Rd 12 (4540662) - Thurs, 6.45-8.15

DATE College of Further Education Dundrum 14 (2964322) - le club 1-4, day/ beginners/ conversational: each 10 wks €66

DIT Faculty: Applied Arts Aungier St 2 (4023465/3445) - language & contemporary culture, 1 yr modular (4024673)

Donahies Community School Streamville Rd 13 (8482217) - beginners/ continuation/ advanced: Mon, 10 wks, €55 each

Dublin City University Registry office Glasnevin 9 (7005338) - applied languages, international business, international marketing

Dun Laoghaire College of Further Education 17 Cumberland St Dun Laoghaire (2809676) - beginners & level 2, Tues, 10 wks, 7.30 & 8.30pm €85

Dun Laoghaire-Rathdown Co Council Public Library Service () - Deansgrange lib, Clonkeen Dr (2850860) - Fr/Eng - informal sessions, Thurs 10.30-12 morn

Foxrock Institute Kill O' the Grange School Kill Lane Blackrock (4939506/4939629) - beginners/improvers 8wks, €85

Greendale Community School Kilbarrack 5 (8322735/6) - beginners/continuation, Thurs, 7-8.30pm/ 8.30-10pm, 10 wks, €50 each

Greenhills College Limekiln Ave Walkinstown 12 (4507779/4507138) - 10 wks, €79

Hartstown Community School Clonsilla 15 (8209863) - beginners, 10wks, €60 each

Inchicore College of Further Education Emmet Rd 8 (4535358) - 10wks each, Thurs

Institute of Technology Tallaght 24 (4042000) - cert, yrs 1 & 2

Killester College of Further Education Collins Ave 5 (8337686) - beginners, Tue 7.30-9, 10 wks 60

Kilroy's College 25 Kingram Place 2 (1850 700700) - tutor supported home study: speak french now, also leaving cert

KLEAR Grange Park View Kilbarrack 5 (8671845) - day only

Kylemore College Kylemore Rd 10 (6265901) - Stage 1 Tue / Stage 2 Mon, each 10 wks

Langtrain International Torquay Rd Foxrock 18 (2893876) - €96 per term

Lucan Community College Esker Drive (6282077) - beginners/ improvers, 10wk, €79 each

Marino College 14-20 Marino Mart 3 (8332100) - beginners/intermediate, 10-20 wks, €50

Maynooth College Language Centre NUI Maynooth Co Kildare (7083737) - all levels, 9wk, €110

Newpark Adult Education Centre Newtownpark Ave Blackrock (2884376) - conversation, 10wks / all levels 1-4, €90 each

Old Bawn Community School Tallaght 24 (4526137) - level 1/2, conversation, 10 wks

Palmerstown Community School 20 (6260116) - level 1&2, Mon 7-10pm 10 wks €60

People's College 32 Parnell Sq 1 (8735879) - all levels, €55

Plunket College Swords Rd, Whitehall 9 (8371689) - leaving cert, 27 wks, €143/ conversation, beginners/ advanced - 10 wks, €66 each

Pobalscoil Rosmini Adult Ed Grace Pk Rd 9 (8371015) - beginners 1&2/ continuation, Mon, 7 & 8.30, 10 wks, €80 each/ advanced Tue €90

Rathmines Snr College Town Hall 6 (4975334) - beginners, Mon, 20 wks €130/ continuation/intermediate, Wed, 25 wks, €165

Ringsend Technical Institute Cambridge Rd 4 (6684498) - beginners, 10wks, €65

Saint Finian's Community College Swords (8402623) - Mon, 10wk, €79

Sandford Language Institute Milltown Pk Sandford Rd 6 (2601296) - all levels, 14 wks, €205

St Mac Dara's Community College Wellington Lane Templeogue 6W (4566216) - Mon cont/ Wed beginners: 7.30-9.30pm, 10 wks, €79

St Mark's Community School Cookstown Road Tallaght 24 (4519399)

St Thomas Community College Novara Ave Bray (2866111) - beginners/ intermediate 10wks €70

St Tiernan's Community School Parkvale Balally 16 (2953224) - absolute beginners, Mon 7.30 10 wks €70

Sth Dublin Co Libraries Languages & Computers: Ballyroan/Clondalkin/ Castletymon, Lucan & Co Library (4597834-admin only) - self learning, beginners, intermediate

Stillorgan Senior College Old Road Stillorgan (2880704) - beginners, Mon, conversational approach, 10 wks €76

TACT St Dominic's School St Dominic's Rd Tallaght 24 (4596757) - conversation, 10 wks €47 day

Tallaght Community School Balrothery 24 (4515566) - basic conversation, 10 wks €45

TARGET St Kevin's School Newbrook Rd, Donaghmede 13 (8671967) - day only, CDVEC , beginners, intermediate, advanced

WORDS Language Services 44 Northumberland Rd 4 (6610240) - individual tuition only

FRENCH - COMMERCIAL / BUSINESS

Alliance Francaise 1 Kildare St 2 (6761632); Alliance-Sud Foxrock Ave 18 (2898760) - business French / also, CORPORATE courses, in-company classes contact Christine Weld for details

Dublin Public Libraries Admin Hq, 138-144 Pearse St 2 (6644800) - central library
Ilac Centre (8734333) or Library HQ for details (6744800), self-learning €free
Sandford Language Institute Milltown Pk Sandford Rd 6 (2601296) - for the work
place, 14 wks, €205
Sth Dublin Co Libraries Languages & Computers: Ballyroan/Clondalkin/
Castletymon, Lucan & Co Library (4597834-admin only) - self learning
WORDS Language Services 44 Northumberland Rd 4 (6610240) - individual
tuition only

FRENCH FOR HOLIDAYS
Donahies Community School Streamville Rd 13 (8482217) - functional - food, trav-
el, holidays, MON 7.30, 10 WKS €55
Dublin Public Libraries Admin Hq, 138-144 Pearse St 2 (6644800) - central library
Ilac Centre (8734333) or Library HQ for details (6744800), self-learning €free
Holy Family Community School Rathcoole (4580766)
Kilroy's College 25 Kingram Place 2 (1850 700700) - tutor supported home study:
speak French now, also leaving cert

FRENCH LITERATURE/CULTURE
Ballsbridge College of Business Studies Shelbourne Rd 4 (6684806) - language &
culture, Tue 6.30, 10 wks €65

FRENCH POLISHING
Cabinteely Community School Johnstown Rd 18 (2857455) - 10wk, €75
Colaiste Dhulaigh Barryscourt Rd Coolock 17 (8481337) - Tues, 8 wks
Greendale Community School Kilbarrack 5 (8322735/6) - & antique repairs, Thurs,
7.30-9.30pm, 10wks, €60

FRENCH TRANSLATION see also Translators Course
FRENCH, LEGAL
Alliance Francaise 1 Kildare St 2 (6761632); Alliance-Sud Foxrock Ave 18
(2898760) - dip in legal French, from October; contact – Louise Stirling for
details

FUNDING / FINANCE see also Banking, Financial Services / Money
European Movement 32 Nassau St 2 (6714300) - European raining course: access
to EU funding

FURNISHINGS see Crafts / Curtain Making / House / Soft Furnishings
FURNITURE MAKING see WOODWORK
FURNITURE RESTORATION Antiques
Ballymun Comprehensive Schools Adult Ed Centre Ballymun Rd 9 (8420654/
8425828 night) - Wed 10 wk, €90
Kilternan Adult Education Group Glencullen Rd Kilternan 18 (2952050)
St Kevins College Clogher Rd Crumlin 12 (4536397) - 10wks
Stillorgan College of Further Education Old Road Stillorgan (2880704) - beginners,
Tue 8 wks €87

GAELIC GAMES (Football, Hurling & Handball) Camogie
Cumann Camogaiochta na nGael Pairc an Chrocaigh St Joseph's Ave 3 (8364619)
GARDA EXAMS
Kilroy's College 25 Kingram Place 2 (1850 700700) - home-study courses

GARDENING see also HORTICULTURE

Ashfield College Main St Templeogue 6W (4900866) - creative gardening, 7.30-9.30 8 wks

Cabinteely Community School Johnstown Rd 18 (2857455) - design & flair, 10wk, €75

Colaiste Dhulaigh Barryscourt Rd Coolock 17 (8481337) - planting & layout, Thurs 10.30 day, 10 wks

Coolmine Community School Clonsilla 15 (8214583) - practical, 9wk, Mon €60

DATE College of Further Education Dundrum 14 (2964322) - the autumn garden, 10 wks €66 day

Dun Laoghaire College of Further Education 17 Cumberland St Dun Laoghaire (2809676) - design, Mon, 7.30-9.30pm, 10 wks, €100

FAS Training Centre Ballyfermot 10 (6055900/ 5933); Finglas Jamestown Rd 11 (8140243); Tallaght 24 (4045284) - maintenance & design 10wk

Foxrock Institute Kill O' the Grange School Kill Lane Blackrock (4939506/4939629) - 8wks, €85

Greendale Community School Kilbarrack 5 (8322735/6) - & horticulture, Tues, 7.30-9.30pm, 8wks, €55

Hartstown Community School Clonsilla 15 (8209863) - & design, 10wks, €60

Kilroy's College 25 Kingram Place 2 (1850 700700) - tutor supported home-study dip course

Kilternan Adult Education Group Glencullen Rd Kilternan 18 (2952050)

Kylemore College Kylemore Rd 10 (6265901) - practical, Tue 10 wks 10.30-1pm/ Tue, 8 wks 7-9pm

Liberties College Bull Alley St 8 (4540044) - garden or window box, Wed 7-9, €110

Marino College 14-20 Marino Mart 3 (8332100) - Thurs, 10wks €50

Newpark Adult Education Centre Newtownpark Ave Blackrock (2884376) - 5.10 & 7.30pm, 10wks, €99

Old Bawn Community School Tallaght 24 (4526137) - beginners, planning a garden, Tues, 7.30-9.30 / garden design, Thurs, 7.30-9.30, 10wks

Palmerstown Community School 20 (6260116) - design, Mon 7.30, 10 wks €60

RAVE Good Shepherd School Churchtown 14 (2981052) - the autumn garden, 10 wks 7.30 €79

St Thomas Community College Novara Ave Bray (2866111) - 8wks, €50

Stillorgan College of Further Education Old Road Stillorgan (2880704) - 8 wks, Tue €73

TACT St Dominic's School St Dominic's Rd Tallaght 24 (4596757) - know your garden, 10wks, €50 day

Taney Parish Centre Taney Rd Dundrum 14 (2985491) - Tues (2809602/086 8920859), day only

Trinity College 2 (6772941) - (6081274), plants & gardens 2003, 8wks €70

UCD Adult Education Office (7061695) - orchid cultivation, 10 wks €120/ a history of gardens 10 wks

GAS INSTALLATION

FAS Training Centre Cabra Bannow Rd 7 (8821400)

GENEALOGY / FAMILY HISTORY

Kilternan Adult Education Centre Glencullen Rd Kilternan 18 (2952050)

Marino College 14-20 Marino Mart 3 (8332100) - Thurs 7.30 10 wks €66

Newpark Adult & Continuing Education Centre Newtownpark Ave Blackrock (2884376) - family history & research, Tues, 20wks €198

Old Bawn Community School Tallaght 24 (4526137) - local & family, Tue 10 wks

Portmarnock Community School Carrickhill Rd (8038056) - genealogy & family history, Thurs 7.20, 8 wks €50

St Thomas Community College Novara Ave Bray (2866111) - 10 wks €70

UCD Adult Education Office (7061695) - family history modules 1&2, 12 wks; also yr 2&3, 24 wks each

GEOGRAPHY see also Surveying

DIT Faculty: Built Environment Bolton St 1 (4023711/3445) - desktop cartography, visualising GIS data, 10 wks / GIS course, 6 modules, 20 wks / GPS course, 3 modules, 10 wks: each €500

Kilroy's College 25 Kingram Place 2 (1850 700700) - tutor supported home study: leaving cert

KLEAR Grange Park View Kilbarrack 5 (8671845) - leaving cert, day only

Plunket College Swords Rd, Whitehall 9 (8371689) - leaving cert, 27 wks, €215

Southside Adult Literacy Scheme 3 Ashgrove Tce Dundrum 14 (2964321) - range of basic one-to-one up to leaving cert courses, FETAC cert foundation & level 1

St Thomas Community College Novara Ave Bray (2866111) - intro to GPS, 10 wks €70

GEOLOGY

Trinity College 2 (6772941) - (6081074) - catastrophic earth, 8 wks €60

GERMAN

Ashfield College Main St Templeogue 6W (4900866) - beginners stage 1 / improvers stage 2 7.30-9.30 8 wks each

Cabinteely Community School Johnstown Rd 18 (2857455) - beginners, Mon, 10 wks, €75

Colaiste Dhulaigh Barryscourt Rd Coolock 17 (8481337) - beginners, Tues 7.15-9.00, 10 wks/ FETAC cert, day Tue & Wed

Colaiste Eanna College of Business & Technical Stu Kilkieran Rd Cabra 7 (8389577) - beginners conversation, 10 wks Tues

College of Further Education Main St Dundrum 14 (2951376) - beginners, Tue

Coolmine Community School Clonsilla 15 (8214583) - beginners, Mon 9wk, €60

DATE College of Further Education Dundrum 14 (2964322) - beginners/ adsvanced/ improvers: each 10 wks €66 day

DIT Faculty: Applied Arts Aungier St 2 (4023465/3445) - language & contemporary culture, 1 yr modular (4024673)

Dublin City University Registry office Glasnevin 9 (7005338) - applied languages, international business, international marketing

Dublin Public Libraries Admin Hq, 138-144 Pearse St 2 (6644800) - central library Ilac Centre (8734333) or Library HQ for details (6744800), self-learning €free

Dun Laoghaire College of Further Education 17 Cumberland St Dun Laoghaire (2809676) - beginners, Mon, 10 wks, 7-9pm, €85

Dun Laoghaire-Rathdown Co Council Public Library Service () - Deansgrange lib, Clonkeen Dr (2850860) - Ger/Eng - informal sessions, Wed 10.30-12 morn

Goethe Institut 62 Fitzwilliam Sq 2 (6801110) - beginners/ intermediate/ advanced, 16wks, also day/ intensive summer courses, 2wks, day/ summer courses, eve & day, 2-6 wks/ pre-junior & pre-leaving cert, 16wks day/ diploma courses, 16wks

Greendale Community School Kilbarrack 5 (8322735/6) - conversation, level 1, Thurs, 7-8.30pm, 10 wks, €50 (see also Cultural Studies)

Holy Family Community School Rathcoole (4580766)

Inchicore College of Further Education Emmet Rd 8 (4535358) - 10wks, each, Mon

Institute of Technology Tallaght 24 (4042000) - beginners/ advanced, cert, yrs 1 & 2

Kilroy's College 25 Kingram Place 2 (1850 700700) - tutor supported home study: leaving cert, incl aural practice

Langtrain International Torquay Rd Foxrock 18 (2893876) - €96 per term

Marino College 14-20 Marino Mart 3 (8332100) - beginners, €66/intermediate, €50, 10-20 wks

Newpark Adult Education Centre Newtownpark Ave Blackrock (2884376) - 3 levels, Mon, 10wks, €90

Old Bawn Community School Tallaght 24 (4526137) - level 1 conversation, 10wks

Palmerstown Community School 20 (6260116) - level 1, Tues 7-8.15 10 wks €60

Plunket College Swords Rd, Whitehall 9 (8371689) - conversation, beginners, Tues, 10 wks, €66/ leaving cert, 27 wks, €143

Pobalscoil Rosmini Adult Ed Grace Pk Rd 9 (8371015) - beginners, Mon, 7pm, 10 wks, €80

Portmarnock Community School Carrickhill Rd (8038056) - beginners, 8wks, €50

Sandford Language Institute Milltown Pk Sandford Rd 6 (2601296) - all levels, 14 wks, €205

St Thomas Community College Novara Ave Bray (2866111) - beginners, 10 wks €70

Sth Dublin Co Libraries Languages & Computers: Ballyroan/Clondalkin/ Castletymon, Lucan & Co Library (4597834-admin only) - self learning

Tallaght Community School Balrothery 24 (4515566) - basic conversation, 10 wks €45

WORDS Language Services 44 Northumberland Rd 4 (6610240) - individual tuition only

GERMAN CULTURE

Goethe Institut 62 Fitzwilliam Sq 2 (6801110) - literature/ translation/ conversation 16wks/ cultural events - programmes on request

Trinity College 2 (6772941) - (6081373) extra mural, masterworks of German lit, 9 wks, €40

GERMAN FOR HOLIDAYS

WORDS Language Services 44 Northumberland Rd 4 (6610240) - individual tuition only

GERMAN, COMMERCIAL

Dublin Public Libraries Admin Hq, 138-144 Pearse St 2 (6644800) - central library Ilac Centre (8734333) or Library HQ for details (6744800), self-learning €free

Goethe Institut 62 Fitzwilliam Sq 2 (6801110) - commercial, business, legal, 16 wks

Language Centre NUI Maynooth Co Kildare (7083737) - 9 wks, €130

Sandford Language Institute Milltown Pk Sandford Rd 6 (2601296) - for the workplace, 14 wks, €205

Sth Dublin Co Libraries Languages & Computers: Ballyroan/Clondalkin/Castletymon, Lucan & Co Library (4597834-admin only) - self learning

WORDS Language Services 44 Northumberland Rd 4 (6610240) - individual tuition only

GLOBALISATION & TRADE Development Studies

Comhlamh 10 Upr Camden St 2 (4783490) - 6wk evening course

GOLF CLASSES

Ballinteer Community School Ballinteer 16 (2988195) - 10 wks, Mon 7.30 & 8.30

Cabinteely Community School Johnstown Rd 18 (2857455) - beginners & improvers, limited class size, 10wk, €75 each

Corporate Club 24 Elmcastle Green Kilnamanagh 24 (4610935)

Dominick Reilly PGA, Leopardstown Pro Shop Foxrock 18 (2893511)

Donahies Community School Streamville Rd 13 (8482217) - Mon, personal tuition, 15 wks œ90

Dun Laoghaire College of Further Education 17 Cumberland St Dun Laoghaire (2809676) - Tues, beginners, 7.30/ improvers, 8.45, €110 each

Elmgreen Golf Course Castleknock 15 (8200797)

Foxrock Institute Kill O' the Grange School Kill Lane Blackrock (4939506/4939629) - beginners/improvers, 8wks, €90 each

Greendale Community School Kilbarrack 5 (8322735/6) - clinic at driving range, Tues/Thurs, 10 wks, €64 each

Hartstown Community School Clonsilla 15 (8209863) - beginners/intermediate, advanced, 6wks, €70 each

Holy Family Community School Rathcoole (4580766)

Kilroy's College 25 Kingram Place 2 (1850 700700) - tutor supported home study: golf psychology,dip course

Kilternan Adult Education Group Glencullen Rd Kilternan 18 (2952050)

Knocklyon Youth & Community Centre, 16 (4943991)

Malahide Community School Malahide (8460949) - 7wks, Tues & Thurs, €90 ea

Network Sports & Social Club 24 Elmcastle Green Kilnamanagh 24 (4524415)

Old Bawn Community School Tallaght 24 (4526137) - beginners/improvers, 10 wks

Palmerstown Community School 20 (6260116) - beginners/improvers, Tues €76 each

Pobalscoil Neasain Baldoyle 13 (8063092) - Mon 3 classes, 10 wks €85/ Tue 3 classes 10 wks €85

St Mark's Community School Cookstown Road Tallaght 24 (4519399)

GOLF COURSES & DRIVING RANGES

Corballis Public Golf Course Donabate (8436583) - 18 hole links

Elmgreen Golf Course Castleknock 15 (8200797)

pobalscoil iosolve

Palmerstown, Dublin 20. Tel: **6260116**

Email: **infor@adulted.ie**   **www.adulted.ie**

Enrol: Sept 8-11 & Sept 15-18: 10am-12pm, 2-4pm

Eve Enrol: Sept 11 & 15: 7-8.30pm

Leopardstown Golf Centre Foxrock 18 (2895341) - head professional, Dominic Reilly

Open Golf Centre Newtown Hse St Margaret's (8640324) - tuition available

Spawell Golf Range Templeogue 6W (4907990)

GOLF, PSYCHOLOGY OF

Kilroy's College 25 Kingram Place 2 (1850 700700) - tutor supported home study

GRAPHIC DESIGN see also Computer Aided Design

Adelaide Computers 14 Pembroke Lane Ballsbridge 4 (2696213) - Photoshop/ Quark, Illustrator, one-to-one training at your office/home or our offices, small groups, beginners to advanced, full training programmes also

CITAS Computer & I.T. Training 54 Middle Abbey St 1 (8782212) - QuarkXpress, photoshop, illustrator, Thurs 6-9pm €600

Crumlin College of Further Education Crumlin Rd 12 (4540662) - Quark Xpress (DTP)/Adobe Photoshop & Illustrator, all Thurs, 10 wks

Crumlin College of Further Education Crumlin Rd 12 (4540662) - photoshop & illustrator, Wed 8.15 10 wks / freehand, Thurs 6.45 10 wks

Dorset College 64a Lr Dorset St/ 8 Belvedere Pl 1 (8309677) - Illustrator, Photoshop

Eden Computer Training Rathfarnham 16, or MACRO Centre, 1 Green St 7 (4953155) - illustrator. photoshop, quark xpress, corell

FAS Training Centre Cabra Bannow Rd 7 (8821400)

Irish Academy of Computer Training 98 St Stephen's Grn 2 (4347600) - dtp course 24 wks €1995, cert/ quarkxpress; corel draw; ms pub; adobe photoshop & illustrator; framemaker: ea 8 wks €695, cert/ frontpage 4 wks cert / also day

New Media Technology Training 13 Harcourt St 2 (4780905) - 3D studio Max/ 2 dreamweaver; 3 java, CGI scripts, style sheets/ digital imaging, adobe photoshop/ animation - flash, director / also p/time day

Pobalscoil Iosolde 20 (6260116) - autocad levels 1&2, c&g cert 10 wks €190 ea

Ringsend Technical Institute Cambridge Rd 4 (6684498) - photoshop, 10 wks €125

Senior College Dun Laoghaire CFE Eblana Ave Dun Laoghaire (2800385) - cert in computer imaging, FETAC 20 wks, €300

GRAPHOLOGY (Handwriting Analysis)

Harvest Moon Centre 24 Lr Baggot St 2 (6627556)

Institute of Graphology 22 Forest Hill Drogheda Co Louth () - by correspondence (send SAE for details)

GREEK - CLASSICAL & MODERN

Dublin Public Libraries Admin Hq, 138-144 Pearse St 2 (6644800) - central library Ilac Centre (8734333) or Library HQ for details (6744800), self-learning €free

Sandford Language Institute Milltown Pk Sandford Rd 6 (2601296) - modern, all levels, 14 wks, €250/ ancient Greek, all levels, 14 wks, €250

Sth Dublin Co Libraries Languages & Computers: Ballyroan/Clondalkin/ Castletymon, Lucan & Co Library (4597834-admin only) - self learning, modern Greek

Trinity College 2 (6772941) - (6081208) - extra mural, beginners modern Greek, €130/intermediate, €78, 22wks each

UCD Adult Education Office (7061695) - modern Greek, beginners/ level 2, 20 wks

GROOMING & MAKE-UP see also Beauty Care/ Make-Up

College of Further Education Main St Dundrum 14 (2951376) - Tue

Colour Connections 4 (087 6288582) - colour, image & style; wardrobe planning; personal shopping/ short courses

Foxrock Institute Kill O' the Grange School Kill Lane Blackrock (4939506/4939629) - colour, image & style, 8wks, €85

Newpark Adult Education Centre Newtownpark Ave Blackrock (2884376) - ladies colour analysis, 5wks, €90

Tallaght Community School Balrothery 24 (4515566) - 8wk, €45

GUITAR see also Music

Abbey School of Music 9b Lr Abbey St 1 (8747908) - Kevin Robinson ALCM / Electric guitar / bass - Trea Breazeale

Bill Brady School of Guitar 92 Pecks Lane Castleknock 15 (8210466 / 8220611)

Bray Music Centre Florence Rd Bray (2866768)

Cabinteely Community School Johnstown Rd 18 (2857455) - folk, beginners/improvers, 10wk, €40 each

Carl Alfred 6 Palmerston Villas, Basement Fl 2 off Upr Rathmines Rd 6 (4972095) - popular, hear-feel teaching method. See display advert

Clontarf School of Music 6 Marino Mart 3 (8330936) - acoustic/Irish trad/jazz /electric, 10wk - also day

Colaiste Eanna College of Business & Technical Stu Kilkieran Rd Cabra 7 (8389577) - beginners, recreation & folk, 10wks, Tue 7-9pm

Coolmine Community School Clonsilla 15 (8214583) - all levels youth, adult, after-noon, eve, 9wk, €50 each

Dublin School of Guitar 26/27 Drury St 2 (6714732) - all styles, individual tuition, grades/dip, 10wk, €170; also day

Dun Laoghaire Music Centre 130A Lr George's St Dun Laoghaire (2844178)

Foxrock Institute Kill O' the Grange School Kill Lane Blackrock (4939506/4939629) - 8wks, €85

Greendale Community School Kilbarrack 5 (8322735/6) - beginners/ continuation, Thurs, 10 wks, €50 each

Greenhills College Limekiln Ave Walkinstown 12 (4507779/4507138) - begin-ners/improvers, 8 wks, €70

Hartstown Community School Clonsilla 15 (8209863) - 10wks, €45

Holy Family Community School Rathcoole (4580766)

James Foy School of Guitar Bel Canto House 21 North Great Georges St 1 (8740184) - individual tuition & seminars, beginners to advanced, phone for appointment

John Murphy Guitar Studio 38 Dellbrook Pk Ballinteer Rd Dundrum 16 (2962797)

John Ward 5 Tibradden Drive Walkinstown 12 (4520918) - popular & classical preparation for TCL grade exams - also day

Kilternan Adult Education Group Glencullen Rd Kilternan 18 (2952050)

Knocklyon Youth & Community Centre, 16 (4943991)

Kylemore College Kylemore Rd 10 (6265901) - beginners, group class, 8 wks

Leinster School of Music Griffith College Campus South Circular Rd 8 (4150467)

Lucan Community College Esker Drive (6282077) - 1&2, 10 wks €66

Marino College 14-20 Marino Mart 3 (8332100) - beginners/intermediate, Tues, 10wks, €50 each

Melody School of Music 178E Whitehall Rd W Perrystown 12 (4650150) - also day; also w/ends Sat-Sun, 12 wks

Newpark Adult Education Centre Newtownpark Ave Blackrock (2884376) - beginners, 10 wks, €80 each

Newpark Music Centre Newtownpark Ave Blackrock (2883740) - jazz guitar, also day

Old Bawn Community School Tallaght 24 (4526137) - beginners/improvers, 10 wks

Palmerstown Community School 20 (6260116) - levels 1&2, Tues 10 wks, €60 each

People's College 32 Parnell Sq 1 (8735879) - classical, €55

Plunket College Swords Rd, Whitehall 9 (8371689) - beginners, Tues, 10 wks, €66

Pobalscoil Rosmini Adult Ed Grace Pk Rd 9 (8371015) - beginners, Mon, 7&8.30, 10 wks, €80

Ringsend Technical Institute Cambridge Rd 4 (6684498) - beginners/ improvers, 10wks, €65 each

St Finian's Community College Swords (8402623) - Mon, for beginners, €79

St Mark's Community School Cookstown Road Tallaght 24 (4519399)

St Thomas Community College Novara Ave Bray (2866111) - beginners/improvers, 10wks, €70

Tallaght Community School Balrothery 24 (4515566) - beginners / intermediate, 10 wks €45 each

Walton's New School of Music 69 Sth Gt George's St 2 (4781884) - classical, acoustic, electric, spanish/ flamenco, jazz, bass, also day, see ad page 173

GYMNASTICS

Irish Amateur Gymnastics Assoc AFAS, House of Sport Long Mile Rd 12 (4501805/4602835)

Marie Oxx Pearse College, Clogher Rd 12 (4536661) - ITEC dip in gym instruction, day

Portobello School Rere 40 Lr Dominick St 1 (8721277) - gym instruction, eve, morn

HAIRDRESSING see also Beauty Care

Ballymun Comprehensive Schools Adult Ed Centre Ballymun Rd 9 (8420654/ 8425828 night) - home, learn to shape & cut, Tue 6wk, €60

Colaiste Dhulaigh & College of Further Education Barryscourt Rd Coolock 17 (8481337) - masters dip, Tues 6.30-9.30 / 3rd & 4th yr apprentices, Mon, 2nd yr Tue, 1st yr Wed, all 9.00-2.30, each 25 wks

Crumlin College of Further Education Crumlin Rd 12 (4540662) - day release, beginners/ junior trade exam class, Mon; senior trade exam class/ advanced practical & theory, Tues; also master dip in hairdressing for qual. hairdressers (2 yrs), Mon/ barbershop techniques (Unisex), Mon; also cutting & styling (uni sex), Wed/ refresher courses in latest techniques

Hartstown Community School Clonsilla 15 (8209863) - & hair care, Weds, 10wks, €60

People's College 32 Parnell Sq 1 (8735879) - & theatrical wig, €50

Tallaght Community School Balrothery 24 (4515566) - haircutting, beginners 8 wks €45

HAND CARE (Therapeutic)

Grange Community College Grange Abbey Rd Donaghmede 13 (8471422) - hand massage with reflexology, 10 wks €66

Irish Red Cross Society 16 Merrion Sq 2 (6765135/6/7) - day, cert, 7hrs, €40

HANDBALL see Gaelic Games

HARMONICA see also Music

Walton's New School of Music 69 Sth Gt George's St 2 (4781884) - also day, see ad page 173

HARP see also Music

Bray Music Centre Florence Rd Bray (2866768)

Comhaltas Ceoltoiri Eireann 32 Belgrave Sq Monkstown (2800295)

Walton's New School of Music 69 Sth Gt George's St 2 (4781884) - also day, see ad page 173

HAUSA (West African Language)

Dublin Public Libraries Admin Hq, 138-144 Pearse St 2 (6644800) - central library Ilac Centre (8734333) or Library HQ for details (6744800), self-learning €free

HEALING see also Alternative

Abbey School of Healing Killester 5 (8310544) - bioenergy therapy, 1 yr incl 9 w/ends, €3800, cert

Acupuncture Foundation Training School Milltown Pk College (1850 577405) -

Chinese herbal medicine, postgrad training for acupuncturists, 16mth, €3800

Ballyfermot College of Further Education Ballyfermot Rd 10 (6269421) - energy healing, Wed 7-9pm, 6 wks, €45

Bi-Aura Foundation De Light House Corlurgan Bailieboro, Co Cavan (087-2317984) - bio-energy dip, 9mth, €3500, w/ends 9mths

Cocoon Reiki Centre Howth (8321255; 086 2312684) - & reiki, levels 1 & 2 mastership, 12 wks, cert

Complementary Healing Therapies 136 New Cabra Rd 7 (8681110) - w/end

Foxrock Institute Kill O' the Grange School Kill Lane Blackrock (4939506/4939629) - & well-being, 8wks, €85

Harvest Moon Centre 24 Lr Baggot St 2 (6627556)

Healing House 24 O'Connell Ave Berkeley Rd 7 (8306413) - healing course intro, Tue €195 / support group teaching healing & visualisation, Mon 8-10 €5-8 donation

Holistic Healing Centre 38 Dame St 2 (6710813)

Institute of Celtic, Shamanic Development Sacred Hoop Lodge 64 Sth William Street 2 (4577839)

Marino College 14-20 Marino Mart 3 (8332100) - holistic awareness & living 10wks, €50 each

Motions Health & Fitness Training City West Leisure Centre (4588179/ 087 2808866)

Moytura Healing Centre 2 Glenageary Rd Dun Laoghaire (2854005) - energy healing, dip, Fri, 10 wks €190

National Training Centre 16a St Joseph's Parade Off Dorset Street 7 (8827777) - neuromuscular therapy, NMT, one w/end per month, 15 mths, €3268, national qualification

Physio Extra 4 Oliver Bond St 8 (6725719) - spineright: yoga with pilates, beginner & intermediate levels; morn, day, eve

Rachel Dempsey (086 3097232) - workshops, courses: various city & co venues

Shiatsu Ireland classes Ranelagh & Leixlip/ individ treatments (6109110) - shiatsu & massage, - beginners & advanced

Shirley McClure, Meitheal (2865997) - shiatsu, also w/end, city centre & Bray

T'ai Chi Energy Centre Milltown Pk Conference Centre Sandford Rd Ranelagh 6 (4961533) - t'ai chi/qi gong - & wkend workshops

Tony Quinn Centre 66/67 Eccles St 7 (8304211)

HEALTH AND SAFETY see also Stress

DIT Faculty: Business Aungier St 2 (4023040/3445) - health, safety & security for business managers, 1 yr €590

DIT Faculty: Tourism & Food Cathal Brugha St 1 (4024349/3445) - hygiene & safety for hospitality & services industry, 1 term €166/ MSc in environmental health risk management, 2 yr €1800pa/ food safety & hygiene, jan-june (4024344)

FAS Training Centre Baldoyle 13 (8167460)

FAS Training Centre Finglas Jamestown Rd 11 (8140243)

Greendale Community School Kilbarrack 5 (8322735/6) - healt safety and risk management in the work place, Thurs 7.30 10 wks €60

Institute of Technology Tallaght 24 (4042000) - cert in safety & health at work (UCD)/ food hygiene, 8 hrs, cert

Keytrainer Ireland 33/34 Dame St 2 (6714000) - VDU risk assessment/ consultancy & training office evaluations/ tailored training

Plunket College Swords Rd, Whitehall 9 (8371689) - in the work place, legislation, risk management, safety statements, Wed, 7-9.30 €66

Ringsend Technical Institute Cambridge Rd 4 (6684498) - health safety & risk management, 10 wks €65

School of Practical Child Care Blackrock Campus Carysfort Ave Blackrock (2886994) - in the creche & playground, 1 day

Westmoreland College for Management Studies 11 Westmoreland St 2 (6795324/7266) - ICM cert in health & safety at work

HEALTH EDUCATION see also Aromatherapy / Diet / Nutrition / Personal Development / Self-Awareness / Stress

AAA Counselling Dr MJ Brennan PhD c/o 48 Connaught St Phibsboro 7 (8380014) - overcoming obesity

Alexander Technique Postural Re-education Frank Kennedy 35 Callary Rd Mt Merrion (2882446) - alexander technique/ stress management - also day

Cocoon Reiki Centre Howth (8321255; 086 2312684) - reiki & healing, cert

Coolmine Community School Clonsilla 15 (8214583) - FETAC cert in health & social care

Health Promotion Unit Dept of Health Hawkins House 2 (6354000) - info, booklets, leaflets

Holistic Healing Centre 38 Dame St 2 (6710813)

Holy Family Community School Rathcoole (4580766)

Irish College of Traditional Chinese Medicine, Dublin (01-4967830) - licentiate in traditional Chinese medicine, 3 yrs, p/time course; also Chinese herbal medicine, post-grad, p/time courses

Irish T'ai Chi Ch'uan Assoc c/o St Andrew's Resource Centre 114 Pearse St 2 (6771930) - energy development, 2nd Sunday monthly

Kilroy's College 25 Kingram Place 2 (1850 700700) - tutor supported home study: diet, fitness & health, dip

KLEAR Grange Park View Kilbarrack 5 (8671845) - health awareness, day

Margaret Macken Stephen's Gr/Adelaide Rd/Clontarf (8332954) - Iyengar Yoga, 6 wk course; also relaxation, stress management and meditation

Motions Health & Fitness Training City West Leisure Centre (4588179/ 087 2808866)

National Training Centre 16a St Joseph's Parade Off Dorset Street 7 (8827777) - bodywork & movement therapies, advanced movement techniques, one w/end every 2 mths, 2 yrs, €6,350, advanced dip

NTC 16a St Joseph's Parade 7 (8827777) - exercise & health studies & personal traning, 18-20 wks, nat qual; day & eve

Pearse College Clogher Rd 12 (4536661/4541544) - holistic health, day

T'ai Chi Energy Centre Milltown Pk Conference Centre Sandford Rd Ranelagh 6 (4961533) - t'ai chi/qi gong - & wkend workshops

Taney Parish Centre Taney Rd Dundrum 14 (2985491) - voluntary stroke scheme, Weds (4941052)/ League of Health Mon, Wed, Fri: 0404-664231/ day only

The Open University Enquiry & Advice Centre Holbrook House, Holles St 2 (6785399) - & social welfare

Time Out (4591038) - also wkend

Trinity College 2 (6772941) - (6082182) - health informatics, 1yr postgrad dip, 24wks/MSc, 1 further yr, 24wk; also Sat

Trinity College 2 (6772941) - (6081588) understanding & facilitating communication in the adult stroke patient

Westmoreland College for Management Studies 11 Westmoreland St 2 (6795324/7266) - ICM dip health services management/ICM health & safety at work

HEALTH FOOD & COOKERY

Dun Laoghaire College of Further Education 17 Cumberland St Dun Laoghaire (2809676) - health & alternative nutrition therapy/ Irish eating plan, 10 wks, Wed, 7.30-9.30pm, €100

Ringsend Technical Institute Cambridge Rd 4 (6684498) - food hygiene 1, 6.30 10 wks €65, cert/ level 2, 7pm 10 wks €120, cert in HACCP principles/ level 3, 7pm 20 wks €240

Time Out (4591038) - also wkend

HEBREW

Dublin Public Libraries Admin Hq, 138-144 Pearse St 2 (6644800) - central library Ilac Centre (8734333) or Library HQ for details (6744800), self-learning €free

Sandford Language Institute Milltown Pk Sandford Rd 6 (2601296) - modern and biblical, all levels, each 14 wks, €250

Sth Dublin Co Libraries Languages & Computers: Ballyroan/ Clondalkin/ Castletymon, Lucan & Co Library (4597834-admin only) - self learning

HERBALISM

Lucan Community College Esker Drive (6282077) - 10wk, €79

HERITAGE STUDIES

Saor-Ollscoil na hEireann 55 Prussia St 7 (8683368) - heritage studies, celtic studies, BA in the Liberal Arts

HIKING & HILL WALKING

An Oige 61 Mountjoy Street 7 (8304555)

Colaiste Dhulaigh Barryscourt Rd Coolock 17 (8481337) - skills & theory, Mon 7-8.15 & Sat 10-2.00, 3/4 wks

Corporate Club 24 Elmcastle Green Kilnamanagh 24 (4610935)

Network Sports & Social Club 24 Elmcastle Green Kilnamanagh 24 (4524415)

Time Out (4591038) - also wkend

HINDI

Dublin Public Libraries Admin Hq, 138-144 Pearse St 2 (6644800) - central library Ilac Centre (8734333) or Library HQ for details (6744800), self-learning €free

Sth Dublin Co Libraries Languages & Computers: Ballyroan/Clondalkin/ Castletymon, Lucan & Co Library (4597834-admin only) - self learning

HIP HOP see MODERN DANCE / Dance

HISTORY see also Archaeology / Architecture / Art / Classical

Adult Education Centre Adult Ed Centre Ballymun Rd 9 (8420654/ 8425828 night) - early man to modern dy politics, with jnr cert option, 30wk, €free/ UCD courses (7068097), 10 wks

All Hallows college Gracepark Rd Drumcondra 9 (8373745) - church history 1&2, Wed 6.50 24 wks, €350; ECTS credits option

Ballsbridge College of Business Studies Shelbourne Rd 4 (6684806) - monarchies of Britain, Mon, 6pm 10 wks €65

Colaiste Dhulaigh Barryscourt Rd Coolock 17 (8481337) - Mon 7.00-9.00 / history & heritage explored, day Thurs 10am, 25wks, FETAC cert optional/ Junior cert, 20 wks/ Leaving cert (O+H), 20 wks

Colaiste Eanna Kilkieran Rd Cabra 7 (8389577) - birth of a nation, 1860-1960, Thurs 10 wks 7-9/ Europe in crisis, 1860-1950 [Jan 2004]

Kilroy's College 25 Kingram Place 2 (1850 700700) - tutor supported home study: leaving cert

KLEAR Grange Park View Kilbarrack 5 (8671845) - leaving cert, day only/ understanding history/ decades of Irish history; day

Old Dublin Society The Secretary c/o City Assembly Hse 58 Sth William St 2 (6794260) - lectures, visits, tours

Plunket College Swords Rd, Whitehall 9 (8371689) - junior cert, 25 wks/ leaving cert, 27 wks, €143

Pobalscoil Neasain Baldoyle 13 (8063092) - UCD course: history makers of the 20th century, Mon 10 wks, day

Royal Soc of Antiquaries of Ireland 63 Merrion Sq 2 (6761749) - individual lectures, outings, talks

Saor-Ollscoil na hEireann 55 Prussia St 7 (8683368) - BA, Irish History Local & Maritime

Southside Adult Literacy Scheme 3 Ashgrove Tce Dundrum 14 (2964321) - range of basic one-to-one up to leaving cert courses incl. FETAC cert foundation & level 1

Trinity College 2 (6772941) - (6081791) the renaissance in Italy, 9 wks, €60

UCD Adult Education Office (7061695) - history of the Arab-Israeli conflict/ the world of Islam/ USA in 2oth century / Russia under the Czars/ History Makers of the 20th century/ the First World War 1 − each 10 wks

HISTORY, LOCAL

Colaiste Eanna College of Business & Technical Stu Kilkieran Rd Cabra 7 (8389577) -day (tel 8688342/8389577)

Department of Adult & Community Education NUI Maynooth (7084500) - NUI cert; also at Malahide (8460949)

Malahide Community School Malahide (8460949) - NUI Maynooth cert, 25 wks, eve €760

People's College 32 Parnell Sq 1 (8735879)

St Thomas Community College Novara Ave Bray (2866111) - discover co Wicklow, 10 wks €70/ 30 wks FETAC cert, €200

UCD Adult Education Office (7061695) - hist of Dublin via walks & talks: each 10 wks

HOCKEY

Irish Hockey Association 6a Woodbine Pk Blackrock (2600028)

Women's Morning Hockey Rathfarnham 14 (2835296) - Thurs am

HOLISTIC MEDICINE - Healing

Rathmines Snr College Town Hall 6 (4975334) - lifestyle: aromatherapy, stress management, reflexology, yoga & shiatsu, indian head massage: Wed 10 wks, €65

Walmer College & Holistic Centre First Floor, Raheny SC Howth Rd 5 (8475410/338) - holistic studies, ITEC dip

HOMOEOPATHY

Balbriggan Community College Pine Ridge Chapel St (8412388/9) - how it works, how to use it, Thurs, 7.30-9.60, 8 wks, 73

Dun Laoghaire College of Further Education 17 Cumberland St Dun Laoghaire (2809676) - in the home, Wed 7-9.30 10 wks €115

Hartstown Community School Clonsilla 15 (8209863) - Tues, 6wks, €40

Pobalscoil Neasain Baldoyle 13 (8063092) - Mon, 7.30 10 wks €85

The Irish School of Homoeopathy Milltown Pk College Ranelagh 6 (8682581) - Practitioner's 4yr course part-time weekends/ 1 wkend workshop -Introductory, €130/ Short Course -6 wkends 'The Power of Homoeopathy' - commencing Autumn €650

HORSE CARE / EQUESTRIAN

FAS Training Centre Ballyfermot 10 (6055900/ 5933) - riding school instructor, day; Finglas 11 (8140243) - instructors & grooms, day

National Training Centre 16a St Joseph's Parade Off Dorset Street 7 (8827777) - equine massage, various, 150 hrs, €2,030, national qualification

Old Bawn Community School Tallaght 24 (4526137) - cert/dip in Equine Science, distance learning programme from International Equine Inst. UL (apply 061-202430)

HORSE RIDING

Brennanstown Riding School Hollybrook Kilmacanogue Bray (2863778)

Broadmeadows Equestrian Centre Bullstown, Ashbourne Co Meath (8352823)

Callaighstown Riding Centre Rathcoole (4588322) - also day/ holiday courses/ BHS exams

Corporate Club 24 Elmcastle Green Kilnamanagh 24 (4610935)

Killegar Stables The Scalp Enniskerry (2860919)

Network Sports & Social Club 24 Elmcastle Green Kilnamanagh 24 (4524415)

Thornton Pk Equestrian Centre Thornton Killsallaghan (8351164) - beginners & advanced/c. 25 mins from city centre/in & outdoor arenas/group concessions

HORTICULTURE see also Gardening

Dublin School of Horticulture 28 Spencer Villas Dun Laoghaire (2148469) - RHS general & advanced cert, 4 yrs

FAS Training Centre Baldoyle 13 (8167460)

Kilroy's College 25 Kingram Place 2 (1850 700700) - tutor supported home study: gardening, dip

Kylemore College Kylemore Rd 10 (6265901) - practical, Tue 10 wks 10.30-1pm

Pearse College Clogher Rd 12 (4536661/4541544) - amenity horticulture, day

Portmarnock Community School Carrickhill Rd (8038056) - introduction to, Thurs 7.30, 8 wks €50

Trinity College 2 (6772941) - (6081274) - extra mural, plants & gardens 2003, 8wks, €70

HOSPITAL AND HEALTH SERVICES ADMINISTRATION

Westmoreland College for Management Studies 11 Westmoreland St 2 (6795324/7266) - ICM dip health services management/ICM cert health & safety at work

HOSPITALITY MANAGEMENT

DIT Faculty: Tourism & Food Cathal Brugha St 1 (4024349/3445) - hospitality & services management, 2 yrs €800pa, cert/ management principles level 1 & 2, 1 term, €166 each/ MSc in hospit managment, 2 yr €1645pa / revenue management, 12 wks €256

Griffith College Dublin Sth Circular Rd 8 (4150400) - BA in International Hospitality management, 3 yr NTU f/time/ Dip in travel & hospitality, ABE cert

Institute of Technology Tallaght 24 (4042000) - supervisory hospitality industry, 1 yr, cert/ national cert in hospitality operations & supervision, 2 yrs p/time, cert

HOSTELLING

An Oige 61 Mountjoy Street 7 (8304555)

HOTEL AND CATERING

DIT Faculty: Tourism & Food Cathal Brugha St 1 (4024349/3445) - hotel

management (IHCI), 3 yr 1 day wkly, €800pa/ dip hotel & catering management, 3 yrs €800pa/
Portobello School Rere 40 Lr Dominick St 1 (8721277) - full time course

HOTEL MANAGEMENT
American College Dublin 2 Merrion Sq 2 (6768939) - modular, €470 per module
Griffith College Dublin Sth Circular Rd 8 (4150400) - BA in International Hospitality management, 3 yr NTU f/time/ Dip in travel & hospitality, ABE cert

HOUSE FURNISHINGS & CRAFTS see Crafts / DIY
Kylemore College Kylemore Rd 10 (6265901) - decorating & improvement, 12 wks day

HOUSE MAINTENANCE & IMPROVEMENTS Building Construction / DIY / Interior Design / Plumbing
FAS Training Centre Tallaght 24 (4045284) - building maintenance, 10wk
Newpark Adult Education Centre Newtownpark Ave Blackrock (2884376) - DIY, 10wks, €99

HUMAN DEVELOPMENT
AAA Counselling Dr MJ Brennan PhD c/o 48 Connaught St Phibsboro 7 (8380014) - relationship harmonisation, also day

HUMAN RELATIONS / BEHAVIOUR Communications / Industrial Relations / Psychology
HUMAN RESOURCES see Personnell / Management
HUMANITY STUDIES
Oscail - National Distance Education Centre DCU 9 (7005481) - dip in Arts (Humanities), 2-3 years, awarded by one of 6 participating Irish Universities, distance learning

HUNGARIAN
Dublin Public Libraries Admin Hq, 138-144 Pearse St 2 (6644800) - central library Ilac Centre (8734333) or Library HQ for details (6744800), self-learning €free
Sandford Language Institute Milltown Pk Sandford Rd 6 (2601296) - all levels, 14 wks, €250

HURLING see Gaelic Games
HYPNOSIS see also Hypnotherapy
Holistic Sourcing Centre 67 Lr Camden St 2 (4785022) - self-hypnosis, intensive 1 day (086 2959678)

HYPNOTHERAPY
IICH Education (Irish Institute of Counselling & Hypnotherapy) 118 Stillorgan Road 4 (2600118) - 3-day foundation skills course, €245. Thought Field Therapy (Algorithms Levels I &II), Applied Behavioural Medicine/ Health Crisis Counselling. Classes at Milltown Pk, 6 and other south-city locations
Institute of Clinical Hypnotherapy & Psychotherapy Therapy Hse 6 Tuckey St Cork (021-4273575) - theory dip by correspondence, advanced practical dip/workshops in Dublin & Cork - prospectus & demo cassette free
Newpark Adult & Continuing Education Centre Newtownpark Ave Blackrock (2884376) - intro to, Mon, €99
St Thomas Community College Novara Ave Bray (2866111) - 10 wks €70

ICELANDIC

Dublin Public Libraries Admin Hq, 138-144 Pearse St 2 (6644800) - central library
Ilac Centre, (8734333) or Library HQ for details (6744800), self-learning €free
Sth Dublin Co Libraries Languages & Computers: Ballyroan/Clondalkin/
Castletymon, Lucan & Co Library (4597834-admin only) - self learning

ILLUSTRATION see Sketching

INCOME TAX see PAYE

INDONESIAN

Dublin Public Libraries Admin Hq, 138-144 Pearse St 2 (6644800) - central library
Ilac Centre (8734333) or Library HQ for details (6744800), self-learning €free
Sth Dublin Co Libraries Languages & Computers: Ballyroan/Clondalkin/
Castletymon, Lucan & Co Library (4597834-admin only) - self learning

INDUSTRIAL ENGINEERING

Institute of Technology Tallaght 24 (4042000) - dip

INDUSTRIAL RELATIONS

Campaign Against Bullying 72 Lakelands Ave Stillorgan (2887976) - anti-bullying courses in workplace/school

Lucan Community College Esker Drive (6282077) - & HRM, 8wk, €73

Malahide Community School Malahide (8460949) - employer relations & management NCI dip, 2yrs

National College of Ireland Mayor St IFSC 1 (4060500/ 1850 221721) - BA in Industrial Relations & Personnel Management, HETAC, 4 yrs, 2 eve wkly

INDUSTRIAL SAFETY see Health & Safety

INFORMATION CENTRES See also Community / Consumer / Library

Youth Info Centres - info on youth activities: education, training, jobs, rights & entitlements, travel sport & leisure: Main St, Blanchardstown (8212077) Monastery Rd, Clondalkin (4594666) Bell Tower, Dun Laoghaire (2809363); Main Rd, Tallaght

INFORMATION TECHNOLOGY / IT see also Computers

ABM Computer Training 54 North St, Swords (8902348) - all yr, also day, Sats

Ashfield Computer Training Main St Templeogue 6W (4926708) - Ms - MCP, MCSA, MCSE / CompTia - A+, Network+, security+, Linux+, Server+/ Linux-linux+, SAIR 1, 2, 3/ Cisco - CCNA, CCNP/ Citrix- CCA/ CIW - webmaster track/ Oracle - OCP

Business Computer Training Institute Central Dublin (6616838 LoCall 1890 564039) - dip in information technology, 48 wks, €2245

CITAS Computer & IT Training 54 Middle Abbey St 1 (8782212) - diploma in IT,

1 yr f/time €2000

DIT Faculty: Science Kevin St 8 (4024585/3445) - BSc in IT, 3 yr dip + 2 yr BSc:€313 per module

DIT Faculty: Tourism & Food Cathal Brugha St 1 (4024349/3445) - for the hospitality industry levels 1 & 2, 1 term €166 each

Dublin Business School 13/14 Aungier St 2 (4177500) - dip in IT, 1 eve per wk, 1 yr/14 wks/ JEB teachers dip in IT, 2 eves - 10 wks, both 6.30-9.30pm/ graduate dip in business studies/ IT, 2 eves per wk plus some Sats, 6.15-9.30pm, 16 mths/ / dip in web design, 1 eve a wk, 10 wks. / advanced dip in PC aplications, 1 eve wk, 1 yr 6.30-9.30

Dublin City University Registry office Glasnevin 9 (7005338)

Eden Computer Training Rathfarnham 16, or MACRO Centre, 1 Green St 7 (4953155) - JEB teacher's dip; word, excel, powerpoint, access, mcse, mcsa, A+, network+ beginners to advanced

FAS Training Centre Ballyfermot 10 (6055900/ 5933)

Institute of Technology, Blanchardstown Blanchardstown Road North 15 (8851100) - IT & business interdisciplinary studies HETAC cert: modules - business management; human resource management; psychology; operating systems; softward development; networking & maths - from 240 to 485 per module/

Irish Academy of Computer Training 98 St Stephen's Grn 2 (4347600) - computer appreciation cert/ word processing; spreadsheets; €275 cert ea/ databases €645 cert/ programming €795 cert/ operating systems; networking; graphics; dtp; presentation tools; new technologies: cert each/ also day

Kilroy's College 25 Kingram Place 2 (1850 700700) - tutor supported home study: PC repair, assembly & A+, ECDL, MOUS, networking, visual basic 6.0

Moresoft Computers Ltd 44 Lr Lesson St 2 (6621711) - ebci IT cert & E-cert, 10 wks €550 each

National College of Ireland Mayor St IFSC 1 (4060500/ 1850 221721) - BSc in Software Systems, 4 yrs eves & Sats/NCI Dip in eCommerce, 12 wks/Grad Dip in eLearning, 1 yr

Oscail - National Distance Education Centre DCU 9 (7005481) - dip in IT, 2-3 years, awarded by DCU, distance learning

Plunket College Swords Rd, Whitehall 9 (8371689) - FETAC info tech, levels 1&2, 20 wks, 7pm, €133 per subject

School of Computer Technology 21 Rosmeen Gdns Dun Laoghaire (2844045) - unix/linux LPI cert, €825/ java; C++; visual basic: C&G certs/ SQL; perl; PHP; website design: all 36 hrs, €750 ea/ also day/ dip in networking C&G cert 4 wks €1600 day

Senior College Dun Laoghaire CFE Eblana Ave Dun Laoghaire (2800385) - teacher's dip in IT skills, JEB 25wks, €500/ single subject €150

The Open University Enquiry & Advice Centre Holbrook House, Holles St 2 (6785399)

Trinity College 2 (6772941) - (6081039/1072) - info systems, dip, 2yr, 22wks/BSc hons 4yr, 22wks per yr/ in Education, MSc, 2 yrs, 24 wks per yr (6082182)

Whitehall College of Further Education Swords Rd 9 (8376011) - PC specialist

PART-TIME COURSES

At National College of Ireland we realise that lifelong learning for career progression is vital. You probably do too. We realise that life is for learning and for living. We offer a range of full-time and part-time courses at National Certificate, National Diploma Degree, Postgraduate, Masters and Doctorate levels in:

- **Business Studies**
- **Management**
- **Financial Services**
- **eCommerce**
- **Business Law**
- **Human Resource Management**
- **Software Systems**
- **eLearning**
- **Maritime Management**
- **Enterprise Studies**

Why choose National College of Ireland?

You will enjoy small interactive classes and a unique supportive learning environment. *You* can choose from a range of courses at a time, place and pace that suit you. *You* will learn from highly qualified, experienced lecturers who are business practitioners.
You will benefit from leading-edge I.T. facilities and the excellent gym, creche, library and restaurant at our IFSC campus.

1850 221 721

National College of Ireland, Mayor St, IFSC, Dublin 1

National College of Ireland

LIVE+LEARN
www.LIVEanDLEarn.ie

training/ internet skills/ desktop publishing/ software systems business info systems - day

INSTRUCTOR TRAINING see also Teachers Courses

Fingall Sailing School Malahide (8451979)

Irish Academy of Computer Training 98 St Stephen's Grn 2 (4347600) - train the trainer, cert / also day

Litton Lane Studios PO Box 123 Greystones Co Wicklow (8728044) - leisure & recreational studies, NCEF Instructor courses, venue DCU - 30 wks, 2 eves per week, all courses begin mid Sept

Motions Health Centre City West Leisure Centre (4588179/ 087 2808866) - fitness instructor training course (NCEF), Fri 7-10pm, Sat 9-4pm, starts 3 Oct

National College of Exercise & Health Studies 16a St Joseph's Parade Dorset St 7 (8827777) - spin cycle, national qual.in Spincycle, 1 day / pilates, national qual, 18 wks, €1640/ Gym instruction Nat Qual, 18 wks, €1640 - all p/time

NTC 16a St Joseph's Parade 7 (8827777) - aqua fitness, w/ends, instructors only/ personal trainers, advanced dip, also day - nat qual

INSURANCE

DIT Faculty: Business Aungier St 2 (4023040/3445) - BBS (Insurance), 4 yrs €1350 pa

Pearse College Clogher Rd 12 (4536661/4541544) - insurance business & computrer studies, day, 1 yr, FETAC/Insurance Inst of Ireland

Plunket College Swords Rd, Whitehall 9 (8371689) - insurance foundation, In Inst of I cert, 25 wks, Tues €159

INTERIOR DESIGN & DECOR

Ashfield College Main St Templeogue 6W (4900866) - prelim/improvers, 7.30-9.30, 8 wks / Ass0ciate dip 1 yr p/time, from Oct

Ballsbridge College of Business Studies Shelbourne Rd 4 (6684806) - Mon & Thurs, 10 wks, 7pm €75

Ballyfermot College of Further Education Ballyfermot Rd 10 (6269421) - 10 wks, Mon, 7-9pm, €65

Ballymun Comprehensive Schools Adult Ed Centre Ballymun Rd 9 (8420654/ 8425828 night) - Mon 10wk, €80

Cabinteely Community School Johnstown Rd 18 (2857455) - 10wk, €75

Colaiste Dhulaigh Barryscourt Rd Coolock 17 (8481337) - Tues, 8 wks, 7.30-9.30

Colour Connections 4 (087 6288582) - short courses

Coolmine Community School Clonsilla 15 (8214583) - 9 wks, Wed €60

Crumlin College of Further Education Crumlin Rd 12 (4540662) - Limperts Academy Dip, Mon 6.45-9.45 25 wks

DATE College of Further Education Dundrum 14 (2964322) - 10 wks €66 day

Donahies Community School Streamville Rd 13 (8482217) - for your home, Tues, 10 wks, €55/ Limperts Academy Dip, Wed 7.30-10pm, 30 wks €1100

Dublin Institute of Design 25 Sufflok St 2 (6790286) - your designer home, 8 wks, €340; also morn/ Rhodec dip, 2-yr, €2300; also day/ Rhodec Assoc dip, 15 or 25 wks, €1100; also day/ retail interiors, cert 25 wks, €1100 / cert in AutoCad 2D design, 12 wks, €550

FAS Training Centre Baldoyle 13 (8167460)

FAS Training Centre Finglas Jamestown Rd 11 (8140243)

Foxrock Institute Kill O' the Grange School Kill Lane Blackrock (4939506/4939629) - 8wks, €85

Greendale Community School Kilbarrack 5 (8322735/6) - general introduction & assignments, Thurs, 10 wks €55

Greenhills College Limekiln Ave Walkinstown 12 (4507779/4507138) - 8wks, €73

Griffith College Dublin Sth Circular Rd 8 (4150400) - B DES & Dip in design & interior architecture, 3 yrs each, HETAC, f/time / Nat Dip, HETAC 3 yr f/time/ dip in interior design, 2 yrs, GCD dip, f/t, Mon to Fri; also 2 eves per wk

Hartstown Community School Clonsilla 15 (8209863) - 8wks, €60

Holy Family Community School Rathcoole (4580766)

Killester College of Further Education Collins Ave 5 (8337686) - intro to, Tues 7-9, 10 wks €75; Mon morn 10-12, 10 wks €85

Malahide Community School Malahide (8460949) - introductory, 10 wks €75

Marino College 14-20 Marino Mart 3 (8332100) - Thurs, 10wks, €50/ founddationi, dip, 1 yr €132

National College of Interior Design & Art 18 Butterfield Ave Rathfarnham 14 (4943303) - foundation course, 8 wks, €160/ cert in interior design, 22 wks, €1,050/ dip in interior architecture & design & fine arts, 50 wks, €1990, day/ european decor, French res holiday, 1 wk €365

Newpark Adult Education Centre Newtownpark Ave Blackrock (2884376) - 10wks,

€120,Mon & Tue 7.30

Old Bawn Community School Tallaght 24 (4526137) - Thurs, 7.30-9.30pm, 10 wks/ Limpert's Academp dip, 1 yr Tue

Palmerstown Community School 20 (6260116) - Thurs 7-9pm, 10wks €65

Phil McNally Portmarnock (8462259) - foundation

Plunket College Swords Rd, Whitehall 9 (8371689) - intro, Tues, 10 wks, €66/ Limperts Academy of Design Dipl, Tue 7-10pm, 30 wks €775

Pobalscoil Rosmini Adult Ed Grace Pk Rd 9 (8371015) - Wed, 7.30-9.30pm, 10 wks, €95

Portobello School Rere 40 Lr Dominick St 1 (8721277) - foundation cert, c&g, part time eve

Rathmines Snr College Town Hall 6 (4975334) - Mon, 10 wks, €65

RAVE Good Shepherd School Churchtown 14 (2981052) - practical, 10 wks 7.30 €79

Senior College Dun Laoghaire CFE Eblana Ave Dun Laoghaire (2800385) - cert in interior design, C&G RAFA, 25 wks, €400

St Finian's Community College Swords (8402623) - household, Mon €79

St Kevins College Clogher Rd Crumlin 12 (4536397) - 10wks

St MacDara's Community College Wellington Lane Templeogue 6W (4566216) - intro, Tue, 7.30-9.30pm, 10 wks, €76

St Mark's Community School Cookstown Road Tallaght 24 (4519399)

St Thomas Community College Novara Ave Bray (2866111) - intro to home interior design C&G/ Regent Academy FA, 1 yr €500

St Tiernan's Community School Parkvale Balally 16 (2953224) - colour, space, light, practical, Wed 7.30-9.30 10 wks, €70

INTERNATIONAL TRADE & MARKETING

American College Dublin 2 Merrion Sq 2 (6768939) - BA in International Business

Colaiste Dhulaigh Barryscourt Rd Coolock 17 (8481337) - dip in international trade & e-Business, 22 wks, Mon & Tues, 6.45-9.15

Dublin City University Registry office Glasnevin 9 (7005338) - international business & marketing/French, German, Spanish, Japanese

electronic Business School of Ireland (094-81444) - elearning course

Institute of International Trade of Ireland 28 Merrion Square 2 (6612182) - prof. dip in Global Trade & e-Business/ documentary credit compliance, 1 day/ customs obligations, 2 day; various locations

Pearse College Clogher Rd 12 (4536661/4541544) - & business studies, day

UCD Adult Education Office (7061695) - & export practice, 12 wks

Westmoreland College for Management Studies 11 Westmoreland St 2 (6795324/7266) - ICM dip marketing, advertising & PR

INTERNET & E-MAIL see also Computers, Introduction to

ABM Computer Training 54 North St, Swords (8902348) - intro to internet, web design, all yr, also day, Sats

Adelaide Computers 14 Pembroke Lane Ballsbridge 4 (2696213) -& web design, one-to-one training at youroffice/home or our offices, small groups, beginners to advanced, full training programmes also

Ashfield Computer Training Main St Templeogue 6W (4926708) - intro to effective web page, CIW

Ballsbridge College of Business Studies Shelbourne Rd 4 (6684806) - beginners, Thurs, 6 & 7.45, 10 wks, €100

Blackrock College (2888681) - with word processing, 7.30-9, 6 wks €65

Cabinteely Community School Johnstown Rd 18 (2857455) - 7-8.25, 10wks €95

Colaiste Dhulaigh Barryscourt Rd Coolock 17 (8481337) - for beginners, Mon 6.15-7.45, 10 wks

Colaiste Eanna College of Business & Technical Stu Kilkieran Rd Cabra 7 (8389577) - set-up, 10wks, Tue 7-9pm

Colaiste Ide Cardiffsbridge Rd Finglas West 11 (8342333) - skills for beginners, Tue, 7.30 5 wks €50

College of Further Education Main St Dundrum 14 (2951376) - intro to, 8 wks, €99

Computeach Computer Centre AXIS, Main St Ballymun 9 (8832167)

Connolly House Nth Strand (by 5 Lamps) 1 (8557116) - introduction to, 10 wks Wed, 8pm €81

DIT Faculty: Business Aungier St 2 (4023040/3445) - 10 wks course [start Oct/Jan/March], €240

Donahies Community School Streamville Rd 13 (8482217) - beginners welcome, Tues/Wed, 10 wks 7.30, €100

Dorset College 64a Lr Dorset St/ 8 Belvedere Pl 1 (8309677) - c&g e-Quals cert

Dublin Public Libraries Admin Hq, 138-144 Pearse St 2 (6644800) - public access to internet facilities in city branch libraries, free, booking essential; contact your local branch library

Dun Laoghaire-Rathdown Co Council Public Library Service () - free internet & email access: the library at: Blackrock (2888117), Cabinteely (2855363), Dalkey (2855277), Deansgrange (2850860), Dun Laoghaire (2801147), Dundrum (2985000), Sallynoggin (2850127), Shankill (2823081), Stillorgan (2889655)

Eden Computer Training Rathfarnham 16, or MACRO Centre, 1 Green St 7

(4953155) - beginners/ advanced incl. web design/ maintenance - front page & dreamweaver

FAS Training Centre Baldoyle 13 (8167460)

Inchicore College of Further Education Emmet Rd 8 (4535358) - intro, wks, Mon

Irish Academy of Computer Training 98 St Stephen's Grn 2 (4347600) - intro to internet & html; frontpage & html; website development; using frontpage: ea 6 wks €645, cert/ ms publisher 8 wks €695 cert/ visual basic 8 wks €795/ java primer, 10 wks €795/ java 10 wks €1295; IACT webmaster 12 wks €1995 dip/ ecommerce &

Keytrainer Ireland 33/34 Dame St 2 (6714000) - tailored & scheduled training on Internet & web design

Kilroy's College 25 Kingram Place 2 (1850 700700) - tutor supported home study: computer basics, ECDL (incl internet & email); i.Net+

Kylemore College Kylemore Rd 10 (6265901) - internet, email, powerpoint, file management, 10 wks Mon 7-9pm

Newpark Adult & Continuing Education Centre Newtownpark Ave Blackrock (2884376) - Tue, 10 wks €130

Old Bawn Community School Tallaght 24 (4526137) - introduction to, 5 wks

Oscail - National Distance Education Centre DCU 9 (7005481) - Internet Systems, graduate dip, 1-2 yrs; MSc Internet Systems, 2-3 yrs; awarded by DCU

Pearse College Clogher Rd 12 (4536661/4541544) - e-Business (dip)

Pitman Training Centre 6-8 Wicklow St 2 (6768008) - 10 hrs €195, cert; day eve Sats

Pobalscoil Neasain Baldoyle 13 (8063092) - getting to know, morns, 10 wks €120

Ringsend Technical Institute Cambridge Rd 4 (6684498) - intro, 10wks, €95

South Dublin Co Libraries Languages & Computers: Ballyroan/Clondalkin/ Castletymon, Lucan & Co Library (4597834-admin only) - €free internet & email access, Ballyroan Library (4941900), Lucan Library (6216422), Castletymon Library (4524888), Clondalkin Library (4593315), County Library (4620073)

St Mark's Community School Cookstown Road Tallaght 24 (4519399)

Stillorgan College of Further Education Old Road Stillorgan (2880704) - intro, Mon, 7.30-9.30pm, 6 wks, €75

The Open University Enquiry & Advice Centre Holbrook House, Holles St 2 (6785399)

INTERVIEWING / INTERVIEWS

AAA Counselling Dr MJ Brennan PhD c/o 48 Connaught St Phibsboro 7 (8380014) - interview skills, also day

Colour & Image Professionals 2 Terenure Rd Nth 6W (4905751) - techniques, CV prep, personal presentation, one-to-one

Communication & Personal Development 30/31 Wicklow St 2 (6713636/6613225)

Eden Computer Training Rathfarnham 16, or MACRO Centre, 1 Green St 7 (4953155) - interviewing techniques, cv prep, job seeking skills

Kilroy's College 25 Kingram Place 2 (1850 700700) - home-study dip course

Leinster School of Music & Drama Griffith College Campus South Circular Rd 8 (4150467) - interview preparation

MD Communications 38 Spireview Lane off Rathgar Rd 6 (4975866)

INVESTMENT see MONEY / STOCK / FINANCE
IRISH (All levels) Basic / Leaving Cert / Languages

Balbriggan Community College Pine Ridge Chapel St (8412388/9) - beginners, pronounciation, oral, Tues, 7-9pm, 8wks, €73

Ballymun Comprehensive Schools Adult Ed Centre Ballymun Rd 9 (8420654/8425828 night) - beginners Tue, 10wk, €60

Colaiste Dhulaigh Barryscourt Rd Coolock 17 (8481337) - Leaving cert (foundation/O), Mon, 20 wks/ for beginners, Mon, 10 wks, 7.15-9.15

Colaiste Eanna College of Business & Technical Stu Kilkieran Rd Cabra 7 (8389577) - conversation, 10 wks Thurs 7-9pm

College of Further Education Main St Dundrum 14 (2951376) - beginners. spoken, Tue

Comhaltas Ceoltoiri Eireann 32 Belgrave Sq Monkstown (2800295) - conversation

Conradh na Gaeilge 6 Sr Fhearchair (Harcourt St) BAC 2 (4757401) - for adults, Tues/Wed/Thurs, 7 levels; Leaving Cert classes on Mon - all classes commence last wk Sept until April

DATE College of Further Education Dundrum 14 (2964322) - beginners/improvers, day €66

Dublin Public Libraries Admin Hq, 138-144 Pearse St 2 (6644800) - central library Ilac Centre (8734333) or Library HQ for details (6744800), self-learning €free

Dun Laoghaire College of Further Education 17 Cumberland St Dun Laoghaire (2809676) - beginners, Tue, 10 wks, 7-9pm, €100

Dun Laoghaire-Rathdown Co Council Public Library Service () - Deansgrange lib, Clonkeen Dr (2850860) - Ir/Eng - informal sessions, Tues 10.30-12 morn

Gael Linn 35 Dame St 2 (6751200) - classes held @ Tri-D Cafe, 3 Dawson St

Greenhills College Limekiln Ave Walkinstown 12 (4507779/4507138) - beginners only, 10 wks, €79 / conversation, Tue, 10wks, €79

Hartstown Community School Clonsilla 15 (8209863) - beginners, 10wks, €60

Institute of Technology Tallaght 24 (4042000) - advanced level only

Killester College of Further Education Collins Ave 5 (8337686) - Mon 7.30-9, 10 wks 60

Kilroy's College 25 Kingram Place 2 (1850 700700) - tutor supported home study: junior cert, leaving cert

Kilternan Adult Education Group Glencullen Rd Kilternan 18 (2952050)

KLEAR Grange Park View Kilbarrack 5 (8671845) - conversation - beginners, improvers, advanced, day only

Liberties College Bull Alley St 8 (4540044) - Ciorcal Gaeilge, Wed 7.30-9, €50

Marino College 14-20 Marino Mart 3 (8332100) - language, 10-20 wks, €50

Maynooth College Language Centre NUI Maynooth Co Kildare (7083737) - 9wk, €110

Newpark Adult & Continuing Education Centre Newtownpark Ave Blackrock (2884376) - for absolute beginners, 10 wks, €90

Old Bawn Community School Tallaght 24 (4526137) - basic conversation, Thurs, 10 wks

Palmerstown Community School 20 (6260116) - for everyone, Tues 8.15, 10 wks €60

People's College 32 Parnell Sq 1 (8735879) - €45

Plunket College Swords Rd, Whitehall 9 (8371689) - leaving cert, 27 wks, €215

Pobalscoil Rosmini Adult Ed Grace Pk Rd 9 (8371015) - adult beginners, Tue, 10 wks, €80

Sandford Language Institute Milltown Pk Sandford Rd 6 (2601296) - all levels, 14 wks, €250/ Irish for foreigners, 14 wks, €250

Saor-Ollscoil na hEireann 55 Prussia St 7 (8683368) - BA, Mon

St Thomas Community College Novara Ave Bray (2866111) - re-discover Irish, 10 wks, €70

Sth Dublin Co Libraries Languages & Computers: Ballyroan/Clondalkin/ Castletymon, Lucan & Co Library (4597834-admin only) - self learning

Sult Teoranta (086 1594140) - 6 levels, 20 wks each €190

TARGET St Kevin's School Newbrook Rd, Donaghmede 13 (8671967) - conversation beginners, improvers, day only, CDVEC

UCD Adult Education Office (7061695) - Gaeilge 1 & 2 / Irish language & culture: 10 wks each

IRISH CULTURE see also Art History / Heritage / Traditional etc

DIT Faculty: Applied Arts Aungier St 2 (4023465/3445) - Irish cultural studies, 1 yr (4024673)

IRISH DANCING - CEILI/FIGURE

Brooks Academy 15 Henrietta St 1 (8730093) - set dancing

Comhaltas Ceoltoiri Eireann 32 Belgrave Sq Monkstown (2800295) various venues, sets & ceili
Corporate Club 24 Elmcastle Green Kilnamanagh 24 (4610935)
Dublin Folk Dance Group 48 Ludford Drive Ballinteer 16 (2987929) - set dancing various centres, ongoing
Network Club, The 24 Elmcastle Green Kilnamanagh 24 (4524415)
Palmerstown Community School 20 (6260116) - ceili, Mon 8.30, 10wks €60
St Kevin's College Clogher Rd Crumlin 12 (4536397) - set, 10wks
IRISH HISTORY see History / Heritage / Archeology
Pearse College Clogher Rd 12 (4536661/4541544) - day
IRISH MUSIC see Music / Folk Music / Traditional
IT see INFORMATION TECHNOLOGY / COMPUTER / INTERNET / TEACHING

ITALIAN (COMMERCIAL)
Sandford Language Institute Milltown Pk Sandford Rd 6 (2601296) - for the workplace, 14 wks, €205
ITALIAN FOR HOLIDAYS
Malahide Community School Malahide (8460949) - beginners - designed to enable visitor communicate effectively, 10 wks €75
ITALIAN LANGUAGE & CULTURE
Aisling Ireland Languages for Business & Pleasure 137 Lr Rathmines Rd 6 (4971902) - beginners + post beginners, 10 wks €145
Ashfield College Main St Templeogue 6W (4900866) - beginners 1, 6.30-8pm, 10 wks / improvers 2, 8-9.30, 10 wks
Ballymun Comprehensive School Adult Ed Centre Ballymun Rd 9 (8420654/ 8425828 night) - beginners/ advanced, Wed 10wk, €75 ea
Cabinteely Community School Johnstown Rd 18 (2857455) - beginners, 10wk, €75
Colaiste Dhulaigh Barryscourt Rd Coolock 17 (8481337) - FETAC cert, Mon, 20 wks/ for beginners, Mon, 10 wks, 8.00-9.00
Colaiste Eanna College of Business & Technical Stu Kilkieran Rd Cabra 7 (8389577) - beginners conversation, 10 wks Thurs 7-9pm
College of Further Education Main St Dundrum 14 (2951376) - beginners Tue/ continuation Thurs, 8 wks
Coolmine Community School Clonsilla 15 (8214583) - beginners Mon, improvers Tue: 18wk, €120/ beginners Wed €60
DATE College of Further Education Dundrum 14 (2964322) - beginners, to III, each10 wks, day €66
Donahies Community School Streamville Rd 13 (8482217) - beginners/ continuation, Mon Tue Wed, 10 wks €55 each
Dublin Public Libraries Admin Hq, 138-144 Pearse St 2 (6644800) - central library Ilac Centre, (9734333) or Library HQ for details (6744800), self-learning €free
Dun Laoghaire College of Further Education 17 Cumberland St Dun Laoghaire (2809676) - beginners / level 1: each 10 wks, Wed, 7 & 8.30 €85
Dun Laoghaire-Rathdown Co Council Public Library Service () - Deansgrange lib, Clonkeen Dr (2850860) - Ital/Eng - informal sessions, Mon 10.30-12 morn;
Foxrock Institute Kill O' the Grange School Kill Lane Blackrock (4939506/4939629) - beginners/for fun, 8 wks, €85 each
Greendale Community School Kilbarrack 5 (8322735/6) - beginners/continuation, Thurs, 10 wks, €50 each
Hartstown Community School Clonsilla 15 (8209863) - 10wks, €60
Inchicore College of Further Education Emmet Rd 8 (4535358) - 10wks each, Tue
Killester College of Further Education Collins Ave 5 (8337686) - beginners, Mon 7.30-9, 10 wks 60
Kilroy's College 25 Kingram Place 2 (1850 700700) - tutor supported home study: leaving cert
Kylemore College Kylemore Rd 10 (6265901) - beginners, Wed, stage 2, Thurs, 7-9pm, 10 wks each
Langtrain International Torquay Rd Foxrock 18 (2893876) - €96 per term

St. Thomas Community College
Bray Senior College

web: www.bife.ie • email: Braynightschool@Hotmail.com

Co. Wicklow
V.E.C.

Full range of daytime or evening courses

tel: (01) 2866 111 / 2829 668 • fax: 2760 653

Lucan Community College Esker Drive (6282077) - Mon, 10 wks €79

Marino College 14-20 Marino Mart 3 (8332100) - beginners/intermediate, €10-20 wks, €50

Maynooth College Language Centre NUI Maynooth Co Kildare (7083737) - beginners/intermediate, 9wk, €110

Newpark Adult Education Centre Newtownpark Ave Blackrock (2884376) - all levels, 10wks, €90; also conversation

Old Bawn Community School Tallaght 24 (4526137) - conversation for beginners, Tues, improvers, Thurs

Palmerstown Community School 20 (6260116) - levels 1&2, Tues, 10wks €60

People's College 32 Parnell Sq 1 (8735879) - language classes, €55

Pobalscoil Rosmini Adult Ed Grace Pk Rd 9 (8371015) - beginners 1 & 2, 10 wks, €80 each

Rathmines Snr College Town Hall 6 (4975334) - all levels, Mon, Tue, Wed: 7pm 20 wks €130/ 25 wks €165

Ringsend Technical Institute Cambridge Rd 4 (6684498) - conversational, 10 wks €65

Saint Tiernan's Community School Parkvale Balally 16 (2953224) - conversation, beginners, Tues, 7.30-9.30pm, 10 wks, €70

Sandford Language Institute Milltown Pk Sandford Rd 6 (2601296) - all levels, 14 wks, €205

St Thomas Community College Novara Ave Bray (2866111) - beginners/stage 2, 10wks, €70 each

Sth Dublin Co Libraries Languages & Computers: Ballyroan/Clondalkin/Castletymon, Lucan & Co Library (4597834-admin only) - self learning

Stillorgan Snr College Old Road Stillorgan (2880704) - beginners, 8 wks, €73

UCD Adult Education Office (7061695) - beginners, 20 wks / spoken workshop, 10 wks

WORDS Language Services 44 Northumberland Rd 4 (6610240) - individual tuition only

JAPANESE Language, Art & Culture

Aisling Language Services Languages for Business & Pleasure 137 Lr Rathmines Rd 6 (4971902) - beginners, 10 wks €185

Dublin City University Registry office Glasnevin 9 (7005338) - applied languages, international business/marketing

Dublin Public Libraries Admin Hq, 138-144 Pearse St 2 (6644800) - central libary Ilac Centre (8734333) or Library HQ for details (6744800), self-learning €free

Sandford Language Institute Milltown Pk Sandford Rd 6 (2601296) - all levels, 14 wks, €250/ Japanese for the workplace, all levels, 14 wks, €250

St Thomas Community College Novara Ave Bray (2866111) - beginners, 10 wks, €70

Sth Dublin Co Libraries Languages & Computers: Ballyroan/Clondalkin/ Castletymon, Lucan & Co Library (4597834-admin only) - self learning

Trinity College 2 (6772941) - (6081560) - extra mural, intro, 24wks, €320/ post-beginners-intermediate/ language, 24wks, €320 each

JAZZ see also Music

Dance Theatre of Ireland Bloomfields Centre, Lr George St Dun Laoghaire (2803455) - Thurs, 8.30-9.30

Dun Laoghaire Music Centre 130A Lr George's St Dun Laoghaire (2844178)

Newpark Music Centre Newtownpark Ave Blackrock (2883740) - improvisation

Walton's New School of Music 69 Sth Gt George's St 2 (4781884) - improvisantion/ ensemble, also day, see ad page

JAZZ BALLET see Ballet

JET SKI

Irish Sailing Assoc 3 Park Rd Dun Laoghaire (2800239) -beginners - intermediate/ personal watercraft handling: apply for provider list

JEWELLERY

Cormac Cuffe Blackrock (2846037) - designing & making; also day; see www.irish-jewelleryclasses.com; in Blackrock

FAS Training Centre Baldoyle 13 (8167460) - stone setting

Gemcraft Design Studio 5 Herbert St 2 (2883796) - making jewellery & art metal-work, 2 eve per wk, 7-9.30, 10 wks

Killester College of Further Education Collins Ave 5 (8337686) - jewellery making, Mon 7-8.30, 10 wks €70

Liberties College Bull Alley St 8 (4540044) - design & make your own, Mon 7-9, €110

Marino College 14-20 Marino Mart 3 (8332100) - & beadmaking, Tue 10wks, €50

National College of Art & Design in Art & Design 100 Thomas Street 8 (6364214) - intro & all levels, c22 wks /art jewellery & metalwork, c. 22wk

Ringsend Technical Institute Cambridge Rd 4 (6684498) - beadmaking 10 wks €65

St Thomas Community College Novara Ave Bray (2866111) - 10 wks €70

Yellow Brick Road 8 Bachelors Wlk 1 (8730177) - heirloom beadwork, wkend workshops €150/ jewellery making all levels, €250 incl materials, 8 wks Wed 7.30-9.30; multimedia necklace / netting & chips, Wed €25 not incl mats / also in Spring 2004

JIVE - Rock 'n' Roll see also Dance

Dance Club Rathmines & Rathgar (2893797)

JOB-SEEKING SKILLS see also Careers

Kilroy's College 25 Kingram Place 2 (1850 700700) - home study: interview techniques, aptitude & intelligence tests

MD Communications 38 Spireview Lane off Rathgar Rd 6 (4975866)

St Tiernan's Community School Parkvale Balally 16 (2953224) - successful job hunting, Tues, 7.30 6 wks €50

JOINERY see Woodwork

JOURNALISM see also Broadcasting / Communications / Media

Ballyfermot College of Further Education Ballyfermot Rd 10 (6269421) - print, 22 wks, Wed, 7-9.30pm, €180

Ballymun Comprehensive School Adult Ed Centre Ballymun Rd 9 (8420654/ 8425828 night) - how the media works, Tue, 7-9pm €90

Colaiste Dhulaigh & College of Further Education Barryscourt Rd Coolock 17 (8481337) - intro to, Mon 7.30-9.15, 10 wks

Dublin Business School 13/14 Aungier St 2 (4177500) - ICM dip, journalism & media studies, p/time, 1yr

Dublin City University Registry office Glasnevin 9 (7005338)

Griffith College Dublin Sth Circular Rd 8 (4150400) - dip in journalism & media studies, 3 yrs, HETAC, f/t Mon to Fri/ journalism & media communications, 18 mths, GCD dip, p/t, 3 eves per wk/ cert in radio broadcasting/ print journalism, 1 yr, p/t, 2 eves per wk/ BA in journalism & media commun, 3 yr HETAC f/time/ grad dip, 18 mth p/t & 1 yr f/t

Irish Academy of Public Relations (2780802) - basics: practical cert, UCD/UCC / GMIT, correspondence or e-mail, 8wks, €355/advanced: practical dip, UCD/UCC / GMIT, 1yr, €1400

Killester College of Further Education Collins Ave 5 (8337686) - intro to, Mon 8.30, 10 wks €60

Kilroy's College 25 Kingram Place 2 (1850 700700) - tutor supported home study: freelance

Marino College 14-20 Marino Mart 3 (8332100) - intro, Tues, 6pm 10 wks €50

UCD Adult Education Office (7061695) - intro to print journalism, 10 wks

Westmoreland College for Management & Business 11 Westmoreland St 2 (6795324/7266) - ICM dip in journalism & media

JUDO

Portmarnock Sports & Leisure Club Blackwood Lane Carrickhill Portmarnock (8462122)

JUNIOR CERT

Ashfield College Main St Templeogue 6W (4900866) - higher, English, Business, French, German, Irish, Maths, Science, p/time

Ballymun Comprehensive School Adult Ed Centre Ballymun Rd 9 (8420654/ 8425828 night) - English/ History, 30wk, €free

Bray Music Centre Florence Rd Bray (2866768) - music

Colaiste Dhulaigh Barryscourt Rd Coolock 17 (8481337) - history(o), Mon 6.45-9, 20 wks/ Spanish(o) Mon 7.15-9.15, 18 wks/ Maths(o) Tues, 20 wks, 6.30-8.45

Colaiste Eanna College of Business & Technical Stu Kilkieran Rd Cabra 7 (8389577) - English, Maths, day (tel 8688342/8389577

Colaiste Eoin Cappagh Rd 11 (8340893) - English/ maths/ history, CSPE, 20wk, also day

DATE College of Further Education Dundrum 14 (2964322) - English Lr, H 28 wks day, free/ English (H); classical studies: each 28 wks €79 day

Dublin Adult Learning Centre 3 Mountjoy Sq 1 (8787266) - English, maths

Dun Laoghaire Music Centre 130A Lr George's St Dun Laoghaire (2844178) - music

Finglas Adult Reading & Writing Scheme Colaiste Eoin Finglas 11 (8340893) - English, day, eve / Maths Basic (also FETAC) day / CSPE, day / all free

Goethe Institute 62 Fitzwilliam Sq 2 (6801110) - German, 16wks, day

Institute of Education 82/85 Lr Leeson St 2 (6613511)

Kilroy's College 25 Kingram Place 2 (1850 700700) - tutor supported home study: Maths, English, Irish

KLEAR Grange Park View Kilbarrack 5 (8671845) - English, maths; day only

Kylemore College Kylemore Rd 10 (6265901) - second chance, English Wed, Math Mon, Technical graphics Thurs, all 7-9pm, 1 yr

Pearse College Clogher Rd 12 (4536661/4541544) - 1yr, for adults, day

Plunket College Swords Rd, Whitehall 9 (8371689) - most subjects incl. English, Maths, Bus Org, History, Computers, 25 wks; also day

Southside Adult Literacy Scheme 3 Ashgrove Tce Dundrum 14 (2964321) - range of basic one-to-one up to leaving cert courses incl. English, maths, geography, history: FETAC cert foundation & level 1

St Kevins College Clogher Rd Crumlin 12 (4536397) - day

TARGET St Kevin's School Newbrook Rd, Donaghmede 13 (8671967) - English, 10wks, CDVEC

KARATE see also Martial Arts / Self-Defence

Clondalkin Sports & Leisure Centre Nangor Rd Clondalkin 22 (4574858)

Dublin Shotokan Karate International (Dublin SKI) St Paul's College Sybil Hill Road Raheny 5 (087 2215685) - Mon & Wed/ also St Vincent's & St Joseph's

Kempo Karate Club, PSLC Carrick Hill, Portnarnock (8462122) – adult & juniors

Shotokan Clubs 087 8197785/ 8570353, Mon, Tue & Thurs, Fairview & Marino

Martial Arts Federation of Ireland 20 Oakpark Ave Santry 9 (8625065) - kenpo, Tues & Thurs

Rathgar Kenpo Karate Studios Garville Rd Rathgar 6 (8423712)

St Vincent's Shotkan Karate Club St Vincent's GAA Club Malahide Road Marino 3 (8570353/ 087 8197785) - Mon, Tue (Juniors), Thurs; also at St Joseph's PS, Fairview

Taney Centre Taney Rd Dundrum 14 (2985491) - Fri (2986046)

Yang's Martial Arts Assoc Newpark Sports Centre, Blackrock (2814901) - white crane & long fist kung fu, all levels

KEEP FIT CLASSES see also Aerobics / Exercise etc

Bodyline Studio Rere Brady's Terenure Pl 6W (4902038) - for women, 6 days, membership from €199

Cabinteely Community School Johnstown Rd 18 (2857455) - taebo (with kickboxing techniques), Mon 7.30-8.30, 10wks €40/ ultimate fat burning class, Tues, 1hr 10wks €40

Clondalkin Sports & Leisure Centre Nangor Rd Clondalkin 22 (4574858) - Khaibo/aerobics/step aerobics/combination work-out/total fitness/great abs, buns'n thighs - also day

The League of Health

Estd. 1934

Whatever your job — whatever your age

Health Exercise to Music for women. Enjoyable classes given by fully qualified teachers improve posture, mobility and fitness. Classes for: Mother & Toddler, Adults & Active Retired Men and Women. Join now and stay in shape with the League. *Free trial class for non-members with this ad. ref. 112.*

REMEMBER MOVEMENT IS LIFE
Enquiries: Phone 01-8333569 / 01-2806376/ 01-2807775

Coolmine Community School Clonsilla 15 (8214583) - get fit 1 & 2, each 9 wks, €40

Greenhills College Limekiln Ave Walkinstown 12 (4507779/4507138) - women, 10 wks, €46

Harmony Yoga Ireland Ballinteer/Dundrum Dalkey / Killiney (087 8263778) - pilates, beginners, 6 & 12 wk, morn & eve / for pregnancy , 6 & 12 wks €15 per class / also pilates 1 to 1

Hartstown Community School Clonsilla 15 (8209863) - circuit training - 10wk, €45 each

Hegarty Fitness Centre 53 Middle Abbey St 1 (8723080) - cellulite removal/ slimming/ figure threapy, 10-15 wks, from €120 each, also day

Inchicore College of Further Education Emmet Rd 8 (4535358) - 10wks

Jackie Skelly's Fitness 42 Clarendon St, 2; Park West Bus Pk, Nangor Rd, 12 & Applewood Village, Swords (6770040 / 6301456 / 8075620) - gym membership, €47-59 per mth incl classes - keep fit, step, pump, aerobics, spin, toning

Killester College of Further Education Collins Ave 5 (8337686) - intro to, Mon 7 & 8.30, 10 wks €60

Kilroy's College 25 Kingram Place 2 (1850 700700) - tutor supported home study: diet, fitness & health dip courses

KLEAR Grange Park View Kilbarrack 5 (8671845) - day only

League of Health (Irl) 17 Dundela Pk Sandycove (2807775) AT: Ballinteer-2988550; Blackrock/Booterstown-2896162; Bray-2807775; Clondalkin-4974539; Clontarf-8333569; Dalkey-2807775; Donnybrook-2888761; Dundrum-4903091; Dun Laoghaire-2806376/2841187; Enniskerry-2824463; Glasnevin-2888761; Glenageary-2841187; Greystones -2896162,2888761; Killothe Grange 2858588; Lucan 2988576; Malahide 8363186; Monkstown 2896162; Mount Merrion 2888761; Newbridge 4974539; Raheny 2807257; Rathgar 2941328; Rathmichael 2824463; Rathmines 2988550

League of Health (Irl) 17 Dundela Pk Sandycove (2807775) - Sandymount-2807257; Santry-8363186; Stillorgan-2807775; Templeogue-2988576; Terenure-2988550; Wicklow, 087 4195494

Lucan Community College Esker Drive (6282077) - callanetics 1&2/exercise time / Kai-Bo: 10 wks €46 each

Marino College 14-20 Marino Mart 3 (8332100) - body conditioning, Thurs 7-8pm 10 wks €33/ pilates, Thurs 8pm €50

Melt, Temple Bar Natural Healing Centre 2 Temple Ln 2 (6798786) - pilates, 8 wks €82; also day

Motions Health Centre City West Leisure Centre (4588179/ 087 2808866)

Newpark Adult Education Centre Newtownpark Ave Blackrock (2884376) - pilates plus, €80

Palmerstown Community School 20 (6260116) - level 1 Mon 7pm 10 wks €45

Phibsboro Gym 1st floor, Phibsboro SC 7 (8301849) - & boxercise

Pilates Institute (NTC) 16a St Joseph's Parade 7 (8827777) - pilates matwork day, wkends, 14 wks, nat qual/ on ball, 1 day; and pregnancy, 1 day; pilatres H2O 1 day: ea €225, nat qual

Pobalscoil Rosmini Adult Ed Grace Pk Rd 9 (8371015) - ladies/men, Mon, 10 wks, €80 each

Portmarnock Sports & Leisure Club Blackwood Lane Carrickhill Portmarnock (8462122) - also fully equipped gym

Ringsend Technical Institute Cambridge Rd 4 (6684498) - aerobics/ circuits/ BLT: 10wks, €50 each

Saint Anthony's House St Lawrence Rd Clontarf 3 (8335300) - League of Health, 15wks, also day

St Thomas Community College Novara Ave Bray (2866111) - step & tone, 8 wks €40

Taney Parish Centre Taney Rd Dundrum 14 (2985491) - pilates, Wed (087 6638487

The Sanctuary Stanhope Street 7 (6705419) - pilates beginners, intermediate, 8 wks €60

Tony Quinn Centre 66/67 Eccles St 7 (8304211) - weight training & body building

KEYBOARD OPERATIONS see also Computers / Typing / Word Processing

Ballsbridge College of Business Studies Shelbourne Rd 4 (6684806) - Mon, 10 wks, €50 each

Ballymun Comprehensive School Adult Ed Centre Ballymun Rd 9 (8420654/ 8425828 night) - learn to type, Tue 10 wks, €75

Bray Business College Florence Rd Bray (2829936) - €80 per wk

Cabinteely Community School Johnstown Rd 18 (2857455) - & typing, 10wk, €75

CITAS Computer & IT Training 54 Middle Abbey St 1 (8782212) - keyboard skills, 5 sessions, €130, ongoing Mon & Thurs 10am, 2-4pm

Colaiste Dhulaigh Barryscourt Rd Coolock 17 (8481337) - Thurs, 10-11am, 13 wks/ beginners, intermediate, Mon 10 wks, 6.15-8.15

Computeach AXIS, Main St Ballymun 9 (8832167)

Crumlin College of Further Education Crumlin Rd 12 (4540662) - Mon, 10 wks, 6.45-8.45

Dorset College 64a Lr Dorset St/ 8 Belvedere Pl 1 (8309677) - keyboarding, Fri 12 wks

Grange Community College Grange Abbey Rd Donaghmede 13 (8471422) -

computers/typing 10wks, €93

Irish Academy of Computer Training 98 St Stephen's Grn 2 (4347600) - becoming computer literate, 4 wks €295/ word; wordpro: 4 wks €275 ea cert/ also day

Keytrainer Ireland 33/34 Dame St 2 (6714000) - data entry/computer keyboard skills, public & tailored

Kilroy's College 25 Kingram Place 2 (1850 700700) - tutor supported home-study dip courses

Kylemore College Kylemore Rd 10 (6265901) - Tues, Wed, 10 wks, 7-9pm/ also day

Newpark Adult Education Centre Newtownpark Ave Blackrock (2884376) - type-writing

Pitman Training Centre 6-8 Wicklow St 2 (6768008) - speed/ audio, 16-20 hrs €170, cert

Pobalscoil Rosmini Adult Ed Grace Pk Rd 9 (8371015) - 10 wks Wed 8.30 €130

Rathmines Snr College Town Hall 6 (4975334) - Tues, 20 wks, €210

St Thomas Community College Novara Ave Bray (2866111) - 10 wks €70

Tallaght Community School Balrothery 24 (4515566) - & typing skills, cert, beginners & improvers, 10wk, €55

KEYBOARD Tuition see also Music

Abbey School of Music 9b Lr Abbey St 1 (8747908) - John Hunter

Clontarf School of Music 6 Marino Mart 3 (8330936) - modern, 12wk - also day

Colaiste Eanna College of Business & Technical Stu Kilkieran Rd Cabra 7 (8389577) - introductory, Thurs, 10 wks 7-9pm

Dun Laoghaire Music Centre 130A Lr George's St Dun Laoghaire (2844178)

Hartstown Community School Clonsilla 15 (8209863) - 10wks, €40

John Ward 5 Tibradden Drive Walkinstown 12 (4520918) - prep for RIAM grade exams/ also day

Melody School of Music 178E Whitehall Rd W Perrystown 12 (4650150) - also day; also w/ends Sat-Sun, 12 wks

Nolan School of Music 3 Dean St 8 (4933730) - also day

Walton's New School of Music 69 Sth Gt George's St 2 (4781884) - also day, see ad page

KICK BOXING

Phibsboro Gym 1st floor, Phibsboro SC 7 (8301849) - all levels, Sat 4-6pm, Tues 8.45, Sun 11-3pm

Taney Parish Centre Taney Rd Dundrum 14 (2985491) - bushido, Mon/Wed (6262261)

KINESIOLOGY see also Health Education

Kinesiology Institute 84 Cappaghmore Clondalkin 22 (4571183) - dip course, Sept 03 to June 04: 13 w/end workshops, practices, exams, fees: €175 per w/end or €2,225

KNITTING / MACHINE KNITTING

Balbriggan Community College Pine Ridge Chapel St (8412388/9) - & crochet, basic, modern, 8 wks, Mon 7.30-9.30, €73

Grafton Academy of Dress Design 6 Herbert Place 2 (6763653) - machine, basic, 4-day €498

KNOW YOUR RIGHTS see also Consumer Education / Law
Campaign Against Bullying 72 Lakelands Ave Stillorgan (2887976) - anti-bullying in workplace & school
KOREAN
Dublin Public Libraries Admin Hq, 138-144 Pearse St 2 (6644800) - central library Ilac Centre, (8734333) or Library HQ for details (674800), self-learning €free
Sth Dublin Co Libraries Languages & Computers: Ballyroan/Clondalkin/ Castletymon, Lucan & Co Library (4597834-admin only) - self learning
KUNG FU
Oakwood Community Centre Eugene Murphy Jamestown Road 11 (8347895) - wing tsun self-defence, Tue, Thurs, 7.30-9pm. 6wks, €50, cert
Yang's Martial Arts Assoc Newpark Sports Centre, Blackrock (2814901) - white crane & long fist, all levels
LACE-MAKING see Embroidery / Crafts
LANDSCAPE PAINTING see also Art / Painting
Brian Byrnes Art Studio 3 Upr Baggot St 4 (6671520 / 6711599) - 8wk, €130, also day
LANGUAGES see also Translation and under individual languages
Aisling Ireland Languages for Business & Pleasure 137 Lr Rathmines Rd 6 (4971902) - Chinese/ English/ French/ German/ Italian/ Japanese/ Russian/ Spanish/ other languages & one-to-one tuition
Bluefeather School of Languages 35 Montpelier Parade Monkstown (2806288) - short inexpensive foreign language courses abroad @ www.tandemlink.com
Dublin City University Registry office Glasnevin 9 (7005338) - applied, French/German/Spanish/Japanese/ Fiontar- entrepreneurship & computing through Irish
Dublin Public Libraries Admin Hq, 138-144 Pearse St 2 (6644800) - self-learning €free - see separate headings & also Lakota/ Lithuanian/ Romanian/ Scots Gaelic/ Somali/ Ukranian/ Urdu/ Vietnamese/ Zulu
Dun Laoghaire-Rathdown Co Council Public Library Service - free self-learning

language facilities: the library at: Blackrock (2888117), Cabinteely (2855363), Dalkey (2855277), Deansgrange (2850860), Dun Laoghaire (2801147), Dundrum (2985000), Sallynoggin (2850127), Shankill (2823081), Stillorgan (2889655)

Esperanto Assoc of Ireland 9 Templeogue Wood 6W (4945020) - Esperanto correspondence course, €free

Fingal Co Libraries County Hall Main St Swords (8905520) - self-learning, free, Ballbriggan: 8411128; Blanchardstown: 8905563; Howth: 8322130; Malahide: 8452026; Rathbeale: 8404179; Mobile Library HQ: 8221564; Schools Library Service: 8225056; Housebound Services: 8604290

Foxrock Institute Kill O' the Grange School Kill Lane Blackrock (4939506/4939629) - French/ Italian/ Spanish, 8 wks, €85

Goethe Institut 62 Fitzwilliam Sq 2 (6801110) - German

Greenhills College Limekiln Ave Walkinstown 12 (4507779/4507138) - French, German, Irish, Spanish, 10 wks, €79 each

Hartstown Community School Clonsilla 15 (8209863) - French, beginners/ Irish, beginners/ Italian, beginners, intermediate/ Spanish beginners, intermediate: 10 wks, €60 each

Inchicore College of Further Education Emmet Rd 8 (4535358) - modern languages & business studies

Institute of Technology Tallaght 24 (4042000) - French/German/Irish (advanced)/Italian/ Spanish/ English - certs, yrs 1&2

Kilroy's College 25 Kingram Place 2 (1850 700700) - ome study: leaving cert & travel - Spanish, German, Irish, French & Italian

Linguaphone Institute Unit 10, Stables Office Pk Portmarnock (8038828) - various

Pearse College Clogher Rd 12 (4536661/4541544) - for travel & tourism, day

Taney Parish Centre Taney Rd Dundrum 14 (2985491) - Macdus (childrens), Sat (2883992; 4905679)

The Open University Enquiry & Advice Centre Holbrook House, Holles St 2 (6785399)

WORDS Language Services 44 Northumberland Rd 4 (6610240) - individual tuition in various languages

LAPIDARY see Crafts

LATIN

Dublin Public Libraries Admin Hq, 138-144 Pearse St 2 (6644800) - central library Ilac Centre (8734333) or Library HQ for details (6744800), self-learning €free

Sandford Language Institute Milltown Pk Sandford Rd 6 (2601296) - all levels, 14 wks, €250

UCD Adult Education Office (7061695) - for beginners, 24 wks

LATIN AMERICAN DANCE see also Dance

Beginners Dance Centre 54 Parnell Sq W 1 (8304647) - €7 per class

Cabinteely Community School Johnstown Rd 18 (2857455) - samba, cha cha, rumba & jive, 10wk, €35

Dance Club Rathmines & Rathgar (2893797)

Morosini-Whelan School of Dancing 46 Parnell Sq W 1 (8303613)

Pobalscoil Iosolde 20 (6260116) - ballroom, Tues 8.15, 10 wks €60

LAW Industrial Relations / Legal Aid / Secretarial

Colaiste Dhulaigh Barryscourt Rd Coolock 17 (8481337) - introduction to legal studies, Tue 7.30-9.30, 8wks

Crumlin College of Further Education Crumlin Rd 12 (4540662) - Legal Studies - Constitutional law: contract law (Mon) & criminal law (Wed)/ Company law: land law (Mon) & law of torts (Wed); passes in 3 subjects - cert in legal studies/ passes in 6 subjects - dip in legal studies, 2 yr course, ICM exam

DIT admissions office Dublin (4023445) - foundations in civil &/or criminal law litigation, 1 eve weekly, €473 ea

DIT Faculty: Applied Arts Aungier St 2 (4023465/3445) - dip in legal studies, 2 yr p/time, €800 pa

Dorset College 64a Lr Dorset St/ 8 Belvedere Pl 1 (8309677) - cert/dip ICM in legal studies, Mon & Wed, 6.30-9pm, 1-2yrs

Dublin Business School 13/14 Aungier St 2 (4177500) - dip legal studies, 2 eves a wk, 6.30-9.30pm, 1 yr/14 wks / BA in business management (law), 2 eves a wk, 4 yrs 6.30-9.30/ dip in employment law, 1 eve a wk, 10 wks, 6.30-9.30/ dip in commercial law, 1 eve a wk + 3 wkend workshops, 6.30-9.30, 1 yr/ dip in family law, 1 eve a wk, 10 wks + 2 wkend workshops, 6.30-9.39pm

Dublin School of Law 23 Upper Fitzwilliam St 2 (2953595) - LLB (Uni of London) 30wk - also day/Law Soc final exam part 1, 12wk

Griffith College Dublin Sth Circular Rd 8 (4150400) - dip in legal studies, 3 yrs, HETAC, Mon to Fri/ dip in professioinal legal studies, 1 yr ILEX/ LLB in Irish Law, 3 yrs, f/t, Mon to Fri; also 3 eves per wk/ BA Law with Business, 4 yrs, HETAC, f/t / BA Business & Law, 3yr, 3 eve per wk; also f/time

Inchicore College of Further Education Emmet Rd 8 (4535358) - business admin with legal studies, day

People's College 32 Parnell Sq 1 (8735879) - legal studies

Pitman Training Centre 6-8 Wicklow St 2 (6768008) - legal studies, 10 hrs €210, cert, day eve Sats/ legal secretarial, 9 wks €1955, dip; day eve Sats

Pobalscoil Rosmini Adult Ed Grace Pk Rd 9 (8371015) - intro to contract, criminal, tort, property & EU law, Thurs 8.30 €80

St Thomas Community College Novara Ave Bray (2866111) - legal studies, 30 wks, €200, FETAC

The Open University Enquiry & Advice Centre Holbrook House, Holles St 2 (6785399) - English

Trinity College 2 (6772941) - (6081007) - construction law & contract admin, postgrad dip, 24wks, also Sat

Westmoreland College for Management Studies 11 Westmoreland St 2 (6795324/7266) - ICM dip legal studies

LAW FOR THE LAYPERSON see also Know Your Rights

Cabinteely Community School Johnstown Rd 18 (2857455) - for beginners, Tues, 10wks, €75

DIT admissions ofice Dublin (4023445) - short law courses (CPD foundation): contract/ property/ tort/ EU law/ equity/ criminal/ constitutional/ company/ family /

employment: 1 night or morn weekly, €334 ea

Hartstown Community School Clonsilla 15 (8209863) - know your rights, Tues, 10wks, €60

Marino College 14-20 Marino Mart 3 (8332100) - Ten relevant topics, Thurs, 10wks €50

Saor-Ollscoil na hEireann 55 Prussia St 7 (8683368) - BA, legal studies

St Mac Dara's Community College Wellington Lane Templeogue 6W (4566216) - Wed, 7.30-9.30pm, 10 wks, €79

UCD Adult Education Office (7061695) - Irish family law, 12 wks cert

LEARNING DISABILITIES see also Disabilities

Dyslexia Association of Ireland 1 Suffolk St 2 (6790276) - individual remedial tuition for adults / group or individual tuition for children

LEAVING CERTIFICATE / PRE-LEAVING

Ashfield College Main St Templeogue 6W (4900866) - choice of subjects, p/time higher, lower /taking an extra subject / intensive summer language courses

Balymun Comprehensive School Adult Ed Centre Ballymun Rd 9 (8420654/ 8425828 night) - English/ Maths/ History 25 wks €150 ea

Bray Music Centre Florence Rd Bray (2866768) - music

Colaiste Dhulaigh Barryscourt Rd Coolock 17 (8481337) - LC basic educ & voc awards course, Irish, French, English(o); Maths(o), history(h&o); Spanish(o)

Colaiste Eanna College of Business & Technical Stu Kilkieran Rd Cabra 7 (8389577) - English, history - day (tel 8688342/8389577)

Colaiste Eoin Cappagh Rd 11 (8340893) - English/ maths/ also day

College of Further Education Main St Dundrum 14 (2951376) - English(h) Tue 8 wks

Conradh na Gaeilge 6 Sr Fhearchair (Harcourt St) BAC 2 (4757401) - Irish

Crumlin College of Further Education Crumlin Rd 12 (4540662) - English, Geography, History, Irish, Maths ord level/also LC prep in Maths

DATE College of Further Education Dundrum 14 (2964322) - English Lr 28 wks

Dublin Adult Learning Centre 3 Mountjoy Sq 1 (8787266) - English

Dun Laoghaire College of Further Education 17 Cumberland St Dun Laoghaire (2809676) - technical drawing (H+O)7-9.30 Mon: 24 wks, €220/ maths (o), (O), 24 wks, 7.30 €220/ 2ye, 5.15 €200

Dun Laoghaire Music Centre 130A Lr George's St Dun Laoghaire (2844178)

Finglas Adult Reading & Writing Scheme Colaiste Eoin Finglas 11 (8340893) - art, day / English, day, eve / Maths basic, day / all 30 wks, free

Goethe Institute 62 Fitzwilliam Sq 2 (6801110) - leaving cert German, 16wks, day

Grange Community College Grange Abbey Rd Donaghmede 13 (8471422) - maths

Greenhills College Limekiln Ave Walkinstown 12 (4507779/4507138) - maths (O)/ English (O) 10wks, €76 each

Kilroy's College 25 Kingram Place 2 (1850 700700) - tutor supported home study, all major subjects/ full rapid revision courses

KLEAR Grange Park View Kilbarrack 5 (8671845) - English, History, day only

Kylemore College Kylemore Rd 10 (6265901) - second chance, 1 yr 7-9pm: Accounting (o), Geography (o,h), Irish (o) - Mon; maths (o) Tue; Business (o), History (o) - Wed; English (o,h) - Thurs

Leinster School of Music Griffith College Campus South Circular Rd 8 (4150467)

Pearse College Clogher Rd 12 (4536661/4541544) - also repeat, day

Plunket College Swords Rd, Whitehall 9 (8371689) - 27 wks, most subjects

Rathmines Snr College Town Hall 6 (4975334) - Maths, 25 wks, life drawing

Ringsend Technical Institute Cambridge Rd 4 (6684498) - English, Maths,, 25wks

Southside Adult Literacy Scheme 3 Ashgrove Tce Dundrum 14 (2964321) - range of basic one-to-one up to leaving cert courses incl. English, maths, geography, history: FETAC cert foundation & level 1

St Kevins College Clogher Rd Crumlin 12 (4536397) - also post-jnr, day

St Thomas Community College Novara Ave Bray (2866111) - maths(o), English(o)

TACT St Dominic's School St Dominic's Rd Tallaght 24 (4596757) - English (o) art (o)/ history math: 30 wks, day, free

Walton's New School of Music 69 Sth Gt George's St 2 (4781884) - music, also day, see ad page 173

LEISURE & RECREATIONAL STUDIES
Inchicore College of Further Education Emmet Rd 8 (4535358) - leisure & recreation management; leisure & disability studies; travel & tourism management
Kilroy's College 25 Kingram Place 2 (1850 700700) - tutor supported home study
Litton Lane Studios PO Box 123 Greystones Co Wicklow (8728044) - exercise & fitness (NCEF cert) - day 12wks/wkend 18wks, €1330 +€395 exam fees

LIBERAL ARTS / STUDIES
The Open University Enquiry & Advice Centre Holbrook House, Holles St 2 (6785399)
Saor-Ollscoil na hEireann 55 Prussia St 7 (8683368) - BA in Liberal Arts

LIBRARIES see also Information Centres / Music Library
Central Library Ilac Centre 1 (8734333)
National Library of Ireland Kildare St 2 (6030200)

LIFE DRAWING & PAINTING see Drawing / Painting / Sketching

LIFE SAVING see Water Safety

LIFE SKILLS / COACHING see also Personal Development, Coaching / Creative Thinking
AAA Counselling Dr MJ Brennan PhD c/o 48 Connaught St Phibsboro 7 (8380014) - life coaching, mentoring, also day
Colaiste Eanna Kilkieran Rd Cabra 7 (8389577) - Wed, 10-12am
Communication & Personal Development 30/31 Wicklow St 2 (6713636/6613225)
Connolly House Nth Strand (by 5 Lamps) 1 (8557116) - 10 wks Wed, 8pm €50
KLEAR Grange Park View Kilbarrack 5 (8671845) - for positive living, day

Malahide Community School Malahide (8460949) - intro to, 10 wks €70

Newpark Adult & Continuing Education Centre Blackrock (2884376) - stress mgmnt, & assertiveness coaching, 10 wks, 99/ be your own life coach, 10 wks €99

Old Bawn Community School Tallaght 24 (4526137) - live your best life, 10 wks

Positive Success Group Mary O'Driscoll NPL (087 7640385) - business & life coaching, dip course (incl foundation, start your own business, branding & marketing, getting clients, NPL core skills)

LINE DANCING see also Dancing

Ballymun Comprehensive Schools Adult Ed Centre Ballymun Rd 9 (8420654/ 8425828 night) - & salsa, 10 wks, €75

LINGUISTICS - Applied

Dublin City University Registry office Glasnevin 9 (7005338) - computational

LITERACY (BASIC) see also Adult / English Literacy

Department of Adult & Community Education NUI Maynooth (7084500) - NUI cert in Integrating Literacy

Hartstown Community School Clonsilla 15 (8209863) - for adults, improve spelling, 10 wks, €20

Kilroy's College 25 Kingram Place 2 (1850 700700) - general education - English, work study, spelling & arithmetic, tutor supported home-study dip course

LITERATURE see also German Culture / Creative Writing

Colaiste Eanna College of Business & Technical Stu Kilkieran Rd Cabra 7 (8389577) - Irish drama introduction, 1890-1950, Wilde, O'Casey, Behan/ intro to anglo-Irish lit, 1890-1930, Yeats, Synge, O'Casey [Jan 2004]

DATE College of Further Education Dundrum 14 (2964322) - NUI cert in English literature, 10 wks, €160/€215, day/ enjoying English lit, 10 wks day

Dun Laoghaire-Rathdown Co Council Public Library Service - free monthly book clubs; novels discussed, informal, new members welcome: the library at: Cabinteely (2855363), Dalkey (2855277), Deansgrange (2850860) Dun Laoghaire (2801147), Dundrum (2985000), Shankill (2823081), Stillorgan (2889655)

James Joyce Centre 35 Nth Gt George's St 1 (8788547) - Reading Joyce, Sept - May

Kilroy's College 25 Kingram Place 2 (1850 700700) - tutor supported home study: English, dip

Marino College 14-20 Marino Mart 3 (8332100) - appreciation of English lit, Thurs

People's College 32 Parnell Sq 1 (8735879) - €40

Plunket College Swords Rd, Whitehall 9 (8371689) - exploring the world of lit €66

Pobalscoil Neasain Baldoyle 13 (8063092) - UCD course modules 1 & 2, 10 wks

Saor-Ollscoil na hEireann 55 Prussia St 7 (8683368) - BA in Lib Arts, European

Trinity College 2 (6772941) - (6082885) - English, 9 wks, €40

UCD Adult Education Office (7061695) - 20th century English & Irish lit/ literature history & romance/ modern Arabic lit / reading Joyce's Ulysse/ Literature module 1 & 2/ New courses in Literature/ mind. body spirit in literature/ modern Irish writing, constructing & deconstructing/ the legends of Camelot - Arthurian literature, art & film/ modern drama/: each 10 wks

LITURGY

All Hallows College Gracepark Rd Drumcondra 9 (8373745) - liturgy 1, Mon 6.50pm, 24 wks, €190 / Liturgy 2 Tues; ECTS credits option

LONE PARENT see also Parents

MAKE-UP (for Stage, Television and Film)

1000 Faces - International School of Stage, TV & Film: (8368201/ 087 2261479) - fashion, special effects, costume, etc, diploma course

Inchicore College of FE, Emmet Rd 8 (4535358) - costume design & wardrobes, day

Portobello School Rere 40 Lr Dominick St 1 (8721277) - fashion theatre & media make-up, p/time eve; also 1 day release/ special effects make-up, p/time eve

MANAGEMENT Business / Computer / Financial / Industrial Relations / Money / Personnel / Teamwork

Colaiste Dhulaigh Barryscourt Rd Coolock 17 (8481337) - practical communication for managers, Tue 7pm, 7 wks

Colaiste Eanna College of Business & Technical Stu Kilkieran Rd Cabra 7 (8389577) - business management attributes, human resources, international environment, 10 wks Tues

Colaiste Ide Cardiffsbridge Rd Finglas West 11 (8342333) - supervisory, 7-10pn, Tue & Thurs, 25 wks €500 ISRM cert

Coolmine Community School Clonsilla 15 (8214583) - NCI dip in management & employee relations, 2yr, €900pa/ NCI dip in first-line management, 2yr, €900pa: contact NCI 4060591

DIT Faculty: Applied Arts Aungier St 2 (4023465/3445) - BSc (Management &

Law), 4 yr p/time, €1350 pa.

DIT Faculty: Business Aungier St 2 (4023040/3445) - BSc in management & law; BSc management of credit; BSc health services management: each 4yrs p/time, €1350 pa/ MSc in strategic management, 5 x 15wk terms, 2yr €2256, or 1 yr f/t €4500

DIT Faculty: Tourism & Food Cathal Brugha St 1 (4024349/3445) - becoming a more effective manager, 12 wks €265, cert/ meat managememnt; bar management dip, each, 2 yrs €500pa / performance management skills, 12 wks €265

Dublin Business School 13/14 Aungier St 2 (4177500) - BA (hons) management & information systems, 3-4 yrs/ dip in management studies, 2 eves, 1 yr/ BA Business Management (Law)/ (HRM) 4 yrs 2 eve a wk 6.30-9.30

Eden Computer Training Rathfarnham 16, or MACRO Centre, 1 Green St 7 (4953155) - business management; start your own business; payroll

FAS Training Centre Baldoyle 13 (8167460); Ballyfermot 10 (6055900/ 5933); Finglas Jamestown Rd 11 (8140243)

FAS Training Centre Tallaght 24 (4045284) - NEBS cert introductory; stores management, intro; effective warehouse management: 10 wks each

Fitzwilliam Institute Ltd Temple Court Temple Rd Blackrock (2834579) - dip in event management, with PR module, 2 eve per wk, Oct-March, €1395 incl AAI exam fees, city centre

Griffith College Dublin Sth Circular Rd 8 (4150400) - International Bus Management: MBA, 1 yr f/t + 2 yr work experience/ MSc, 12 mth NTU f/t or 18 mths p/time / Grad Dipl, 2 semesters f/t or 18 mths p/t 3 eve wkly

Institute of Public Administration 57-61 Lansdowne Rd 4 (6686233)

Institute of Technology Tallaght 24 (4042000) - IMI cert in supervisory management/ cert in production & inventory management/ BBS/ nat dip/ nat cert in management/ postgrad dip in financial management (ACCA), 1 yr

Institute of Technology, Blanchardstown Blanchardstown Road North 15 (8851100) - HETAC project management in business, 13 wk modules, 6-10pm, from €350 to 420

Irish Management Institute Sandyford Rd 16 (2078400) - Henley Diploma in management, 18mth prog, €10500

Kilroy's College 25 Kingram Place 2 (1850 700700) - tutor supported home study: basic, business

Malahide Community School Malahide (8460949) - & employer relations, NCI dip, 2yrs / project management, intro, 10 wks €75

National College of Ireland Mayor St IFSC 1 (4060500/ 1850 221721) - MA in Management & Technology by Research, 2 yrs; MA in Human Resource Management, 2 yrs p/time day; NCI cert in Managing Voluntary Organisations, 1 yr; HETAC Dip and Cert in Personnel & Human Resources Management; NCI Dip and HETAC Cert in Management and Employee Relations, 1 yr each; NCI Certs in Managing Teams/ eCommerce for Managers/ Motivation and Leadership, 12 wks online

Old Bawn Community School Tallaght 24 (4526137) - first-line management, 2 yr dip, 6.30-9pm, 24 wks - National College of Ireland (4060591) - also 1 yr dip, 1.30-6pm

Oscail - National Distance Education Centre DCU 9 (7005481) - graduate diploma/ MSc Management of Operations, 3-4 years, awarded by DCU, distance learning

Palmerstown Community School 20 (6260116) - NCI dip in 1st line management, yr 1

Pearse College Clogher Rd 12 (4536661/4541544) - retail management & business studies, day

Plunket College Swords Rd, Whitehall 9 (8371689) - business, IATI cert, €113.50/
& employee relations dip, National College of Ireland/ dip in first line management
supervisor - 20 wks each

Portmarnock Community School Carrickhill Rd (8038056) - project management,
Thurs, 8 wks, €50

Portobello School Rere 40 Lr Dominick St 1 (8721277) - facilities mgmnt/ event
mgmnt/ HR mgmnt, each p/time eve

Saint Finian's Community College Swords (8402623) - supervisory, IMI cert, 25wk,
Mon & Tue, 7-10pm

St Thomas Community College Novara Ave Bray (2866111) - supervisory, IMI cert,
€400

Tallaght Community School Balrothery 24 (4515566) - transport management cert,
CPC, 30wk, €460

Trinity College 2 (6772941) - (6081007) - project, 1yr postgrad dip, 24wks, also Sat

UCD Adult Education Office (7061695) - entrepreneurship & mgmt theory/ finance for non-financial manager/ HR mgmt/ mgmt techniques/ operations mgmt/ quality mgmt: 12 wks each, certs

Westmoreland College for Management Studies 11 Westmoreland St 2 (6795324/7266) - ICM dip health services management/ICM dipcorporate management/ICM grad dip management/ICM dip HR management/ Adv dip in project management

MANDOLIN see also Music

Comhaltas Ceoltoiri Eireann 32 Belgrave Sq Monkstown (2800295)

Walton's New School of Music 69 Sth Gt George's St 2 (4781884) - also day, see ad page

MANICURE & PEDICURE see also Beauty

Portobello School Rere 40 Lr Dominick St 1 (8721277) - ITEC cert/ also nail technology: each part-time eve, day, wkend

MAP READING see Surveying

MARINE TECHNOLOGY

Cabinteely Community School Johnstown Rd 18 (2857455) - marine engine maintenance, 10wk, €75

Ringsend Technical Institute Cambridge Rd 4 (6684498) - engine maintenance, 10wks, €85

MARKETING see also Sales

Colaiste Eanna College of Business & Technical Stu Kilkieran Rd Cabra 7 (8389577) - intro to, identifying business opportunities market research, Tues, 10 wks

DIT admissions ofice Dublin (4023445) - branding workshops, 4 day (8146091)

DIT Faculty: Business Aungier St 2 (4023040/3445) - foundation cert, 2 yrs €700 pa/ MII dip, 1 yr €700/ graduateship in, final yr MII, €700 pa

DIT Faculty: Tourism & Food Cathal Brugha St 1 (4024349/3445) -intro to for hospitality sector, 1 term €166

Dorset College 64a Lr Dorset St/ 8 Belvedere Pl 1 (8309677) - dip marketing advertising & pr, Mon & Wed, 6.30-9.30 1-2 yrs

Dublin Business School 13/14 Aungier St 2 (4177500) - BA (hons) marketing, 6.15-9.30pm, 3-4 yrs/ dip in marketing, advertising & PR, 2 eves per wk, 6.30-9.30pm, 1 yr/14 wks/ dip in strategic marketing, 2 eves per wk, 1 yr/ 14 wks

Dublin Institute of Design 25 Sufflok St 2 (6790286) - retail & design, c&g dip, 2 eves pw, 1 yr, €2,300 / advertising & design, c&g dip, 2 eves pw, 1 yr, €2,300

Dun Laoghaire College of Further Education 17 Cumberland St Dun Laoghaire (2809676) - ICM cert, 20wks, 7-10pm €520

electronic Business School of Ireland (094-81444) - elearning course

FAS Training Centre Finglas Jamestown Rd 11 (8140243)

Griffith College Dublin Sth Circular Rd 8 (4150400) - dipl in marketing, 15 wks ICM, p/time

Institute of Technology Tallaght 24 (4042000) - BBS/ nat dip/ nat cert

Marketing Institute Sth Co Business Pk, Leopardstown 18 (2952355) - certificate (2 yrs), dip (3 yrs), graduate (4 yrs), also day - by attending college or distance learning

Newpark Adult Education Centre Newtownpark Ave Blackrock (2884376) - marketing & selling cert, 10 wks, €120

Pitman Training Centre 6-8 Wicklow St 2 (6768008) - marketing & PR, 8 wks €1646, dip; day eve Sats

Portobello School Rere 40 Lr Dominick St 1 (8721277) - marketing, davertising & PR, part-time eve

Rathmines Snr College Town Hall 6 (4975334) - & sales, Mon, 20 wks €130

Senior College Dun Laoghaire CFE Eblana Ave Dun Laoghaire (2800385) - MII cert/dip, stages 1-3, 1yr, €400 each; single subject €120/ graduateship stage 4 €470, single subject €150

St Thomas Community College Novara Ave Bray (2866111) - practice, 10 wks, €130/ also 30 wks, €200, cert

Star Consulting PO Box 8796 2 (086 6061639) - healing your business 1 day €200

Westmoreland College for Management Studies 11 Westmoreland St 2 (6795324/7266) - ICM dip marketing, advertising & PR

MARRIAGE GUIDANCE Pre-Marriage

ACCORD (Catholic Marriage Care Service) 39 Harcourt St 2 (4780866) - marriage counselling - appointments & drop-in service

MARTIAL ARTS see also Aikido / Judo / Kung-Fu / Karate / Tae-Kwon-Do / T'ai Chi / Self Defence etc

Irish Martial Arts Commission 23E York St 2 (4783831) - nationwide info service, 350 affiliated instructors

Irish T'ai Chi Ch'uan Assoc c/o St Andrew's Resource Centre 114 Pearse St 2 (6771930) - Chinese Kung Fu, 8wks, competition standard, forms, weapons

Marino College 14-20 Marino Mart 3 (8332100) - khai-Bo, 10 wks, €50

Martial Arts Federation of Ireland 20 Oakpark Ave Santry 9 (8625065) - karate

Natural Health Training Centre 1 Park Lane E Pearse St 2 (6718454) - all levels

Oakwood Community Centre Eugene Murphy Jamestown Road 11 (8347895) - wing tsun self defence, Tue, Thurs, 7.30-9pm. 6wks, €50, cert

St Vincent's Shotkan Karate Club St Vincent's GAA Club Malahide Road Marino 3 (8570353/ 087 8197785) - Mon, Tue (Juniors), Thurs; also at St Joseph's PS, Fairview

Taekwon-Do Centre 10 Exchequer St 2 (6710705)

Tai Chi Ireland PO Box 8276 6 (4968342 a'noon; 087 9795042 day only) - T'ai Chi qigong & daoist breathing, bagua; city centre

Yang's Martial Arts Assoc Newpark Sports Centre, Blackrock (2814901) -white crane & long fist kung fu & yang style t'ai chi ch'uan, all levels

MASSAGE see also Sports Massage

Acupuncture Foundation Training School Milltown Pk College (1850 577405) - dip in Chinese medical massage, postgrad training for acupuncturists, 6mth, €1,625

Ann Prendergast Rosebud Salon Rathgar Ave 6 (4920856) - morning, w/end, €120 Rathgar/Rathfarnham

Aspen's Beauty Clinic & College of Beauty Therapy 83 Lr Camden St 2 (4751079/ 4751940) - body massage, Tues 9.30am-3.30pm, 9 mths, €1695/ aromatherapy,

Sunday 11am-4pm 16 wks, €1,795/ indian head massage, Fri 6.30-9pm, 10 wks, €895 Ballymun Mens Centre LS4 Shangan Rd Ballymun 9 (8623117/8623409) - one-to-one, day

Balymun Comprehensive School Adult Ed Centre Ballymun Rd 9 (8420654/ 8425828 night) - Wed 6.45 & 8.30 10 wks €110

BASE Ballyboden Adult Social Education Whitechurch Library Taylor's Lane 16 (4935953)

Berni Grainger 21 Grangemore Ave 13 (8472943) - holistic body/Indian head, w/end, €140

Bronwyn Conroy Beauty School 10 The Crescent Monkstown (2804020) - anatomy & physiology

Colaiste Ide Cardiffsbridge Rd Finglas West 11 (8342333) - intro to healing massage, Sat, 10-2pm, 10 wks, €50/ teacher's dip Sweedish, ITEC 20 wks €380

Complementary Healing Therapies 136 New Cabra Rd 7 (8681110) - w/end; 7 months, ITEC dip/ w/end, Indian head massage

Crumlin College of Further Education Crumlin Rd 12 (4540662) - ITEC cert in indian head massage, 10 wks, Mon & Wed 6.45-9.45

Galligan College of Beauty 109 Grafton St 2 (6703933) - ITEC & CIBTAC, 30wks

Hartstown Community School Clonsilla 15 (8209863) - massage therapy, 10 wks €60

Hazel Byrne (087-2843079) - baby massage, 5wk course for parents, caregivers: Swords, Stillorgan, & city centre; also private tuition

Indian Head Massage

Indian Head Massage is part of the Ayurvedic bodywork healing system. Learn an authentic massage.

Tutor: Christine Courtney is an accredited tutor to the Institute of Indian Head Massage, of the U.K.

Venue: Obus School, Lucan.   **Phone: 01-628 21 21**

WALMER COLLEGE & HOLISTIC CENTRE

ITEC Diploma courses in: Holistic Massage, Aromatherapy, Reflexology, Anatomy & Physiology, Nutrition & Diet, Stress Management. Massage course in Mullingar. Holistic Studies (1 year Course)

Classes in: T'ai Chi Chuan, Introduction to Mind, Body & Spirit, Introduction to Massage and Aromatherapy.

 Walmer College & Holistic Centre
1st Floor, Raheny SC, Howth Rd, Raheny, D5.
Tel: 8475410/8475338 Fax: 8475363

Healing House 24 O'Connell Ave Berkeley Rd 7 (8306413) - healing massage basic intro, w/end workshop €125/ healing massage ITEC dip, Sept-June, Tue & Thurs 7-10 €1500; also w/end only course/ Indian head ITEC w/ends €695 / ITEC dip Holistic massage, Tue, Thurs or w/end €1500

Holistic Healing Centre 38 Dame St 2 (6710813) - dip course/ Indian head, cert/ deep tissue massage dip/ on-site seated massage/ dip

Holistic Sourcing Centre 67 Lr Camden St 2 (4785022) - indian head, 2 day, cert (086 8032670)/ baby massage (087 2843079)

Irish Academy of Massage & Complementary Therapies 33 Monkstown Lawns, Clondalkin,22 Walkinstown/ Celbridge centres (4640126 /086 8494660) - ITEC dip in advanced Swedish, 150 hrs €1350; also wkends / Indian head massage, 2 wkends 50 hrs €450 ITEC dip. Venues - Walkinstown, Celbridge, Dundrum, Swords, Tullamore

Irish College of Complementary Medicine 6 Main St Donnybrook 4 (2696588/086-2500617) - ITEC holistic massage, dip

Irish Institute for Integrated Psychotherapy 26 Longford Tce Monkstown (2809313)

KLEAR Grange Park View Kilbarrack 5 (8671845) - Shiatsu, Indian head massage, day only

Lucan Community College Esker Drive (6282077) - indian head massage, 6 wks €53

Marie Oxx Pearse College, Clogher Rd 12 (4536661) - ITEC dip, day - massage, indian head; sports massage

Marino College 14-20 Marino Mart 3 (8332100) - & aromatherapy for women, €66/mixed, €50: 10wks each

Melt, Temple Bar Natural Healing Centre 2 Temple Ln 2 (6798786) - w/end, 1 yr, €1,600, cert/ Indian head massage, w/end, €150, cert

Motions Health Centre City West Leisure Centre (4588179/ 087 2808866) - dip in holistic massage (ITEC), Tues 7-10pm, starts Oct 7.

Moytura Healing Centre 2 Glenageary Rd Dun Laoghaire (2854005) - dip, Fri & Sat, 10 wks €660

National Training Centre 16a St Joseph's Parade Off Dorset Street 7 (8827777) - sports massage & remedial therapy, sports injury, one w/end per month, 15 mths, €3268, national qualification/ infant massage, 24 wks, national qualification, also day

Newpark Adult Education Centre Newtownpark Ave Blackrock (2884376) - basic for women, Mon 10wks €99

NTC 16a St Joseph's Parade 7 (8827777) - sports massage, 2 terms, 1 eve p/wk, €3268, Nat Qual

OBUS Aromatherapy Training 53 Beech Grove Lucan (6282121) - aromatherapy, 1yr, dip, also day @ Lucan & Leixlip

Old Bawn Community School Tallaght 24 (4526137) - indian head massage, intro, Thurs, 7.30-9.30pm, 8 wks

Plunket College Swords Rd, Whitehall 9 (8371689) - holistic massage, Mon 7.30 10wks €66

Pobalscoil Rosmini Adult Ed Grace Pk Rd 9 (8371015) - Indian head, beginners, Thurs, 7pm, 10 wks, €80

Portobello School Rere 40 Lr Dominick St 1 (8721277) - holistic massage, ITEC dip part time eve, day, wkend/ sports massage: eve

Seamus Lynch 19 St Patrick's Cresc Monkstown Farm Dun Laoghaire (2846073) - Indian head, w/end, 13 hrs, €150, cert of completion

Senior College Dun Laoghaire CFE Eblana Ave Dun Laoghaire (2800385) - dip in anatomy, physiology, massage, CIBTEC, 25 wks, €475/intro to aromatherapy & massage, 10 wks, €100

Shiatsu Ireland classes Ranelagh & Leixlip/ individ treatments (6109110) - shiatsu beginners & advanced

TACT St Dominic's School St Dominic's Rd Tallaght 24 (4596757) - learn how, 5 wks €24 day

Tallaght Community School Balrothery 24 (4515566) - intro to massage & aromatherapy, 7.30 8 wks €45

Walmer College & Holistic Centre First Floor, Raheny SC Howth Rd 5 (8475410/338) - holistic massage, ITEC dip/ sports massage ITEC dip/

MATHEMATICS see also Basic Education / Junior Cert / Leaving Cert / Parents

Adult Education Centre Adult Ed Centre Ballymun Rd 9 (8420654/ 8425828 night) - numeracy & basic maths, Mon 10wk, €free

Colaiste Dhulaigh Barryscourt Rd Coolock 17 (8481337) - Junior cert(O), Tues, 6.30-8.45, 20 wks/ Leaving cert(O), Mon, 20 wks 7-9.30

Colaiste Eanna College of Business & Technical Stu Kilkieran Rd Cabra 7 (8389577) - day (tel 8688342/8389577), for beginners

DIT Faculty: Science Kevin St 8 (4024585/3445) - MSc applied maths & theoretical physics, 3 yr p/time, €600 per module/ BSc mathematics/ licentiateship of Institute of M, 2 yrs €835pa, BSc hons, 2 yrs €835

Dublin Adult Learning Centre 3 Mountjoy Sq 1 (8787266) - jnr cert

Dublin City University Registry office Glasnevin 9 (7005338) - financial & actuarial/mathematical sciences

Dun Laoghaire College of Further Education 17 Cumberland St Dun Laoghaire (2809676) - leaving cert (O), 24 wks, 7.30 €220/ 2ye, 5.15 €200

FAS Training Centre Finglas 11 (8140243) - craft calculations

Grange Community College Grange Abbey Rd Donaghmede 13 (8471422) - leaving cert, 16 wks, €79

Greenhills College Limekiln Ave Walkinstown 12 (4507779/4507138) - leaving cert(O), 20 wks, €79

Kilroy's College 25 Kingram Place 2 (1850 700700) - tutor supported basic arithmetic for adults, also junior & leaving cert, home-study courses

KLEAR Grange Park View Kilbarrack 5 (8671845) - discovering maths, dau / foundation maths Thurs eve

National Adult Literacy Agency 76 Lr Gardiner St 1 (8554332) - national referral service for adults to get help with reading, writing & maths

Plunket College Swords Rd, Whitehall 9 (8371689) - junior cert, 25 wks, also day/ leaving cert, 27 wks, €215

Ringsend Technical Institute Cambridge Rd 4 (6684498) - leaving cert (O), 25wks, €132

Ringsend Technical Institute Cambridge Rd 4 (6684498) - FETAC cert courses at various times,ongoing, free

The Open University Enquiry & Advice Centre Holbrook House, Holles St 2 (6785399)

MECHANICAL ENGINEERING see also Engineering

DIT Faculty: Engineering Bolton St 1 (4023649/3445) - BE degree, 3 yr p/time €1350; technician cert & dip, 3yr/5yr, €800; general maintenance technology, 1 yr €500, cert; pneumatics/ hydraulics/ mechanical power transmission, cert/ machine tools systems/ plant installation & commissioning/ NC/CNC machine setting & operation, cert/ CNC advanced parts prog, cert/ programmable logic controllers cert: all 1yr, €500 each / certified manufacturing technologist, 1yr €700

Dublin City University Registry office Glasnevin 9 (7005338) - computer-aided mechanical & manufacturing engineering

Institute of Technology Tallaght 24 (4042000) - national cert in mechanical engineering, yrs 1 & 2

St Kevins College Clogher Rd Crumlin 12 (4536397) - engineer technician, NCVA, 1yr, day

MEDIA see also Broadcasting / Journalism / Campaigning

Comhlamh 10 Upr Camden St 2 (4783490) wkend workshop, development issues

DIT admissions ofice Dublin (4023445) - MA in film & TV/ professional level courses for audio visual personnel

DIT admissions ofice Dublin (4023445) - media production unit course (4023108): non-linear edition / productino management for drama / legal & business affairs / budget, costs control - documentary or drama / adobe photoshop/ non-linear audio editing: each 2 - 5 day courses

DIT Faculty: Applied Arts Aungier St 2 (4023465/3445) MA in media studies, 2 yr p/time, €1800 pa

Dublin Business School 13/14 Aungier St 2 (4177500) - BA media & marketing studies, 6.15-9pm, 3-4 yrs / BA (film studies) 4 yrs p/t 2 eve a wk

Dublin City University Registry office Glasnevin 9 (7005338) - & multimedia

Fitzwilliam Institute Ltd Temple Court Temple Rd Blackrock (2834579) - post-grad dip in communications & media skills, 17 wks+ 8wks arranged work experience, f/time day €3990+€190 fees

Gael-Linn 35 Dame St 2 (6751200) - classes held @ Tri-D Cafe, 3 Dawson St

Griffith College Dublin Sth Circular Rd 8 (4150400) - cert in radio broadcasting/ print journalism, 1 yr, p/t, 2 eves per wk/ dipl in media techniques, TV & video, 1 yr, CGLI, f/t / 2 yrs p/t, 3 eve per wk, BA in journalism & media communications, 3 yrs, HETAC degree f/t / HETAC Grad dip in journalis m & communications 18 mths p/time/ also f/time 1 yr /

Irish Academy of Public Relations (2780802) - practical journalism cert, UCD/UCC/GMIT, correspondence or e-mail, 8wks, €355

Kilroy's College 25 Kingram Place 2 (1850 700700) - tutor supported home study: freelance journalism

New Media Technology Training 13 Harcourt St 2 (4780905) - digital video production & online broadcasting/ interactive media production

Pearse College Clogher Rd 12 (4536661/4541544) - & production skills, day

Saor-Ollscoil na hEireann 55 Prussia St 7 (8683368) - media studies, BA in Lib Arts, Weds

St Kevin's College Clogher Rd Crumlin 12 (4536397) - production, Higher National Dip, 2yrs, day

UCD Adult Education Office (7061695) - screenwriting for film/ television/ writing for radio - 10 wks each

Westmoreland College for Management & Business 11 Westmoreland St 2 (6795324/7266) - ICM dip in journalism & media

MEDICAL RECORDS ADMINISTRATION

DIT Faculty: Science Kevin St 8 (4024585/3445) - records admin & patient services management, 1 yr 2 eve weekly €700

Pitman Training Centre 6-8 Wicklow St 2 (6768008) - medical studies, 40 hrs €460, day eve Sats/ medical secretarial dip, 9 wks €1955; dat eve Sats

MEDICINE see also Alternative

Acupuncture Foundation Training School Milltown Pk College (1850 577405) - traditional Chinese acupuncture Licentiate, 3yr p/time, €3533 pa/ also in Belfast

DIT Faculty: Science Kevin St 8 (4024585/3445) - MSc in molecular pathology, 2ye p/t, €3005/ technicians cert in medical physics & physiological measurement, 2 yrs Sats, €850 / intro to cellular pathology & histology, 5 day €320

Irish College of Traditional Chinese Medicine, Dublin (01-4967830) - licentiate in traditional Chinese medicine, 3 yrs, p/time course; Chinese herbal medicine postgraduate p/time courses also

Saint Anthony's House St Lawrence Rd Clontarf 3 (8335300) - Parkinson's association

MEDITATION see also Buddhism / Yoga / Reiki

Ann Slevin 24 Newpark Rd Blackrock (2898019) - angel classes, on-going, also day, 6 wks €120/ channelling, 6wks €120/ magnetic healing w/end 1-day, €160

Ballyfermot College of Further Education Ballyfermot Rd 10 (6269421) - angels in your daily life, 6 wks, Mon 7-9pm, €45

Brahma Kumaris WSU Raja Yoga Centres 61 Morehampton Rd 4 (6687480) - 7wk

Classical Hatha Yoga 61 Morehampton Rd 4 (6687480) - peace & clarity, 4 wks + life long, free, self-rulership - also day

Colaiste Eanna Kilkieran Rd Cabra 7 (8389577) - stress/ tension relief, 10wks, Tues, 6.30-8pm

Divine Rainbow Centre Marino 3 (8333640)

Dublin Meditation Centre 42 Lr leeson St (Basement) 2 (6615934) - 5wk, €120 waged, €50 unwaged

Harvest Moon Centre 24 Lr Baggot St 2 (6627556)

Holistic Healing Centre 38 Dame St 2 (6710813)

International Society for Krishna Consciousness ISKCON, 4 Aungier St 2 (086 1608108) - cultivating inner strength with mantras, 7 wks, €70/€48 cons

Irish T'ai Chi Ch'uan Assoc c/o St Andrew's Resource Centre 114 Pearse St 2 (6771930) - t'ai chi prep, level 1-4 breathing/ relaxation/ stretching/ meditation, 2mths

Knocklyon Youth & Community Centre, 16 (4943991)

Melt, Temple Bar Natural Healing Centre 2 Temple Ln 2 (6798786) - 6 wks, €36/ also drop-in €8

Rigpa Tibetan Buddhist Meditation Centre 12 Wicklow St, 3rd Floor 2 (6703358) -

discovering the natural mind, 10wks, €70 course donation or €10 per class, Jan, April, July & October

Shambhala Meditation Group Upstairs at The Davis Gallery 11 Capel St 1 (8533782) - Meditation & Shambhala teachings, Wed, 8pm, €free

St Thomas Community College Novara Ave Bray (2866111) - learn to meditate 10 wks no fee/ angel connections, 10 wks €70

T'ai Chi Energy Centre Milltown Pk Conference Centre Sandford Rd Ranelagh 6 (4961533) - t'ai chi/qi gong - & wkend workshops

TACT St Dominic's School St Dominic's Rd Tallaght 24 (4596757) - working with angels, 10wks, €53 day

TACT St Dominic's School St Dominic's Rd Tallaght 24 (4596757) - working with angels, 10 wks €53

Tai Chi Ireland PO Box 8276, D 6 (4968342 a'noon; 087 9795042 day only) - T'ai Chi qigong & daoist breathing, bagua; city centre

Tara Buddhist Centre 32 Whitebarn Rd Churchtown 14 (2983314) - €8 per class: at 67 Lr Camden St 2, Tue, 7.30 / Chinese Med Centre, Clarinda Pk W, Dun Laoghaire, Thurs, 7.30 / Northside - phone for details

The Sanctuary Stanhope Street 7 (6705419) - the art of being still 8 wks €60

Walmer College & Holistic Centre First Floor, Raheny SC Howth Rd 5 (8475410/338) - & relaxation

Yang's Martial Arts Assoc Newpark Sports Centre, Blackrock (2814901) - yang style, t'ai chi ch'uan/qigong - all levels

MEN, COURSES/ACTIVITIES FOR

Ballymun Mens Centre LS4 Shangan Rd Ballymun 9 (8623117/8623409) - social events, group outings, drop-in centre, day

MENTAL HEALTH / ILLNESS, UNDERSTANDING

Kilroy's College 25 Kingram Place 2 (1850 700700) - tutor supported home study: adult & child psychology, dip

METAL WORK see also Art Metal Work

DIT Faculty: Engineering Bolton St 1 (4023649/3445) - pipe fabrication, 20 wks 1 eve weekly €500, cert

Newpark Adult Education Centre Newtownpark Ave Blackrock (2884376) - Tue, metalcraft, 10 wks, €130

MIDI see also Music Technology

Walton's New School of Music 69 Sth Gt George's St 2 (4781884) - also day, see ad page 173

MILLINERY

Grafton Academy of Dress Design 6 Herbert Place 2 (6763653) - Tues, 6 classes, €240

MIME see also Acting

Betty Ann Norton Theatre School 11 Harcourt St 2 (4751913)

MODEL PLANES / CARS see Aeromodelling / Motor Sports

MODEL ENGINEERING

St Kevins College Clogher Rd Crumlin 12 (4536397) - 10wks

MODERN DANCE see also Dance

Dance Theatre of Ireland Bloomfields Centre, Lr George St Dun Laoghaire (2803455) - hip-hop Wed 8-9PM; also Saturdays for adults, teen-to-adult, young people various times

Marino College 14-20 Marino Mart 3 (8332100) - hip-hop, Tue 5-6pm, €33

MONEY MANAGEMENT / PERSONAL ACCOUNTS see also Accountancy

Ballsbridge College of Business Studies Shelbourne Rd 4 (6684806) - personal finance, Thurs 6.30 10 wks €50

Donahies Community School Streamville Rd 13 (8482217) - how to get the most out of your money, invertment, planning, pensions etc, Mon 7.30 6wks €50

Donahies Community School Streamville Rd 13 (8482217)

Newpark Adult & Continuing Education Centre Newtownpark Ave Blackrock (2884376) - successful investing, 10 wks €120

Old Bawn Community School Tallaght 24 (4526137) - personal finances, Thurs, 10 wks

MONTESSORI COURSE

College of Further Education Main St Dundrum 14 (2951376) - intro to, 20 wks

Montessori Education Centre 41-43 Nth Gt George's St 1 (8780071) - Montessori teacher training dip: course (1) 0-6 yrs, (2) 6-9 yrs, (3) 9-12 yrs: 29 wks, €1800 each/ also by distance learning, 36 wks, €1250

Old Bawn Community School Tallaght 24 (4526137) - Montessori foundation dip,

St Nicholas Montessori College Ireland, Tues & Thurs, 6.45-9.45pm, 30 wks

Portobello School Rere 40 Lr Dominick St 1 (8721277) - dip in montessori teaching, full time; also part time eve, day, wkend also higher dip/

St Nicholas Montessori College 16 Adelaide St Dun Laoghaire (2806064) - national dip/ BA degree/ postgrad

MORRIS DANCING

Dublin City Morris Dancers c/o Alan Corsini 38 Meadow Mount 16 (2985068)

MOSAIC see crafts

MOTOR BOAT TRAINING

Colaiste Dhulaigh & College of Further Education Barryscourt Rd Coolock 17 (8481337) - powerboating, Sat 9.30-12.30

Irish Sailing Assoc 3 Park Rd Dun Laoghaire (2800239) - motorboat handling coastal, offshore; powerboat inland, coastal: apply for provider list

MOTOR CYCLE MAINTENANCE

DIT Faculty: Engineering Bolton St 1 (4023649/3445) - motor cycle studies, 3yrs 2 eve wkly, €700pa

Kylemore College Kylemore Rd 10 (6265901) - Tues, Wed, 10 wks each / restoration, Thurs 8 wks

Pobalscoil Rosmini Adult Ed Grace Pk Rd 9 (8371015) - beginners, Tues, 10 wks, €100

MOTOR INDUSTRY MANAGEMENT AND RELATED COURSES Garage Management

DIT Faculty: Engineering Bolton St 1 (4023649/3445) - management, 3 yr dip €700 yr 1; 2 yr cert €700 yr 1

MOTOR MAINTENANCE - Know Your Car, NTC

Ballymun Comprehensive Schools Adult Ed Centre Ballymun Rd 9 (8420654/8425828 night) - Wed 10wk, €95

Cabinteely Community School Johnstown Rd 18 (2857455) - 10wk, €75

Coolmine Community School Clonsilla 15 (8214583) - 7.30-9.30, 9 wks, €60

DIT Faculty: Engineering Bolton St 1 (4023649/3445) - vehicle parts personnel, distance learning prog, €500/ motor compressed air systems, 3 10wk modules €500/ auto engineering technician, 1 yr €700/ technological cert in auto engineering, elementary, intermediate, advanced, 1 yr each €700 per stage

FAS Training Centre Finglas Jamestown Rd 11 (8140243)

FAS Training Centre Tallaght 24 (4045284) - basic, 10wk

Greendale Community School Kilbarrack 5 (8322735/6) - 10wks, Tues, 7.30-9.30pm, €55

Greenhills College Limekiln Ave Walkinstown 12 (4507779/4507138) - 8wks, €73

Hartstown Community School Clonsilla 15 (8209863) - beginners/intermediate, 10wks, €60 each

Kylemore College Kylemore Rd 10 (6265901) - workshop, Mon, 8 wks

Newpark Adult Ed Centre Newtownpark Ave Blackrock (2884376) - 10wks, €99

Plunket College Swords Rd, Whitehall 9 (8371689) - beginners, Tues, 10 wks, €66

Pobailscoil Iosolde 20 (6260116) - Mon 10 wks €65

Pobalscoil Rosmini Adult Ed Grace Pk Rd 9 (8371015) - beginners & prep for NCT, Mon, 10 wks, €85

Ringsend Technical Institute Cambridge Rd 4 (6684498) - 10wks €85

Saint Finian's Community College Swords (8402623) - Mon, 10wk, €79

St Kevins College Clogher Rd Crumlin 12 (4536397) - 10wks

St Tiernan's Community School Parkvale Balally 16 (2953224) - basic care, national car test, Tues, 7.30-9.30pm, 10 wks, €70

Stillorgan College of Further Education Old Road Stillorgan (2880704) - Thurs, 7.30-9.30pm, 8 wks, €70

MOTOR SPORTS

Motor Cycle Union of Ireland (Sth Centre) Ltd, BEAT Centre Stephenstown Bus Pk Balbriggan (8020480)

Taney Centre Taney Rd Dundrum 14 (2985491) - model cars, Sat (4944345)

Training Associates DIT Bolton St 7 (086 2544364) - intro to Rallying, 10 wks, 7-10pm, €195 - theory, framework, techniques, ideas relevant to stage rallying

MOUNTAINEERING see Adventure Sports

MUSIC see also Music Appreciation and under individual instruments

Abbey School of Music 9b Lr Abbey St 1 (8747908)

Bray Music Centre Florence Rd Bray (2866768) - string quartet / also Music Initiation (Kindergarten)

Carl Alfred 6 Palmerston Villas, Basement Fl 2 off Upr Rathmines Rd 6 (4972095) - guitar, popular, hear-feel teaching method. See display ad at Guitar

Clontarf School of Music 6 Marino Mart 3 (8330936) - music for fun, intro, 10wk - also day

DCU Registry office Glasnevin 9 (7005338) - BA in music performance, RIA/DCU

DIT Faculty: Applied Arts Aungier St 2 (4023465/3445) - individual &or class instrumental/vocal tuition: incl most instruments/ leaving & junior cert courses/ jazz improvisation/ musicianship/ singing, etc: at DIT Adelaide Rd (4023552)

Donahies Community School Streamville Rd 13 (8482217) - explore world of classical music, Mon 7.30-9.30, 10 wks €200

Dun Laoghaire Music Centre 130A Lr George's St Dun Laoghaire (2844178)

Hartstown Community School Clonsilla 15 (8209863) - tin whistly & flute, 10 wks €60

Leinster School of Music Griffith College Campus South Circular Rd 8 (4150467)

Melody School of Music 178E Whitehall Rd W Perrystown 12 (4650150) - wkend courses all instruments, Sat & Sun, 12 wks

Merriman School of Singing and Music Bel Canto House 21 North Great George's St 1 (874 2034)

Metropolitan College of Music 59 Lr Baggot St 2 (4540753) - private, all instruments, 30wks

Na Piobairi Uilleann 15 Henrietta St 1 (8730093) - see various instruments/ also recitals Sat nights

Pobalscoil Rosmini Adult Ed Grace Pk Rd 9 (8371015) - joy of classical, Wed, 7pm, 10 wks/ tin whistle & flute, Thurs 7.30 €80

Rachel Dempsey (086 3097232) - workshops, courses: various city & co venues

Sound Training Centre Temple Bar Music Centre Curved Street Temple Bar 2 (6709033) - song school, cert, for pre-leaving, 1 week summer €350

Walton's New School of Music 69 Sth Gt George's St 2 (4781884) - also day, see ad page 173

MUSIC APPRECIATION

Ballymun Comprehensive School Adult Ed Centre Ballymun Rd 9 (8420654/ 8425828 night) - hooked on classics, Wed 7.30, 10 wks €90

DATE College of Further Education Dundrum 14 (2964322) - listening with an expert, 10 wks, €66 day

KLEAR Grange Park View Kilbarrack 5 (8671845) - enjoying mujsic, day

Leinster School of Music & Drama Griffith College Campus South Circular Rd 8 (4150467) - for adults

Newpark Adult Education Centre Newtownpark Ave Blackrock (2884376) - music for pleasure, 10wks, €130

People's College 32 Parnell Sq 1 (8735879) - €50

Rachel Dempsey (086 3097232) - workshops, courses: various city & co venues

UCD Adult Education Office (7061695) - 8 wks

Walton's New School of Music 69 Sth Gt George's St 2 (4781884) - classical, also day, see ad page 173

MUSIC BUSINESS

Dun Laoghaire College of Further Education 17 Cumberland St Dun Laoghaire (2809676) - the industry explained, Tue 7-9pm 12 wks €590

Sound Training Centre Temple Bar Music Centre Curved Street Temple Bar 2 (6709033) - intro to music industry, STC cert 1 wk €320

MUSIC LIBRARY

Central Library Ilac Centre 1 (8734333)

MUSIC TECHNOLOGY

Dun Laoghaire Music Centre 130A Lr George's St Dun Laoghaire (2844178)

Kylemore College Kylemore Rd 10 (6265901) - post-leaving FETAC 2, day: music technology; performance & tech;

New Media Technology Training 13 Harcourt St 2 (4780905)

Sound Training Centre Temple Bar Music Centre Curved Street Temple Bar 2 (6709033) - sound engineering music technologies C&G 1&2, 32 weeks €3000 p/time/€4200 f/time / advanced course, C&G 3, 32 weeks €4200/ sound engineer, lighting & stage production, C&G 1 32 wks €4000/ recording techniques, STC cert 15 wks €950/ MIDI & desktop audio, STC cert, 8 wks €400/ Pro-tools hard-disk recording sys; professional studio recording: 2 wkends, all yr, €200 each

Waltons New School of Music 69 Sth Gt George's St 2 (4781884) - also day, see ad page 173

MUSIC THEATRE

Dun Laoghaire Music Centre 130A Lr George's St Dun Laoghaire (2844178)

Walton's New School of Music 69 Sth Gt George's St 2 (4781884) - see ad page 173

MUSIC THEORY & HARMONY

Abbey School of Music 9b Lr Abbey St 1 (8747908) - Kevin Robinson

Bray Music Centre Florence Rd Bray (2866768)

John Ward 5 Tibradden Drive Walkinstown 12 (4520918) - prep for Assoc board grade exams - also day

Metropolitan College of Music 59 Lr Baggot St 2 (4540753) - private, 30wks

Newpark Music Centre Newtownpark Ave Blackrock (2883740)

Walton's New School of Music 69 Sth Gt George's St 2 (4781884) - also day, see ad page 173

MUSICAL INSTRUMENT REPAIR

Na Piobairi Uilleann 15 Henrietta St 1 (8730093) - reed making classes

NATURAL HISTORY / NATURE STUDY see also Ornithology / Wildlife

Dublin Naturalists Field Club Fridolin Kerr, Membership Sec. 31 Cherrywood Pk Clondalkin 22

NAVIGATION

Ballsbridge College of Business Studies Shelbourne Rd 4 (6684806) - yachtmaster coastal, 7pm 20 wks €165

Colaiste Dhulaigh Barryscourt Rd Coolock 17 (8481337) - introduction, Tue 7pm, 8 wks

Fingall Sailing School Malahide (8451979)

Glenans Irish Sailing Club 5 Lr Mount St 2 (6611481) - coastal cert

Irish Sailing Assoc 3 Park Rd Dun Laoghaire (2800239) - navigation & pilotage courses, all levels, apply for provider list

Newpark Adult & Continuing Education Centre Newtownpark Ave Blackrock (2884376) - yachtmaster offshore cert, intermediate & advanced, 20 wks, €260/ coastal skipper intermediate/ navigation basics, 10 wks, €130

Ringsend Technical Institute Cambridge Rd 4 (6684498) - coastal & offshore, 20 wks €200 ISA cert

Sea-Craft 3 Newcourt Ave Bray (2863362) - ISA Yachtmaster coastal, 21 wk €335, cert/ Yachtmaster offshore, 21 wks €397/ celestial, yachtmaster ocean, 20 wks €440, cert/ RYA HCA SRC Short Range cert, GMDSS, 1 day €129/ GMDSS LRC Long Range cert, 5 day €635/

St Thomas Community College Novara Ave Bray (2866111) - basic coastal/ intro to GPS: 10wks, €70 ea

NEEDLEWORK / NEEDLE CRAFT see also Crafts

KLEAR Grange Park View Kilbarrack 5 (8671845) - day

NEGOTIATION SKILLS

Hartstown Community School Clonsilla 15 (8209863) - 10 wks, €60

NEUROLINGUISTIC PROGRAMMING

Ballsbridge College of Business Studies Shelbourne Rd 4 (6684806) intro to NLP,

Mon 7pm 10 wks 475

IICH Education 118 Stillorgan Road 4 (2600118) - 3-day foundation skills course, €245. Thought Field Therapy (Algorithms Levels I &II), Applied Behavioural Medicine/ Health Crisis Counselling. Classes at Milltown Pk, 6 and other south-city locations

NORWEGIAN

Dublin Public Libraries Admin Hq, 138-144 Pearse St 2 (6644800) - central library Ilac Centre (8734333) or Library HQ for details (6744800), self-learning, €free

Sandford Language Institute Milltown Pk Sandford Rd 6 (2601296) - all levels, 14 wks, €250

Sth Dublin Co Libraries Languages & Computers: Ballyroan/Clondalkin/ Castletymon, Lucan & Co Library (4597834-admin only) - self learning

NUMEROLOGY

Healing House 24 O'Connell Ave Berkeley Rd 7 (8306413) - & tarot/ w/end workshop €80

NURSERY TRAINING Childcare / Montessori

Hazel Byrne (087-2843079) - baby massage, 5wk course for parents & caregivers: Swords, Stillorgan & cith centre

Inchicore College of Further Education Emmet Rd 8 (4535358) - nursery nursing & child care - day

Kilroy's College 25 Kingram Place 2 (1850 700700) - tutor supported home study: child care, dip course

UCD Adult Education Office (7061695) - nursery management, day, NCNA dip

NURSING STUDIES

Crumlin College of Further Education Crumlin Rd 12 (4540662) - ITEC dip in anatomy & physiology & body massage, for registered nurses

Dublin City University Registry office Glasnevin 9 (7005338)

Inchicore College of Further Education Emmet Rd 8 (4535358) - pre-nursing studies/ nursery studies & child care

Kilroy's College 25 Kingram Place 2 (1850 700700) - home-study: entrance exam

Oscail - National Distance Education Centre DCU 9 (7005481) - Bachelor of Nursing Studies, 2-3 years, awarded by DCU, distance learning

St John's Ambulance Brigade of Ireland 29 Upr Leeson St 4 (6688077) - home nursing, 7 wks, cert, various venues

NUTRITION see also Diet / Food Science / Health

AAA Counselling Dr MJ Brennan PhD c/o 48 Connaught St Phibsboro 7 (8380014) - obesity factors

Holistic Healing Centre 38 Dame St 2 (6710813)

Kilroy's College 25 Kingram Place 2 (1850 700700) - tutor supported home study

KLEAR Grange Park View Kilbarrack 5 (8671845) - day

Kylemore College Kylemore Rd 10 (6265901) - FETAC food, cookery nutrition, cert, 12 wks, Wed 1.30-4pm

Portobello School Rere 40 Lr Dominick St 1 (8721277) - & diet, ITEC dip, eve

St Thomas Community College Novara Ave Bray (2866111) - 30 wks €200 FETAC

Time Out (4591038) - & food intolerances, also wkend

Walmer College & Holistic Centre First Floor, Raheny SC Howth Rd 5 (8475410/338) - & diet, ITEC dip

OBOE see Music

OFFICE PROCEDURES / OFFICE TECHNOLOGY see also Secretarial / Computer Training / ECDL etc

ABM Computer Training 54 North St, Swords (8902348) - all yr, also day, Sats / ms office specialist modules

CITAS Computer and IT Training, 54 Middle Abbey St 1 (8782212) – pitman's C&G 1 yr f/time

Colaiste Ide Cardiffsbridge Rd Finglas West 11 (8342333) - cert of professional competence, Tues & Thurs, 7.30, 20 wks €400 CIT cert

Computeach AXIS, Main St Ballymun 9 (8832167) - ECDL pitman / internet, email

Dorset College 64a Lr Dorset St/ 8 Belvedere Pl 1 (8309677) - office technology: , keyboarding, ECDL job prep, comp accounts, Mon-Fri 10 wks/ MOS & e-Quals core level & expert adv dip

FAS Net College www.fas-netcollege.com (info@fas-netcollege.com/ 2043600) - elearning: computer fundamentals €free

FAS Training Centre Cabra Bannow Rd 7 (8821400); Finglas (8140243);

Irish Academy of Computer Training 98 St Stephen's Grn 2 (4347600) - MOUS master - ms office user specialist 20 wks €1496, cert/ MOS/MOUS master book camp, 10 wks €995, cert

Keytrainer Ireland 33/34 Dame St 2 (6714000) - office skills incl keyboard/ ECDL/ CV prep

Kilroy's College 25 Kingram Place 2 (1850 700700) - tutor supported keyboarding & typing, data processing, book-keeping & accounts, computer skills, home-study dip course

Pitman Training Centre 6-8 Wicklow St 2 (6768008) - advanced dip in office technology, 11 wks €2246; day eve Sats

Whitehall College of Further Education Swords Rd 9 (8376011) - ofice admin; tourism-language ofice admin; personnel admin; health admin - day

OIL BURNER SERVICING

DIT Faculty: Built Environment Bolton St 1 (4023711/3445) - oil fired, 10 wks €230

FAS Training Centre Ballyfermot 10 (6055900/ 5933); Cabra Bannow Rd 7 (8821400)

OIL PAINTING see also Drawing & Painting

Ashfield College Main St Templeogue 6W (4900866) - 7.30-9.30, 8 wks

Brian Byrnes Art Studio 3 Upr Baggot St 4 (6671520 / 6711599) - 8wk, €130, also day

Cabinteely Community School Johnstown Rd 18 (2857455) - beginners/improvers, 10wk, €75 each

DATE College of Further Education Dundrum 14 (2964322) - 10 wks, €66 day

Donahies Community School Streamville Rd 13 (8482217) - & soft pastels, Tues, 10 wks, €55

Holy Family Community School Rathcoole (4580766)

Jean Strong (2892323) - ongoing beginners improvers, 10 wks €140/also day - Blackrock

Kilternan Adult Education Group Glencullen Rd 18 (2952050) oils/ acrylics, Mon, Tue, Wed, Fri: - day 10 wks €79

Lucan Community College Esker Drive (6282077) - 10wk, €79

Marino College 14-20 Marino Mart 3 (8332100) - & watercolours, Tue & Thurs, beginners/intermediate, 10wks €66 each

Meridian Art Group c/o St Paul's College Raheny 5 (8310688)

National College of Art & Design in Art & Design 100 Thomas Street 8 (6364214) - aspects of, introductory & intermediate, 21wk

Pobalscoil Neasain Baldoyle 13 (8063092) - Wed 2-4pm, 10 wks €140

Pobalscoil Rosmini Adult Ed Grace Pk Rd 9 (8371015) - oils & pastels, Wed €100

St Thomas Community College Novara Ave Bray (2866111) - 10wks, €70

OLD-TIME DANCING see also Ballroom / Dance

Dance Club Rathmines & Rathgar (2893797)

ONLINE EDUCATION see also Distance Learning

FAS Net College www.fas-netcollege.com (info@fas-netcollege.com/ 2043600) - variety of courses online with optional tutor support

OPERA

St Thomas Community College Novara Ave Bray (2866111) - Maria Callas & Italian Lyric Opera, 10 wks, €70

ORCHESTRA

Walton's New School of Music 69 Sth Gt George's St 2 (4781884) - see ad page

ORGAN see Music

ORIENTEERING see also Adventure Sports

Corporate Club 24 Elmcastle Green Kilnamanagh 24 (4610935)

Network Sports & Social Club 24 Elmcastle Green Kilnamanagh 24 (4524415)

ORNITHOLOGY

Birdwatch Ireland (2804322)

UCD Adult Education Office (7061695) - Irish birds, 10 wks

OUTDOOR EDUCATION

St Kevin's College Clogher Rd Crumlin 12 (4536397) - BTEC dip, day, ICU/BTEC, 2yr, day

PAIN MANAGEMENT / BACKPAIN see also HEALING

Physio Extra 4 Oliver Bond St 8 (6725719) - spineright: yoga with pilates, beginner & intermediate levels; morn, day, eve

PAINTING see also Art / Art History / Drawing / Landscape / Oil Painting / Pastel / Portrait / Sketching / Watercolour

Brenda Bigger Killiney (2849675) - hand-painted porcelain, 5wk, 2.5 hours per class, €85, materials extra, day

Brian Byrnes Art Studio 3 Upr Baggot St 4 (6671520 / 6711599) - water colour, oil, 8wk, €130, also day

Colaiste Eanna Vocational School Kilkieran Rd Cabra 7 (8389577) - Tues, 7-9pm, 10 wks

DIT Faculty: Applied Arts Aungier St 2 (4023465/3445) - painting a shifting horizon, 6 wks; responding to your landscape 10 wks/ (4024138)

Foxrock Institute Kill O' the Grange School Kill Lane Blackrock (4939506/4939629) - watercolours for pleasure, 8wks, €85

Jean Strong (2892323) - ongoing, beginners-improvers, 10wks, €140/also day - Blackrock

KLEAR Grange Park View Kilbarrack 5 (8671845) - painting & drawing 1, day

National College of Art & Design in Art & Design 100 Thomas Street 8 (6364214) - from life/new perspectives, intermediate & advanced/ painting the figure/ portrait painting

Newpark Adult Education Centre Newtownpark Ave Blackrock (2884376) - & drawing/ watercolour painting, 10wks, €99 each

People's College 32 Parnell Sq 1 (8735879) - €50

Pobalscoil Rosmini Adult Ed Grace Pk Rd 9 (8371015) - landscape, beginners & improvers, Mon €85

RAVE Good Shepherd School Churchtown 14 (2981052) - painting with Hazel / painting & drawing, each 10 wks Mon 7.30, €79

Saint Tiernan's Community School Parkvale Balally 16 (2953224) - water colour/acrylic, 10wks, €70

St Thomas Community College Novara Ave Bray (2866111) - & sketching, 10wks, €70

UCD Adult Education Office (7061695) - mixed media painting, 10 wks morns

PARACHUTING AND SKY-DIVING Adventure Sports

Parachute Assoc of Ireland Moyne Lodge Moyne Rd Baldoyle 13 (087-2906492)

PARENTS, COURSES FOR see also Child / Drugs / Family / Pre-School / Psychology / Single Parents

Campaign Against Bullying 72 Lakelands Ave Stillorgan (2887976) - anti-bullying courses

Froebel College of Education Sion Hill, Blackrock & Nurture Inst 140 Meadowgrove Dundrum (2963795) - parenting: family management Tue, 30 wks cert/ dip, €290/ what a parent can do/ Teen parenting/ from pram to primary/ assertiveness for parents: Tues, 7 wks, €80 each

Further Education & Training Awards Council (FETAC East Point Plaza East Point Business Park 3 (8659500) - national certification body

Gail Bovenizer 52 Walkinstown area (087 7590685) - learn how to massage your baby, Wed, Thurs morn & pm

Harmony Yoga Ireland Ballinteer/Dundrum Dalkey / Killiney (087 8263778) - how to massage your baby, day 5 wks €95 / post-natal yoga, Sat morn €15 per class / pregnancy yoga, €15 per class / birthing from within, wk/end 1 day €100 /

Kilroy's College 25 Kingram Place 2 (1850 700700) - tutor supported home study: childcare/ psychology, dip

KLEAR Grange Park View Kilbarrack 5 (8671845) - parent to parent/ day

Lucan Community College Esker Drive (6282077) - Mon, 10 wks €79

Newpark Adult Education Centre Newtownpark Ave Blackrock (2884376) - effective parenting for 0-12 yrs Mon 7.30, 10 wks, €99, 20 wks €198/ managing my child's education, Wed, €99

Parental Equality 54 Middle Abbey St 1 (8740999) - shared parenting course

Pobalscoil Rosmini Adult Ed Grace Park Rd 9 (8371015) - safe passage prog, children & drugs, Wed 7.30 10 wks €40/ teenage issues, Tue €40/ family studies, Thurs €80

Portmarnock Community School Carrickhill Rd (8038056) - coping with adolescents, Dr V Moloney, Tues 7.20, 6 wks €90

Ringsend Technical Institute Cambridge Rd 4 (6684498) - parenting skills, 10 wks €65

Saint Anthony's House St Lawrence Rd Clontarf 3 (8335300) - mother & toddler group

St Thomas Community College Novara Ave Bray (2866111) - practical parenting. - 10 wks €80

Taney Parish Centre Taney Rd Dundrum 14 (2985491) - parenting, Tues (2832141)

TARGET St Kevin's School Newbrook Rd, Donaghmede 13 (8671967) - day only, NAHB

Transactional Analysis in Ireland (4511125) - in everyday situations, mthly workshop, donation

UCD Adult Education Office (7061695) - parenting & gifted child, 10 wks morns

PASTELS: PAINTING & DRAWING see also Art

Jean Strong (2892323) - ongoing, beginners, improvers, 10 wks €140/also day - Blackrock

National College of Art & Design in Art & Design 100 Thomas Street 8 (6364214) - drawing with, c. 22wk

PASTORAL CARE

All Hallows College Gracepark Rd Drumcondra 9 (8373745) - pastoral education, Tue 6.50 12 wks €190; ECTS credits option

PATCHWORK & QUILTING see also Embroidery

Ballymun Comprehensive Schools Adult Ed Centre Ballymun Rd 9 (8420654/ 8425828 night) - & lace-making, Mon, Tue, 10 wks €75

Quilt Art Workshops 4 Mill Wood Naas (045-876121) - classes & workshops, SAE for info

St Tiernan's Community School Parkvale Balally 16 (2953224) - make a quilt, covers, cushions, Wed, 7.30-9.30pm, 10 wks, €70

PATTERNMAKING / PATTERN CUTTING see FASHION

PAYE, VAT & WAGES see also Book-Keeping / Business Studies / Taxation

Marino College 14-20 Marino Mart 3 (8332100) - Tues 8pm 10 wks €50

PAYROLL / ACCOUNTS see also Accountancy
Irish Payroll Association (IPASS) Clifton House Lower Fitzwilliam St 2 (6617200) - certified payroll technician, 1 eve x 10 wks, stage 1 & 2/ dip in payroll management, 4 modules, 2 day each: various venues: city centre, Griffith Ave, Blanchardstown, Tallaght, Dun Laoire

PC REPAIR, ASSEMBLY see also COMPUTER MAINTENANCE
Irish Academy of Computer Training 98 St Stephen's Grn 2 (4347600) - pc troubleshooting & repair, 8 wks €755 cert/ A+ cert, 8 wks €1995 / also day
Kilroy's College 25 Kingram Place 2 (1850 700700) - tutor supported home study

PERCUSSION see also Music
Walton's New School of Music 69 Sth Gt George's St 2 (4781884) - Latin percussion/African/drum kit, also day, see ad page

PERSIAN
Dublin Public Libraries Admin Hq, 138-144 Pearse St 2 (6644800) - central library Ilac Centre (8734333) or Library HQ for details (6744800), self-learning €free

PERSONAL DEVELOPMENT see also Assertiveness / Enneagram / Self-Awareness / Beauty Care / Teamwork
Balbriggan Community College Pine Ridge Chapel St (8412388/9) - for women, 8 wks, 7.30-9.30, Thurs, €73
Ballsbridge College of Business Studies Shelbourne Rd 4 (6684806) - intro to NLP, Mon 7pm, 10 wks €75
Ballymun Comprehensive Schools Adult Ed Centre Ballymun Rd 9 (8420654/ 8425828 night) - voyage of self-discovery, Tue, 10wk, €75
Ballymun Mens Centre LS4 Shangan Rd Ballymun 9 (8623117/8623409) - courses & social activities, day
Bi-Aura Foundation De Light House Corlurgan Bailieboro, Co Cavan (087-2317984) - bio-energy dip, 9mth, €3,500, w/ends 9mths
Brahma Kumaris WSU Raja Yoga Centres 61 Morehampton Rd 4 (6687480) - 7wk, day
Business Coach Ireland 28 Grange Pk Walk Raheny 5 (8478391) - dip business

& executive coaching, 1 yr eves, €2500

Cabinteely Community School Johnstown Rd 18 (2857455) `- unlocking your creative potential, Tues, 10wks, €75

Centre for Professional & Personal Development Coach Centre 44 Westland Row 2 (6612291) - find the career you love, eve, w/end, 6 wks, €400, cert

Colaiste Dhulaigh Barryscourt Rd Coolock 17 (8481337) - Tues, 8 wks, 7-9.15

Colaiste Eanna College of Business & Technical Stu Kilkieran Rd Cabra 7 (8389577) - day (tel 8688342/8389577) / self-esteem, goal setting, etc, 10 wks Tues / life skills, Wed 10-12am

Communication & Personal Development 30/31 Wicklow St 2 (6713636/6613225) - confidence building & personal development for women

Complementary House 91 Terenure Rd N 6W (4929077) - angel workshop, w/end, 2 days €150

DIT Faculty: Applied Arts Aungier St 2 (4023465/3445) - self-esteem enhancement skills, 76 hrs over 36 wks plus 16 hrs training (4023312)

Donahies Community School Streamville Rd 13 (8482217) - self-confidence for men & women, Mon, 8 wks, €45

Eden Computer Training Rathfarnham 16, or MACRO Centre, 1 Green St 7 (4953155) - time management, assertiveness, communication skills, motivation: customised

FAS Net College www.fas-netcollege.com (info@fas-netcollege.com/ 2043600) - elearning: appraisals series €80; business writing basic €80; online tutor option €80

Finglas Adult Reading & Writing Scheme Colaiste Eoin Finglas 11 (8340893) - day, 30wks, free

Geraldine Brand Style Image Consultant City Centre (8327332) - courses or individual consultation for men, women & teenagers

Greenhills College Limekiln Ave Walkinstown 12 (4507779/4507138) - winning ways, Mon, 10wks, €79

Hartstown Community School Clonsilla 15 (8209863) - intro/continuing/life enrichment - 10wks, €60 each

Healing Arts Centre International 46 Walnut Rise Drumcondra 9 (8370831 / 087 2749701)

Hegarty Fitness Centre 53 Middle Abbey St 1 (8723080) - yogametrics, also home/office/city centre, from €120, also day

Holistic Healing Centre 38 Dame St 2 (6710813)

Holistic Sourcing Centre 67 Lr Camden St 2 (4785022) - life & social skills, 6 wks (087 6431796)

KAIROS Therapy Training Ellen Smith (6286466) Kairos emotioinal release therapy

Kilroy's College 25 Kingram Place 2 (1850 700700) - tutor supported home study: adult & child psychology, diet & fitness, and others

KLEAR Grange Park View Kilbarrack 5 (8671845) - self-esteem, group facilitation & advanced facilitation/ confidence building/ mindpower; day

Marino College 14-20 Marino Mart 3 (8332100) - levels 1 €20/ & 2 €26: 10wks

MD Communications 38 Spireview Lane off Rathgar Rd 6 (4975866)

Milltown Institute of Theology & Philosophy Milltown Pk 6 (2698388) - intro to philos/ to theolog: each - dip, Tue/Thurs, 2yrs, 26 wks €1420 pa/ - intro to spirituality, dip, Mon, 26 wks €530/ personal opportunity to explore alternative leadership styles, 6 wks, Wed, €530, cert

New Directions 16 Carmichael Cntr Nth Brunswick St 7 (8723181) - public speaking

Newpark Adult & Continuing Education Centre Newtownpark Ave Blackrock (2884376) - stress mamagement & life skills, €99/ Louise L Hay workshop, tyes, €99

Palmerstown Community School 20 (6260116) - Mon 7.30-9, 10wks €65

People's College 32 Parnell Sq 1 (8735879) - €50

PRH Personality & Human Relations 6 Hazelwood Crescent Clondalkin 22 (4593275) - awareness for beginners, cert, 10 wks €150

Quantum Communications Ken McCready 39 Emerald Sq, Dolphin's Barn 8 (086 1502604) - courses in city centre, 6 wk

Rachel Dempsey (086 3097232) - workshops, courses: various city & co venues

Rathcoole Community School Rathcoole (4580766)

Rathmines Snr College Town Hall 6 (4975334) - & assertiveness, Mon, 10 wks, €65

Rigpa Tibetan Buddhist Meditation Centre 12 Wicklow St, 3rd Floor 2 (6703358) - discovering the natural mind, 10wks, €70 course donation or €10 per class, Jan, April, July & October

Ringsend Technical Institute Cambridge Rd 4 (6684498) - living with confidence, 10wks, €65

St Finian's Community College Swords (8402623) - make it 'your best year yet', 10 wks €79

St Kevin's College Clogher Rd Crumlin 12 (4536397) - social workplace relationship skills, 1 yr, NCVA 2, NUI, cert Maynooth

St Mark's Community School Cookstown Road Tallaght 24 (4519399)

St Thomas Community College Novara Ave Bray (2866111) - journey through the rainbow; energy field & chacras, psycic potential: ea 10 wks €70

Star Consulting PO Box 8796 2 (086 6061639) - 2 day €350

TACT St Dominic's School St Dominic's Rd Tallaght 24 (4596757) - enrichment, 5wks, €24 day

The Professional Training and Coaching Consultancy (087 6379765/ 045 865783) - assertiveness / confidence building/ achieving your goals: 6 wks

Tony Quinn Centre 66/67 Eccles St 7 (8304211) - & relaxation & stress management

Transactional Analysis in Ireland (4511125) - in everyday situations, mthly workshop, donation

UCD Adult Education Office (7061695) - focusing & personality, 8 wks/

Yvonne Stewart Park House Library Road Dun Laoire (2802150) - assertiveness training for women, 8wk, €70, day

PERSONNEL PRACTICE / HR MANAGEMENT see also Management

AAA Counselling Dr MJ Brennan PhD c/o 48 Connaught St Phibsboro 7 (8380014) - life coaching, mentorship, also day

ABM Business Training 54 North St, Swords (8902348) - staff appraisals; also day, Sat

Colaiste Ide Cardiffsbridge Rd Finglas West 11 (8342333) - CIPD cert, Tues & Thurs, 7-10pm, 25 wks, €450

DIT Faculty: Business Aungier St 2 (4023040/3445) - BSc in human resource management, 4 yrs p/time €1350 pa/ CIPD cert in personnel practice, 1 yr €800/ cert in training & development, 1 yr €800

Dorset College 64a Lr Dorset St/ 8 Belvedere Pl 1 (8309677) - human resource development dip, Tues & Thurs, 6.30-9pm, 1 yr

Griffith College Dublin Sth Circular Rd 8 (4150400) - dipl in HRM, 15 wks, ICM, p/time

Institute of Technology Tallaght 24 (4042000) - cert in personnel practice

National College of Ireland Mayor St IFSC 1 (4060500/ 1850 221721) - Management & Employee Relations, 1 yr cert; also day release/NCI Dip in Management and Employee Relations, 2 yr, 1 eve wkly/ Also HETAC Cert, 2 yrs 1 day wkly/NCI Dip in First-Line Management (Supervision), 1 yr, p/time, also day release and Off- Campus/BA in Industrial Relations & Personnel Management, HETAC, 4 yrs, 2 eves wkly/ National Dip in Personnel Management, 4 years, 2 eves wkly/HETAC Dip in Business Studies, 1 yr, 2 eves wkly/ Cert in Personnel Practice, 1 yr, 2 eves wkly/ MA in Human Resource Management, 2 yrs, p/time day

Portobello School Rere 40 Lr Dominick St 1 (8721277) - human resource mgmnt, p/time eve

UCD Adult Education Office (7061695) - HR management, 12 wks

Westmoreland College for Management Studies 11 Westmoreland St 2 (6795324/7266) - ICM dip corporate management/ ICM dip health services management/ICM grad dip management/ICM dip HR management/ Adv dip in project management

PERSONNEL/ HUMAN RESOURCES

Dublin Business School 13/14 Aungier St 2 (4177500) - dip in human resource management, 1 eve per wk, 1 yr/ 14 wks/ graduate dip in Business Studies/Human Resource Management, 2 eves plus some Sats, 16 months - both 6.30-9.30pm

Old Bawn Community School Tallaght 24 (4526137) - management & employee relations, 2 yr dip, National College of Ireland (4060591); course in Old Bawn, Tues, 6.30-9pm, 24 wks

Pitman Training Centre 6-8 Wicklow St 2 (6768008) - 8 wks €1446, dip; day eve Sats

St Tiernan's Community School Parkvale Balally 16 (2953224) - management & employee relations, NCI dip

PHARMACY

DIT Faculty: Science Kevin St 8 (4024585/3445) - MSc pharmaceutical quality assurance, 2/4 yr p/t or 1yr f/t: €2000

PHILOSOPHY see also Buddhism / Religion

All Hallows College Gracepark Rd Drumcondra 9 (8373745) - philos of religion, Mon 6.50-8.25, 24 wks €350 / logic & philosophical anthropology, Wed 6.50, 24 wks €540 / theory of knowledge, Thurs, 6.50 24 wks €350 / contemporary philosophy, Thurs 6.50, 24 wks €350: all offer ECTS credits option

Brahma Kumaris WSU Raja Yoga Centres 61 Morehampton Rd 4 (6687480) - 5wk,Yoga philosophy

Colaiste Dhulaigh Barryscourt Rd Coolock 17 (8481337) - intro to, Mon, 8 wks, 7.15-9.15

DATE College of Further Education Dundrum 14 (2964322) - 10 wks €79 day

International Society for Krishna Consciousness (ISKCON) 4 Aungier St 2 (086 1608108) - Bhagavad Gita: the gem of Eastern Philosophy, 7 wks €70 / €48cons

Irish T'ai Chi Ch'uan Assoc c/o St Andrew's Resource Centre 114 Pearse St 2 (6771930) - taoist tao te ching, 2mths

Killester College of Further Education Collins Ave 5 (8337686) - intro to, Tues 7.30, 10 wks €60

Marino College 14-20 Marino Mart 3 (8332100) - intro, 10 wks, €66

Milltown Institute of Theology & Philosophy Milltown Pk 6 (2698388) - intro to philos, dip. Tue/Thurs, 2yrs, 26 wks €1420 pa

Plunket College Swords Rd, Whitehall 9 (8371689) - overview of western philos, Mon 7.30, 10 wks €66

Saor-Ollscoil na hEireann 55 Prussia St 7 (8683368) - BA in Lib Arts, Mon
School of Philosophy & Economic Science 49 Northumberland Rd 4 (6603788) -
practical philosophy, each eve, Sat & Thurs morn, 12 wks 7.30, €100/ €50
concession
Tara Buddhist Centre 32 Whitebarn Rd Churchtown 14 (2983314) - €8 per class: at
67 Lr Camden St 2, Tue, 7.30 / Chinese Med Centre, Clarinda Pk W, Dun Laoghaire,
Thurs, 7.30 / Northside - phone for details
Trinity College 2 (6772941) - (6081529) - philos & society, 9wks, €50
UCD Adult Education Office (7061695) - philos & knowledge module 2; philos &
religion; philos for everyday life; philos of adult ed; philos of happiness/ the ques-
tion of ethics: 12 wks each
PHOTOGRAPHY
An Oige 61 Mountjoy Street 7 (8304555) - group
Cabinteely Community School Johnstown Rd 18 (2857455) - beginners, 10wk, €75
Colaiste Dhulaigh Barryscourt Rd Coolock 17 (8481337) - for beginners, Mon 7.30-
9.30, 9 wks/ digital for beginners, Tue: 7.30-9.30, 8 wks
Computeach Computer Centre AXIS, Main St Ballymun 9 (8832167) - digital cam-
era & scanner workshop
Connolly House Nth Strand (by 5 Lamps) 1 (8557116) - beginners, Wed, 7.30pm
€66/ intermediate Wed 6pm €50
Crumlin College of Further Education Crumlin Rd 12 (4540662) - digital

imaging (own camera necessary), Thurs 8.15 10 wks

DIT admissions ofice Dublin (4023445) - media production unit course (4023108), 10 wks; police studies photography, 3 days

Dublin Camera Club 10 Lr Camden St 2 (6624464)

Dun Laoghaire College of Further Education 17 Cumberland St Dun Laoghaire (2809676) - beginners, Mon/ intermediate, Tue: each 10 wks, 7.30, €100/ portfolio preparation, Mon, 22 wks, 7.30pm, €220, FETAC level 2/ digital photo & image processing, 10wks €150

Gallery of Photography Meeting House Square 2 (6714654) - black & white (beginners/ advanced)/ colour printing/ refresher courses/ studio portraiture/ artist documentation workshops/ digital photography. Also Sats

Greenhills College Limekiln Ave Walkinstown 12 (4507779/4507138) - Mon, 10wks, €79

Griffith College Dublin Sth Circular Rd 8 (4150400) - cert, 2 yrs, CGLI, p/t, 2 eves per wk/ also 1 yr, CGLI, f/t, Mon to Fri

Hartstown Community School Clonsilla 15 (8209863) - 10wks, €60

Holy Family Community School Rathcoole (4580766)

Killester College of Further Education Collins Ave 5 (8337686) - beginners Mon/ improvers Tue: 7-10 10 wks €120

Kilroy's College 25 Kingram Place 2 (1850 700700) - tutor supported home study: practical, dip

Lucan Community College Esker Drive (6282077) - beginners/advanced, 8wk, €99

Marino College 14-20 Marino Mart 3 (8332100) - beginners, €66/intermediate, €50 - Thurs, 10 wks each

National College of Art & Design in Art & Design 100 Thomas Street 8 (6364214) - intro/advanced, c. 22wk each

New Media Technology Training 13 Harcourt St 2 (4780905) - digital

Newpark Adult Education Centre Newtownpark Ave Blackrock (2884376) - beginners, 10wks, €99

Old Bawn Community School Tallaght 24 (4526137) - beginners, 35mm SLR, b/w, Tue 10 wks/ studio, Thurs 10 wks

Palmerstown Community School 20 (6260116) - Thurs 7.30, 10wks €55

Palmerstown Photographic Classes 20 (6265243) - beginners, 10wk, €55

People's College for Continuing Education & Traini 32 Parnell Sq 1 (8735879) - €50

Photographic Society of Ireland PO Box 3817 Parnell Square 1 (8730263) - beginners, cert, 10wks, €150

Plunket College Swords Rd, Whitehall 9 (8371689) - beginners, 10 wks, €66

Pobalscoil Rosmini Adult Ed Grace Pk Rd 9 (8371015) - beginners, Wed, 7pm, 10 wks, €95

Ringsend Technical Institute Cambridge Rd 4 (6684498) - beginners €75 / intermediate €100, 10 wks each

Ringsend Technical Institute Cambridge Rd 4 (6684498) - darkroom techniques, 10 wks €120

St Kevins College Clogher Rd Crumlin 12 (4536397) - media production, NCVA, 1yr, day

St MacDara's Community College Wellington Lane Templeogue 6W (4566216) - beginners, Mon, Tue, 7.30 10 wks €79

St Thomas Community College Novara Ave Bray (2866111) - 10wks, €70

Stillorgan College of Further Education Old Road Stillorgan (2880704) - beginners, dark room facility, Mon, 7.30-9.30pm, 8 wks, €70/ intermediate 5 wks

Tallaght Photographic Society 26 Alderwood green Springfield 24 (2440649) - beginners, 10 wks €65

TARGET St Kevin's School Newbrook Rd, Donaghmede 13 (8671967) - day only, 10 wks

UCD Adult Education Office (7061695) - digital photog, intro, morns 5 wks

PHYSICAL EDUCATION see Aikido / Body Building / Keep Fit etc

PHYSICS

DIT Faculty: Science Kevin St 8 (4024585/3445) - MSc applied math & theoretical physics, 3 yr p/time €600r module/ technicians cert in medical physics & physiological measurement, 2 yrs Sats, €850

Dublin City University Registry office Glasnevin 9 (7005338) - applied/ German/ French/ astronomy

Kilroy's College 25 Kingram Place 2 (1850 700700) - tutor supported home study: leaving cert

Plunket College Swords Rd, Whitehall 9 (8371689) - leaving cert, 27 wks, €215

PHYSIOLOGY see also Nursing

Coogan-Bergin Clinic & College of Beauty Therapy Glendenning Hse 6-8 Wicklow St 2 (6794387) - anatomy, physiology & massage, CIBTAC, Thurs 6-9pm, €1263

Trinity College 2 (6772941) - (6082723) - extra mural, exercise physiology & fitness evaluation, 10wks, €200

Walmer College & Holistic Centre First Floor, Raheny SC Howth Rd 5 (8475410/338) - & anatomy, ITEC dip

PIANO see also Keyboards / Music

Abbey School of Music 9b Lr Abbey St 1 (8747908) - Linda Butler, John Hunter

Bray Music Centre Florence Rd Bray (2866768)

Clontarf School of Music 6 Marino Mart 3 (8330936) - classical & modern, 12wk - also day

Dun Laoghaire Music Centre 130A Lr George's St Dun Laoghaire (2844178)

John Ward 5 Tibradden Drive Walkinstown 12 (4520918) - prep for RIAM grade exams - also day

Leinster School of Music Griffith College Campus South Circular Rd 8 (4150467) - group piano for adult beginners & intermediate, 10 wks / also individual lessons

Melody School of Music 178E Whitehall Rd W Perrystown 12 (4650150) - also day; also w/ends Sat-Sun, 12 wks

Newpark Music Centre Newtownpark Ave Blackrock (2883740) - also day

Walton's New School of Music 69 Sth Gt George's St 2 (4781884) - also day, see ad page 173

PICTURE FRAMING

Colaiste Dhulaigh Barryscourt Rd Coolock 17 (8481337) - Mon 7pm, 6 wks

Newpark Adult & Continuing Education Centre Newtownpark Ave Blackrock (2884376) - Mon, 10 wks €102

Newpark Adult Education Centre Newtownpark Ave Blackrock (2884376) - 10wks, €99

Old Bawn Community School Tallaght 24 (4526137) - frame your own, Thurs, 10 wks

PILATES see also KEEP-FIT

Ballymun Comprehensive School Adult Ed Centre Ballymun Rd 9 (8420654/ 8425828 night) - Wed, 7-8pm, 10 wks €80

Harmony Yoga Ireland, Ballinteer/ Dundrum/ Dalkey / Killiney (087 8263778) - pilates, beginners, 6 & 12 wk, morn & eve / for pregnancy , 6 & 12 wks €15 per class / also pilates 1 to 1

Physio Extra 4 Oliver Bond St 8 (6725719) - spineright: yoga with pilates, beginner & intermediate levels; morn, day, eve

Pilates Institute (NTC) 16a St Joseph's Parade 7 (8827777) - pilates matwork day, wkends, 14 wks, nat qual/ on ball, 1 day; and pregnancy, 1 day; pilatres H2O 1 day: ea €225, nat qual

PITCH AND PUTT Golf

Corporate Club 24 Elmcastle Green Kilnamanagh 24 (4610935)

Elmgreen Golf Course Castleknock 15 (8200797)

Network Sports & Social Club 24 Elmcastle Green Kilnamanagh 24 (4524415)

Pitch & Putt Union of Ireland House of Sport Long Mile Rd Walkinstown 12 (4509299)

Spawell Golf Range Templeogue 6W (4907990)

PITMANSCRIPT see Shorthand

PLANNING

DIT Faculty: Built Environment Bolton St 1 (4023711/3445) - MSc in planning & development, 2 yr p/time, €1800 pa/ MSc in spacial planning, 3 yr p/time, yr 1&2 €2800, yr 3 €1500

PLASTERING

DIT Faculty: Built Environment Bolton St 1 (4023711/3445) - decorative plaster-work, 30 wks €500

PLAY GROUPS see Pre-School

Ballyfermot College of Further Education Ballyfermot Rd 10 (6269421) - 10wks, IPPA courses, Mon 7-9.30pm €65

School of Practical Child Care Blackrock Campus Carysfort Ave Blackrock (2886994) - themes & topics through play, SPCC 1 day

PLUMBING

DIT Faculty: Built Environment Bolton St 1 (4023711/3445) - advanced plumbing, mechanical services, 12 modules, 2 yr €700

FAS Training Centre Cabra Bannow Rd 7 (8821400)

Newpark Adult Education Centre Newtownpark Ave Blackrock (2884376) - beginnners, 10wks, €99

POETRY see also CREATIVE WRITING / Creative Thinking/ Writing

Ballymun Comprehensive School Adult Ed Centre Ballymun Rd 9 (8420654/ 8425828 night) - intro to poetry appreciation, Tue 7.30 free

UCD Adult Education Office (7061695) - the art of reading & writing poetry, 10 wks

POLISH

Dublin Public Libraries Admin Hq, 138-144 Pearse St 2 (6644800) - central library Ilac Centre (8734333) or Library HQ for details (6744800), self-learning €free

Polish Social & Cultural Society 20 Fitzwilliam Pl 2 (2954058) - all levels, cert, 12wks, €153

Sandford Language Institute Milltown Pk Sandford Rd 6 (2601296) - all levels, 14 wks, €250

Sth Dublin Co Libraries Languages & Computers: Ballyroan/Clondalkin/ Castletymon, Lucan & Co Library (4597834-admin only) - self learning

Trinity College 2 (6772941) - (6081896) - extra mural, beginners/intermediate, 22wks, €225

POLITICAL STUDIES / POLITICS Current Affairs / European Studies

DATE College of Further Education Dundrum 14 (2964322) - 8 wks, €53 day

Saor-Ollscoil na hEireann 55 Prussia St 7 (8683368) - BA, politics/ peace & world order, Weds

UCD Adult Education Office (7061695) - the Arab-Israeli conflict

PONY TREKKING see Horse Riding

POPULAR CULTURE see also Cultural Studies

Irish Centre for Popular Culture 30/31 Wicklow St 2 (6713636)

PORTFOLIO PREPARATION see also Art

Marino College 14-20 Marino Mart 3 (8332100) - for art college, 10wks, €66, Thurs

Meridian Art Group c/o St Paul's College Raheny 5 (8310688)

National College of Art & Design in Art & Design 100 Thomas Street 8 (6364214) - pre-third level, 16 wks

Plunket College Swords Rd, Whitehall 9 (8371689) - Mon, 20wks, €128 - still life & observation

Pobalscoil Rosmini Adult Ed Grace Pk Rd 9 (8371015) - art, 10 wks, Thurs, 7pm, €85

Ringsend Technical Institute Cambridge Rd 4 (6684498) - drawing course, 10 wks €75

St Kevins College Clogher Rd Crumlin 12 (4536397) - 20wks

TACT St Dominic's School St Dominic's Rd Tallaght 24 (4596757) - 30 wks, free

PORTRAIT PAINTING / SKETCHING see also Art

Botanic Art School 28a Prospect Avenue Glasnevin 9 (8304720) - Mon, 6.30-9pm

Brian Byrnes Art Studio 3 Upr Baggot St 4 (6671520 / 6711599) - 8wk, €130, also day/ pen & ink, 8wk, €130

National College of Art & Design in Art & Design 100 Thomas Street 8 (6364214) - intro & intermediate/ human figure/ painting the figure

PORTUGUESE Languages

Dublin Public Libraries Admin Hq, 138-144 Pearse St 2 (6644800) - central library

Ilac Centre, (8734333) or Library HQ for details (6744800), self-learning €free

Language Centre NUI Maynooth Co Kildare (7083737) - for beginners, 9 wks, €110

Marino College 14-20 Marino Mart 3 (8332100) - beginners/ continuation, 10-20 wks, €50 each

Sandford Language Institute Milltown Pk Sandford Rd 6 (2601296) - all levels, 14 wks, 250/ for the workplace, 14 wks, €250

Sth Dublin Co Libraries Languages & Computers: Ballyroan/Clondalkin/ Castletymon, Lucan & Co Library (4597834-admin only) - self learning

WORDS Language Services 44 Northumberland Rd 4 (6610240) - beginners, advanced, commercial, individual tuition only

POTTERY, PORCELAIN, CERAMICS see also Art / Crafts

Balbriggan Community College Pine Ridge Chapel St (8412388/9) - pottery, 8wks, Mon, 7.30-9.30, €73

Ballymun Comprehensive Schools Adult Ed Centre Ballymun Rd 9 (8420654/ 8425828 night) - beginners, Tue 10wk, €100

Cabinteely Community School Johnstown Rd 18 (2857455) - 10wk, €90

Grange Community College Grange Abbey Rd Donaghmede 13 (8471422) - beginners, 8 wks, €87

Greendale Community School Kilbarrack 5 (8322735/6) - practical, incl. raw materials, Thurs, 7.30-9.30pm, €65

Liberties Vocational School Bull Alley St 8 (4540044) - pottery, Mon 7-9pm €110

Lucan Community College Esker Drive (6282077) - 10wk, €79

NCAD in Art & Design 100 Thomas Street 8 (6364214) - introduction

Newpark Adult Education Centre Newtownpark Ave Blackrock (2884376) - 10wks, €125/ cold porcelain for beginners, €102

Palmerstown Community School 20 (6260116) - Thurs 7.30-10, 10wks €65

Plunket College Swords Rd, Whitehall 9 (8371689) - hand pottery, beginners, 10 wks, €66

Ringsend Technical Institute Cambridge Rd 4 (6684498) - level 1&2, 10 wks, €75 each

Saint Tiernan's Community School Parkvale Balally 16 (2953224) - pottery, Mon, 7.30-9.30pm, 10 wks, €90

St Thomas Community College Novara Ave Bray (2866111) - pottery, ceramics, 10 wks, €85

Taney Parish Centre Taney Rd Dundrum 14 (2985491) - Wed (0507 31458; 2956264)

Tracy Miley 13b Dodder View Cottages Ballsbridge 4 (086 8485394) - hand built ceramics, beginners, 7-9pm 8 wks, €115, materials supplied

POWERPOINT see COMPUTER TRAINING / Prsentation Skills

PRE-MARRIAGE / MARRIAGE EDUCATION

ACCORD (Catholic Marriage Care Service) 39 Harcourt St 2 (4780866) - pre-marriage courses, 1 w/end, €100/ inter-church wkend, €100 / also marriage enrichment days

PRE-RETIREMENT

Retirement Planning Council of Ireland 27/29 Lr Pembroke St 2 (6613139) - details on request

PRE-SCHOOL / PLAY SCHOOL see also Child Care / Montessori / Parents

Balbriggan Community College Pine Ridge Chapel St (8412388/9) - play & the developing child, 20wks, Tues 7.30-9.30, €158

Cabinteely Community School Johnstown Rd 18 (2857455) - theory of playgroup management, IPPA approved, 10wk, €75

Colaiste Dhulaigh Barryscourt Rd Coolock 17 (8481337) - Tues, 8wks, IPPA cert, 7-9.30

College of Further Education Main St Dundrum 14 (2951376) - IPPA cert, Thurs 10 wks

Donahies Community School Streamville Rd 13 (8482217) - practical, Tue 10 wks €55

Greenhills College Limekiln Ave Walkinstown 12 (4507779/4507138) - IPPA cert, 10wks, €79

Hartstown Community School Clonsilla 15 (8209863) - play & the developing child, cert, 10wks, €60

IPPA - the Early Childhood Organisation Unit 4 Broomhill Business Complex Dublin 24 (4630010) - play & the developing child, raising awareness, practical ways to support children's play

Kilroy's College 25 Kingram Place 2 (1850 700700) - tutor supported home study: child care, child psychology, dip

Plunket College Swords Rd, Whitehall 9 (8371689) - play & the developing child, Tues, 10 wks, €66

Saint Finian's Community College Swords (8402623) - IPPA play & the developing child, cert, 10wk, €79

St MacDara's Community College Wellington Lane Templeogue 6W (4566216) - intro to playgroups, Tue, 7.30, 10 wks, €79

St Thomas Community College Novara Ave Bray (2866111) - play & the developing child, IPPA cert, 10wks, €70/ early childhood education, 30 wks €200 FETAC

Stillorgan College of Further Education Old Road Stillorgan (2880704) - play & the developing child, 10 wks IPPA cert

Tallaght Community School Balrothery 24 (4515566) - IPPA cert, 10wk, €55

UCD Adult Education Office (7061695) - creche management, cert/ nursery management, dip

PRE-THIRD LEVEL COURSES Return to Learning / Pre-University

Further Education & Training Awards Council (FETAC East Point Plaza East Point Business Park 3 (8659500) - national certification body

Pearse College Clogher Rd 12 (4536661/4541544) - uni access course, mature students, day/ third-level foundation, science & technology, 30wk, VTOS

PRE-UNIVERSITY EDUCATION

Kilroy's College 25 Kingram Place 2 (1850 700700) - tutor supported home study: general education, personal development, computer skills, leaving cert, adult education, dip courses

Newpark Adult Education Centre Newtownpark Ave Blackrock (2884376) - A levels: psychology, sociology, 30wks, €279 pa

PRESENTATION SKILLS see also Portfolio

ABM Business Training 54 North St, Swords (8902348) - effective delivery of presentations; also day, Sat

ABM Computer Training 54 North St, Swords (8902348) - powerpoint

Ballsbridge College of Business Studies Shelbourne Rd 4 (6684806) - powerpoint for beginners, Tues 10 wks €80

CITAS Computer & IT Training 54 Middle Abbey St 1 (8782212) - powerpoint, 1 dat €199

Colour & Image Professionals 2 Terenure Rd Nth 6W (4905751) - corporate/personal image

Communication & Personal Development 30/31 Wicklow St 2 (6713636/6613225)

Kilroy's College 25 Kingram Place 2 (1850 700700) - tutor supported communication skills, home-study dip course

MD Communications 38 Spireview Lane off Rathgar Rd 6 (4975866)

PRIMARY SCHOOL see also Teachers

Alliance Francaise 1 Kildare St 2 (6761632); Alliance-Sud Foxrock Ave 18 (2898760) () - tuition in ps, contact Aude Japy at Alliance for details

PRINTING & BOOK PRODUCTION see also Publishing / Desktop

DIT Faculty: Applied Arts Aungier St 2 (4023465/3445) - digital workflow techniques, 12 wks 100hrs Fri pm & Sat am, credits

FAS Training Centre Jervis St 1 (8044600) - national print museum heritage project, day

PRINTMAKING

National College of Art & Design in Art & Design 100 Thomas Street 8 (6364214) - textile printing, c. 22wk

PRIVATE INVESTIGATION

National College of Communications Park Hse Cabinteely Vlg 18 (2352657) - home study

PSYCHICS

Harvest Moon Centre 24 Lr Baggot St 2 (6627556)

PSYCHOLOGY see also Counselling / Personal Development / Sports / Golf

AAA Counselling Dr MJ Brennan PhD c/o 48 Connaught St Phibsboro 7 (8380014) - stress management, also day / obesity factors

Ballyfermot College of Further Education Ballyfermot Rd 10 (6269421) - intro, 8 wks, Mon 7-9pm, €55

Ballymun Comprehensive Schools Adult Ed Centre Ballymun Rd 9 (8420654/ 8425828 night) - intro, Mon 8wk, €70

Brahma Kumaris WSU Raja Yoga Centres 61 Morehampton Rd 4 (6687480) - 3wk, Yoga psychology

Business Coach Ireland 28 Grange Pk Walk Raheny 5 (8478391) - dip business & executive coaching, 1 yr eves, €2500

Cocoon Reiki Centre Howth (8321255; 086 2312684) - 1yr, cert, NUI Maynooth at Coolmine, The Donaghies & Palmerstown

Coolmine Community School Clonsilla 15 (8214583) - NUI Maynooth cert, Mon 7-10pm, 1 yr, €900

DATE College of Further Education Dundrum 14 (2964322) - for everyday life, NUI credit course, 10 wks, €160/€215

Department of Adult & Community Education NUI Maynooth (7084500) - NUI cert: Arklow (0402-32149); Bray (2866111); Clane (045-868121); Coolmine (8473522); Crumlin (4536397); Donaghies 13 (8473522); Dunlaoghaire (2809676); Old Bawn (4526137); Palmerstown (6260116); Wicklow ((0404-64023)

Donahies Community School Streamville Rd 13 (8482217) - NUI Maynooth cert, 1 yr Tue 7-10pm, €860

Dorset College 64a Lr Dorset St/ 8 Belvedere Pl 1 (8309677) - cert/dip ICM, Tues & Thurs, 6.30-9pm, 1-2yrs

Dublin Business School 13/14 Aungier St 2 (4177500) - BA psychology, eves, 3-4 yrs/ HETAC graduate dip in psychoanalytic studies, 2 eves, both 1 yr, 6.30-9.30pm/ ICM dip in psychology, 1yr / dip in psychology 1 eve a wk, 6.15-9.30, 1 yr/ dip in popular forensic psychology, 1 eve a wk, 6.30-9.30 10 wks/ dip in child psychology, 10 wks 6.30 - 9.30 / Dip in Counselling Skills for Early Childhood Care / Adolescent care, 10 wks

Dun Laoghaire College of Further Education 17 Cumberland St Dun Laoghaire (2809676) - NUI cert psychology, 1 yr: Mon, 25 wks, also 4 Sats, €1090

Killester College of Further Education Collins Ave 5 (8337686) - introduction to, Tue 7pm 10 wks €60

Kilroy's College 25 Kingram Place 2 (1850 700700) - tutor supported home study: sports/golf, adult/child, dip; effective work skills

KLEAR Grange Park View Kilbarrack 5 (8671845) - day

Kylemore College Kylemore Rd 10 (6265901) - intro, Stg 2 behavioural, 8 wks, Wed 7-9pm

Lucan Community College Esker Drive (6282077) - intro, 10wk, €79

Marino College 14-20 Marino Mart 3 (8332100) - beginners, €66/intermediate, €50 - Tue, 10wks each

Newpark Adult & Continuing Education Centre Newtownpark Ave Blackrock (2884376) - A level, 30 wks, €250 pa

Old Bawn Community School Tallaght 24 (4526137) - NUI Maynooth, cert, course in Old Bawn, 1yr, 100hrs, Thurs / child psychology cert SPCC, 15 wks apply 2886994

Pobailscoil Iosolde 20 (6260116) - NUI cert, 1yr, Mon 7.30

Pobalscoil Rosmini Adult Ed Grace Pk Rd 9 (8371015) - for beginners, 8.30pm Wed/ psychology at work, 7pm Wed/ psych of good luck, Tue 7pm / psych for everyone, Thurs 7pm : all €80

Portmarnock Community School Carrickhill Rd (8038056) - introduction to, Thurs 7.30, 8 wks €50

Rathmines Snr College Town Hall 6 (4975334) - the enneagram, Wed 10 wks €65/ UCD course: intro to, Mon module 1, 12 wks €225 cert; special interest only, €165

Saor-Ollscoil na hEireann 55 Prussia St 7 (8683368) - BA, Wed

School of Practical Child Care Blackrock Campus Carysfort Ave Blackrock (2886994) - intro to child psychology, SPCC cert, 30 wks+8 Sats/ understanding children's psychological, behavioural problems, SPCC, 1 day/ play therapy, 1 day/ attention deficit, hyperactivity/ autism, early signs: all SPCC 1 day / Outreach courses available

St MacDara's Community College Wellington Lane Templeogue 6W (4566216) - and assertiveness, Tue, 7.30-9.30pm, 10 wks, €79

St Thomas Community College Novara Ave Bray (2866111) - intro to, 10wks, €70/ NUI cert, 1yr €700 / Open Uni BA & BSc (h) degree course

Tallaght Community School Balrothery 24 (4515566) - intro, 10wk, €55

Transactional Analysis in Ireland (4511125) - in everyday situations, mthly workshop, donation

UCD Adult Education Office (7061695) - psychology introduction/ consciousness & self: each 10 wks / psy of everyday life/ of relationships/ of gifted development: 12&8 wks/ psy of interpersonal communication/ of stress mgmnt/ mental health East & West/ walking with teenagers

PSYCHOTHERAPY see also Counselling

Business Coach Ireland 28 Grange Pk Walk Raheny 5 (8478391) - dip business & executive coaching, 1 yr eves, €2500

Dublin Business School 13/14 Aungier St 2 (4177500) - BA in counselling & psychotherapy, 6.15-9.30pm, 4 yrs

IICH Education 118 Stillorgan Road 4 (2600118) - 3-day foundation skills course, €245. Thought Field Therapy (Algorithms Levels I &II), Applied Behavioural Medicine/ Health Crisis Counselling. Classes at Milltown Pk, 6 and other south-city locations

Irish Association of Holistic Medicine 66 Eccles St 7 (8500493) - psychotherapy &

counselling foundation wkend course €250/ 2 yr dip, 11 wkends pa €2000pa

Irish Institute for Integrated Psychotherapy 26 Longford Tce Monkstown (2809313)

Roebuck Counselling Centre 59 Rathgar Rd 6 (4971929) - dip in counselling & psychotherapy, 3 yrs, Fri 4-10pm; Sat 8am-2pm

PUBLIC ADMINISTRATION see Administration

PUBLIC RELATIONS

Ashfield College Main St Templeogue 6W (4900866) - dip, 2 year, p/time

Dorset College 64a Lr Dorset St/ 8 Belvedere Pl 1 (8309677) - dip marketing advertising & pr, Mon & Wed, 6.30-9.30 1-2 yrs

Dublin Business School 13/14 Aungier St 2 (4177500) - dip in marketing, advertising & PR, 2 eves per wk, 6.30-9.30pm, 1 yr/ 14ks/ also advanced dip, 2 eves wkly, 1 yr 6.30-9.30

Eden Computer Training Rathfarnham 16, or MACRO Centre, 1 Green St 7 (4953155) - dip in pr & marketing, 2 eve per wk, 14 wks

FAS Training Centre Jervis St 1 (8044600)

Fitzwilliam Institute Ltd Temple Court Temple Rd Blackrock (2834579) - dip in PR, 2 yrs, €1355 with €300 PRII exam fees, with optional E-commerce module/ postgrad dip in PR, day, internationally recognised, 17 wks + 8 wks arranged work experience, f/t day, €3390 with €400 regist charge; also PRII dip

Irish Academy of Public Relations (2780802) - basic, intro, cert, correspondence, e-mail, UCD/ UCC/ UCG, 8wks, €355/advanced, practical recognised dip, UCD/UCC, 2yrs, €1200pa

Portobello School Rere 40 Lr Dominick St 1 (8721277) - marketing, advertising & PR, dip

Westmoreland College for Management & Business 11 Westmoreland St 2 (6795324/7266) - ICM dip, marketing, advertising & PR

PUBLIC SPEAKING see also Debating

Ballymun Comprehensive Schools Adult Ed Centre Ballymun Rd 9 (8420654/ 8425828 night) - Mon, 7-8.30 10 wks €70

Communication & Personal Development 30/31 Wicklow St 2 (6713636/6613225)

Coolmine Community School Clonsilla 15 (8214583) - toastmasters, 9wk, €60

DATE College of Further Education Dundrum 14 (2964322) - practical course, 10 wks €66 day

Hartstown Community School Clonsilla 15 (8209863) - presentatin skills, 10 wks €60

Holy Family Community School Rathcoole (4580766)

Leinster School of Music Griffith College Campus South Circular Rd 8 (4150467)

Marino College 14-20 Marino Mart 3 (8332100) - Thurs 6pm 10 wks €50

MD Communications 38 Spireview Lane off Rathgar Rd 6 (4975866)

New Directions 16 Carmichael Cntr Nth Brunswick St 7 (8723181)

Newpark Adult & Continuing Education Centre Newtownpark Ave Blackrock (2884376) - confidence in, 10 wks €99

People's College for Continuing Education & Traini 32 Parnell Sq 1 (8735879) - €50

Peoples College Debating Society 32 Parnell Sq 1 (8735879) - and debating

Plunket College Swords Rd, Whitehall 9 (8371689) - beginners, 10 wks, €49

Pobalscoil Rosmini Adult Ed Grace Pk Rd 9 (8371015) - gain lasting confidence, beginners, Wed, 10 wks, €80

St Tiernan's Community School Parkvale Balally 16 (2953224) - Wed 10 wks €70

Toastmasters International Clubs (2860718 / 087 3542277 - call ans) - Clubs in greater Dublin area: AIB (Ballsbridge), Bray, Castleknock, Clondalkin, Drogheda, Dublin, Dun Laoghaire, East Coast, Eblana, ESB Engineers, Fingal, Glasnevin, Greystones, Hellfire, , Iarnrod Eireann, Lucan, Malahide, Naas, Navan, PRII, Rathfarnham Society, Swords, Tara

UCD Adult Education Office (7061695) - speak with confidnece, 6 wks/ also workshops,1 day

PUBLISHING see also Desk-Top / Printing

BookConsulT 68 Mountjoy Square (8740354) - book publishing - consultancy & tuition

PURCHASING & MATERIALS MANAGEMENT/ CONTROL

Colaiste Dhulaigh Barryscourt Rd Coolock 17 (8481337) - 3 yr cert/dip in purchasing & materials management, 20 wks each: 1st yr cert & 2nd yr advanced Cert, Mon & Tues 7-9.30; 3rd yr Dip, Tues, 6.45-9.30

Colaiste Ide Cardiffsbridge Rd Finglas West 11 (8342333) - dip, 3 yrs, Tues & Thurs, 7-10pm, each 25 wks, IIPMM cert, €500

Crumlin College of Further Education Crumlin Rd 12 (4540662) - IIPMM dip, incl. part 1: logistics - stores, inventory & transport, principles of purchasing, business management, economics; part 2: purchasing & supply management strategy & operations, financial management, marketing; part 3: statistical method , materials & productin, planning & control, business law, purch & management level 2, 2 eves wkly

DIT Faculty: Business Aungier St 2 (4023040/3445) - purchasing & materials management, cert/ advanced cert/ dip: €700 pa each

Dun Laoghaire College of Further Education 17 Cumberland St Dun Laoghaire (2809676) - IIPMM cert in purchasing & materials management, 22 wks, Mon+Wed, €460

FAS Training Centre Baldoyle 13 (8167460) - manual handling

FAS Training Centre Jervis St 1 (8044600) - manual handling

Institute of Technology Tallaght 24 (4042000) - IIPMM - professional exam

St Thomas Community College Novara Ave Bray (2866111) - IIPMM cert, 3yrs, €350pa

QUALITY CONTROL

Colaiste Dhulaigh Barryscourt Rd Coolock 17 (8481337) - ISO 9000 quality systems, Tues, 8 wks/ quality assurance C&G cert, Mon 20 wks

DIT Faculty: Business Aungier St 2 (4023040/3445) - London C&G cert in quality assurance/ cert in quality management: 1 yr €500 each

DIT Faculty: Engineering Bolton St 1 (4023649/3445) -quality assurance, cert pt 1 & 2, 1 yr each/ quality management, cert & dip: each 1 yr €500

FAS Training Centre Finglas Jamestown Rd 11 (8140243) - ISO Q mark, Quantity mark

Trinity College 2 (6772941) - (6081768) - quality improvement, 1yr postgrad dip, 24wks

QUILTING Patchwork

Quilt Art Workshops 4 Mill Wood Naas (045-876121) - classes & workshops, SAE for info

QUIZZES & CROSSWORDS see COMPETITION

RACE ISSUES / ANTI-RACISM see SOCIAL Studies

Trinity College 2 (6772941) - (6082766) extra mural, Theories of 'race' and 'ethnicity', an introduction, 10wks, €130

RADIO - AMATEUR

Blind & Disabled Amateur Radio Group c/o Joseph Dillon PO Box 462 9 (8390812) - ham radio theory, 1yr €12 - B licence / inquiries for Dublin and countrywide

Nth Dublin Radio Club c/o Chanel College Coolock 5 (8313267) - ham radio, theory, B licence/Morse Class, A licence (with theory), €35 each, Oct to May

RADIO AND TV see also Broadcasting / Media

Ballyfermot College of Further Education Ballyfermot Rd 10 (6269421) - deejaying for radio, Wed, 7-9, 8 wks, €55

Colaiste Dhulaigh & College of Further Education Barryscourt Rd Coolock 17 (8481337) - intro to community radio, Tues 7-9.30, 10 wks

RADIO SERVICING / PRODUCTION

DIT admissions ofice Dublin (4023445) - media production unit course (4023108), radio skills, 3 day

Dun Laoghaire College of Further Education 17 Cumberland St Dun Laoghaire (2809676) - radio production techniques, Mon, 10 wks, 7-10pm, €280

Sea-Craft 3 Newcourt Ave Bray (2863362) - RYA HCA SRC Short Range cert, GMDSS, 1 day €129/ GMDSS LRC Long Range cert, 5 day €635/

READING see also Basic Education / English Literacy Scheme

Ballymun Comprehensive School Adult Ed Centre Ballymun Rd 9 (8420654/ 8425828 night) - reading & writing group, free classes tel. 8622402

National Adult Literacy Agency 76 Lr Gardiner St 1 (8554332) - national referral service for adults to get help with reading, writing & maths

Plunket College Swords Rd, Whitehall 9 (8371689) - basic reading & writing, 25 wks Tues, Wed 10-12.30pm

UCD Adult Education Office (7061695) - reading skills, 10 wks

RECEPTIONIST see also Office Procedure / Secretarial Courses

Dorset College 64a Lr Dorset St/ 8 Belvedere Pl 1 (8309677)

Keytrainer Ireland 33/34 Dame St 2 (6714000) - tailored, day, softskills, telephone techniques, customer care, etc

Pitman Training Centre 6-8 Wicklow St 2 (6768008) - telephone reception skills, Thurs, 1 day €250, cert/

Portobello School Rere 40 Lr Dominick St 1 (8721277) - full time course

RECORDER see also Music

Abbey School of Music 9b Lr Abbey St 1 (8747908) - Michael McGrath

Bray Music Centre Florence Rd Bray (2866768)

Dun Laoghaire Music Centre 130A Lr George's St Dun Laoghaire (2844178)

Leinster School of Music Griffith College Campus South Circular Rd 8 (4150467)

Newpark Music Centre Newtownpark Ave Blackrock (2883740) - also day

Nolan School of Music 3 Dean St 8 (4933730) - also day

Palmerstown Community School 20 (6260116) - Mon 7.30-9, 10 wks €60

Walton's New School of Music 69 Sth Gt George's St 2 (4781884) - also day, see ad page 173

REFEREEING

Donahies Community School Streamville Rd 13 (8482217) - foundation level, theoretical & practical, Wed 7.30 7 wks €50

Football Assoc of Ireland 80 Merrion Sq Sth 2 (6766864)

Irish Basketball Assoc National Basketball Arena Tallaght 24 (4590211)

Martial Arts Federation of Ireland 20 Oakpark Ave Santry 9 (8625065) - NRC rules

REFLEXOLOGY

Ann Prendergast Rosebud Salon Rathgar Ave 6 (4920856) - intro, 8wk, €127, w/end mornings, Rathgar/Rathfarnham

Aspen's Beauty Clinic & College 83 Lr Camden St 2 (4751079/ 4751940) - wkend course, Sunday 11am-4pm, 16 wks €1795

Ballymun Comprehensive School Adult Ed Centre Ballymun Rd 9 (8420654/ 8425828 night) - basic training & practice, Tue 6wk, €65

Beaumont Institute of Complementary Therapies Institute of Theology & Philosophy Milltown Pk 6 (8571327/8376741) - starts early Oct for 1 yr

Berni Grainger 21 Grangemore Ave 13 (8472943) - intro, w/end, €140

Colaiste Dhulaigh Barryscourt Rd Coolock 17 (8481337) - Mon, 9 wks, 6.10-7.40

Colaiste Ide Cardiffsbridge Rd Finglas West 11 (8342333) - Sat, 2.30-4.30pm, 10 wks, €50

Complementary Healing Therapies 136 New Cabra Rd 7 (8681110) - ITEC dip, w/end, 10 mths

Coolmine Community School Clonsilla 15 (8214583) - 7.30-9.30, 9 wks €60

Crumlin College of Further Education Crumlin Rd 12 (4540662) - ITEC dip, 25 wks

Donahies Community School Streamville Rd 13 (8482217) - introductory, Tues 8 wks, €55

Foxrock Institute Kill O' the Grange School Kill Lane Blackrock (4939506/4939629) - 8 wks, €85

Galligan College of Beauty 109 Grafton St 2 (6703933) - ITEC & CIBTAC, 30wks

Greenhills College Limekiln Ave Walkinstown 12 (4507779/4507138) - 8wks, €87

Hartstown Community School Clonsilla 15 (8209863) - 10wks, €60

Harvest Moon Centre 24 Lr Baggot St 2 (6627556)

Healing House 24 O'Connell Ave Berkeley Rd 7 (8306413) - international ITEC qualification, Wed 7-10, 1 yr €1500; also w/end only course

Holistic Healing Centre 38 Dame St 2 (6710813) - dip

Irish College of Complementary Medicine 6 Main St Donnybrook 4 (2696588/086-2500617) - ITEC dip

KLEAR Grange Park View Kilbarrack 5 (8671845) - day

Lucan Community College Esker Drive (6282077) - beginners, 10wk, €79

Marie Oxx Pearse College, Clogher Rd 12 (4536661) - ITEC dip, day

Marino College 14-20 Marino Mart 3 (8332100) - Tues, 10wks, €66

Melt, Temple Bar Natural Healing Centre 2 Temple Ln 2 (6798786) - intro, w/end day €150

Newpark Adult & Continuing Education Centre Newtownpark Ave Blackrock (2884376) - for family & friends, Tues €99

Old Bawn Community School Tallaght 24 (4526137) - basics, Tue 7.30

Palmerstown Community School 20 (6260116) - introduction, Mon 7.30 10 wks €55

Portobello School Rere 40 Lr Dominick St 1 (8721277) - ITEC dip, eve, morn, wkends

Suaimhneas Reflexology c/o Walmer Holistic College Raheny Shopping Centre, 1st floor 5 (8475410) - dip, 52wks, €1460

Time Out (4591038) - also wkend

Walmer College & Holistic Centre First Floor, Raheny SC Howth Rd 5 (8475410/338) - ITEC dip

REFRIGERATION AND AIR CONDITIONING

DIT Faculty: Built Environment Bolton St 1 (4023711/3445) - advanced level, 1 yr €500

REFUGEE STUDIES see community development

REHABILITATION STUDIES

UCD Adult Education Office (7061695) - community rehabilitation, Irish Assoc of Rehab Professionals

REIKI see also Healing, Health Education

Ann Slevin 24 Newpark Rd Blackrock (2898019) - introductory talk night & meditation, €10/ w/end workshops 2-day, €225 all levels, cert

Ballyfermot College of Further Education Ballyfermot Rd 10 (6269421) - 6 wks, Mon, 7-9.30pm, €50

Ballymun Comprehensive School Adult Ed Centre Ballymun Rd 9 (8420654/8425828 night) - holisitic healing, level 1& 2 Mon, 10 wks €100, €130

Christine Courtney 53 Beech Grv Lucan (6282121) - levels 1, 2 & 3, cert, day - 1:€95, 2:€95, 3:€330

Cocoon Reiki Centre Howth (8321255; 086 2312684) - levels 1 & 2 mastership, 12 wks, cert

Complementary Healing Therapies 136 New Cabra Rd 7 (8681110) - eves

Hartstown Community School Clonsilla 15 (8209863) - Mon, 10wks, €60

Harvest Moon Centre 24 Lr Baggot St 2 (6627556)

Healing Arts Centre International 46 Walnut Rise Drumcondra 9 (8370831 / 087 2749701) - wkend workshops

Holistic Sourcing Centre 67 Lr Camden St 2 (4785022) - reiki 1, 2, 3 classes/ also wkend workshops (087 7986785 & 087 6209892)

Liberties Vocational School Bull Alley St 8 (4540044) - Mon 7-8.30, €50

Marino College 14-20 Marino Mart 3 (8332100) - Tues, 10 wks €50

Melt, Temple Bar Natural Healing Centre 2 Temple Ln 2 (6798786) - w/end, €120, 1st & 2nd degree cert

OBUS Aromatherapy Training 53 Beech Grove Lucan (6282121) - day

Old Bawn Community School Tallaght 24 (4526137) - traditional Reiki 1 with hands-on technique / working with angels, level 1& 2, 10 wks each

Plunket College Swords Rd, Whitehall 9 (8371689) - beginners, 5 wks, €33

Pobailscoil Iosolde 20 (6260116) - level 1, €76/level 2, €82, 10 wks each, certs

Pobalscoil Rosmini Adult Ed Grace Pk Rd 9 (8371015) - level 1, Wed 7pm €80

School of Reiki Ivy House Sth Main St Naas (045 8982343 086 3084657) - reiki 1, 2 & 3 to master level, cert/ wkend workshops

St Thomas Community College Novara Ave Bray (2866111) - 10 wks €70

St Tiernan's Community School Parkvale Balally 16 (2953224) - healing & self improvement, Mon 7.30-9.30pm, 10 wks, €90

RELAXATION see also Meditation / Stress / Yoga

Brahma Kumaris WSU Raja Yoga Centres 61 Morehampton Rd 4 (6687480) - 3wk

Classical Hatha Yoga 61 Morehampton Rd 4 (6687480) - peace & clarity, 4 wks + life long, free - also day

Donahies Community School Streamville Rd 13 (8482217) - gentle body movement, for all ages, Wed 11.45-1.15, €55

Forde Clinic 316 Howth Road Raheny 5 (8339902) - mind yoga for stress management (breathing, relaxation, meditation, visualistion - not exercise), Tues, 8.15-9.45pm, 6wks, €100

Greenhills College Limekiln Ave Walkinstown 12 (4507779/4507138) - relaxed living, 8wks, Tue, €73

Hartstown Community School Clonsilla 15 (8209863) through art, 10 wks €6-

Holistic Healing Centre 38 Dame St 2 (6710813)

Irish T'ai Chi Ch'uan Assoc c/o St Andrew's Resource Centre 114 Pearse St 2 (6771930) - t'ai chi prep, level 1-4, 2mths/beginners /advanced, chi-kung & t'ai-chi movement 10 wks, various centres

Margaret Macken Stephen's Gr/Adelaide Rd/Clontarf (8332954) - Iyengar Yoga, 6 wk course; also relaxation, stress management and meditation

Pobailscoil Iosolde 20 (6260116) - & de-stress, 10 wks €55

St Paul's College Sybil Hill 5 (Margaret Forde, 8339902) - beginners & intermediate yoga, 6 wks, €70

St Thomas Community College Novara Ave Bray (2866111) - 10 wks €70

T'ai Chi Energy Centre Milltown Pk Conference Centre Sandford Rd Ranelagh 6 (4961533) - t'ai chi/qi gong - & wkend workshops

Tony Quinn Centre 66/67 Eccles St 7 (8304211) - & stress management & personal development; also Dun Laoghaire (2809891)

RELIGION see also Pastoral Care / Philosophy / Scripture

Catholic Youth Care 20-23 Arran Qy 7 (8725055) - Catholic Religious Education - School of Faith for 18-23 yr old

Chris Harkins (045 866710) - bible studies, by e-mail only

Colaiste Dhulaigh Barryscourt Rd Coolock 17 (8481337) - christianity esplored, Tue 10am day

Milltown Institute of Theology & Philosophy Milltown Pk 6 (2698388) - theology/ philosophy/ personal development courses

Pobalscoil Rosmini Adult Ed Grace Pk Rd 9 (8371015) - the catholic faith, foundations & spirit, Wed 7.30 €80

Tara Buddhist Centre 32 Whitebarn Rd Churchtown 14 (2983314) - €8 per class: at 67 Lr Camden St 2, Tue, 7.30 / Chinese Med Centre, Clarinda Pk W, Dun Laoghaire, Thurs, 7.30 / Northside - phone for details

Trinity College 2 (6772941) - (6081297) - charity, friendship and social relations among ancient jews, 3 wks, €15 / war & peace, conflict & its resolution in world religions, 8 wks, €40 / (6080208) Gods & Cult - the religious roots of mediteranean world, 9 wks, €40

UCD Adult Education Office (7061695) - wisdom of the east; old testament studies: world of Islam; the catholic church in modern Ireland, 6 wks

RESCUE TECHNIQUES see also Adventure Sports

Civil Defence Esplanade Wolftone Qy 7 (6772699) - various centres

Sea & Shore Safety Services Ltd Happy Valley Glenamuck Rd 18 (2955991) - personal survival techniques, 1 day €110/ safety & social responsibility, 1 day €65/ elementary fire fighting; crowd management; crisis management:each, half-day €65/ fast rescue boat, €1490/

RETAIL STUDIES see also Sales Persons

Consumers Association of Ireland 45 Upr Mount St 2 (6612466) - professional skills development, CAIRS course, 1 day €280, cert

DIT Faculty: Business Aungier St 2 (4023040/3445) - retail & wholesale management, 2 yrs €700/ retail food management cert, 2yrs €590 pa

Dublin Institute of Design 25 Sufflok St 2 (6790286) - retail interiors, cert 25 wks, €1100 / marketing, retail & design, c&g dip, 2 eves pw, 1 yr, €2,300

RETIREMENT

Newpark Adult & Continuing Education Centre Newtownpark Ave Blackrock (2884376) - successful retirement, 10 wks €99

RETURN TO LEARNING COURSES

AAA Counselling Dr MJ Brennan PhD c/o 48 Connaught St Phibsboro 7 (8380014) - graduate thesis mentoring, also day

Department of Adult & Community Education NUI Maynooth (7084500) - NUI cert; also at Finglas Arts (8343950)

Further Education & Training Awards Council (FETAC East Point Plaza East Point Business Park 3 (8659500) - national certification body

Greendale Community School Kilbarrack 5 (8322735/6) - back to education courses for early school leavers, p/time workers, unemployed in computers, personal skills, communication, maths, work experience / post-leaving cert courses in business studies, web design, tourism & travel, community & health care

Inchicore College of Further Education Emmet Rd 8 (4535358) - various subjects, post leaving cert course/ also VTOS

Kilroy's College 25 Kingram Place 2 (1850 700700) - tutor supported home study: English, word study, spelling & arithmetic, also junior & leaving cert, general adult education

Old Bawn Community School Tallaght 24 (4526137) - Arts/ Humanities/ Social Sciences, NUI foundation course, applications UCD (7068097), 20 wks, Tues, 6.30-9.30, Thurs, 7.30-9.30 + some Sats

Plunket College Swords Rd, Whitehall 9 (8371689) - for the active retired, Art/painting, Bridge for beginners, day - reduced fees apply/ junior cert for adults: English, Maths, Computers - 25 wks; Eng & Maths also eve

Pobalscoil Neasain Baldoyle 13 (8063092) - UCD course, 20 wks, day

UCD Adult Education Office (7061695) - returning to learning access courses: (at Baldoyle, Ballymun, Belfield, Hartstown, Inchicore, Tallaght), 20 wks

Whitehall College of Further Education Swords Rd 9 (8376011)

RETURN TO WORK COURSES

Colaiste Eanna College of Business & Technical Stu Kilkieran Rd Cabra 7 (8389577) - preparation for work, Mon 2-4pm

FAS Training Centre Baldoyle 13 (8167460); Ballyfermot 10 (6055900/ 5933) - day; Loughlinstown Wyatville Rd (2043600)

Kilroy's College 25 Kingram Place 2 (1850 700700) - tutor supported home study: interview techniques, computer skills; aptitude & intelligence tests, dip

RIGHTS see Know Your Rights

ROAD SAFETY see Driving

ROCK CLIMBING see also Adventure Sports / Mountaineering

Kylemore College Kylemore Rd 10 (6265901) - beginners Tues 7-9pm 8 wks

ROCK MUSIC see also Sound Engineering

Abbey School of Music 9b Lr Abbey St 1 (8747908) - Trea Breazeale

Walton's New School of Music 69 Sth Gt George's St 2 (4781884) - also music technology, see ad page

ROMANIAN

Sandford Language Institute Milltown Pk Sandford Rd 6 (2601296) - all levels, 14 wks, €250

ROWING

Irish Amateur Rowing Union House of Sport Long Mile Rd 12 (4509831)

RUGBY

Irish Rugby Football Union 62 Lansdowne Rd 4 (6473800)

RUSSIAN

Aisling Language Services Languages for Business & Pleasure 137 Lr Rathmines Rd 6 (4971902) - beginners + post beginners, 10 wks €185

Colaiste Dhulaigh Barryscourt Rd Coolock 17 (8481337) - beginners, Tues, 8 wks

Dublin Public Libraries Admin Hq, 138-144 Pearse St 2 (6644800) - central library Ilac Centre (8734333) or Library HQ for details (6744800), self-learning €free

Greendale Community School Kilbarrack 5 (8322735/6) - for beginners, Tue 10 wks €50

Marino College 14-20 Marino Mart 3 (8332100) - beginners, €50/improvers, €66

Pobalscoil Neasain Baldoyle 13 (8063092) - Tue 7.30 10 wks €85

Sandford Language Institute Milltown Pk Sandford Rd 6 (2601296) - all levels, 14 wks, €250

St Thomas Community College Novara Ave Bray (2866111) - 10 wks €70

Sth Dublin Co Libraries Languages & Computers: Ballyroan/Clondalkin/Castletymon, Lucan & Co Library (4597834-admin only) - self learning

Trinity College 2 (6772941) - (6081896) - extra mural, beginners, 24wk, €450/lower intermediate / upper intermediate, 24 wks, €225

WORDS Language Services 44 Northumberland Rd 4 (6610240) - individual tuition only

SAILING AND SEAMANSHIP see also Adventure Sports / Navigation / Yachtmaster's Cert

Bray Sailing Club The Harbour Bray (2860272)

Corporate Club 24 Elmcastle Green Kilnamanagh 24 (4610935) - sailing

Fingall Sailing School Malahide (8451979)

Glenans Irish Sailing Club 5 Lr Mount St 2 (6611481) - navigation coastal cert/ ISA yachtmaster/ cruise, catamaran, dinghy, windsurfing instruction/ sailing holidays/ ISA dinghy/ ISA windsurfing

Irish National Sailing School W Pier Dun Laoghaire (2844195) - level 1 & 2 €430; start sailing basic eve & day, 1/2 wks, cert, €430

Irish Sailing Assoc 3 Park Rd Dun Laoghaire (2800239) - sailing - dinghies, open dingies keelboats, catamarans; costal, offshort & ocean cruising yachtmaster courses: beginner to advanced, all yr, apply for provider list

Network Sports & Social Club 24 Elmcastle Green Kilnamanagh 24 (4524415) - sailing

Sea-Craft 3 Newcourt Ave Bray (2863362) - ISA Yachtmaster coastal, 21 wk €335, cert/ Yachtmaster offshore, 21 wks €397/ celestial, yachtmaster ocean, 20 wks €440, cert

Surfdock Grand Canal Dockyard Sth Dock Rd Ringsend 4 (6683945) - level 1&2 /power boating, level 1&2 - also w/end/ corporate groups

SALES PERSONS / SELLING TECHNIQUES

DIT Faculty: Business Aungier St 2 (4023040/3445) - MII cert course, 2 yrs €700 pa

FAS Training Centre Loughlinstown (2043600) - pharmacy sales, day

FAS Training Centre Tallaght 24 (4045284) - pharmacy sales/ sales rep/ customer care day

Pearse College Clogher Rd 12 (4536661/4541544) - retail management & business studies, day

Rathmines Snr College Town Hall 6 (4975334) - sales & marketing skills, 20 wks €130

Sales Institute of Ireland, The 50-52 Pembroke Rd Ballsbridge 4 (6672166) - cert in professional selling, 1 yr p/time, Sept-April,Dublin & Cork/ Dip in professional selling, Dublin 18mths, €2380, members, €2250: at DIT Aungier St 2

Senior College Dun Laoghaire CFE Eblana Ave Dun Laoghaire (2800385) - MII cert, 25 wks, €400, single subject €120

St Thomas Community College Novara Ave Bray (2866111) - cosmetic sales assistant, 10 wks €80

SALSA see also Dance

Adult Education Centre Adult Ed Centre Ballymun Rd 9 (8420654/ 8425828 night) - & latin american, 10 wks, €75

Colaiste Eanna Vocational School Kilkieran Rd Cabra 7 (8389577) - Tues, 10 wks, 7-8 & 8-9pm

Dance Club Rathmines & Rathgar (2893797)

Dance Theatre of Ireland Bloomfields Centre, Lr George St Dun Laoghaire (2803455) - Tues, 7.45-9pm / cardio salsa, 6.30 & 7.30

Just Dance Owen Cosgrave (4628857 087 8473518) - salsa / latino, venues harold's

Cross, Drumcondra, Dunlaoire, Tallaght, Lucan, Sutton

Marino College 14-20 Marino Mart 3 (8332100) - beginners/improvers, Thurs 10wks, €33

Morosini-Whelan School of Dancing 46 Parnell Sq W 1 (8303613)

Newpark Adult & Continuing Education Centre Newtownpark Ave Blackrock (2884376) - beginners, 10 wks, €90

Pobalscoil Iosolde 20 (6260116) - Tues 7pm 10 wks €60

Pobalscoil Neasain Baldoyle 13 (8063092) - tus, 7.30 10 wks €70

Pobalscoil Rosmini Adult Ed Grace Pk Rd 9 (8371015) - & latin american, beginners, 7 & 8.30, 10 wks, €80/ 7-8.20 Thurs 475

Salsa Dublin, East Hill Newtownmountkennedy Co Wicklow (087 9172939) - salsa/ cardiosalsa/ salsa club: various Dublin venues €8 per class

TACT St Dominic's School St Dominic's Rd Tallaght 24 (4596757) - + cha-cha, samba, 10 wks €50

SAXOPHONE see also Music

Abbey School of Music 9b Lr Abbey St 1 (8747908) - Peter Ogram

Bray Music Centre Florence Rd Bray (2866768)

Dun Laoghaire Music Centre 130A Lr George's St Dun Laoghaire (2844178)

Newpark Music Centre Newtownpark Ave Blackrock (2883740) - also day

Nolan School of Music 3 Dean St 8 (4933730) - also day

Walton's New School of Music 69 Sth Gt George's St 2 (4781884) - also day, see ad page 173

SCIENCE see also Biology / Chemistry / Geology / Natural History / Physics

DIT admissions ofice Dublin (4023445) - distance learning unit - foundatin science programme, 8 wks (87837730

Dublin City University Registry office Glasnevin 9 (7005338) - analytical/biotechnology - common entry into science/science education/sport, science & health/ environmental

Dublin Zoo Education Dept Phoenix Pk 8 (6771425) - conservation & wildlife, 4wks Wed eve, Oct

Institute of Technology Tallaght 24 (4042000) - grad dip in pharmaceutical production/ nat dip in pharma technology/ nat cert in science - gmp

Kilroy's College 25 Kingram Place 2 (1850 700700) - tutor supported home study: Physics, Biology, Chemistry - leaving cert

KLEAR Grange Park View Kilbarrack 5 (8671845) - everyday science, day

National College of Ireland Mayor St IFSC 1 (4060500/ 1850 221721) - FETAC Foundation Cert, 1 yr, p/time day

St Kevin's College Clogher Rd Crumlin 12 (4536397) - applied laboratory, NCVA, 1yr

The Open University Enquiry & Advice Centre Holbrook House, Holles St 2 (6785399)

Trinity College 2 (6772941) - (6711759) - polymer science & technology, post-grad dip, 1 yr

UCD Adult Education Office (7061695) - access to science & engineering course, 20 wks, cert

SCREENWRITING see WRITING, CREATIVE
SCRIPTURE STUDY see also Bible Study / Religion
All Hallows College Gracepark Rd Drumcondra 9 (8373745) - introduction to scripture, Tue 8.30 12 wks €190 / pastoral use of & Johannine writings, Tue 24 wks, €350 / the pentateuch (!st sem) & the synoptic gospels (2nd sem), Wed 8.30, 24 wks €350; all offer ECTS credits option

Chris Harkins (045 866710) - bible studies, by e-mail only

SCUBA DIVING
Great Outdoors Chatham St 2 (6727154) - diving lessons, eve & wkend beginner to advanced; PADI cert

Irish Underwater Council 78a Patrick St Dun Laoghaire (2844601) - info on local clubs

National Diving School Marina Village Malahide (8452000) - training, beginners/advanced level

Portmarnock Sub-Aqua Club John Kirwan Diving Instructor (2987932-pm)

SCULPTURE
National College of Art & Design in Art & Design 100 Thomas Street 8 (6364214) - modelling from life, intro/advanced, c22wk

SECONDARY SCHOOL COURSES
Alliance Francaise 1 Kildare St 2 (6761632); Alliance-Sud Foxrock Ave 18 (2898760) () - pre-teen 6th class / secondary 1st & 2nd, Junior cert, 5th yr, Leaving cert

SECRETARIAL COURSES see also Business Methods / Computers / Keyboards / Office Procedure / Receptionist / Shorthand / Typing / Word Processing
Dorset College 64a Lr Dorset St/ 8 Belvedere Pl 1 (8309677) - office technology: ecdl, keyboarding, job prep, comp accounts, Mon-Fri 12 wks/ business studies cert/dip, Tues & Thurs, 1-2 yrs; also day 9.30-2.30 30 wks

Keytrainer Ireland 33/34 Dame St 2 (6714000) - computer office skills including keyboard skills, layout, dictation, CV & job prep, ECDL, 4-8wks, flexible

Kilroy's College 25 Kingram Place 2 (1850 700700) - tutor supported home study: data processing, computer skills, keyboard & typing, dip

Pitman Training Centre 6-8 Wicklow St 2 (6768008) - legal secretarial, 9 wks €1955 dip/ secretarial dip, 8 wks €1646/ intro to office skills, 4 wks €680, cert/ executive PA dip, 15 wks €2946: day eve Sat

SECURITY
DIT Faculty: Business Aungier St 2 (4023040/3445) - health, safety & security for business managers, 1 yr €390 cert

SEICHIM
Cocoon Reiki Centre Howth (8321255; 086 2312684) - levels 1 & 2 mastership, 2 wks, cert

SELF-AWARENESS / REALISATION see also Personal Development
Brahma Kumaris WSU Raja Yoga Centres 61 Morehampton Rd 4 (6687480) - 7wk

Business Coach Ireland 28 Grange Pk Walk Raheny 5 (8478391) - dip business & executive coaching, 1 yr eves, €2500

Divine Rainbow Centre Marino 3 (8333640)

Hartstown Community School Clonsilla 15 (8209863) - personal totem pole process, 10 wks €60

Holistic Healing Centre 38 Dame St 2 (6710813)

Kilroy's College 25 Kingram Place 2 (1850 700700) - tutor supported home study: adult/child psychology dip courses

KLEAR Grange Park View Kilbarrack 5 (8671845) - self-esteem, day

SELF-DEFENCE see also Karate / Judo / Martial Arts

Clondalkin Sports & Leisure Centre Nangor Rd Clondalkin 22 (4574858)

Hartstown Community School Clonsilla 15 (8209863) - 10 wks, €60

Holy Family Community School Rathcoole (4580766)

Irish T'ai Chi Ch'uan Assoc c/o St Andrew's Resource Centre 114 Pearse St 2 (6771930) - Chin Na (joint locking & pressure point strikes) self defence, 8wks

Marino College 14-20 Marino Mart 3 (8332100) - Tue, 5.30 €33

Martial Arts Federation of Ireland 20 Oakpark Ave Santry 9 (8625065) - men & women, intro for over 25s, 8wk

Oakwood Community Centre Eugene Murphy Jamestown Road 11 (8347895) - wing tsun, Tue, Thurs, 7.30-9pm. 6wks, €50, cert

Pobalscoil Rosmini Adult Ed Grace Pk Rd 9 (8371015) - for ladies, (Ir Karate Ass) 8.30pm, 8 wks, €80

Rathgar Kenpo Karate Studios Garville Rd Rathgar 6 (8423712)

Yang's Martial Arts Assoc Blackrock (2814901) - Yang's Martial Arts Association/ white crane & long fist kung fu

SELF-EMPLOYED see also Business Small / Entrepreneurial Skills

Kilroy's College 25 Kingram Place 2 (1850 700700) - tutor supported home study: accounts & tax, dip

SERBO-CROATIAN Languages

Dublin Public Libraries Admin Hq, 138-144 Pearse St 2 (6644800) - central library

Ilac Centre (8734333) or Library HQ for details (6744800), self-learning €free

Sandford Language Institute Milltown Pk Sandford Rd 6 (2601296) - Serbian, Croatian, Bosnian: all levels, 14 wks, €250

Sth Dublin Co Libraries Languages & Computers: Ballyroan/Clondalkin/ Castletymon, Lucan & Co Library (4597834-admin only) - self learning - travel pack only

SET DANCING see also Dance
Brooks Academy 15 Henrietta St 1 (8730093)
Corporate Club 24 Elmcastle Green Kilnamanagh 24 (4610935)
Crossroads Set Dancers Scoil Aine, Raheny 5 (8420662 / 6601898)
Dublin Folk Dance Group 48 Ludford Drive Ballinteer 16 (2987929)
Kilternan Adult Education Group Glencullen Rd 18 (2952050) Mon 8-10pm 10 wks €40
Marino College 14-20 Marino Mart 3 (8332100) - Thurs, 10 wks €40
Na Piobairi Uileann 15 Henrietta St 1 (8730093) Thurs, beginners; Mon & Wed, intermediate
Pobalscoil Rosmini Adult Ed Grace Pk Rd 9 (8371015) - beginners 1 & 2, Tues, 10 wks, €80 each
St Kevin's College Clogher Rd Crumlin 12 (4536397) - 10wks

SEWING see also Dressmaking
Donahies Community School Streamville Rd 13 (8482217) - cross stitch & design, Mon, 10 wks, €55
Hartstown Community School Clonsilla 15 (8209863) - sewing & craftwork, 10wks, €60
Kilroy's College 25 Kingram Place 2 (1850 700700) - tutor supported home study: & dress-making, dip

SHIATSU
Cabinteely Community School Johnstown Rd 18 (2857455) - 10wk, €75
Dun Laoghaire College of Further Education 17 Cumberland St Dun Laoghaire (2809676) - & massage training, Tues, 10 wks, 7.30-9.30pm, €100
Irish School of Shiatsu c/o 6 St Patrick's Tce Naas Co Kildare (045-897052) - see display ad for details of beginners classes & practitioner training
KLEAR Grange Park View Kilbarrack 5 (8671845) - day

Malahide Community School Malahide (8460949) - relax, tune-in, move forward, 10 wks €60

Marino College 14-20 Marino Mart 3 (8332100) - & natural healing, 10wks, €48, Thurs

Natural Health Training Centre 1 Park Lane E Pearse St 2 (6718454)

People's College 32 Parnell Sq 1 (8735879) - intro, €40

Saint Finian's Community College Swords (8402623) - basic, Mon, 10wk, €79

Shiatsu Ireland classes Ranelagh & Leixlip/ individ treatments (6109110) - beginners & advanced

Shirley McClure (2865997) - beginners courses, eves/ w/ends, city centre and Bray

St Tiernan's Community School Parkvale Balally 16 (2953224) - Wed 10 wks €70

The Sanctuary Stanhope Street 7 (6705419) - 8 wks €120

SHOOTING

Fassaroe Sporting Club (087 2243829)

SHORTHAND see also Secretarial

Pitman Training Centre 6-8 Wicklow St 2 (6768008) - 60 hrs, €400, cert

SIGHT SINGING/EAR TRAINING

Walton's New School of Music 69 Sth Gt George's St 2 (4781884) - see ad page

SIGN LANGUAGE

Ballyfermot College of Further Education Ballyfermot Rd 10 (6269421) - 8 wks, Mon, 7-9pm, €55

Ballymun Comprehensive School Adult Ed Centre Ballymun Rd 9 (8420654/ 8425828 night) - beginners/advanced, Mon, Wed, 10wk, €75 each

Colaiste Dhulaigh Barryscourt Rd Coolock 17 (8481337) - cert, Mon 7.30-9.30

Colaiste Eanna Kilkieran Rd Cabra 7 (8389577) - beginners, 10 wks, Thurs, 7-9pm

Colaiste Ide Cardiffsbridge Rd Finglas West 11 (8342333) - intro, Tues, 7.30-9.30pm, 10 wks, €75

College of Further Education Main St Dundrum 14 (2951376) - beginners, Tues, 8 wks

Donahies Community School Streamville Rd 13 (8482217) - level 1 beginners, Tye 7.30 10 wks €45

Foxrock Institute Kill O' the Grange School Kill Lane Blackrock (4939506/4939629) - 8 wks, €85

Grange Community College Grange Abbey Rd Donaghmede 13 (8471422) - intro, 8wks, €53

Greendale Community School Kilbarrack 5 (8322735/6) - beginners 1/ level 2, Thurs, 10 wks €50 each

Greenhills College Limekiln Ave Walkinstown 12 (4507779/4507138) - Tue, 20 wks, €130, cert

Hartstown Community School Clonsilla 15 (8209863) - 10wks, €60

Henry Pollard email: wendyland@eircom.net (Fax: 2853126) - for private tuition, deaf awareness training

Lucan Community College Esker Drive (6282077) - beginners/improvers, 10wks €65 each/ advanced, 10wk, €79

Marino College 14-20 Marino Mart 3 (8332100) - beginners/improvers, 10wks, €50 each

Newpark Adult & Continuing Education Centre Newtownpark Ave Blackrock (2884376) - beginners, 10 wks, €90

Old Bawn Community School Tallaght 24 (4526137) - cert, level 1, beginners, Tues, 7.15-9.30pm, 20 wks

Plunket College Swords Rd, Whitehall 9 (8371689) - 10 wks, €49

Pobalscoil Rosmini Adult Ed Grace Pk Rd 9 (8371015) - beginners, Mon, 7&8.30pm, 10 wks, €80

Ringsend Technical Institute Cambridge Rd 4 (6684498) - Irish sign language, 7-8.30 10 wks €65

St Mark's Community School Cookstown Road Tallaght 24 (4519399)

St Thomas Community College Novara Ave Bray (2866111) - 10wks, €70

Tallaght Community School Balrothery 24 (4515566) - 10wk, €45

Trinity College 2 (6772941) - (6672479) - extra mural, beginners / post-beginners / intermediate (ISL), 24 wks, €185 each / intro to Irish Sign Language (ISL), 10 wks €100

SILK PAINTING

Jean Strong (2892323) - ongoing, beginners-improvers, 10wks, €140/also day - Blackrock

SINGING see also Music

Abbey School of Music 9b Lr Abbey St 1 (8747908) - Conor Farren (8747909)

Bel Canto School of Singing Bel Canto House 21 Nth Gt George's St 1 (8742460/8740184) - vocal analysts/ coaches, all fields of singing, modern and classical

Bray Music Centre Florence Rd Bray (2866768) - individual singing & instrumental, 2.30-9pm, 10 wks x 3, approx €120 per half hr x 10, exams: Royal Irish Academy & Associated Board

Comhaltas Ceoltoiri Eireann 32 Belgrave Sq Monkstown (2800295) - traditional

Donahies Community School Streamville Rd 13 (8482217) - for fun, Wed, 10 wks, €55

Dublin Airport Singers (8403539) - at Griffith Ave, Tue eve, Sats

Dun Laoghaire Music Centre 130A Lr George's St Dun Laoghaire (2844178)

Edwin Williamson School of Singing Bel Canto House 21 Nth Gt George's St 1 (874 2034) - singing teacher, vocal analysis & coaching, all fields of singing, modern and classical

Inchicore College of Further Education Emmet Rd 8 (4535358) - singing club, Wed, 10 wks, 7.30-9

Leinster School of Music Griffith College Campus South Circular Rd 8 (4150467) - group singing for adult beginners, 6 wks/ also individual lessons

Marino College 14-20 Marino Mart 3 (8332100) - singing made easy, Tue 6pm €66

Melody School of Music 178E Whitehall Rd W Perrystown 12 (4650150) - also day; also w/ends Sat-Sun, 12 wks

Merriman School of Singing and Music Bel Canto House 21 North Great George's St 1 (874 2034)

Newpark Music Centre Newtownpark Ave Blackrock (2883740) - also day

Rachel Dempsey (086 3097232) - workshops, courses: various city & co venues/ global harmonies holistic singing

The Sanctuary Stanhope Street 7 (6705419) - global harmonies - explore your voice regardless of singing ability, 10 wks €100

Walton's New School of Music 69 Sth Gt George's St 2 (4781884) - see ad page 173

SKETCHING see also Art / Drawing / Landscape / Oil Painting / Still Life

DATE College of Further Education Dundrum 14 (2964322) - painting & sketching, 10 wks, €79 day

Dun Laoghaire College of Further Education 17 Cumberland St Dun Laoghaire (2809676) - Wed 7.30 10 wks €100

Marino College 14-20 Marino Mart 3 (8332100) - pencil, Tue, 10wks €66

Newpark Adult & Continuing Education Centre Newtownpark Ave Blackrock (2884376) - in pen & ink, 10 wks €99

St Thomas Community College Novara Ave Bray (2866111) - & painting, 10wks, €70

SKIING

Ski Club of Ireland Kilternan (2955658)

SKIN CARE see also Beauty Care

Colaiste Dhulaigh Barryscourt Rd Coolock 17 (8481337) - & make up, Tues, 10 wks

Crumlin College of Further Education Crumlin Rd 12 (4540662) - CIBTAC dip, 20 wks

Holy Family Community School Rathcoole (4580766)

SKIN DIVING see Scuba Diving

SKY-DIVING see Parachuting

SLIMMING

Hegarty Fitness Centre 53 Middle Abbey St 1 (8723080) - cellulite removal/slimming/figure therapy, 10-15wks, from €120 ea, also day

Kilroy's College 25 Kingram Place 2 (1850 700700) - tutor supported home study: diet, fitness, health, dip

Saint Anthony's House St Lawrence Rd Clontarf 3 (8335300) - also day

Tony Quinn Centre 66/67 Eccles St 7 (8304211)

Unislim 49 Lr Dorset St 1 (8556111) - weekly, all areas

SNOOKER

Network Sports & Social Club 24 Elmcastle Green Kilnamanagh 24 (4524415)

SOCCER

Clondalkin Sports & Leisure Centre Nangor Rd Clondalkin 22 (4574858) - also day

Corporate Club 24 Elmcastle Green Kilnamanagh 24 (4610935)

Donahies Community School Streamville Rd 13 (8482217) - indoor football for men, Mon/ Tues, 10 wks, €48

Football Assoc of Ireland 80 Merrion Sq Sth 2 (6766864)

Network Sports & Social Club 24 Elmcastle Green Kilnamanagh 24 (4524415)

Portmarnock Sports & Leisure Club Blackwood Lane Carrickhill Portmarnock (8462122) - outdoor 5-a-side/ indoor

Women's Football Assoc of Ireland 80 Merrion Sq 2 (6611131)

SOCIAL EVENTS

An Oige 61 Mountjoy Street 7 (8304555)

Ballymun Mens Centre LS4 Shangan Rd Ballymun 9 (8623117/8623409) - group outings & with other groups, day

Corporate Club / Network Sports & Social Club 24 Elmcastle Green Kilnamanagh 24 (4524415) - barbecues, treasure hunts, parties, camping, quizzes, music groups, dances, cinema, theatre, set dancing

Saint Anthony's House St Lawrence Rd Clontarf 3 (8335300) - club, day

SOCIAL STUDIES/ AFFAIRS see also Law / Psychology / Sociology

Ballymun Comprehensive School Adult Ed Centre Ballymun Rd 9 (8420654/ 8425828 night) civic, social & political studies, Tue, 7.30 free

Department of Adult & Community Education NUI Maynooth (7084500) - NUI cert: Hartstown (8209863); Old Bawn (4526137);

DIT Faculty: Applied Arts Aungier St 2 (4023465/3445) - drama in education (for social/community workers), 1 yr, also level 2, each €500, Rathmines, cert

Dublin Business School 13/14 Aungier St 2 (4177500) - national cert in Applied Social Studies/ Counselling Skills, eves, 6.30-9.30pm, 2 yrs

European Movement 32 Nassau St 2 (6714300) - European training course - EU employment & social policy

Hartstown Community School Clonsilla 15 (8209863) - & human studies, cert (NUI Maynooth) 25wks €860

I.T. Blanchardstown Blanchardstown Road North 15 (8851100) - HETAC cert for employees in social care industry - psychology, communications, sociology, personal development, health & well-being, 2 full days wkly, 3 yr €2960 pa

Inchicore College of Further Education Emmet Rd 8 (4535358) - social studies cert

International Foundation of Adult Education PO Box 93 Eglinton St Cork (022-29358/ 0818 365305) - dip, distance learning, IFAE-Netherlands

National College of Ireland Mayor St IFSC 1 (4060500/ 1850 221721) - FETAC Foundation Cert, 1 yr, p/time day

Old Bawn Community School Tallaght 24 (4526137) - social & human studies, NUI cert, how modern Irish society functions, Tues, 6.45-9.45 + some Sats, 100hrs

Pobailscoil Iosolde 20 (6260116) - social psychology & sociology, levels 1&2, Thurs 10 wks €60

St Thomas Community College Novara Ave Bray (2866111) - 30 wks, €200, FETAC cert/ Open Uni BA, BSc (h) in social science, health & social care

The Open University Enquiry & Advice Centre Holbrook House, Holles St 2 (6785399)

UCD Adult Education Office (7061695) - conflict resolution & mediation skills 1 & 2/ drugs, conselling & intervention skills / project & community development/ community rehabilitation/ sociology of sex & gender; of health care/ community drugs work

SOCIAL WORKERS SERVICES / AGENCIES see also Voluntary

DIT Faculty: Applied Arts Aungier St 2 (4023465/3445) - multi-element behavioural support, 7 units (4023533)

Trinity College 2 (6772941) - (6082001) contemporary social work perspectives, 8 wks, €50 - for professionally qualified social workers

Whitehall College of Further Education Swords Rd 9 (8376011) - national dip in social care/ health & social care/ working in childcare/ childcare supervisor - day

SOCIOLOGY

DATE College of Further Education Dundrum 14 (2964322) - human society NUI cert, day, 10 wks €160/ 215

International Foundation of Adult Education PO Box 93 Eglinton St Cork (022-29358/ 0818 365305) - dip, distance learning, IFAE-Netherlands

Newpark Adult Education Centre Newtownpark Ave Blackrock (2884376) - A levels, 30wks, €250 pa

UCD Adult Education Office (7061695) - contemporary Irish society; comparative social policy; social analysis; crime & criminality 1 & 2; human societies; Irish social policy; project development; research & evaluation; sociology

SOFT FURNISHINGS see also Patchwork

Colaiste Dhulaigh Barryscourt Rd Coolock 17 (8481337) - & curtains, Tues, 8 wks

Dun Laoghaire College of Further Education 17 Cumberland St Dun Laoghaire (2809676) - patchwork, dressmaking, Tues, 10 wks, 7.30-9.30pm, €100

SONG WRITING see also Music

Sound Training Centre Temple Bar Music Centre Curved Street Temple Bar 2 (6709033) - song school, cert, for pre-leaving, 1 week summer €350

SOUND ENGINEERING

Kylemore College Kylemore Rd 10 (6265901) - FETAC level 2 cert, Mon 7-9, 20 wks

Pulse Recording Studios 67 Pleasants Place 8 (4784045) - intro, cert, 8wk, €610/ also C&G 1820 Part 1, 8 mths, Sat, €1,500; part 1&2 day 9 mths, €3,820; part 2 eve 7 mths €1,500 / part 3, sept-Jan, 2eve wkly, €1500

Sound Training Centre Temple Bar Music Centre Curved Street Temple Bar 2 (6709033) - sound engineering music technologies C&G 1&2, 32 weeks €3000 p/time/€4200 f/time / advanced course, C&G 3, 32 weeks €4200/ sound engineer, lighting & stage production, C&G €4000/ recording techniques, STC cert 15 wks €950/ MIDI & desktop audio, STC cert, 8 wks €400/ Pro-tools hard-disk recording sys; professional studio recording: 2 wkends, all yr, €200 each

Waltons New School of Music 69 Sth Gt George's St 2 (4781884) - also day, see ad page 173

SPANISH

Aisling Ireland Languages for Business & Pleasure 137 Lr Rathmines Rd 6 (4971902) - beginners to intermediate, 10 wks €145

Ashfield College Main St Templeogue 6W (4900866) - beginners / improvers 7.30-9.30 8 wks

Ballinteer Community School Ballinteer 16 (2988195) - Tue 8pm, 15 her €100

Ballsbridge College of Business Studies Shelbourne Rd 4 (6684806) - conversational, beginners, Mon 6.30 10 wks €85

Ballymun Comprehensive School Adult Ed Centre Ballymun Rd 9 (8420654/ 8425828 night) - continuation, Tue 10wk, €65

BASE Ballyboden Adult Social Education Whitechurch Library Taylor's Lane 16 (4935953) - beginners/ improvers/ FETAC

Blackrock College (2888681) - Tue, beginners 7pm/ advanced 8.30, 6 wks €65 each

Cabinteely Community School Johnstown Rd 18 (2857455) - beginners/improvers, 10wk, €75 each

Colaiste Dhulaigh Barryscourt Rd Coolock 17 (8481337) - Mon 7-9.15, 18 wks, Junior cert/ Leaving cert(O), 20 wks, 7-9.30

Colaiste Eanna College of Business & Technical Stu Kilkieran Rd Cabra 7 (8389577) - beginners conversation, 10 wks Thurs 7-9pm

Coolmine Community School Clonsilla 15 (8214583) - beginners, Mon/ improvers, Tue: 18wk, €120 each/ for holidays, Tue-Wed €60

Crumlin College of Further Education Crumlin Rd 12 (4540662) - Tues, 6.45-8.15

DATE College of Further Education Dundrum 14 (2964322) - continuation 10 wks €66 day

DIT Faculty: Applied Arts Aungier St 2 (4023465/3445) - language & contamporary culture, 1 yr modular (4024673)

Donahies Community School Streamville Rd 13 (8482217) - beginners & continuation, Tue 10 wks €55 each

Dublin City University Registry office Glasnevin 9 (7005338) - applied languages/international business/marketing

Dublin Public Libraries Admin Hq, 138-144 Pearse St 2 (6644800) - & Latin American Spanish, central library Ilac Centre (8734333) or Library HQ for details (6744800), self-learning €free

Dun Laoghaire College of Further Education 17 Cumberland St Dun Laoghaire (2809676) - beginners & level 3, Tue 7 & 8.30; Wed level 1 & 2: each 10 wks €85

Dun Laoghaire-Rathdown Co Council Public Library Service () - Deansgrange lib, Clonkeen Dr (2850860) - Spanish/Eng - informal sessions, Fri & Sat 10.30-12 morn;

Foxrock Institute Kill O' the Grange School Kill Lane Blackrock (4939506/4939629) - for fun, 8 wks, €85

Grange Community College Grange Abbey Rd Donaghmede 13 (8471422) - beginners; improvers; each 10wks, €66

Greendale Community School Kilbarrack 5 (8322735/6) - conversation, intro/ beginners, Thurs, 10 wks, €50 each

Greenhills College Limekiln Ave Walkinstown 12 (4507779/4507138) - beginners, 10 wks, €79

Hartstown Community School Clonsilla 15 (8209863) - 10wks, €60

Holy Family Community School Rathcoole (4580766)

Inchicore College of Further Education Emmet Rd 8 (4535358) - beginners, continuation, Mon, 7 & 8.30, 10 wks each

Institute of Technology Tallaght 24 (4042000) - cert, yrs 1 & 2

Instituto Cervantes Spanish Cultural Inst 58 Northumberland Rd 4 (6682024)

Killester College of Further Education Collins Ave 5 (8337686) - beginners, Tue 7.30-9, 10 wks 60

Kilroy's College 25 Kingram Place 2 (1850 700700) - tutor supported home study: speak Spanish now, also leaving cert

Kilternan Adult Education Centre Glencullen Rd 18 (2952050) Tue 7.30 10 wks €66

Knocklyon Youth & Community Centre, 16 (4943991)

Kylemore College Kylemore Rd 10 (6265901) - stage1 Mon, 2 Wed, 3 Tues, 4 Thurs: eqach 10 wks

Lucan Community College Esker Drive (6282077) - beginners / improvers, 10wk, €79

Malahide Community School Malahide (8460949) - beginners, Tues/improvers, Thurs - 10wks €75 each

Marino College 14-20 Marino Mart 3 (8332100) - beginners/ continuation/ intermediate: 10-20 wks €50 each

Maynooth College Language Centre NUI Maynooth Co Kildare (7083737) - beginners/intermediate, 9wk, €110

Newpark Adult Education Centre Newtownpark Ave Blackrock (2884376) - all levels, 10wks, €90

Palmerstown Community School 20 (6260116) - level 1&2, Thurs 10 wks €60 ea

People's College 32 Parnell Sq 1 (8735879) - €55

Plunket College Swords Rd, Whitehall 9 (8371689) - beginners/ intermediate, conversation, 10 wks, €66 each

Pobalscoil Neasain Baldoyle 13 (8063092) - Mon 7.30 10 wks €85/ Wed morn 10.30-12pm 10 wks €65

Pobalscoil Rosmini Adult Ed Grace Pk Rd 9 (8371015) - beginners, Mon, Tues, 7 & 8.30pm, 10 wks, €80

Portmarnock Community School Carrickhill Rd (8038056) - beginners / improvers / conversation, 8wks, €50

Rathmines Snr College Town Hall 6 (4975334) - beginners/improvers, Tues; continuation/ intermediate Wed: 7pm 20 wks €130/ 25 wks €165

Ringsend Technical Institute Cambridge Rd 4 (6684498) - beginners/ intermediate, 10wks, €65 each

Saint Finian's Community College Swords (8402623) - beginners, Mon, Tue, €79

Sandford Language Institute Milltown Pk Sandford Rd 6 (2601296) - all levels, 14 wks, €205

St Mac Dara's Community College Wellington Lane Templeogue 6W (4566216) - Mon/ Tue, 7.30-9.30pm, 10 wks, €79

St Mark's Community School Cookstown Road Tallaght 24 (4519399)

St Thomas Community College Novara Ave Bray (2866111) - beginners/intermediate, 10 wks, €70 each

St Tiernan's Community School Parkvale Balally 16 (2953224) - conversation, Levels 1-3, Mon, Tue, Wed, 10 wks, €70 each

Sth Dublin Co Libraries Languages & Computers: Ballyroan/Clondalkin/Castletymon, Lucan & Co Library (4597834-admin only) - Latin American, self learning

Stillorgan Senior College Old Road Stillorgan (2880704) - beginners, conversational, Tue 10 wks, €73

TACT St Dominic's School St Dominic's Rd Tallaght 24 (4596757) - beginners/intermediate, conversation, 10wks, €30, day only

TARGET St Kevin's School Newbrook Rd, Donaghmede 13 (8671967) - 10 wks, day only, beginners, improvers

WORDS Language Services 44 Northumberland Rd 4 (6610240) - individual tuition only

SPANISH COMMERCIAL

Donahies Community School Streamville Rd 13 (8482217) - for business, Tye 7.30, 10 wks €55

Sandford Language Institute Milltown Pk Sandford Rd 6 (2601296) - for the workplace, 14 wks, €205

WORDS Language Services 44 Northumberland Rd 4 (6610240) - individual tuition only

SPANISH CULTURE

Instituto Cervantes Spanish Cultural Inst 58 Northumberland Rd 4 (6682024)

SPANISH FOR HOLIDAYS

Ballymun Comprehensive School Adult Ed Centre Ballymun Rd 9 (8420654/8425828 night) - beginners & continuation, Tue 7 & 8.30 €75 ea

Colaiste Dhulaigh Barryscourt Rd Coolock 17 (8481337) - for property owners, Mon, 10 wks

Kilroy's College 25 Kingram Place 2 (1850 700700) - tutor supported home-study

Old Bawn Community School Tallaght 24 (4526137) - beginners/improvers, 10 wks

Pobalscoil Rosmini Adult Ed Grace Pk Rd 9 (8371015) - beginners, Tues, 7pm, 10 wks, €80

SPECIAL NEEDS see Child Care / Teachers/ Classroom Assistant

SPEECH AND DRAMA see also Drama / Public Speaking / Voice Production

Betty Ann Norton Theatre School 11 Harcourt St 2 (4751913) - all levels, all ages

Leinster School of Music Griffith College Campus South Circular Rd 8 (4150467)

Taney Parish Centre Taney Rd Dundrum 14 (2985491) - Thurs (4069758), day only

Trinity College 2 (6772941) - (6081588) - voice care for teachers, 8wks €100

SPEECH TRAINING see also Public Speaking / Voice Production
Betty Ann Norton Theatre School 11 Harcourt St 2 (4751913)
Marie Barrington 26 Iona Cres Glasnevin 9 (8305389)
MD Communications 38 Spireview Lane off Rathgar Rd 6 (4975866)
SPEED READING
Reading Speed Centre 25 Sandford Rd 6 (4975239) - one-to-one 6hr session
SPEED WRITING
SPIRITUAL DEVELOPMENT / SPIRITUALITY
Ballymun Comprehensive School Adult Ed Centre Ballymun Rd 9 (8420654/
8425828 night) - spirituality & modern living, Wed, 8-9pm, 10 wks €40
Brahma Kumaris WSU Raja Yoga Centres 61 Morehampton Rd 4 (6687480)
Divine Rainbow Centre Marino 3 (8333640)
Institute for Feminism & Religion www.instituteforfeminismandreligion.org 6w
(4624504)
Milltown Institute of Theology & Philosophy Milltown Pk 6 (2698388) - intro to
study of, dip, Mon, 26 wks €530
SPORT
Colaiste Dhulaigh Barryscourt Rd Coolock 17 (8481337) - injury prevention &
management, Tue 7-9, 6 wks
Dublin City University Registry office Glasnevin 9 (7005338) - sport science & health
FAS Training Centre Jervis St 1 (8044600) `- football player training; soccer coad-
hing; football skills - day
Pearse College Clogher Rd 12 (4536661/4541544) -soccer coaching, day, 1 yr
FETAC/FAI cert
UCD Adult Education Office (7061695) - horseracing in Ireland, 10 wks
SPORTS MASSAGE
Marino College 14-20 Marino Mart 3 (8332100) - sports massage therapy, Tues
6pm 10 wks €66
National Training Centre 16a St Joseph's Parade Off Dorset Street 7 (8827777) -
and remedial therapy, national qualification, 15mths, 1 eve per wk, €3268
NTC 16a St Joseph's Parade 7 (8827777) - w/ends, 15 mths, nat qual, neuromuscu-
lar therapy
Portobello School Rere 40 Lr Dominick St 1 (8721277) - diploma, p/time eve
SPORTS PSYCHOLOGY / THERAPY see also Golf, psychology of
Kilroy's College 25 Kingram Place 2 (1850 700700) - tutor supported home-study
dip courses
UCD Adult Education Office (7061695) - for golfers, 8 wks
SPREADSHEETS see also computer training
ABM Computer Training 54 North St, Swords (8902348) - beginners to advances;
all yr, also day, Sat
CITAS Computer & I.T. Training 54 Middle Abbey St 1 (8782212) - Excel,1day, €199
Grange Community College Grange Abbey Rd Donaghmede 13 (8471422) - ms
excel, 10wks, €93
Kilroy's College 25 Kingram Place 2 (1850 700700) - ECDL (incl. Excel 2000),
computer basics, tutor supported home-study

SQUASH

Irish Squash House of Sport Longmile Rd 12 (4501564) - see www.leinster-squash.ie/clubs.htm for list

Portmarnock Sports & Leisure Club Blackwood Lane Carrickhill Portmarnock (8462122)

STAINED GLASS

Ballymun Comprehensive Schools Adult Ed Centre Ballymun Rd 9 (8420654/8425828 night) - & mosaics, beginners, Tue 10wk, €95

Cabinteely Community School Johnstown Rd 18 (2857455) - glass & equip supplied, 10wk, €95

Colaiste Dhulaigh & College of Further Education Barryscourt Rd Coolock 17 (8481337) - Thurs 10.30-12.30, 10 wks

Greendale Community School Kilbarrack 5 (8322735/6) - stained glass for beginners, 7.30 Thurs 10 wks €60

Hartstown Community School Clonsilla 15 (8209863) - stained glass skills, 10 wks, €80

Killester College of Further Education Collins Ave 5 (8337686) - making stained glass, Mon 8.30, 10 wks €70

Knocklyon Youth & Community Centre, 16 (4943991)

Malahide Community School Malahide (8460949) - beginners/ improvers, 10 wks €80

Marino College 14-20 Marino Mart 3 (8332100) - beginners, €66/improvers, €50: Thurs 10wks each

National College of Art & Design in Art & Design 100 Thomas Street 8 (6364214) - intro/advanced, c. 22wk

Old Bawn Community School Tallaght 24 (4526137) - tiffany/stained glass, intro, Thurs, 7.30, 10 wks

Pangur Bawn Crafts 40 Finglas Business Centre Jamestown Rd 11 (8568191) - intro to goass, Tue or Sat, 6 wks, €125 / also fusing

Pobalscoil Iosolde 20 (6260116) - intro, 10 wks €65

Ringsend Technical Institute Cambridge Rd 4 (6684498) - 8.30-10pm, 10 wks €65

St Thomas Community College Novara Ave Bray (2866111) - 10wks, €70

Tracy Miley 13b Dodder View Cottages Ballsbridge 4 (086 8485394) - beginners, 7pm 8 wks €130

STATISTICS see also Mathematics

Trinity College 2 (6772941) - (6081768) - postgrad dip, 24wks

STOCK MARKET see also Financial services / Banking

St Tiernan's Community School Parkvale Balally 16 (2953224) - the stock market & online trading, learn how, Tue 8 wks €279

UCD Adult Education Office (7061695) - introduction to the stock market, 10 wks

STORES

FAS Training Centre Tallaght 24 (4045284) - management intro, 10wk

STRESS MANAGEMENT see also Health

Alexander Technique Postural Re-education Frank Kennedy 35 Callary Rd Mt Merrion (2882446) - alexander technique/ health education - also day

Ballsbridge College of Business Studies Shelbourne Rd 4 (6684806) - Thurs, 7.30 10 wks €50

Brahma Kumaris WSU Raja Yoga Centres 61 Morehampton Rd 4 (6687480) - 3wk

Complementary Healing Therapies 136 New Cabra Rd 7 (8681110) - ITEC dip, 4 w/ends

Crumlin College of Further Education Crumlin Rd 12 (4540662) - ITEC dip, Tues 6.45-9.45

Dun Laoghaire College of Further Education 17 Cumberland St Dun Laoghaire (2809676) - with meditation mantra, 7.30-9.30 10 wks Wed, €85

Forde Clinic 316 Howth Road Raheny 5 (8339902) - mind yoga for stress management (breathing, relaxation, meditation, visualistion - not exercise), Tues, 8.15-9.45pm, 6wks, €100

Healing Arts Centre International 46 Walnut Rise Drumcondra 9 (8370831 / 087 2749701)

LIFEWORKS Yoga Margaret Forde (8339902) - a yoga class in your workplace?

Margaret Macken Stephen's Gr/ Adelaide Rd/ Clontarf (8332954) - Iyengar Yoga, 6 wk course; also relaxation, stress management and meditation

Marino College 14-20 Marino Mart 3 (8332100) - Tues, 10wks €66

Newpark Adult Education Centre Newtownpark Ave Blackrock (2884376) - 10wks, €95/ & life skills, €190

Plunket College Swords Rd, Whitehall 9 (8371689) - coping with stress, Tues 7.30

Pobalscoil Rosmini Adult Ed Grace Pk Rd 9 (8371015) - holistic lifestyles, Thurs 7pm €73

Shirley McClure (2865997) - & relaxation, workshops and courses for community groups & voluntary organisations, also day

St MacDara's Community College Wellington Lane Templeogue 6W (4566216) - Tue, 7.30-9.30pm, 10 wks, €79

Star Consulting PO Box 8796 2 (086 6061639) - 1 day, €200

T'ai Chi Energy Centre Milltown Pk Conference Centre Sandford Rd Ranelagh 6 (4961533) - t'ai chi/qi gong - & wkend workshops

Tai Chi Ireland PO Box 8276, D6 (4968342 a'noon; 087 9795042 day only) - T'ai Chi qigong & daoist breathing, bagua; city centre

The Professional Training and Coaching Consultancy (087 6379765/ 045 865783) - how to manage stress effectively, 1-day workshop

Time Out (4591038) - also wkend

Tony Quinn Centre 66/67 Eccles St 7 (8304211) - & relaxation & personal development; also Dun Laoghaire (2809891)

UCD Adult Education Office (7061695) - psychology of, 10 wks

Walmer College & Holistic Centre First Floor, Raheny SC Howth Rd 5 (8475410/338) - ITEC dip

SUPERVISION Management

Colaiste Dhulaigh Barryscourt Rd Coolock 17 (8481337) - IMI supervisory management, level 1, Mon & Tues, 20wks/ IMI level 2, 22 wks

Coolmine Community School Clonsilla 15 (8214583) - cert, supervisory management, 1 yr, €360

Crumlin College of Further Education Crumlin Rd 12 (4540662) - IMI cert, 2 yr course: Yr 1: management theory & practice, psychology & work, mangagement techniques Pt 1, practical communication; Yr 2: business environment, personnel management, management techniques Pt 2, 2 eve per wk

DIT Faculty: Business Aungier St 2 (4023040/3445) - IMI cert in supervisory management, 2 pts, €700

DIT Faculty: Engineering Bolton St 1 (4023649/3445) - maintenance organisation, 1 yr cert €500

Dun Laoghaire College of Further Education 17 Cumberland St Dun Laoghaire (2809676) - cert in supervisory management (IMI), 22 wks, 7-10pm, Mon+Tue, €520

FAS Training Centre Baldoyle 13 (8167460); Jervis St 1 (8044600)

Marino College 14-20 Marino Mart 3 (8332100) - supervisory management, 2 yr Tue & Thurs €295

National College of Ireland Mayor St IFSC 1 (4060500/ 1850 221721) - NCI Dip in First-Line Management, 1 yr p/time; also day release and at Off-Campus Centres

SURFING see Board Sailing

SURVEYING

DIT Faculty: Built Environment Bolton St 1 (4023711/3445) - desktop cartography, visualising GIS data, 10 wks / GIS course, 6 modules, 20 wks / GPS course, 3 modules, 10 wks: each €500

SWAHILI

Dublin Public Libraries Admin Hq, 138-144 Pearse St 2 (6644800) -central library Ilac Centre (8734333) or Library HQ for details (6744800), self-learning €free

SWEDISH

Dublin Public Libraries Admin Hq, 138-144 Pearse St 2 (6644800) - central library Ilac Centre (8734333) or Library HQ for details (6744800), self-learning €free

Sandford Language Institute Milltown Pk Sandford Rd 6 (2601296) - all levels, 14 wks, €250

Sth Dublin Co Libraries Languages & Computers: Ballyroan/Clondalkin/ CastletyMon, Lucan & Co Library (4597834-admin only) - self learning

Taney Parish Centre Taney Rd Dundrum 14 (2985491) - Sat (2814747)

SWIMMING see also Adventure Sports / Water Safety

Blackrock College (2888681) - lessons, 7.30-9, 6 wks €65

Clondalkin Sports & Leisure Centre Nangor Rd Clondalkin 22 (4574858) - also day

Clontarf Swimming Club N O'Meara 5 Grange Pk Cl 5 (086-8116566) - Guinness swimming pool, Sun, 6 - 7pm

Colaiste Dhulaigh Barryscourt Rd Coolock 17 (8481337) - for beginners, Mon 11-12 / improvers, Mon 10-11

Corporate Club 24 Elmcastle Green Kilnamanagh 24 (4610935)

Network Sports & Social Club 24 Elmcastle Green Kilnamanagh 24 (4524415)

Portmarnock Sports & Leisure Club Blackwood Lane Carrickhill Portmarnock (8462122)

Public Pools () Ballyfermot (6266504); Ballymun (8421368); Coolock, Northside Shopping Centre (8477743); Crumlin (4555792); Rathmines (4961275); Sean McDermott St (8720752); Townsend St (6729121)

Saint Paul's Swimming Pool Sybil Hill Raheny 5 (8316283) - competitive/adult & children/public sessions

Stewart's Sport Centre Waterstown Ave Palmerstown 20 (6269879) - club & classes, teenage lengths class, Masters Training

Swim Ireland House of Sport Long Mile Rd Walkinstown 12 (4568698 / 4501739) - assistant teacher cert/ teacher (2 parts)/ Aquafit (2 parts)/ adult & child

SYSTEMS ANALYSIS see also Computer Programming

Irish Academy of Computer Training 98 St Stephen's Grn 2 (4347600) - website development & HTML 6 wks €645/ access 8 wks €645/ visual basic; C: 8 wks ea €795/ programming; structured prog design & development, 4-8 wks, €795/ C++; visual C++; java; visual J++: each 12 wks €1295, cert/ also day

T'AI CHI see also Meditation / Relaxation / Stress management / Health / Healing

Balbriggan Community College Pine Ridge Chapel St (8412388/9) - Tues 7.30-9.30, 10 wks €66

Balymun Comprehensive School Adult Ed Centre Ballymun Rd 9 (8420654/ 8425828 night) - Wed 2.30-3.30 10 wks €65

Cabinteely Community School Johnstown Rd 18 (2857455) - yang style, Tues, 10 wks, €60

Connolly House Nth Strand (by 5 Lamps) 1 (8557116) - 10 wks Wed, 8.30pm €33

Coolmine Community School Clonsilla 15 (8214583) - Mon, Tue, Wed, 7-8.20, 8.30-9.50 9 wks €45

Crumlin College of Further Education Crumlin Rd 12 (4540662) - Thurs, 6.45 & 8.15, 10 wks each

DATE College of Further Education Dundrum 14 (2964322) - 10 wks €66 day

Dun Laoghaire College of Further Education 17 Cumberland St Dun Laoghaire (2809676) - Wed, 10 wks, 7 & 8.30, €85 each

Foxrock Institute Kill O' the Grange School Kill Lane Blackrock (4939506/4939629) - plus healing, 8 wks, €85

Frank Dunphy (6777258 086 8308757) - chuan, beginners/ intermediate, Thurs morn , eve 7pm, 8.30, 10 wks €100 Dublin 3; Mon 8pm, Dublin 12; Swords, Tues

Greendale Community School Kilbarrack 5 (8322735/6) - Thurs, 7.30-9.30pm

Hartstown Community School Clonsilla 15 (8209863) - 10 wks, €50

Hu Ming Yue Tai Ji Association – (8646619) (085 7176292) Terry or Jo – regular foundation courses, various venues

Harvest Moon Centre 24 Lr Baggot St 2 (6627556)

Irish T'ai Chi Ch'uan Assoc c/o St Andrew's Resource Centre 114 Pearse St 2 (6771930) - preparation, level 1-4, 2mths/beginners, 2hrs /short form, long form, sword form and other aspects, 10 wks, various centres

Knocklyon Youth & Community Centre, 16 (4943991)

Melt, Temple Bar Natural Healing Centre 2 Temple Ln 2 (6798786) - 8 wks, €100

Newpark Adult Education Centre Newtownpark Ave Blackrock (2884376) - beginners €99 / improvers €80

Old Bawn Community School Tallaght 24 (4526137) - beginners, energy awareness, Tues/Thurs, 10 wks

Phibsboro Gym 1st floor, Phibsboro SC 7 (8301849)

Pobalscoil Neasain Baldoyle 13 (8063092) - Tue eve 3 classes, 10 wks €65

Pobalscoil Rosmini Adult Ed Grace Pk Rd 9 (8371015) - chen style, 10 wks, Tues, 7.30-9.30 €90/ Wed 7pm & 8.30 €80/ / Wed 1.30&3pm €85

Priory Institute, The St Mary's Tallaght 24 (4048124) - beginners, 10 wks, €75

Rathmines Snr College Town Hall 6 (4975334) - Mon, 10 wks, €50

Ringsend Technical Institute Cambridge Rd 4 (6684498) - beginners / improvers: each 10 wks €65

School of T'ai Chi Chuan 10 Winton Ave Rathgar 6 (2695281) - classes, city centre

School of Traditional Reiki Ivy House Sth Main St Naas (045 8982343 086 3084657) - T'ai chi chi gong

St Mark's Community School Cookstown Road Tallaght 24 (4519399)

St Tiernan's Community School Parkvale Balally 16 (2953224) - Mon 10 wks €70

T'ai Chi Energy Centre Milltown Pk Conference Centre Sandford Rd Ranelagh 6 (4961533) - t'ai chi/qi gong - & wkend workshops

TACT St Dominic's School St Dominic's Rd Tallaght 24 (4596757) - beginners, 10wks, €50 day

Tai Chi Ireland PO Box 8276, D6 (4968342 a'noon; 087 9795042 day only) - T'ai Chi qigong & daoist breathing, bagua; city centre

Taney Parish Centre Taney Rd Dundrum 14 (2985491) - Fri (2783188), also day

The Sanctuary Stanhope Street 7 (6705419) - beginners/ advanced, 8 wks €80

Walmer College & Holistic Centre First Floor, Raheny SC Howth Rd 5 (8475410/338)

Yang's Martial Arts Assoc Blackrock (2814901) - & qi gong - all levels

TABLE-TENNIS

Corporate Club 24 Elmcastle Green Kilnamanagh 24 (4610935)

Irish Table Tennis Assoc House of Sport Long Mile Rd 12 (4507559) - leagues, tournaments, coaching

Network Sports & Social Club 24 Elmcastle Green Kilnamanagh 24 (4524415)

St Anthony's House St Lawrence Rd Clontarf 3 (8335300) - 7.30-9.30p.m.

TAE KWON DO

Taekwon-Do Centre 10 Exchequer St 2 (6710705)

Taney Parish Centre Taney Rd Dundrum 14 (2985491) - Mon, Thurs 087 9067387

TAP DANCING

St Thomas Community College Novara Ave Bray (2866111) - Wed 9-10pm, 10 wks, €40

Tapestry Dance Company 309 Errigal Rd Drimnagh 12 (087- 7438923) - rhythm tap

TAROT CARDS

Catherine Woods - Prof Tarot Card Reader 12 Church St E East Wall 3 (8552799)

Healing House 24 O'Connell Ave Berkeley Rd 7 (8306413) - numerology & Tarot, w/end workshop €80

Marino College 14-20 Marino Mart 3 (8332100) - beginners/ advanced, Tues

Old Bawn Community School Tallaght 24 (4526137) - 10 wks/ higher + numerology

TACT St Dominic's School St Dominic's Rd Tallaght 24 (4596757) - 10 wks €50

TAXATION see also Accounts / PAYE

Institute of Taxation in Ireland 19 Sandymount Ave 4 (6688222)

Kilroy's College 25 Kingram Place 2 (1850 700700) - tutor supported home study: farm, self-employed accounts, dip

Plunket College Swords Rd, Whitehall 9 (8371689) - IATI cert, p/time day, €113.50

TEACHING / TEACHERS COURSES see also Adult Educators / Classroom Assistant / English Teaching / Sailing

ABM Business Training 54 North St, Swords (8902348) - deliver effective training; all yr, also day, Sat / ABM Computer Training - JEB teachers ITdip 1 eve pre wk; all yr also day, Sat

Ballyfermot College of Further Education Ballyfermot Rd 10 (6269421) - IT dip, Mon & Wed 7-10pm, 22 wks, €450, JEB cert / skills & principles of teaching and training (ICS Skills), Mon 7-9.30, 15 wks €500, ECDL cert

Betty Ann Norton Theatre School 11 Harcourt St 2 (4751913) - speech & drama dip

Colaiste Dhulaigh Barryscourt Rd Coolock 17 (8481337) - JEB dip in IT

Colaiste Eanna College of Business & Technical Stu Kilkieran Rd Cabra 7 (8389577) - literacy tutor training, Tues 7-9pm

Colaiste Ide Cardiffsbridge Rd Finglas West 11 (8342333) - IT, Tues & Thurs, 6.30pm, 25 wks, €650, JEB cert/

Coolmine Community School Clonsilla 15 (8214583) - FETAC cert: in classroom assistant's training, 12 eve c. €400/ in special needs assistant 20 eve+5 Sats c €770

DIT admissions ofice Dublin (4023445) - postgrad in third level learning & teaching, 3 modules, p/time: halfday weekly, cert & dip €1500pa; masters €1500 (4027881)

Donahies Community School 13 (8482217) - special needs assistant, cert,

Dorset College 64a Lr Dorset St/ 8 Belvedere Pl 1 (8309677) - teachre's dip information communication technology, JEB, Wed or Sat - sept/ Mon - Jan

Dublin Adult Learning Centre 3 Mountjoy Sq 1 (8787266) - tutor training

Dublin Business School 13/14 Aungier St 2 (4177500) - JEB teacher's dip in IT, 2 eves, 6.30-9.30pm, 15 wks

Dublin School of English 10-12 Westmoreland St 2 (6773322) - TEFL 4 wks, 6 lesson wkly € 180/ 12 lesson €360 - also p/time day

Dyslexia Association of Ireland 1 Suffolk St 2 (6790276) - remedial tuition

Eden Computer Training Rathfarnham 16, or MACRO Centre, 1 Green St 7 (4953155) - JEB teacher's dip in IT

FAS Training Centre Tallaght 24 (4045284) - JEB dip in IT, 20 wks

Finglas Adult Reading & Writing Scheme Colaiste Eoin Finglas 11 (8340893) - literacy tutor training, eve, 10wks, free

I.T. Blanchardstown Blanchardstown Rd Nth 15 (8851100) - language teaching (French/ German) for promary teachers, 4 hrs wkly, 2 yrs €450pa

Irish Health Culture Association 66 Eccles St 7 (8500493/ 8304211) - yoga teacher's dip/ eve, wkend, & concentrated courses/ ask for prospectus

Irish Yoga Asociation (4929213 / 087 2054489) - teacher & tutor training

Montessori Education Centre 41-43 Nth Gt George's St 1 (8780071) - Montessori teacher training dip: course (1) 0-6 yrs, (2) 6-9 yrs, (3) 9-12 yrs: 29 wks, €1800

Motions Health & Fitness Training City West Leisure Centre (4588179/ 087 2808866) - fitness instructor training course (NCEF), Fri 7-10, Sat 9-4pm, starts 3 Oct

Palmerstown Community School 20 (6260116) - special needs assistant, cert Mon 7pm 20 wks €750

Portobello School Rere 40 Lr Dominick St 1 (8721277) - home study courses: Montessori teaching cert, dip & higher dip/ playgroup leader cert, dip;

Prodancer Presentation Primary School Terenure 6 (6211514/ 087 2484890) - ballroom dancing all levels, teacher's courses, medal certif

Senior College Dun Laoghaire CFE Eblana Ave Dun Laoghaire (2800385) - JEB IT dip, 1 yr €500

Swim Ireland House of Sport Long Mile Rd Walkinstown 12 (4568698 / 4501739) - teacher's swimming courses: adult & child, aquafit, assistant teacher, various dates

Trinity College 2 (6772941) - (6081989/ 1290 am only) - career programmes for teachers, also w/end/ IT in education, MSc, 2 yrs, 24 wks per yr (6082182)

UCD Adult Education Office (7061695) - courses on: adults teaching adults learning, 10 wks; course delivery; philosophy of adult ed; supporting the adult learner; facilitation skills, group learning; new ideas in adult ed; contemporary issues: all 12 wk

TEAMWORK see also Management

ABM Business Training 54 North St, Swords (8902348) - team leader skills

Department of Adult & Community Ed NUI Maynooth (7084500) - cert, group work theory & practice: Ballymun Axis Centre (8832134) day; Old Bawn, Tallaght (4526137)

DIT admissions office Dublin (4023445) - Nat Institute for transport & Logistics courses (4023115): management course: teamwork & communication, 20 hrs

Eden Computer Training Rathfarnham 16, or MACRO Centre, 1 Green St 7 (4953155) - team management, motivation, leadership

FAS Net College www.fas-netcollege.com (info@fas-netcollege.com/ 2043600) - elearning: teamworking, €80; leading teams, €80; online tutor option €80

National College of Ireland Mayor St IFSC 1 (4060500/ 1850 221721) - NCI Cert in Managing Teams, 12 wks online/NCI Cert in Motivation and Leadership, 12 wks online

Old Bawn Community School Tallaght 24 (4526137) - teamwork ethic 10wks

TECHNOLOGY

Institute of Technology Tallaght 24 (4042000) - BSc in Tech Management/ national dip in Tech Management

The Open University Enquiry & Advice Centre Holbrook House, Holles St 2 (6785399)

TELECOMMUNICATIONS see also Electronics / Radio

DIT Faculty: Engineering Bolton St 1 (4023649/ 3445) - applied optoelectronics centre courses include: introduction to telecommunications; data cabling installation; optic fibre tech; sdh networks; isdn introduction & intermediate; safety issues; advanced optical network design; labview for instrumentation and data acquisition (4024959)

Dublin City University Registry office Glasnevin 9 (7005338) - engineering/ information & communications engineering

Irish Academy of Computer Training 98 St Stephen's Grn 2 (4347600) - networking 12 wks €1995/ windows NT; novell; internet: each 12 wks €1295, cert/ also day

TELEPHONE TECHNIQUES & SELLING
ABM Business Training 54 North St, Swords (8902348) - to increase business; also day, Sat
Eden Computer Training Rathfarnham 16, or MACRO Centre, 1 Green St 7 (4953155) - sales, telesales, reception, call centre training
Pitman Training Centre 6-8 Wicklow St 2 (6768008) - telephone/ reception skills, Thurs 1 day €250, cert

TELEVISION PRODUCTION see also Broadcasting
Ballyfermot College of Further Education Ballyfermot Rd 10 (6269421) - intro to, 5 wks, Mon 7-10pm & Sat 10-3pm, €100
St Kevins College Clogher Rd Crumlin 12 (4536397) - TV & video, 20wks

TENDERING & ESTIMATING
DIT Faculty: Built Environment Bolton St 1 (4023711/3445) - tendering & estimating practice, cert 1 yr, €500

TENNIS
Corporate Club 24 Elmcastle Green Kilnamanagh 24 (4610935)
Network Sports & Social Club 24 Elmcastle Green Kilnamanagh 24 (4524415)
Portmarnock Sports & Leisure Club Blackwood Lane Carrickhill Portmarnock (8462122)
Tennis Ireland Dublin City University Glasnevin 9 (8844010) - information

TEXTILE PAINTING
Jean Strong (2892323) - ongoing/beginners, improvers, 10 wks, €140/also day - Blackrock

TEXTILE PRINTING
National College of Art & Design in Art & Design 100 Thomas Street 8 (6364214)
- c. 22wk
THAI
Dublin Public Libraries Admin Hq, 138-144 Pearse St 2 (6644800) - central library
Ilac Centre (8734333) or Library HQ for details (6744800) self-learning €free
Sth Dublin Co Libraries Languages & Computers: Ballyroan/Clondalkin/
Castletymon, Lucan & Co Library (4597834-admin only) - self learning
THEATRE see also Acting / Drama / Literature / Speech & Drama
Betty Ann Norton Theatre School 11 Harcourt St 2 (4751913) - acting dip / teachers dip / performance
Corporate Club 24 Elmcastle Green Kilnamanagh 24 (4610935)
Inchicore College of Further Education Emmet Rd 8 (4535358) - art & design, day/
Core School of Theatre studies: acting & foundation; set design & construction;
stage management; sound & lighting; costume & wardrobe - day courses
KLEAR Grange Park View Kilbarrack 5 (8671845) - enjoying theatre, day
People's College 32 Parnell Sq 1 (8735879) - theatrical wig & hairdressing, €50
Saor-Ollscoil na hEireann 55 Prussia St 7 (8683368) - BA, film & theatre studies
THEOLOGY
All Hallows College Gracepark Rd Drumcondra 9 (8373745) - intro to systematic
theology, Thurs, 6.50pm/ sacramental theology /The God of the Christians, Tues
6.50 / intro to moral theology, Mon 7.40 / the person in relationship & theology of
life/ ; justice, peace & ecology 1, Mon 6.50 / theological aesthetics - module: each
24 wks €350; ECTS credits option
Brahma Kumaris WSU Raja Yoga Centres 61 Morehampton Rd 4 (6687480) - the
theology of yoga, 3 wk
Institute of Technology Tallaght 24 (4042000) - nat dip in humanities (theology)
Milltown Institute Milltown Pk 6 (2698388) - intro to theology, dip. Tue/Thurs,
2yrs, 26 wks €1420 pa/ adult ed dip in theology, 2 yrs, 26 wks €530pa

THIRD WORLD STUDIES See Development Studies

THOUGHT FIELD THERAPY see also Counselling

IICH Education 118 Stillorgan Road 4 (2600118) - 3-day foundation skills course, €245. Thought Field Therapy (Algorithms Levels I &II), Applied Behavioural Medicine/ Health Crisis Counselling. Classes at Milltown Pk, 6 and other south-city locations

TIMBER TECHNOLOGY

DIT Faculty: Built Environment Bolton St 1 (4023711/3445) - CNC machining, 10 wks €230/ woodcutting machinery, 1 yr €700

TIME MANAGEMENT

ABM Business Training 54 North St, Swords (8902348)

Dorset College 64a Lr Dorset St/ 8 Belvedere Pl 1 (8309677) 5940

Kilroy's College 25 Kingram Place 2 (1850 700700) - tutor supported home study: dip course

Old Bawn Community School Tallaght 24 (4526137) - interactive, Thurs, 10wks

TIN WHISTLE see also Music

Abbey School of Music 9b Lr Abbey St 1 (8747908) - Michael McGrath

Catherine Cooney TTCT Dip Forrest Road Swords (086 8386797) - tin whistle & flute

Clontarf School of Music 6 Marino Mart 3 (8330936) - Irish, 10wk - day only

Comhaltas Ceoltoiri Eireann 32 Belgrave Sq Monkstown (2800295)

Holy Family Community School Rathcoole (4580766)

Old Bawn Community School Tallaght 24 (4526137) - for beginners, Thurs, 10 wks

People's College 32 Parnell Sq 1 (8735879) - €55

Pobalscoil Rosmini Adult Ed Grace Pk Rd 9 (8371015) - tin whistle and flute, 7.30 Thurs 10 wks €80

Walton's New School of Music 69 Sth Gt George's St 2 (4781884) - also day, see ad page 173

TOASTMASTERS CLUBS see Public Speaking

TOURISM see also Travel Management

Colaiste Ide Cardiffsbridge Rd Finglas West 11 (8342333) - standard & advanced dip in Travel & Tourism, Tues & Thurs, 7-10pm, 18 wks, €550 each, IATA/UFTAA

DIT Faculty: Tourism & Food Cathal Brugha St 1 (4024349/3445) - MSc in tourism management, 2yrs p/t, 1 yr f/t: €1645pa

Dublin Business School 13/14 Aungier St 2 (4177500) - dip in tourism management & marketing, 2 eves per wk, 6.30-9.30pm, 1 yr

Inchicore College of Further Education Emmet Rd 8 (4535358) - travel & tourism management; adventure tourism; Tourism NCVA 2 award

Institute of Technology Tallaght 24 (4042000) - cert in Tourism & Customer Care

Pearse College Clogher Rd 12 (4536661/4541544) - languages for travel & tourism, day

Portobello School Rere 40 Lr Dominick St 1 (8721277) - tourism & travel studies, fares & ticketing 1 & 2, wkend/ Galileo/ Sabre: eve/ airline studies, f/time & p/time/ travel agency skills, eve p/time

Stillorgan College of Further Education Old Road Stillorgan (2880704) - gallileo travel agency course

Westmoreland College for Management Studies 11 Westmoreland St 2 (6795324/7266) - ICM cert, dip travel & tourism

TRADITIONAL MUSIC see also Music

Catherine Cooney TTCT Dip Forrest Road Swords (086 8386797) - tin whistle & flute

Comhaltas Ceoltoiri Eireann 32 Belgrave Sq Monkstown (2800295) - all traditinal instruments / group playing/ singing: venues at: Artane, Beaumont, Ballymun, Clontarf, Kinsealey, Monkstown, Malahide, Navan Rd, Portmarnock, Raheny, Santry

Dun Laoghaire Music Centre 130A Lr George's St Dun Laoghaire (2844178)

Walton's New School of Music 69 Sth Gt George's St 2 (4781884) - also day, see ad page

TRANSACTIONAL ANALYSIS

Transactional Analysis in Ireland (4511125) - in everyday situations, mthly workshop, donation

TRANSITION YEAR COURSES

School of Practical Child Care Blackrock Campus Carysfort Ave Blackrock (2886994) - Cert in Babysitting / Cert in Caring For Children with Special Needs/ Cert in Working With Young Children FETAC Child Development & Play/ Outreach courses available

TRANSLATION / TRANSLATORS, COURSES FOR

Alliance Francaise 1 Kildare St 2 (6761632); Alliance-Sud Foxrock Ave 18 (2898760) () - contact Alliance for details of translators courses

DIT Faculty: Applied Arts Aungier St 2 (4023465/3445) - online, theory & practice, French, German, Spanish, 1 yr €950, Kevin St 8 (4024673 / 4024944)

DIT Online Kevin St 8 (4024944) - online courses leading to Dip Inst Linguists London: German/ French/ Spanish; 27 wks; 5 ECTS credits

WORDS Language Services 44 Northumberland Rd 4 (6610240) - French/German/Italian/Portugese/Spanish, by correspondence & e-mail

TRANSPORT see also Distance learning

DIT admissions ofice Dublin (4023445) - various courses re supply chain operations & management

DIT admissions ofice Dublin (4023445) - Nat Institute for transport & Logistics courses (4023115): management courses - supply chain / purchasing/ warehousing & inventory/ quality / production planning/ project/ distribution/ EU logistic stragtegies/ 20 hrs each

DIT Faculty: Engineering Bolton St 1 (4023649/3445) - road transport studies, yr 1 & 2, €500; yr 3 €700, cert

FAS Training Centre Baldoyle 13 (8167460)

Institute of International Trade of Ireland 28 Merrion Square 2 (6612182) - dangerous goods safety advisor (road), 4 day/ movement of dangerous goods by sea IMDG code, 2 day

Kylemore College Kylemore Rd 10 (6265901) - post lc, day, FETAC 2, transport technology (motor engineering)

St Thomas Community College Novara Ave Bray (2866111) - CPC in road trasport, cert, 20 wks, €400

Tallaght Community School Balrothery 24 (4515566) - transport management, cert, CPC, 30wk, €460

TRAVEL MANAGEMENT see also Tourism

Inchicore College of Further Education Emmet Rd 8 (4535358) - travel & tourism management

Pearse College Clogher Rd 12 (4536661/4541544) - languages for travel & tourism, day

Portobello School Rere 40 Lr Dominick St 1 (8721277) - tourism & travel studies, fares & ticketing 1 & 2, wkend/ Galileo/ Sabre: eve/ airline studies, f/time & p/time/ travel agency skills, eve p/time

Westmoreland College for Management Studies 11 Westmoreland St 2 (6795324/7266) - ICM cert, dip travel & tourism

TROMBONE

Bray Music Centre Florence Rd Bray (2866768)

Newpark Music Centre Newtownpark Ave Blackrock (2883740) - also day

TRUMPET

Bray Music Centre Florence Rd Bray (2866768)

Newpark Music Centre Newtownpark Ave Blackrock (2883740) - also day

Walton's New School of Music 69 Sth Gt George's St 2 (4781884) - also day, see ad page 173

TURKISH

Dublin Public Libraries Admin Hq, 138-144 Pearse St 2 (6644800) - central library Ilac Centre (8734333) or Library HQ for details (6744800), self-learning €free

Sandford Language Institute Milltown Pk Sandford Rd 6 (2601296) - all levels, 14 wks, €250

TYPESETTING & PHOTOSETTING see Desk Top Publishing / Printing
TYPING see also Keyboard / Teachers / Word Processing

Cabinteely Community School Johnstown Rd 18 (2857455) - & keyboard skills, 10wk, €75

Dublin Public Libraries Admin Hq, 138-144 Pearse St 2 (6644800) - self-learning €free

Keytrainer Ireland 33/34 Dame St 2 (6714000) - intro/advanced/refresher/ dictaphone, day & eve

Kilroy's College 25 Kingram Place 2 (1850 700700) - tutor supported home study, dip courses

Newpark Adult Education Centre Newtownpark Ave Blackrock (2884376) - 10wks, €99

Pitman Training Centre 6-8 Wicklow St 2 (6768008) - keyboard, speed/ audio16-20 hrs €170 cert; day eve Sats

People's College

EVENING COURSES
October 2003 to March 2004

AROMATHERAPY &
   INDIAN HEAD MASSAGE
COMPUTERS
COUNSELLING
CREATIVE WRITING
CURRENT AFFAIRS
ENGLISH (Basic)
ENGLISH FOR FOREIGNERS
EXPLORING MODERN ART
GUITAR (Classical)
LEGAL STUDIES
LITERATURE
ENVIRONMENT

EUROPE
MUSIC APPRECIATION
PAINTING
PERSONAL DEVELOPMENT
PUBLIC SPEAKING
SHIATSU
   (Introduction to)
TIN WHISTLE
THEATRICAL WIG &
   HAIRDRESSING
   (Jan. 2004)
YOGA
LOCAL HISTORY

LANGUAGE COURSES
FRENCH, ENGLISH, IRISH, ITALIAN, SPANISH
Cost of Courses: €20.00 to €90.00
Prospectus available (mid-August) for collection from:
**People's College, 32 Parnell Square,
Liberty Hall, Dublin 1,**
and
Central Library, Ilac Centre.
or S.A.E. (60c) to
32 Parnell Square, Dublin 1.

ENROLMENTS

Dates:	**Monday 8th to Thursday 11th September 2003**
Time:	**5.30 p.m. to 8.30 p.m.**
Dates:	**Monday 15th to Friday 26th September 2003**
Time:	**10.00 a.m. to 5.00 p.m. (including lunch-time)**
Venue:	**People's College, 32 Parnell Square, Dublin 1.**

Tel: 8735879 Fax: 8735164 E-mail: peopcoll@iol.ie

Portmarnock Community School Carrickhill Rd (8038056) - beginners / improvers 8wks, €50 each

TACT St Dominic's School St Dominic's Rd Tallaght 24 (4596757) - typing on computer, day 10 wks €38

Tallaght Community School Balrothery 24 (4515566) - & keyboard skills, cert, beginners & improvers, 10wk, €55

UILLEANN PIPES see also Music / Traditional Music

Comhaltas Ceoltoiri Eireann 32 Belgrave Sq Monkstown (2800295)

Na Piobairi Uilleann 15 Henrietta St 1 (8730093) Tues, 7.30-10pm, beginners, intermediate, advanced

Waltons New School of Music 69 Sth Gt George's St 2 (4781884) - also day, see ad page

UPHOLSTERY

College of Further Education Main St Dundrum 14 (2951376) - 8 wks, €87

Newpark Adult Education Centre Newtownpark Ave Blackrock (2884376) - beg/advanced, 10wks, €99

VEGETARIAN COOKERY

Cafe Fresh Mary Farrell Powerscourt Townhouse Centre 2 (6719669/ 086 8115519) - 6 wks

Greendale Community School Kilbarrack 5 (8322735/6) - the exotic way, Thurs, 10 wks €70

International Society for Krishna Consciousness (ISKCON) 4 Aungier St 2 (086 1608108) - Govinda's vegetarian cookery - our secrets disclosed, 6 wks €60, ph 087 9921332

Marino College 14-20 Marino Mart 3 (8332100) - Tues, 10wks €66

VIDEO PRODUCTION

Ballyfermot College of Further Education Ballyfermot Rd 10 (6269421) - camcorder video editing, Wed, 7-10, 10 wks €100

New Media Technology Training 13 Harcourt St 2 (4780905) - digital video production & online broadcasting

Newpark Adult Education Centre Newtownpark Ave Blackrock (2884376) - camcorder beginners, 6 wks €85

St Kevins College Clogher Rd Crumlin 12 (4536397) - tv & video, 20wks

St Thomas Community College Novara Ave Bray (2866111) - camcorder know-how, 5wks, €35

VIOLA see also Music

Bray Music Centre Florence Rd Bray (2866768)

Dun Laoghaire Music Centre 130A Lr George's St Dun Laoghaire (2844178)

Walton's New School of Music 69 Sth Gt George's St 2 (4781884) - also day, see ad page

VIOLIN see also Music

Abbey School of Music 9b Lr Abbey St 1 (8747908) - Mary Fahy

Bray Music Centre Florence Rd Bray (2866768)

Clontarf School of Music 6 Marino Mart 3 (8330936) - classical, 12wk - day only

Dun Laoghaire Music Centre 130A Lr George's St Dun Laoghaire (2844178)

Leinster School of Music Griffith College Campus South Circular Rd 8 (4150467)

Melody School of Music 178E Whitehall Rd W Perrystown 12 (4650150) - all day W/S & Sat; w/ends, Sat-Sun, 12 wks

Newpark Music Centre Newtownpark Ave Blackrock (2883740) - also day

Walton's New School of Music 69 Sth Gt George's St 2 (4781884) - also day, see ad page 173

VOICE PRODUCTION see also Music / Singing

Betty Ann Norton Theatre School 11 Harcourt St 2 (4751913)

Dun Laoghaire Music Centre 130A Lr George's St Dun Laoghaire (2844178)

Leinster School of Music Griffith College Campus South Circular Rd 8 (4150467)

MD Communications 38 Spireview Lane off Rathgar Rd 6 (4975866)

Walton's New School of Music 69 Sth Gt George's St 2 (4781884) - also day, see ad page 173

VOLLEYBALL / MINI VOLLEYBALL

Corporate Club 24 Elmcastle Green Kilnamanagh 24 (4610935)

Network Sports & Social Club 24 Elmcastle Green Kilnamanagh 24 (4524415)

VOLUNTARY WORK / VOLUNTEERING MANAGEMENT Community Development

Dublin Simon Community Margaret Dent Volunteer Coordinator 1 (6749200) - training for Simon volunteers

National Adult Literacy Agency 76 Lr Gardiner St 1 (8554332) - info on becoming a voluntary literacy tutor

Sli Eile Volunteers 20 Upr Gardiner Street 1 (8787166) - opportunities for 18-35 yr olds to work as volunteers in educational projects in North Inter City. Training on 'Working for Justice' and Christian basis for 'social justice work' also provided

Volunteering Ireland Coleraine House Coleraine St 7 (8722622) - volunteering management courses: developing vol policy, €50 / supporting vols,17 Sept, €50 / retaining vols, 22 Oct €80 / designing volunteer roles, 1 day €80 / vols on management cttees, 8 Nov; screening & selection, €50 / all 1 day

VTOS COURSES

FAS Training Centre Ballyfermot 10 (6055900/ 5933) - various for people with disabilities

Pearse College Clogher Rd 12 (4536661/4541544) - leaving cert/university foundation studies, science & technology, 30wk - day

WALKING see also Adventure Sports / Hiking / Mountaineering

Corporate Club 24 Elmcastle Green Kilnamanagh 24 (4610935)

Network Club, The 24 Elmcastle Green Kilnamanagh 24 (4524415)

WALTZING

Dance Club Rathmines & Rathgar (2893797)

WARDEN SERVICE

Civil Defence Esplanade Wolftone Qy 7 (6772699) - various centres

WATER COLOURS see also Art

Ashfield College Main St Templeogue 6W (4900866) - 7.30-9.30, 8 wks

Ballsbridge College of Business Studies Shelbourne Rd 4 (6684806) - intro, Thurs 6pm, 10 wks, €50

Blackrock College (2888681) - watercolour painting, Mon, 7.30-9, 6 wks €65

Botanic Art School 28a Prospect Avenue Glasnevin 9 (8304720) - for adults & children, also day

Brian Byrnes Art Studio 3 Upr Baggot St 4 (6671520 / 6711599) - 8wk, €130, also day

Cabinteely Community School Johnstown Rd 18 (2857455) - beginners/improvers, 10wk, €75 each

Colaiste Eanna College of Business & Technical Stu Kilkieran Rd Cabra 7 (8389577) - 10wks, Tue 7-9pm

College of Further Education Main St Dundrum 14 (2951376) - beginners, Thurs

Donahies Community School Streamville Rd 13 (8482217) - beginners/ improvers, Mon, 10 wks, €55

Dun Laoghaire College of Further Education 17 Cumberland St Dun Laoghaire (2809676) - Wed, 10 wks, 7.30-9.30pm, €100

Greendale Community School Kilbarrack 5 (8322735/6) - Tues, Thurs, Wed (day),10 wks, €55, also day

Hartstown Community School Clonsilla 15 (8209863) - 10wks, €60

Holy Family Community School Rathcoole (4580766)

Jean Strong (2892323) - ongoing, beginners-improvers, 10wks, €140/also day - Blackrock

Kilternan Adult Education Group Glencullen Rd 18 (2952050) Mon, Fri, day, 10 wks €72; beginners, Thurs, 10 wks €79

Kylemore College Kylemore Rd 10 (6265901) - Wed, 10 wks

Lucan Community College Esker Drive (6282077) - & sketching, 8wk, €79

Malahide Community School Malahide (8460949) - Tue, Thurs, 10 wks, beginners/ improvers €75

Meridian Art Group c/o St Paul's College Raheny 5 (8310688)

National College of Art & Design in Art & Design 100 Thomas Street 8 (6364214) - intro& advanced/ techniques of, c.22wk

Newpark Adult Education Centre Newtownpark Ave Blackrock (2884376) - 10wks, €99

Palmerstown Community School 20 (6260116) - level 1&2, Thurs, 10 wks €65 ea

Pobalscoil Rosmini Adult Ed Grace Pk Rd 9 (8371015) - & oils, 10 wks, €90/ landscape, Tue €80

St Finian's Community College Swords (8402623) - watercolours & drawing, Tue €79

St Tiernan's Community School Parkvale Balally 16 (2953224) - Wed 10 wks, €70

UCD Adult Education Office (7061695) - beginners 10 wks

WATER POLO

Irish Water Polo Association N O'Meara, Leinster Branch, 5 Grange Pk Close Raheny 5 () - Clontarf swimming club, Guinness swimming pool, Sundays, 6-7pm Nicky O' Meara, 086 8116566

Saint Paul's Swimming Pool Sybil Hill Raheny 5 (8316283)

WATER SAFETY

Clondalkin Sports & Leisure Centre Nangor Rd Clondalkin 22 (4574858)

Sea & Shore Safety Services Ltd. Happy Valley Glenamuck Rd 18 (2955991) - personal survival techniques, 1 day €110/ safety & social responsibility, 1 day €65/

elementary fire fighting; crowd management; crisis management:each, half-day €65/ fast rescue boat, €1490/ CPSC 5 day €425

WATER SKIING
Golden Falls Waterski Club Ballymore Eustace Co Kildare (2855205)

WEB DESIGN See also Computer / Graphics / Web Development
ABM Computer Training 54 North St, Swords (8902348) - web design using Front Page; all yr, also day, Sat

Adelaide Computers 14 Pembroke Lane Ballsbridge 4 (2696213) - one-to-one training at youroffice/home or our offices, small groups, beginners to advanced, full training programmes also

Ballsbridge College of Business Studies Shelbourne Rd 4 (6684806) - html, java & dreamweaver, Tues 6.30, 10 wks €200

Balymun Comprehensive School Adult Ed Centre Ballymun Rd 9 (8420654/ 8425828 night) - web page design basics, Thurs 10 wks €140

Business Computer Training Central Dublin (6616838 LoCall 1890 564039) - site design, 12 wks cert €570/ I-NET+ Internet Technical Professional, 11 wks, CompTia iNet cert, €660/ CIW site designer, 11 wks, cert €760/ CIW e-commerce designer, 10 wks, €760 cert

CITAS Computer & IT Training 54 Middle Abbey St 1 (8782212) - HTML/ Dreamweaver, 6 wks Tue 6.30-9pm, €600; also day

Colaiste Ide Cardiffsbridge Rd Finglas West 11 (8342333) - incl. graphics & digital repro, Thurs, 7-10pm, 13 wks, €200

Crumlin College of Further Education Crumlin Rd 12 (4540662) - multimedia authoring (macromedia director), Tues/ Dreamweaver, Tues/ using HTML & Javascript, Thurs/ Flash/ Fireworks graphics, both Wed - all 10 wks/ animation / interactive, Thurs 8.45 10 wks

Dorset College 64a Lr Dorset St/ 8 Belvedere Pl 1 (8309677) - CompTIA I-net, CIW site designer, e-commerce: master designer

Dublin Business School 13/14 Aungier St 2 (4177500) - dip in web design, 1 eve per wk, 6.30-9.30pm, 10 wks

Dun Laoghaire College of Further Education 17 Cumberland St Dun Laoghaire (2809676) - Mon, 20 wks, 7.30-9.30 FETAC cert, €270

Eden Computer Training Rathfarnham 16, or MACRO Centre, 1 Green St 7 (4953155) - effective, using dreamweaver, fireworks

FAS Net College www.fas-netcollege.com (info@fas-netcollege.com/ 2043600) - design & programming: e-commerce designer, cert, dreamweaver & ultra dev; dynamic server pages & CGI using perl, cert; flash, java 2 enterprise connectivity/ programming fundamentals/ javascript cert €120 each; object oriented analysis & design with UML, cert; site designer cert; dreamweaver 4; SQL server 7 - database implement; warehouses; Visual C++6 appli; Online tutor option €80

FAS Training Centres: Baldoyle 13 (8167460); Ballyfermot 10 (6055900/ 5933); Cabra Bannow Rd 7 (8821400); Finglas Jamestown Rd 11 (8140243); FAS Training Services Wyatville Rd (2043600)

Fitzwilliam Institute Ltd Temple Court Temple Rd Blackrock (2834579) - postgrad dip in software development, networking & website development, ICM,f/time day,

€3810/ 4540 Eu non-resident/ 5835 non EU nationals, all + €190 exam fees

Irish Academy of Computer Training 98 St Stephen's Grn 2 (4347600) - IACT webmaster course, in web design, 12 wks dip, €1995

Keytrainer Ireland 33/34 Dame St 2 (6714000) - scheduled & tailored training in web design & internet

New Media Technology Training 13 Harcourt St 2 (4780905) - web authoring 1 html; 2 dreamweaver; 3 java, CGI scripts, style sheets/ digital imaging, adobe photoshop/ animation - flash, director/ also p/time day/ web programming active server pages

Pitman Training Centre 6-8 Wicklow St 2 (6768008) - 12-18 hrs, €280, cert/ business skills dip & web design, 8 wks €1646; day eve Sats

Pobalscoil Iosolde 20 (6260116) - dreamweaver, Mon 7-9pm 10 wks

Pobalscoil Rosmini Adult Ed Grace Pk Rd 9 (8371015) - for beginners, Thurs, 7pm €130

Rathmines Snr College Town Hall 6 (4975334) - Wed, 10 wks €80

Ringsend Technical Institute Cambridge Rd 4 (6684498) - introduction to, 10 wks €95

School of Computer Technology 21 Rosmeen Gdns Dun Laoghaire (2844045) - C&G cert 36 hrs €750/ also day

Senior College Dun Laoghaire CFE Eblana Ave Dun Laoghaire (2800385) - cert in web authoring, FETAC 25 wks, €330

St Thomas Community College Novara Ave Bray (2866111) - C&G cert, web design, 20 wks, €250

Whitehall College of Further Education Swords Rd 9 (8376011) - Tue & Thurs, 6.30-9.30pm, 10 wks

WEBSITE DEVELOPMENT see also Web Design

Connolly House Nth Strand (by 5 Lamps) 1 (8557116) - website design, 10 wks Wed, 6.30pm €81

Crumlin College of Further Education Crumlin Rd 12 (4540662) - build your own, Tues 6.45 10 wks

FAS Net College www.fas-netcollege.com (info@fas-netcollege.com/ 2043600) - elearning: e-Commerce €120; intro HTML €40; online tutor option €80

FAS Training Centre Tallaght Cookstown Indl Est 24 (4045284) - levels 1 & 2

Fitzwilliam Institute Ltd Temple Court Temple Rd Blackrock (2834579) - postgrad dip in software development, networking & website development, ICM,f/time day, €3810/ 4540 Eu non-resident/ 5835 non EU nationals, all + €190 exam fees

Institute of Technology Tallaght 24 (4042000) - website construction, 8 wks

WEIGHT LIFTING / TRAINING

Irish Amateur Weightlifting Assoc 4 (6601390, Fax: 6680486)

Motions Health & Fitness Training City West Leisure Centre (4588179/ 087 2808866)

Tony Quinn Centre 66/67 Eccles St 7 (8304211)

WELDING see also Art Metal Work

DIT Faculty: Engineering Bolton St 1 (4023649/3445) - MMA & oxy-acetylene welding; gas shielded arc; MMA advanced plate & pile; pipe fabrication; inspection & testing NDT; welding repair & maintenance: each course 20 wks, cert, 1 eve weekly, €500

FAS Training Centre Ballyfermot 10 (6055900/ 5933)

FAS Training Centre Tallaght 24 (4045284) - basic gas shielded arc 1 & 2, 10wk

WELFARE SERVICE

Civil Defence Esplanade Wolftone Qy 7 (6772699) - various centres

The Open University Enquiry & Advice Centre Holbrook House, Holles St 2 (6785399) - & health studies

WELSH

Dublin Public Libraries Admin Hq, 138-144 Pearse St 2 (6644800) - central library

Ilac Centre (8734333) or Library HQ for details (6744800), self-learning €free

Sth Dublin Co Libraries Languages & Computers: Ballyroan/Clondalkin/ Castletymon, Lucan & Co Library (4597834-admin only) - self learning

WILDLIFE see also Conservation / Natural History / Ornithology

St Thomas Community College Novara Ave Bray (2866111) - 30 wks €200 FETAC

WIND-SURFING see also Board Sailing

Colaiste Dhulaigh Barryscourt Rd Coolock 17 (8481337) - Sat, 5 wks, 9.30-12.30

Corporate Club 24 Elmcastle Green Kilnamanagh 24 (4610935)

Fingall Sailing School Malahide (8451979)

Irish Sailing Assoc 3 Park Rd Dun Laoghaire (2800239) - all levels, all yr, all ages, apply for provider list

Network Sports & Social Club 24 Elmcastle Green Kilnamanagh 24 (4524415)

Surfdock Grand Canal Dockyard Sth Dock Rd Ringsend 4 (6683945) - level 1-4, also w/end/ corporate groups

WINE APPRECIATION / MAKING see also Cookery

Ashfield College Main St Templeogue 6W (4900866) - tasting & appreciation, / gourmet cookery & wine selection, 8 wks each

Cabinteely Community School Johnstown Rd 18 (2857455) - Tues, 8 wks, €100

Coolmine Community School Clonsilla 15 (8214583) - 6 wks, Mon & Tue, €80 each

DIT Faculty: Tourism & Food Cathal Brugha St 1 (4024349/3445) - cert in wine studies, 1 yr €700/ wine course 10 wks Sommelier cert €230 / oenology, jan-june (4024344)

Dun Laoghaire College of Further Education 17 Cumberland St Dun Laoghaire (2809676) - Wed 10 wks 7-9.30 €150

Hartstown Community School Clonsilla 15 (8209863) - appreciation, 10wks, €140

Institute of Technology Tallaght 24 (4042000) - intro to wine, 8 wks

Knocklyon Youth & Community Centre, 16 (4943991)

Liberties Vocational School Bull Alley St 8 (4540044) - Wed 7-9.30, €175

Malahide Community School Malahide (8460949) - tasting, 6 wks, Tues €80

Marino College 14-20 Marino Mart 3 (8332100) - beginners 10wks, €66 incls wine/ varietal, €132

Newpark Adult Education Centre Newtownpark Ave Blackrock (2884376) - beginners/ improvers, €140

Old Bawn Community School Tallaght 24 (4526137) - introduction to, Tue 8 wks

WOMEN'S STUDIES/ ISSUES

TACT St Dominic's School St Dominic's Rd Tallaght 24 (4596757) - women in literature, 10 wks €50

WOMEN, COURSES / ACTIVITIES FOR
KLEAR Grange Park View Kilbarrack 5 (8671845) - various, day only

League of Health (Irl) 17 Dundela Pk Sandycove (2807775) - individual centres listed under KEEP FIT

Yvonne Stewart Park House Library Road Dun Laoire (2802150) - assertiveness, 8wks €70, day

WOODCARVING / CRAFT
Hartstown Community School Clonsilla 15 (8209863) - carving & marquetry, 10 wks €70

Newpark Adult Education Centre Newtownpark Ave Blackrock (2884376) - 10wks, €99

Saint Tiernan's Community School Parkvale Balally 16 (2953224) - native Irish wood, Tues 7.30-9.30, 10 wks, €70

St Thomas Community College Novara Ave Bray (2866111) - carving, 10 wks, €70

WOODWIND
Dun Laoghaire Music Centre 130A Lr George's St Dun Laoghaire (2844178)

Walton's New School of Music 69 Sth Gt George's St 2 (4781884) - also day, see ad page 173

WOODWORK
Ballymun Comprehensive Schools Adult Ed Centre Ballymun Rd 9 (8420654/8425828 night) - woodturning, Mon 10wk, level 1 / Tue level 2, ; €100 ea

Blackrock College (2888681) - diy course, 7.30-9, 6 wks €65

Colaiste Dhulaigh Barryscourt Rd Coolock 17 (8481337) - wood turning, Tue 7.15, 8 wks

DIT admissions ofice Dublin (4023445) - Timber Dev Centre, FurnCert - prog for furniture & Wood industry, and advanced level / also wood machining introductory, 80 hrs contact 8729020

DIT Faculty: Built Environment Bolton St 1 (4023711/3445) - wood turning, Mon 7-10pm, 10 wks €230

FAS Training Centre Finglas Jamestown Rd 11 (8140243)

FAS Training Centre Tallaght 24 (4045284) - 10 wks

Greenhills College Limekiln Ave Walkinstown 12 (4507779/4507138) - woodturning, 8wks, €146

Hartstown Community School Clonsilla 15 (8209863) - woodturning, 10wks, €70

Holy Family Community School Rathcoole (4580766)

Kylemore College Kylemore Rd 10 (6265901) - FETAC: craft foundation level, woodcraft, woodwork Fri, 1.30-4.30; improvers, Thurs / furniture making, Thurs, 9.30-12.30/

Newpark Adult Education Centre Newtownpark Ave Blackrock (2884376) - beginners/improvers,10wks, €99

Pobalscoil Rosmini Adult Ed Grace Pk Rd 9 (8371015) - beginners, Tue, 7&8.30pm, 10 wks, €95

Ringsend Technical Institute Cambridge Rd 4 (6684498) - beginners, €75/ intermediate €100, 10 wks each

Saint Tiernan's Community School Parkvale Balally 16 (2953224) - basic & DIY,

Mon, 7.30-9.30pm, 10 wks, €70/ woodturning, 10 wks, €120

St Thomas Community College Novara Ave Bray (2866111) - woodturning, 10 wks, €70

WORD PROCESSING see also Computers / Keyboard / Secretarial / Typing

ABM Computer Training 54 North St, Swords (8902348) - intro to WP, intermediate & advanced ECDL

Balbriggan Community College Pine Ridge Chapel St (8412388/9) - basic skills, 8 wks, Thurs, 7.30-9.30, €99

Blackrock College (2888681) - with internet & email, 7.30-9, 6 wks €65

CITAS Computer & I.T. Training 54 Middle Abbey St 1 (8782212) - ms word, 1 day €199

Colaiste Eanna College of Business & Technical Stu Kilkieran Rd Cabra 7 (8389577) - intro to, 10wks Thurs 7-9pm/ intro to ms applications, 10 wks

College of Further Education Main St Dundrum 14 (2951376) - beginners/ improvers, Tue, Thurs

Computeach AXIS, Main St Ballymun 9 (8832167) - Pitman - essential, intermediate & advanced

Coolmine Community School Clonsilla 15 (8214583) - Mon 2 terms 18 wks €180/ Tue €90; Wed, beginners €90: 9wks, 7.30-9.30

Crumlin College of Further Education Crumlin Rd 12 (4540662) - for beginners/ ms office, Mon 6.45-9.45/ also excel & access

Donahies Community School Streamville Rd 13 (8482217) - intro to WP & keyboard skills/ wp & internet Mon, day: each 10 wks €100

Eden Computer Training Rathfarnham 16, or MACRO Centre, 1 Green St 7 (4953155) - beginners to advanced; also ECDL, MOS

FAS Training Centre Baldoyle 13 (8167460)

FAS Training Centre Ballyfermot 10 (6055900/ 5933)

Grange Community College Grange Abbey Rd Donaghmede 13 (8471422) - ms word, 10wks, €93

Griffith College Dublin Sth Circular Rd 8 (4150400) - Word, ITEB cert, p/t, end user, 1 eve per wk

Keytrainer Ireland 33/34 Dame St 2 (6714000) - intro to advanced levels, day, incl ECDL

Kilroy's College 25 Kingram Place 2 (1850 700700) - tutor supported home study: computer basics, ECDL, keyboard & typing

Kylemore College Kylemore Rd 10 (6265901) - FETAC foundation level, Thurs & level 2 Mon: 12 wks, day 10-12

Plunket College Swords Rd, Whitehall 9 (8371689) - NCVA level 2, Tues 20wks, €133

Rathmines Snr College Town Hall 6 (4975334) - keyboarding & wp, Tue, 7pm 20 wks €210

Ringsend Technical Institute Cambridge Rd 4 (6684498) - word for windows, 10wks, €95

Ringsend Technical Institute Cambridge Rd 4 (6684498) - 10 wks, MOUS core cert, €185

St Kevins College Clogher Rd Crumlin 12 (4536397) - word for windows level 2, NCVA, 20wks

St Thomas Community College Novara Ave Bray (2866111) - 30 wks, €200, cert, day only

Stillorgan Senior College Old Road Stillorgan (2880704) - beginners/ continuation, 8 wks, €95 each

Whitehall College of Further Education Swords Rd 9 (8376011) - MOS 10 wks, Tue & Thurs 6.30-9.30

WORKOUT see Keep Fit

WRESTLING

Irish Amateur Wrestling Assoc Michael McAuley, 9 (8315522/ 087-2627452) - olympic freestyle; Hercules, 9 Lurgan St, Dublin 1, Tues-Thurs, 6.30-7.30 juniors, 7.30-8.45 seniors, Sun 11-1pm; Spartan, Tue 6-8pm, Sat, 6-8pm Firhouse Scount Den Ballycullen Dr; Vulcan, Westland Row, 1.30-3pm Wed. / also: Gladiators, UCD, Larkin community college/ St Andrews resource centre, Pearse St

WRITING (CREATIVE) see also Songwriting / Creative Thinking

Ashfield College Main St Templeogue 6W (4900866) - & getting published, 7.30-9.30, 8 wks

Balymun Comprehensive School Adult Ed Centre Ballymun Rd 9 (8420654/ 8425828 night) - workshops, beginners, continuation, Mon 10 wks €80/ poetry appreciation, Tue 10 wks free

BASE Ballyboden Adult Social Education Whitechurch Library Taylor's Lane 16 (4935953) - for women

BookConsulT 68 Mountjoy Square (8740354) - occasional courses/ tuition/ getting published

Cabinteely Community School Johnstown Rd 18 (2857455) - 10wk, €85

Colaiste Dhulaigh & College of Further Education Barryscourt Rd Coolock 17 (8481337) - you can write your own play, Mon 7-9pm, 10 wks

Coolmine Community School Clonsilla 15 (8214583) - Mon, 9wk, €60

DATE College of Further Education Dundrum 14 (2964322) - writers group/ beginners/ improvers, 10 wks, day €79

Dublin Writer's Workshop meet at Bowes Fleet St 2 ()

Dun Laoghaire College of Further Education 17 Cumberland St Dun Laoghaire (2809676) - for the novice & established, Tue 7.30-9.30, 10wks €100

Dun Laoghaire-Rathdown Co Council Public Library Service () - Dalkey Writer's Group, Thurs 6-7.45, fortnightly, free, new members always welcome (2781788)

Finglas Adult Reading & Writing Scheme Colaiste Eoin Finglas 11 (8340893) - day, 30 wks, free

Foxrock Institute Kill O' the Grange School Kill Lane Blackrock (4939506/4939629) - 8 wks, €85

Gaiety School of Acting Sycamore St Meeting House Sq Temple Bar 2 (6799277) - creative writing/ page to stage/ advanced page to stage: each €290

Greenhills College Limekiln Ave Walkinstown 12 (4507779/4507138) - beginners/improvers, writers workshop, 10 wks, €79

Greenhills College Limekiln Ave Walkinstown 12 (4507779/4507138) - writers workshop, Tue, 10 wks €79

Irish Writers' Centre 19 Parnell Sq 1 (8721302)

Kilroy's College 25 Kingram Place 2 (1850 700700) - tutor supported home study: for adults & children, dip courses

KLEAR Grange Park View Kilbarrack 5 (8671845) - beginners/advanced; writers group; day

Lucan Community College Esker Drive (6282077) - & literature appreciation 8wk, €79

Marino College 14-20 Marino Mart 3 (8332100) - Thurs 6pm, 10wks, €66

Newpark Adult Education Centre Newtownpark Ave Blackrock (2884376) - memoir writing/ writers' workshop, beginners/improvers, 10wks, €99/ filmscript, Thurs €99

People's College 32 Parnell Sq 1 (8735879) - €50

Ringsend Technical Institute Cambridge Rd 4 (6684498) - writing & journalism workshop, 10wks, €65

St MacDara's Community College Wellington Lane Templeogue 6W (4566216) - Tue, 7.30-9.30pm, 10 wks, €79

St Peter's College Collins Ave 5 (8337686) - beginners Mon/ improvers, Tue: 7.30-10, 10 wks €60

St Thomas Community College Novara Ave Bray (2866111) - screen writing, 10 wks €70

Tallaght Community School Balrothery 24 (4515566) - 8wk, €45

UCD Adult Education Office (7061695) - screenwriting for film & tv; writing for radio/ unlocking the creative skills, intro to & continuation workshop/ writing fiction - short story & beyond/ poetry reading & writing/ intro to creative writing for everyone: all 10 wks

WRITING SKILLS

Hartstown Community School Clonsilla 15 (8209863) - write your own story, 10 wks €60

Irish Academy of Public Relations (2780802) - practical journalism, cert, UCD/UCC/UCG, correspondence or e-mail, 8wks, €355

Keytrainer Ireland 33/34 Dame St 2 (6714000) - tailored courses in report writing

Kilroy's College 25 Kingram Place 2 (1850 700700) - tutor supported home study: freelance journalism, creative, dip

Pobalscoil Rosmini Adult Ed Grace Pk Rd 9 (8371015) - practical, letter, essauy assignments, 10 wks Thurs €80

WRITING, BASIC and READING see Basic Education / Adult / English Literacy

Ballymun Comprehensive School Adult Ed Centre Ballymun Rd 9 (8420654/ 8425828 night) - spellwell, a new approach, Mon. Tue 7.30, free

FAS Net College www.fas-netcollege.com (info@fas-netcollege.com/ 2043600) - business writing basic series €80; online tutor option €80

Kilroy's College 25 Kingram Place 2 (1850 700700) - tutor supported home study: English, word study & spelling, general adult education

National Adult Literacy Agency 76 Lr Gardiner St 1 (8554332) - national referral service for adults/literary resource room available

Plunket College Swords Rd, Whitehall 9 (8371689) - basic reading & writing, Tue, Wed, 10-12.30pm

Ringsend Technical Institute Cambridge Rd 4 (6684498) - spellwell, various times ongoing, free

YACHTMASTER'S CERTIFICATE / OFFSHORE / OCEAN

Glenans Irish Sailing Club 5 Lr Mount St 2 (6611481) - ISA coastal yachtmaster

Irish Sailing Assoc 3 Park Rd Dun Laoghaire (2800239) - apply for list of providers

Sea-Craft 3 Newcourt Ave Bray (2863362) - ISA Yachtmaster coastal, 21 wk €335, cert/ Yachtmaster offshore, 21 wks €397/ celestial, yachtmaster ocean, 20 wks €440, cert

YOGA

Alan Pelly Dominican College 9 & Mercy College 5 (8476440 / 087 2749011) - Iyengar, Wed, Thurs; & Astanga Tues; 7 wks €80 each,

Balbriggan Community College Pine Ridge Chapel St (8412388/9) - 8wks, Tues, 7.30-9.30, Stage 2 8.30-10pm, €53 each

Ballyfermot College of Further Education Ballyfermot Rd 10 (6269421) - manoyoga from southern India, Wed, 7.30 5 wks €50

Ballymun Comprehensive Schools Adult Ed Centre Ballymun Rd 9 (8420654/ 8425828 night) - Mon 6.30 & 8pm 10wk, €75

BASE Ballyboden Adult Social Education Whitechurch Library Taylor's Lane 16 (4935953)

Blackrock College (2888681) - Wed, 7.30-9, 6 wks €65

Brahma Kumaris WSU Raja Yoga Centres 61 Morehampton Rd 4 (6687480) - raja, 7wk

Cabinteely Community School Johnstown Rd 18 (2857455) - beginners/continuing 10wk, 1.5 hrs, €60 each

Classical Hatha Yoga 61 Morehampton Rd 4 (6687480) - Hatha 6wk, €75 small groups - also day

Colaiste Dhulaigh Barryscourt Rd Coolock 17 (8481337) - Mon 7.30-9, Tues 6.30-8, 10 wks beginners/ continuation/ also day Wed 10.30am, 10 wks

Colaiste Eanna Kilkieran Rd Cabra 7 (8389577) - beginners, Thurs,6.30 & 8pm, 10wk

College of Further Education Main St Dundrum 14 (2951376) - beginners/ continuation, Tue & Thurs

Connolly House Nth Strand (by 5 Lamps) 1 (8557116) - beginners, 10 wks Wed, 6.30 & 8pm €50 each

Coolmine Community School Clonsilla 15 (8214583) - Mon, Tue, Wed: 9wk, €60

Crumlin College of Further Education Crumlin Rd 12 (4540662) - beginners/continuation, 10 wks Mon, Tue, Wed

Dance Theatre of Ireland Bloomfields Centre, Lr George St Dun Laoghaire (2803455) - Hatha Yoga, Fri, 6.30 & 8; 8-9pm; mornings, Wed, 10-11.30

DATE College of Further Education Dundrum 14 (2964322) - beginners/ intermediate/ mixed ability: eqach 10 wks, €66 day

Donahies Community School Streamville Rd 13 (8482217) - beginners/ improvers, Tues 7 & 8.30, 10 wks, €50

Dublin Meditation Centre 42 Lr leeson St (Basement) 2 (6615934) - 5wks, €60

Dun Laoghaire College of Further Education 17 Cumberland St Dun Laoghaire (2809676) - beginners Mon 7.30-8.30/ mixed ability 8.30-10, Tues, 10 wks, €85 each

Foxrock Institute Kill O' the Grange School Kill Lane Blackrock (4939506/4939629) - healing and Yoga, 8 wks, €85

Grange Community College Grange Abbey Rd Donaghmede 13 (8471422) - for relaxation, 8 wks, €53

Greendale Community School Kilbarrack 5 (8322735/6) - beginners Tue 7pm/ continuation Thurs, 8.30pm, 10wks, €50 each/ workshop, Sat €35

Greenhills College Limekiln Ave Walkinstown 12 (4507779/4507138) - 8wks, €77

Harmony Yoga Ireland Ballinteer/Dundrum Dalkey / Killiney (087 8263778) - beginners, intermediate, advanced; 12 wk; also pay-as-you-come; morn, eve / pregnancy yoga / post natal yoga / pregnancy yoga dip / baby yoga dip

Hartstown Community School Clonsilla 15 (8209863) - 10wks, €50

Healing House 24 O'Connell Ave Berkeley Rd 7 (8306413) - beginners & improvers, 6 wks / morning courses from 7.30; also evenings

Holistic Healing Centre 38 Dame St 2 (6710813)

Holistic Sourcing Centre 67 Lr Camden St 2 (4785022) - hatha 8 wk (4547310)

Holy Family Community School Rathcoole (4580766)

Inchicore College of Further Education Emmet Rd 8 (4535358) - beginners, continuation, 10 wks each, Mon/Tue

Irish Aikido Federation 1 Parklane E Pearse St 2 (6718454) - 10wk, €100/ 3 Months, €150

Irish Health Culture Association 66 Eccles St 7 (8500493/ 8304211) - yoga teacher's dip/ eve, wkend, & concentrated courses/ ask for prospectus

Irish Health Culture Association Yoga Teachers 66 Eccles St 7 (8500493/ 8304211) - see display listing: MIHCA yoga teachers, classes mainly 1.25-1.5 hrs, 6-8 wks, fees c €60-80; contact individual teachers

Irish Yoga Asociation (4929213 / 087 2054489) - various locations / teacher's course for EU of Yoga standard

Jackie Skelly's Fitness 42 Clarendon St, 2; Park West Bus Pk, Nangor Rd, 12 & Applewood Village, Swords (6770040 / 6301456 / 8075620) - gym membership, €47-59 per mth incl classes

Jean McDonald IYA (2722317) - KRIYA Yoga small groups, various locations, dip / mixed ability IYA dip courses at: Glen Druid Marriot, Newtownmountkennedy Co Wicklow, 6.15 (6634750); Shelbourne Club, St Stephens Green 2 6pm (6634750)

Karen Ward Classes, Dublin 4 (6704905) - as seen on RTE TV's 'The Health Squad'; also workshops & yoga holidays

Kilternan Adult Education Group Glencullen Rd 18 (2952050) Mon, Tue, day 10 wks €66

KLEAR Grange Park View Kilbarrack 5 (8671845) - beginners, intermediate, 10 wks, day only

Knocklyon Youth & Community Centre, 16 (4943991)

Liberties Vocational School Bull Alley St 8 (4540044) - beginners &improvers, all ages, Mon 7-8.3- €65

LIFEWORKS Yoga Margaret Forde (8339902) - a yoga class in your workplace?

Lucan Community College Esker Drive (6282077) - 10 wk 1 hr, €46/ 1.25 hr €56

Malahide Community School Malahide (8460949) - beginners, 10 wks Tues & Thurs, 7.30 & 8.30, €70 ea

Margaret Macken Stephen's Gr/Adelaide Rd/Clontarf (8332954) - Iyengar Yoga, 6 wk course; also relaxation, stress management and meditation

Marino College 14-20 Marino Mart 3 (8332100) - Tues, beginners/intermediate, 10wks €50

Melt, Temple Bar Natural Healing Centre 2 Temple Ln 2 (6798786) - 8 wks, Iyengar/Astanga yoga, €82/ hata yoga/ pregnancy yoga, 10.30-11.30 €12 per session; also day

Natural Health Training Centre 1 Park Lane E Pearse St 2 (6718454) - basic method, 10 wks, €100

Newpark Adult Education Centre Newtownpark Ave Blackrock (2884376) - beginners, improvers, 10wks, €80

Old Bawn Community School Tallaght 24 (4526137) - level 1& 2, 7,30-9.30, Tues 10wks

Palmerstown Community School 20 (6260116) - levels 1&2, Tues & Thurs 10 wks €55 ea

People's College 32 Parnell Sq 1 (8735879) - €80

Phibsboro Gym 1st floor, Phibsboro SC 7 (8301849) - beginners, Fri 6.30-7.30, 8 wks

Physio Extra 4 Oliver Bond St 8 (6725719) - spineright: yoga with pilates, beginner & intermediate levels; morn, day, eve

Pinewood 76 Butterfield Ave Rathfarnham 14 (4947003) - all levels, eve, 8wk, €90

Plunket College Swords Rd, Whitehall 9 (8371689) - beginners, Tues, 10 wks, €49

Pobalscoil Neasain Baldoyle 13 (8063092) - Mon & Tue 8-9.30, 10 wks €65/ also pregnancy yoga, Tue/ Mon morn 10.30, 10 wks €65

Pobalscoil Rosmini Adult Ed Grace Pk Rd 9 (8371015) - beginners/continuation, Mon-Thurs, 10 wks, €80 each

Portmarnock Community School Carrickhill Rd (8038056) - beginners / improvers 8 wks €45

Rathmines Snr College Town Hall 6 (4975334) - beginners, Wed; yoga AI Tue, 10 wks €50 ea

Ringsend Technical Institute Cambridge Rd 4 (6684498) - beginners/improvers, 10wks, €65

Saint Finian's Community College Swords (8402623) - beginners, Tue/ continuation, Mon, €79 each

Saint Tiernan's Community School Parkvale Balally 16 (2953224) - beginners with Mella, Mon, 7.30-9.30pm, 10 wks, €65/ advanced Wed

Seamus Lynch 19 St Patrick's Cresc Monkstown Farm Dun Laoghaire (2846073) - yoga of the heart, continuous, €12.50 per session, 26 Longford Tce Monkstown, Wed mornings

St Anthony's House St Lawrence Rd Clontarf 3 (8335300)

St Kevin's College Clogher Rd Crumlin 12 (4536397) - 10wks

St Mac Dara's Community College Wellington Lane Templeogue 6W (4566216) - beginners, Mon/ easy yoga, Tue: 7.30-8.30pm, 10 wks, €66 each

St Mark's Community School Cookstown Road Tallaght 24 (4519399)

St Paul's College Sybil Hill 5 (Margaret Forde, 8339902) - beginners & intermediate, 6 wks, €70

St Peter's College Collins Ave 5 (8337686) - Mon, Thurs, 10wk, 7.30 & 8.30, €60 ea

St Thomas Community College Novara Ave Bray (2866111) - beginners/continuation, 10wks, €70 each

Stillorgan Senior College Old Road Stillorgan (2880704) - beginners/improvers, 8 wks, €70 each

Susan Church (087 6210402) - hatha yoga: Phibsboro, Church St, Baggot St, Sandymount

TACT St Dominic's School St Dominic's Rd Tallaght 24 (4596757) - beginners/advanced, 10wks, €47 day

Tallaght Community School Balrothery 24 (4515566) - beginners/ improvers, 10wk, €45 each

Taney Centre Taney Rd Dundrum 14 (2985491) - Tue, Thurs: 2982880; Tue: 6767551; Mon, Wed, Thurs: 2962608/ also day

TARGET St Kevin's School Newbrook Rd, Donaghmede 13 (8671967) - 10 wks, day only, beginners, improvers

The Sanctuary Stanhope Street 7 (6705419) - beginners /& intermediate: satyanda, hata 8 wks €80 ea/ astanga 10 wks €100

Tony Quinn Centre 66/67 Eccles St 7 (8304211) - 6 wk courses, lunchtime courses, drop-in classes, individual tuition

Valerie Ward, Yoga Teacher city centre & southside (087 2852293) - 6wks, €65 / pregnant yoga classes / also yoga kids

Yoga Therapy Ireland 20 Auburn Drive Killiney (2352120) - classes with fully qualified & insured Yoga teachers / accredited teacher training dip, 20 wkends, 2yrs / tutor training, 10 wkends, 1 yr / yoga therapy open days; workshops / seminars 2-day w/end

YOUTH COURSES / INFORMATION CENTRES

Catholic Youth Care 20-23 Arran Qy 7 (8725055) - centres at: Bray (2828324); Swords (8405100); Clondalkin (4594666); Dun Laoghaire (2806147); E Wicklow (0402-39646); Finglas (8341436); Lucan/Nth Kildare (6280465); Ronanstown (4570363)

Department of Adult & Community Education NUI Maynooth (7084500) - NUI cert Youth Studies: Blanchardstown (8209550); Bray (2869607); Liberties College (4542100)

Kilroy's College 25 Kingram Place 2 (1850 700700) - tutor supported home study: English, word study & spelling, arithmetic, computer skills, junior & leaving cert, return to education, sports psychology, dip

Youth Info Centres () - info on education, training, employment, careers, rights & entitlements, travel, sport & leisure - Main St, Blanchardstown (8212077) Monastery Rd, Clondalkin (4594666) Bell Tower, Dun Laoghaire (2809363); Main Rd, Tallaght

YOUTH INFORMATION CENTRES YOUTH COURSES

Catholic Youth Care 20-23 Arran Qy 7 (8725055) - Bray (2762818); Clondalkin (4594666); Dun Laoghaire (2809363) - info on careers, employment, entitlements, sports & leisure, talks & exhibitions.

ZOO

Dublin Zoo Education Dept Phoenix Pk 8 (6771425) - conservation & wildlife, 4wks, Wed eve, Oct

ZCOLOGY see Natural History

Directory of E-mail addresses & websites
Relating to courses at most of the centres listed

Abbey School of Healing: – bioenergy@eircom.net
ABM Business Training: – training@abm.ie – www.abm.ie
ABM Computer Training: – training@abm.ie – www.abm.ie
ACCA: – – recruit.dublin@accaglobal.com
ACCORD: – marriagepreparation@dublin.accord.ie – www.dublin.accord.ie
Acupuncture Foundation Trn Sch: – acufound@eircom.net –
    www.acupuncturefoundation.com
Addiction Training Institute: – ati@indigo.ie – www.addiction.ie
Adelaide Computers: – adelaide@esatclear.ie
Aisling Ireland: – aisirl@iol.ie: – aisling-ireland.com
Alan Pelly: – discoveryoga@eircom.net – www.discover-yoga.com
Alexander Technique: – frankkennedy@eircom.net – www.alexandertech-dublin.com
All Hallows College: – jcleary@allhallows.ie
Alliance Francaise: – info@alliance-francaise.ie – www.alliance-francaise.ie
Alpha College of English: – admin@alphacollege.com – www.alphacollege.com
American College Dublin: – degree@amcd.ie
An Oige: – mailbox@anoige.ie
An Taisce - The National Trust: – info@antaisce.org – www.antaisce.org
Ashfield Computer Training: – info@ashfieldcomputer-train.ie
Aspen's College of Beauty: – neelaminfo@aspensireland.com – www.aspensireland.com
Astronomy Ireland: – info@astronomy.ie – www.astronomy.ie
Athletics Association: – admin@athleticsireland.ie – www.athleticsireland.ie
Badminton Union of Ireland: – lbbui@indigo.ie – www.badmintonireland.com
Ballinteer Community School: – ballcom@eircom.net – www.ballinteercs.ie
Ballyfermot College of FE: – night school@bcfe.cdvec.ie
Ballymun Comprehensive School: – compaded@eircom.net
Ballymun Men's Centre: – menscentre@oceanfree.net
Bel Canto School of Singing: –
    reception@thesingingschool.com – www.thesingingschool.com
Betty Ann Norton Theatre School: –
    bettyannnorton@eircom.net – www.bettyann-nortontheatreschool.com
Bi-Aura Foundation: – bio@iol.ie – www.bi-aura.com
Bill Brady School of Guitar: – bbguitar@eircom.net
Birdwatch Ireland: – info@birdwatchireland.org – www.birdwatchireland.ie
Blackrock College: – rpdalton1@eircom.net – www.blackrockcollege.com
Bluefeather School of Languages: – TEFL@bluefeather.ie – www.bluefeather.ie
Bodyline Studio: – – www.bodyline.ie
BookConsulT: – cashmanprojects@eircom.net
Brahma Kumaris WSU Raja Yoga: – bknick@indigo.ie
Bray Music Centre: – artemiskent@esatclear.ie
Bray Sailing Club: – training@braysailingclub.ie – www.braysailingclub.ie
Broadmeadows Equestrian Centre: – broadmeadow@eircom.net
Bronwyn Conroy Beauty School: – – www.bronwynconroy.com
Business Coach Ireland: – mjohalloran@eircom.net
Business Computer Training Inst: – info@bct.ie
C Harkins: – cato@esatclear.ie
Cafe Fresh: – mary@cafe-fresh.com – www.cafe-fresh.com
Caitriona Mitchell: – caitrionamitchell@hotmail.com
Calliaghstown Riding Centre: – info@calliaghstownridingcentre.com

Campaign against Bullying: – odonnellb@indigo.ie: – www.indigo.ie/~odonnellb/cabullying/
Catholic Youth Care: – info@cyc.ie – www.cyc.ie
Central Library: – cicelib@iol.ie
Centre for Professional & Personal Development: –
    marycurran@coachcentre.ie – www.coachcentre.ie
CITAS Computer & IT Training: – citas@iol.ie
Clanwilliam Institute: – training@clanwilliam.ie – www.clanwilliam.ie
Classical Hatha Yoga: – bknick@indigo.ie
Clondalkin Sports & Leisure: – scdls@eircom.net – www.clondalkin.co.cslc
Clontarf School of Music: – csmusic@eircom.net
Clontarf Swimming Club: – nicholasomeara@entemp.ie
Cocoon Reiki Centre: – annfaherty@esatclear.ie
Colaiste Dhulaigh & College of FE: – info@accd.net – www.accd.net
Colaiste Eanna: – info@colaiste-eanna.com: – www.colaiste-eanna.com
Colaiste Eoin: – info@eoin.cdvec.ie – www.colaisteeoin.ie
Colaiste Ide: – general.enquiries@ide.cdvec.ie – www.colaisteide.ie
College of FE, Dundrum: – info@cfedundrum.com – www.cfedrundrum.com
Comhaltas Ceoltoiri Eireann: – enquiries@comhaltas.com – www.comhaltas.com
Comhlamh: – info@comhlamh.org
Community & Youth Info Centres: – ycinfo@iol.ie
Complementary House: – courses@complementaryhouse.com – www.spiritireland.com
Computeach Computer Centre: – computech@axis-ballymun.ie
Conradh na Gaeilge: – eolas@cnag.ie: – ww.cnag.ie
Consumers Association of Ireland: –
    cai@consumerassociation.ie – www.consumerassociation.ie
Coolmine Community School: – adulted@coolmine.ie
Cormac Cuffe: – cormaccuffe@oceanfree.net – www.irishjewelleryclasses.com
Corporate Club: – reply@corporateclub.ie – www.corporateclub.ie
Crescent Flower Studios: – ior@crescentstudios.com
Crossroads Set Dancers: – jgryan@eircom.net
Crumlin College of FE: – adulted@ccfe.cdvec.ie
Cumann Camogaiochta na nGael: – camogie@gofree.indigo.ie – www.camogie.ie
Dance Theatre of Ireland: –
    info@dancetheatreireland.com: – www.dancetheatreireland.com
Dept of Adult & Community Ed, Maynooth – josephine.w.finn@may.ie
Development Studies Centre: – info@dsckim.ie – www.dsckim.ie
DIT admissions ofice: – admissions@dit.ie – www.dit.ie
DIT School of Languages: – denise.murray@dit.ie
Donahies Community School: – donahcs@eircom.net
Dorset College: – info@dorset-college.ie: – dorset-college.ie
Drama League of Ireland: – dli@eircom.net
Driving Instructor Register: – info@dir.ie – www.dir.ie
Dublin Adult Learning Centre: – info@dalc.ie – www.dalc.ie
Dublin Business School: – admissions@dbs.edu: – www.dbs.edu
Dublin Camera Club: – pauls@eircom.net – www.dublincameraclub.ie
Dublin City Council Arts Office: – arts@dubc@iol.ie
Dublin City Council Public Lib: –
    dublinpubliclibraries@dublincity.ie – www.iol.ie/dublincitylibrary/
Dublin City Morris Dancers: – alancorsini@eircom.net
Dublin City University / DCU: – registry@dcu.ie – www.dcu.ie
Dublin Folk Dance Group: – : – dublinfolkdancegroup.com
Dublin Inst of Design: – info@dublindesign.ie – www.dublindesign.ie
Dublin Media Centre: – info@dublinmediacentre.com

Dublin Meditation Centre: – – www.dublinmeditationcentre.org
Dublin School of Art: – artistica@eircom.net
Dublin School of Classical & Contemporary Dance: – inybco@inybco.com
Dublin School of Horticulture: – bacus@indigo.ie
Dublin Shotokan Karate Int: – – www.dublinski.com
Dublin Simon Community: – mdent@dubsimon.ie
Dun Laoghaire College of FE: – eddieoriordan@decfe.ie
Dun Laoghaire-Rathdown Co Co: – – www.dlrcoco.ie/library
Dunboyne Village: – marysiahz@eircom.net
Dunsink Observatory: – astro@dunsink.dias.ie – www.dunsink.dias.ie
Dyslexia Association of Ireland: – info@dyslexia.ie – www.dyslexia.ie
Eden Computer Training: – info@eden.ie
Educational Multimedia Corp: –
      info-ire@educationalmultimedia – www.educationalmultimedia.com
Edwin Williamson Sch of Singing: –
      reception@thesingingschool.com – www.thesingingschool.com
EireCopter Helicopters: – eirecopter@oceanfree.net
electronic Business School: – info@ebsi.ie: – – www.ebsi.ie
ENFO, Dept of Environment: – info@enfo.ie – www.enfo.ie
English Language Institute: – elin@iol.ie
Esperanto Assoc of Ireland: – – www.esperanto.ie
ETC Consult: – etcc@iol.ie
European Movement: – info@europeanmovement.ie – www.europeanmovement.ie
FACTS Training: – facts@indigo.ie
FAS Net College: – info@fas-netcollege.com
FAS Training Centre Tallaght: – tallaghtnight@fas.ie
FE & Training Awards Council: – information@fetac.ie: – fbrennan@fetac.ie – www.fetac.ie
Film Inst of Ireland: – education@fii.ie
Finglas Adult Reading Scheme: – info@eoin.cdvec.ie
Fitzwilliam Inst Ltd: – fitzinst@iol.ie – www.fitzwilliam-institute.ie
Football Assoc of Ireland: – www.fai.ie
Forde Clinic: – yogalife@eircom.net
Froebel College of Education: – chairman@nurture.ie – www.nurture.ie
Gaiety School of Acting: – info@gaietyschool.com – www.gaietyschool.com
Gail Bovenizer: – gail13@oceanfree.net
Gallery of Photography: – gallery@irish-photography.com
Geraldine Brand Consultant: – info@geraldinebrand.com
Glenans Irish Sailing Club: – info@glenans-ireland.com – www.glenans-ireland.com
Goethe Institute: – goethela@iol.ie
Grafton Academy of Dress Design: –
      info@graftonacademy.com – www.graftonacademy.com
Great Outdoors: – greatod@indigo.ie – www.greatoutdoors.ie
Greendale Community School: – admin@greendalecs.com – www.iol.ie/~gcs
Griffith College Dublin: – admissions@gcd.ie
Hanly Centre: – info@thehanleycentre.com – www.thehanleycentre.com
Harmony Yoga Ireland: – harmonyyogaireland@utvinternet.ie
Hartstown Community School: – adedu@hotmail.com
Hazel Byrne: – – www.infantmassage.com
Healing House: – info@healinghouse.ie
Healing Pages – – www.the healing pages.com
Health Promotion Unit – – www.doh.ie
Hegarty Health Systems: – yogametrics@eircom.net – www.yogametrics.com
Henry Pollard: – wendyland@eircom.net

Hi-Tech Training: – hitech@indigo.ie – www.hitechtraining.ie
Holistic Healing Centre: – – www.hhc.ie
Holistic Sourcing Centre: –
    info@holisticsourcingcentre.com – www.holisticsourcingcentre.com
Holy Family Community School: – hfcs@iol.ie
House of Astrology: – mail2@astroleg.dk
I.T. Blanchardstown: – student.helpline@itb.ie – www.itb.ie
IICH Education: – iich@eircom.net – www.therapyireland.org
Inchicore College of FE: – enquiries@inchicore.cdvec.ie
Inst for Feminism & Religion: –
    irish-femrel@ntlworld.com – www.instituteforfeminismandreligion.org
Inst of Accounting Technicians: – info@iati.ie – www.iati.ie
Inst of Celtic, Shamanic Dev: – celticshaman@druidic.com – www.celticshaman.com
Inst of Certified Public Acc: – cpa@cpaireland.ie – www.cpaireland.ie
Inst of Creative Counselling & Psychotherapy: – iccp@eircom.net
Inst of International Trade: – iiti@irishexporters.ie – www.irishexporters.ie
Inst of Professional Auctioneers & Valuers: – info@ipav.ie – www.ipav.ie
Inst of Technology Tallaght: – – www.it-tallaght.ie
Instituto Cervantes: – cendub@cervantes.es – www.dublin.cervantes.es
International Society for Krishna Consciousness: – lotus108@eircom.net – www.iskcon.com
International Study Centre: – isc@indigo.ie – www.iscdublin.com
IPPA - the Early Childhood Organisation: – info@ippa.ie – www.ippa.ie
Irish Academy of Computer Training: – info@iact.ie – www.iact.ie
Irish Academy of Massage: – derek@massagecourses.net – www.massagecourses.net
Irish Academy of Public Relations: – info@irishacademy.com – www.irishacademy.com
Irish Amateur Boxing Assoc: – iaba@eircom.net
Irish Amateur Gymnastics Assoc: – irishgymnastics@eircom.net – www.irishgymnastics.ie
Irish Amateur Rowing Union: – info@iaru.ie – www.iaru.ie
Irish Astrological Assoc: – irishastrology@dublin.ie
Irish Astronomical Society: – jgoneill@indigo.ie
Irish Auctioneers & Valuers Inst: – education@iavi.ie – www.realestate.ie
Irish Basketball Assoc: – info@iba.ie
Irish Canoe Union: – office@irishcanoeunion.com
Irish Chinese Cultural Society: – iccs@oceanfree.net – www.ucd.ie/~iccs
Irish College of English: – ice@indigo.ie – www.irishcollegeofenglish.ie
Irish Deaf Society (Linkup): – linkupids@eircom,net
Irish Federation of Sea Anglers: – ifsa@gofree.indigo.ie – www.ifsa.ie
Irish Georgian Society: – info@irishgeorgiansoc.org – www.irish-architecture.com/igs/
Irish Hockey Association, The: – info@hockey.ie – www.hockey.ie
Irish Management Institute: – – www.imi.ie
Irish Martial Arts Commission: – i.m.a.c.@iol.ie – www.martialarts.ie
Irish National Sailing School: – ssailing@inss.ie
Irish Payroll Association (IPASS): – ask@ipass.ie – www.ipass.ie
Irish Peatland Conservation Council: – bogs@ipcc.ie – www.ipcc.ie
Irish Red Cross Society: – info@redcross.ie – www.redcross.ie
Irish Rugby Football Union: – info@irishrugby.ie – www.irishrugby.ie
Irish Sailing Assoc: – training@sailing.ie – www.sailing.ie
Irish School of Ecumenics (TCD): – aerisec@tcd.ie – www.tcd.ie/ise
Irish School of Homoeopathy: – ishom@indigo.ie – www.homoeopathy.ie
Irish School of Shiatsu: – shiatsu@eircom.net – www.shiatsu.ie
Irish Squash: – irishsquash@eircom.net – www.irishsquash.com
Irish Table Tennis Assoc: – owne@ttireland.com
Irish Underwater Council: – scubairl@indigo.ie – www.scubaireland.com

Irish Water Polo Assoc: – nicholas_omeara@entemp.ie
Irish Writers' Centre: – info@writerscentre.ie – www.writerscentre.ie
Irish Yoga Association: – iya@eircom.net
Jackie Skelly's Fitness: – info@jackieskellyfitness.com – www.jackieskellyfitness.com
James Foy School of Guitar: –
    reception@thesingingschool.com – www.thesingingschool.com
James Joyce Cultural Centre: – joycecen@iol.ie
Just Dance: – danceireland@hotmail.com
KAIROS Therapy Training: – ellensmith@oceanfree.net
Karen Ward: – kward@iol.ie – www.karenwardholistictherapist.com
Keytrainer Ireland: – mcazabon@iol.ie
Killester College of FE: – nightcourses@kcfe.cdvec.ie – www.killestercollege.ie
Kilroy's College: – homestudy@kilroyscollege.ie
Kinesiology Institute: – kinesiologyinstitute@eircom.ne
KLEAR: – klear@eircom.net
Kylemore College: – info@kylemore.cdvec.ie
Lakelands Folk Dance Club: – odonnellb@indigo.ie
Langtrain International: – info@langtrain.ie
Language Centre: – language.centre@may.ie – www.may.ie/language
Language Learning International: – info@lli.ie – www.lli.ie
Leinster School of Music & Drama: – leinster.school@gcd.ie
Liberties College: – info@liberties.cdvec.ie – www.libertiescollege.cdvec.ie
LIFEWORKS Yoga: – yogalife@eircom.net
Linguaphone Institute: – learn@linguaphone.ie – www.linguaphone.ie
Malahide Community School: – adulted@malahidecs.ie
Marino College: – info@marino.cdvec.ie – www.marino.college.com
Marketing Institute: – info@mii.ie – www.mii.ie
McKeon Murray Business Training: – mck@conlancrottymurray.com
Melody School of Music: – tumi@gofree.indigo.ie
Melt, Temple Bar Natural Healing: – info@2melt.com
Merriman Sch of Singing & Music: –
    reception@thesingingschool.com – www.thesingingschool.com
Milltown Institute: – admissions@milltown-institute. – www.milltown-institute.ie
Montessori Education Centre: – mec@iol.ie
Moresoft IT Institute: – training@moresoftit.com: – – www.moresoftit.com
Motions Health & Fitness Training: – motions@iol.ie
Motorcycling Ireland: –
    office@motorcycling-ireland.co – www.office@motorcycling-ireland.com
Na Piobairi Uilleann: – mail@pipers.ie: – – www.pipers.ie
Nat Col of Interior Design & Art: – indesarch@eircom.net
National Adult Literacy Agency: – literacy@nala.ie – www.nala.ie.
National College of Communications: – natcolcom@aol.com – www.theopencollege.com
National College of Ireland: – info@ncirl.ie – www.liveandlearn.ie
National Community Games: – info@communitygames.ie
National Diving School: – natdive@nds.ie – www.nds.ie
National Flight Centre Flight Sch: – – www.nfc.ie
National Gallery of Ireland: – artgall@tinet.ie
National Library of Ireland: – info@nli.ie – www.nli.ie
National School of Sports Massage: – info@ntc.ie – www.ntc.ie
National Training Authority: – ntahomestudy@aol.com
National Training Centre: – info@ntc.ie – www.ntc.ie
Natural Health Training Centre: – aikido@indigo.ie – www.aikido.ie
NCAD Centre for Continuing Ed: – cead@ncad.ie

Network Club, The: – reply@networkclub.ie: – – www.networkclub.ie
New Media Technology Training: – info@hypermedia7.com – www.hypermedia7.com
Newpark Adult & Continuing Ed: – newparkedu@eircom.net
Newpark Sports Centre: – pm@scmaa.ie – www.scmaa.ie
Nth Dublin Radio Club: – fammads@iol.ie
OBUS Healing Centre: – obus@eircom.net
Old Bawn Community School: – obcsaded@indigo.ie
Open Golf Centre, The: – opengolf@iol.ie
Open University, The: – – www.open.ac.uk/ireland
Order of Malta Ambulance Corps: – info@orderofmalta.ie
Oscail - Nat Distance Ed Centre: – oscail@dcu.ie – www.oscail.ie
Palmerstown Community School: – info@adulted.ie – www.adulted.ie
Pangur Bawn Crafts: – onfo@pangurbaw.com – www.pangurbaw.com
Parachute Assoc of Ireland: – pai@indigo.ie
Parental Equality: – – www.parentalequality.ie
Pearse College: – information@pearse.cdvec.ie
People's College Debating Soc: – peopcoll@iol.ie
People's College: – peopcoll@iol.ie
Phoenix A.B.C. TEFL: – info@phoenixtefl.com – www.phoenixtefl.com
Physio-Extra: – physioextra@eircom.net – www.e-physio.ie
Pilates Inst (NTC): – info@ntc.ie
Pitch & Putt Union of Ireland: – ppui@iol.ie
Pitman Training Centre: – pitmand@iol.ie – www.pitman-training.ie
Pobalscoil Rosmini: – rosmini@internet-ireland.ie
Portmarnock Community School: – office@portcs.iol.ie
Portobello School: – info@portobelloschool.ie
Positive Success Group: – maryo'driscoll@PositiveSuccessGroup
Priory Institute, The: – enquiries@prioryinstitute.com
Prism Computer Training: – prismct@indigo.ie – www.prismcomputertraining.ie
Prodancer: – info@silver-slipper.com – www.silver-slipper.com
Professional Training and Coaching Consultancy: – g.kingston@esatclear.ie
Public Service Aikido Club: – psac@akidoinireland.org – www.akidoinireland.org
Pulse Recording College: – pulse@clubi.ie – www.pulserecording.com
Rachel Dempsey: – racheldempsey@hotmail.com
Rakassah Sch Egyptian Belly Dance: – valerie@emailfast.com
Rathmines Snr College: – info@rsc.cdvec.ie
Retirement Planning Council: – information@rpc.ie
Rigpa Tibetan Buddhist Medit Centre: – dublin@rigpa.ie: – – www.rigpa.ie
Ringsend Technical Institute: – info@ringtec.cdvec.ie
Roebuck Counselling Centre: – roebuckcounsellingcentre@eircom.net
Royal Society of Antiquaries: – rsai@gofree.indigo.ie
Sales Inst of Ireland: – catherine@salesinstitute.ie – www.salesinstitute.ie
Salsa Dublin: – hilclarke@hotmail.com – www.salsadublin.com
Sanctuary: – enquiries@sanctuary.ie – www.anctuary.ie
Sandford Language Institute: – info@sandfordlanguages.ie – www.sandfordlanguages.ie
School of Computer Technology: – info@sct-ireland.com – www.sct-ireland.com
School of Practical Child Care: – info@practicalchildcare.com
Sea & Shore Safety Services Ltd: – seaandshore@eircom.net – www.seaandshoresafety.com
Seamus Lynch: – – www.iol.ie/~Seamus Lynch
Shiatsu Ireland: – enquiries@shiatsuireland.com
Shirley McClure: – mcclures@gofree.indigo.ie
Ski Club of Ireland: – ski@skiclub.ie – www.skiclub.ie
Sli Eile Volunteers: – volunteering@sli-eile.com

Sound Training Centre: – info@soundtraining.com – www.soundtraining.com
South Dublin Co Libraries: – – www.south-dublin.ie
Southside Adult Literacy Scheme: – sals@eircom.net
St Kevin's College: – info@stkevins.cdvec.ie
St Thomas Community College: – braynightschool@hotmail.com: – – www.bife.ie
St Vincent's Shotkan Karate Club: –
        gearoid.quinn@mail.esb.ie – www.karateireland.com/stvincents
Star Consulting: – info@star-consulting.net – www.star-consulting.net
Suaimhneas Reflexology: – carol@suimhneas.com – www.suimhneas.com
Surfdock: – courses@surfdock.ie – www.surfdock.ie
Susan Church: – schurch@gofree.indigo.ie
Swim Ireland: – swimireland@iolfree.ie – www.swimireland.ie
TACT: – tact@oceanfree.net
Tagnrye Dog Services: – tagnrye@eircom.net
T'ai Chi Ireland: – taichi@indigo.ie – www.taichi-ireland.com
Tallaght Community School: – tallaghtcs@eircom.net
Tallaght Photographic Society: – j.byrne@ntlworld.ie
Tapestry Dance Company: – info@tapestry.ie – www.tapestry.ie
Tara Buddhist Centre: – taracentre@ireland.com – www.meditateinireland.com
TARGET: – targeteducation@eircom.net
TEFL Training Inst of Ireland: – dublang@iol.ie – www.tefl.ie
Tennis Ireland: – info@tennisireland.ie – www.tennisireland.ie
Thornton Pk Equestrian Centre: – info@thorntonpark.ie – www.thorntonpark.ie
Toastmasters International Clubs: – – www.toastmasters.org.uk
Tracy Miley: – tracy@gofree.indigo.ie
Training Associates: – trainingassociates@eircom.net
Transactional Analysis in Ireland: – liztai@eircom.net
Trinity College: – – www.tcd.ie
U-Learn Language Centre: – ulearn@eircom.net – www.u-learn.ie
Unislim: – info@unislim.ie – www.unislim.ie
Valerie Larkin, Bellydance Irl: – info@bellydance-irl.com
Volunteering Ireland: – anne-marie@volunteeringireland – www.volunteeringireland.com
Walmer College & Holistic Centre: – walmer@indigo.ie
Walton's New School of Music: – info@newschool.ie – www.newschool.ie
Watchtower Bible & Tract Society: – – www.watchtower.org
Westmoreland College: –
        admissions@westmorelandcollege.ie – www.westmorelandcollege.ie
Whitefriar Aikido Dojo: – brd@iol.ie – www.akidoireland.ie
Whitehall College of FE: – general.enquiries@whsc.cdvec.i – www.whitehallcollege.com
WORDS Language Services: – info@wls.ie – www.wls.ie
Yellow Brick Road: – stacey@yellowbrickroad.ie – www.yellowbrickroad.ie
Yoga Therapy Ireland: – yti@eircom.net – www.yogatherapyireland.com
Yvonne Stewart: – ystewart@gofree.indigo.ie